What's the Best Trivia Book? Mega Edition

Over 6,000 Questions in 12 Categories

David Fickes

Printed in the United States of America

First Printing: 2020

Introduction

What you find in most trivia is a lot of erroneous or outdated information or questions that are so simple or esoteric that they aren't interesting. It is difficult to come up with interesting questions that are at the right level of difficulty that a wide variety of people can enjoy them, and they are something that you feel you should know or want to know.

I have tried to ensure that the information is as accurate as possible, and to retain its accuracy, I have also tried to avoid questions whose answers can quickly change with time. Since the simple answer is often not all you want to know, the answers also frequently include additional details to put them in context and provide further information.

There are over 6,000 questions in 12 wide-ranging categories – Animals, Arts, History, Literature, Miscellaneous, Movies, Science and Nature, Sports, Television, U.S. Geography, U.S. Presidents, and World Geography. To make it quick and easy to test yourself or others without initially seeing the answers, each category is divided into quizzes with 20 questions followed by their answers.

If you enjoyed this book and learned a little and would like others to enjoy it also, please put out a review or rating. If you scan the QR code below, it will take you directly to the Amazon review and rating page.

Contents

Animals

Quiz 1

1) What is the offspring of a cob and a pen?
2) What is a monotreme?
3) What is a bird's vocal organ called?
4) What is the largest venomous snake?
5) How many toes does a rhinoceros have on each foot?
6) What order of mammals has the most species?
7) The Komodo dragon is native to what country?
8) What was the first animal placed on the endangered species list?
9) What two islands are the natural habitat of the orangutan?
10) How many eyelids do camels have?
11) What color is octopus blood?
12) What is the fastest swimming fish?
13) Only one species of bear is almost exclusively carnivorous, and only one species is almost exclusively herbivorous; what are these two species?
14) What male fish species give birth?
15) Ribbon worms will do what if they can't find food?
16) What bird has the largest wingspan?
17) How many pairs of legs does a shrimp have?

18) What two animals are on the Australian coat of arms?
19) Alligators are naturally found in the United States and what other country?
20) What is the only female animal that has antlers?

Quiz 1 Answers

1) Swan
2) Egg laying mammal
3) Syrinx
4) King cobra
5) Three
6) Rodents
7) Indonesia
8) Peregrine falcon
9) Borneo and Sumatra
10) Three – for sand protection
11) Blue – A copper-rich protein carries oxygen instead of the iron-rich protein in other animals.
12) Sailfish – 68 mph
13) Polar bear and giant panda
14) Seahorse and pipefish
15) Eat themselves; they can eat a substantial portion of their own body and still survive.
16) Albatross – up to over 11 feet
17) Five
18) Emu and kangaroo
19) China
20) Caribou or reindeer

Quiz 2

1) What fish's name is thought to derive from the Latin meaning "to leap"?
2) What is the largest species of deer?
3) What lives in a formicary?
4) What did ancient Egyptians do to mourn the deaths of their cats?
5) What is a rhinoceros horn made of?
6) What animal has the world's longest distance migration?
7) What animal lives in a drey?

8) Along with some species of sharks, what common ocean fish needs to swim continuously to breathe?
9) What is the heaviest snake?
10) What is the only snake that builds a nest?
11) Fireflies are what kind of insect?
12) What fish is known as poor man's lobster?
13) What breed of dog can't bark?
14) What type of creature lives in a sett?
15) What kind of animal does cashmere come from?
16) What do insects do with their spiracles?
17) Other than elephants, what is the heaviest land animal?
18) What is the only insect that can turn its head?
19) The male of what species testicles explode on mating and then dies?
20) What kind of whale is Moby Dick?

Quiz 2 Answers

1) Salmon
2) Moose – up to 7 feet tall and 1,500 pounds
3) Ants
4) They shaved off their own eyebrows.
5) Hair
6) Sooty shearwater – It is one of the most common seabirds in the world and has been electronically tracked migrating 40,000 miles.
7) Squirrel
8) Tuna – They can't pump water through their gills without swimming.
9) Anaconda – up to 550 pounds
10) King cobra – It lays up to 40 eggs at once and builds a nest from vegetation to help keep the eggs safe.
11) Beetle
12) Monkfish
13) Basenji
14) Badger
15) Goat
16) Breathe
17) Rhinoceros
18) Praying mantis
19) Honeybee
20) Sperm whale

Quiz 3

1) What animal has the most taste buds?
2) Of all the animal species scientists have studied, what is the only one that shows no outward signs of conciliatory behavior?
3) What breed of dog, known for its thick white coat, is named for the nomadic people of Siberia who bred it?
4) What creature can be Indian, White, or Broad Lipped?
5) What mammal has the shortest known gestation period with an average of just 12 days?
6) What is the largest land predator?
7) What is the more common name of the chaparral cock?
8) Owls have how many eyelids?
9) What species of animal has sub-species including Masai, Reticulated, and Rothschild's?
10) Armadillos are good swimmers, but what other method do they use to cross bodies of water?
11) Oysters can change what about themselves based on environmental conditions?
12) What animal's name translates from Arabic as "fast walker"?
13) What is the largest invertebrate (animal without a backbone) species?
14) What animal has the longest known lifespan of all vertebrate (animals with a backbone) species?
15) An elephant is a pachyderm; what does pachyderm mean?
16) What is unique about a crocodile's tongue?
17) A female cat is called a molly; after she has become a mother, what is she called?
18) What is the heaviest bird capable of flight?
19) What is unusual about a cat's jaw?
20) Besides elephants and rhinoceroses, what other animals are considered pachyderms?

Quiz 3 Answers

1) Catfish – It has over 100,000 taste buds both in its mouth and all over its body, about 10 times more than humans.
2) Domestic cat
3) Samoyed
4) Rhinoceros
5) Opossum

6) Polar bear – up to 11 feet long and 1,700 pounds
7) Roadrunner
8) Three – They have one for blinking, one for sleeping, and one for keeping their eyes clean.
9) Giraffe
10) They walk underwater; they can hold their breath for six to eight minutes.
11) Gender – It can change back and forth based on conditions.
12) Giraffe
13) Colossal squid
14) Greenland shark – 400 years
15) Thick skinned
16) They can't stick it out; it is attached to the roof of their mouth; their tongue helps keep their throat closed underwater, so they can open their mouth to hunt prey.
17) A queen
18) Kori bustard – It is from Africa and can weigh over 40 pounds.
19) It can't move sideways, so they can't chew large chunks.
20) Hippopotamuses

Quiz 4

1) What is the name for a group of elk?
2) Adult domestic cats meow for what purpose?
3) At what age does a filly become a mare?
4) What is a group of rhinoceros called?
5) Where is a shrimp's heart located?
6) Birds don't have what basic body function of most animals?
7) Horses can't do what normal body function through their mouths?
8) What is the only animal that naturally has an odd number of whiskers?
9) Why are bald eagles called bald when they aren't?
10) How many legs do butterflies have?
11) Including hunting dives, what is the fastest bird in the world?
12) Where is the only place in the world that alligators and crocodiles exist together naturally in the wild?
13) What is the largest lizard?
14) What is the national animal of Scotland?
15) What country has the largest population of poisonous snakes?
16) What is the most common group of insects?

17) Iguanas have three of something that most animals have two; what is it?
18) Lemurs are native to what island nation?
19) What animal has the longest tongue relative to its size?
20) What is the sleepiest animal in the world?

Quiz 4 Answers

1) Gang
2) To communicate with humans - They don't meow to each other.
3) Five
4) Crash
5) In its head
6) They don't urinate. Birds convert excess nitrogen to uric acid instead of urea; it is less toxic and doesn't need to be diluted as much. It goes out with their other waste and saves water, so they don't have to drink as much.
7) Breathe – A soft palate blocks off the pharynx from the mouth except when swallowing.
8) Catfish
9) Bald comes from the old English word piebald, meaning white-headed.
10) Six
11) Peregrine falcon – 242 mph
12) Southern Florida
13) Komodo dragon – up to 10 feet long and 250 pounds
14) Unicorn
15) Australia
16) Beetles – followed by flies
17) Eyes – A third parietal eye on top of their head can just distinguish light and dark.
18) Madagascar
19) Chameleon
20) Koala – It sleeps 22 hours per day.

Quiz 5

1) What shark is thought to be the largest to have ever lived?
2) What is the world's largest reptile?
3) What animal can survive temperatures from -458 to 300 degrees Fahrenheit, 1,000 atmospheres of pressure, radiation 1,000 times

higher than the lethal dose for humans, the vacuum of space, and can live for 30 years without food or water?
4) What kind of animal lives in a holt?
5) What is the world's largest rodent?
6) What is the fastest moving land snake?
7) What animal has the world's largest egg?
8) What color is a polar bear's skin?
9) What happens to a bear's urine when they hibernate?
10) What is the largest animal ever known to have lived on the earth?
11) What is the largest current day shark?
12) What animal has the largest brain?
13) What bird species is the highest flying ever recorded?
14) Why is a giraffe's tongue black or purple?
15) What animal has the most legs?
16) A flamboyance is a group of what animals?
17) What do sea otters do while they are sleeping, so they don't drift apart?
18) In terms of the senses, what do most birds lack?
19) What is the fastest two-legged animal?
20) If cats are feline, what are sheep?

Quiz 5 Answers

1) Megalodon – It became extinct about 2.6 million years ago and was up to 59 feet long and 65 tons.
2) Saltwater crocodile – up to 20 feet long and 3,000 pounds
3) Tardigrade – They are water-dwelling, eight-legged micro animals (about 0.02 inches long) that were discovered in 1773 and are found everywhere from mountain tops to the deep sea and from tropical rainforests to the Antarctic.
4) Otter
5) Capybara – up to 150 pounds
6) Black mamba – 12 mph
7) Whale shark – The ostrich has the largest laid egg.
8) Black
9) They don't urinate in hibernation; their body converts the urine into protein, and they use it as food.
10) Blue whale – up to 100 feet long and 200 tons
11) Whale shark – up to 41 feet long and 47,000 pounds
12) Sperm whale – 17 pounds

13) Ruppell's griffon vulture – It has been spotted at 37,000 feet; they have special hemoglobin that makes their oxygen intake more effective.
14) To prevent sunburn - It is exposed a lot of the time while they eat.
15) Millipede – up to 750
16) Flamingos
17) Hold hands
18) Sense of smell
19) Ostrich – over 40 mph
20) Ovine

Quiz 6

1) The United States has the most dogs of any country in the world; what country has the second most?
2) The United States has the most domestic cats of any country in the world; what country has the second most?
3) What land animal has the longest tail?
4) What part of their bodies do butterflies taste with?
5) What is the V-shaped formation of a flock of geese called?
6) What is nidification?
7) You can tell the age of a whale by counting the rings in its what?
8) What is unusual about grey whale mating habits?
9) What animal produces the loudest sound?
10) The okapi belongs to what family of animals?
11) Killer whales aren't whales; what are they?
12) What percent of kangaroos are left-handed?
13) During WWI, the British army tried to train what animal to battle submarines?
14) When a woodpecker's beak hits a tree, how many times the force of gravity does it experience?
15) What animal has the greatest bite force?
16) What is the only insect considered kosher?
17) How many species of insects are native to Antarctica?
18) How old was the world's oldest dog?
19) How many blood types do dogs have?
20) What are the only two animal species known to seek visual clues from another animal's eyes?

Quiz 6 Answers

1) Brazil
2) China
3) Giraffe – up to eight feet long
4) Feet
5) Skein
6) Nest building
7) Earwax
8) They always mate in a threesome with two males and one female. One of the males is dominant, and the other assists.
9) Sperm whale – 230 decibels
10) Giraffe
11) Dolphins – The similarities with dolphins include teeth, streamlined bodies, rounded head, beak, echolocation, living in pods, and group hunting.
12) Almost 100%
13) Seagulls – They were supposed to poop on periscopes.
14) 1,000 times
15) Nile crocodile – 5,000 psi
16) Locust
17) One – Antarctic midge
18) 29 years
19) 13
20) Humans and dogs

Quiz 7

1) Humans need 16 to 20 images per second to perceive something as a moving picture rather than a flickering image; how many images per second do dogs need?
2) On average, how many people do sharks kill per year?
3) What happens as soon as sand tiger shark embryos develop teeth while still in the womb?
4) Female Greenland sharks reach sexual maturity at what age?
5) Why don't sharks get cavities?
6) What country has the world's largest feral camel herd?
7) What country has all 10 of the deadliest snakes in the world?
8) How many species of bear are alive today?

9) What is a group of bears called?
10) Scientists believe that herrings use what unusual method to communicate?
11) Based on oxygen usage, what animal is the most efficient swimmer?
12) Which of the basic tastes can't cats taste?
13) How many eyes do bees have?
14) Relative to its weight, what is the strongest organism known?
15) Why is horseshoe crab blood worth $14,000 per quart?
16) What mammal needs the least sleep?
17) What blood type do mosquitoes like most?
18) What species of animal (not microscopic) has the largest size difference between males and females?
19) Excluding man, what animal species has the longest tested memory?
20) Research has shown that most mammals on average live for about the same number of heartbeats; how many?

Quiz 7 Answers

1) 70 – Older televisions could only produce 50 images per second, so dogs would only see flickering images; modern televisions are fast enough to appear as moving pictures to dogs.
2) 12
3) The largest of the embryos in each of the two uteruses attacks and eats its siblings, leaving just two pups to be born.
4) 150 – Greenland sharks grow to a similar size as great whites and can live up to 400 years.
5) The outside of their teeth is made of fluoride.
6) Australia – There were as many as 1 million camels at one time; they were imported in the 19th century and many were later set free as the automobile took over. They roam freely with no natural predators.
7) Australia
8) Eight – sun, sloth, spectacled, American black, Asian black, brown, polar, giant panda
9) A sloth
10) Farts – Herrings have excellent hearing, and their farts produce a high-pitched sound; the farts aren't from flatulence but from gulping air at the surface and storing it in their swim bladder.
11) Jellyfish – It uses 48% less oxygen than any other known animal; they never stop moving.
12) Sweet – They don't have taste receptors for sweet; this applies to all

cats, domestic and wild.

13) Five
14) Gonorrhea bacterium – They can pull with a force of 100,000 times their body weight, comparable to a 150-pound person pulling 7,500 tons.
15) Its unique chemical properties make it very valuable in the health care industry for bacterial testing. It can coagulate around as little as one part in a trillion of bacterial contamination, and the reaction only takes 45 minutes, instead of two days with mammalian blood.
16) Giraffes – On average, they only sleep 30 minutes a day, just a few minutes at a time.
17) Type O
18) Blanket octopus – Females are 10,000 to 40,000 times larger than males; females can be 6.5 feet in length; males are 1 inch.
19) Dolphins – Bottlenose dolphins have unique whistles like names; studies have shown that they remember the whistle of other dolphins they have lived with even after 20 years of separation.
20) 1.5 billion – Larger animals have slower heartbeats, so they live longer; humans used to fit the pattern before health and medical improvements.

Quiz 8

1) What land mammal has the most teeth?
2) What land animal has the most teeth?
3) Some snakes, Komodo dragons, sharks, and turkeys are all capable of what biblical feat?
4) What female mammal can die if she doesn't mate?
5) What is a group of owls called?
6) What was the first domesticated animal?
7) Humans only have 1, but leeches have 32 what?
8) What is a group of cats called?
9) What bird can only eat when its head is upside down?
10) What is the only creature that can turn its stomach inside out?
11) What animal has the largest eye?
12) An elephant has 40,000 what in its trunk?
13) What animal produces its own sunscreen?
14) In ancient China, what dog breed was restricted to the aristocracy?
15) What insect may be the most efficient predator and possibly has the best vision of any animal?

16) What animal always gives birth to four identical offspring?
17) The nine-banded armadillo and humans have what in common?
18) The minnow is the smallest member of what fish family?
19) Based on AKC registrations, what are the three most popular purebred dog breeds in the United States?
20) What land mammal has the best sense of smell?

Quiz 8 Answers

1) Opossum – 50
2) Giant armadillo – up to 100
3) Virgin births
4) Ferret – The female stays in heat until she mates; if she doesn't, very high levels of estrogen remain in her blood for a long time and can cause aplastic anemia and death. She doesn't have to get pregnant, but she must mate.
5) Parliament
6) Dog
7) Brains – Each controls a different segment of their body.
8) Clowder
9) Flamingo
10) Starfish
11) Giant and colossal squid - up to an 11-inch diameter
12) Muscles – Humans only have about 650 muscles in their entire body.
13) Hippopotamus – They produce a mucus-like secretion that keeps them cool and acts as a powerful sunscreen.
14) Pekingese
15) Dragonfly - Humans have three light-sensitive proteins in the eye for red, blue, and green (tri-chromatic vision); dragonflies have up to 33. Their bulbous eyes have 30,000 facets and can see in all directions at once. Studies have also shown that they catch as much as 95% of their intended prey.
16) Armadillo - A single embryo splits into four as part of their normal reproduction.
17) Leprosy – They are the only animals known to be infected.
18) Carp or cyprinid
19) Labrador Retrievers, German Shepherds, and Golden Retrievers
20) Bear – Black bears have been observed to travel 18 miles in a straight line to a food source; grizzlies can find an elk carcass underwater, and polar bears can smell a seal through 3 feet of ice.

Quiz 9

1) A horse's height is measured from the ground to what part?
2) What would happen to you if you ate a polar bear's liver?
3) A newborn Bactrian camel has how many humps?
4) What biological aspect of a mouse is bigger than an elephant's?
5) What animal has the highest blood pressure?
6) What is the only native North American marsupial?
7) What organ accounts for up to 30% of a shark's total body mass?
8) How many compartments does a cow's stomach have?
9) What is the longest living land mammal after man?
10) What is the longest living land animal of any kind?
11) Where are a snail's reproductive organs?
12) What is a newly hatched swan called?
13) How many rows of whiskers does a cat have?
14) What resin used in varnish is a secretion of an insect?
15) What is the largest cat in the Americas?
16) What fish's skin was once used commercially as sandpaper?
17) Which leg of a chicken is more tender, left or right leg?
18) What can't rats do that makes them particularly vulnerable to poison?
19) What does the horned toad squirt from its eyes when attacked?
20) The cheetah is the fastest land animal; what is the second fastest?

Quiz 9 Answers

1) Withers - base of the neck above the shoulders
2) You would get vitamin A poisoning and could die. Polar bears have 50-60 times the normal human levels of vitamin A in their liver, and it is about 3 times the tolerable level that a human can intake.
3) Zero - Baby camels don't get their humps until they start eating solid food.
4) Sperm - Large animals tend to have high numbers of smaller sperm.
5) Giraffe – about 300 over 200
6) Opossum
7) Liver – Sharks don't have gas-filled swim bladders for buoyancy; they rely on a large oil-filled liver.
8) Four
9) Elephant – up to 86 years
10) Tortoise – up to 250 years

11) Head
12) Cygnet
13) Four
14) Shellac – lac insect
15) Jaguar – It is the third-largest cat after the tiger and lion.
16) Shark
17) Left leg – Chickens scratch with their right leg, building up more muscle in that leg and making it tougher than the left.
18) Vomit
19) Blood
20) Pronghorn antelope – 55 mph

Quiz 10

1) What bird has the biggest brain relative to its body size?
2) What was the first bird domesticated by man?
3) For animals, what is the summer equivalent to hibernation?
4) How many claws does a normal house cat have?
5) What is the only known animal to regularly prey on adult bears?
6) How many hearts does an octopus have?
7) What is the only dog breed specifically mentioned in the Bible?
8) What color is a polar bear's fur?
9) Napoleon's life was saved by what breed of dog?
10) A cat is feline; what kind of animal is leporine?
11) Where are a cricket's ears located?
12) What order of insects contains the most species?
13) What species of whale dives deeper and stays underwater the longest?
14) What is a group of rattlesnakes called?
15) What is the closest living relative to the Tyrannosaurus Rex?
16) Silkworms live on a diet of leaves from only what plant?
17) What was the penalty in ancient Egypt for killing a cat even accidentally?
18) Dalmatian dogs originated in what country?
19) What is the only land mammal native to New Zealand?
20) Humans and what two other species of animals are the only ones to go through menopause?

Quiz 10 Answers

1) Hummingbird – over 4% of its body weight

2) Goose
3) Estivation – Animals slow their activity for the hot, dry summer months.
4) 18 – five on each front paw and four on each back paw
5) Tiger
6) Three
7) Greyhound
8) It has no color; it is transparent and appears white only because it reflects visible light.
9) Newfoundland – It saved him from drowning.
10) Rabbit
11) Front legs
12) Beetles
13) Sperm whale – They can dive for more than an hour and more than 4,000 feet deep.
14) A rhumba
15) Chicken
16) Mulberry
17) Death
18) Croatia – Dalmatia region
19) Bat
20) Killer whales and short-finned pilot whales

Quiz 11

1) What is the fleshy protuberance above a turkey's bill called?
2) What animal's fingerprints are virtually indistinguishable from human fingerprints even with careful analysis under a microscope?
3) What body part do frogs use to force food down their throats?
4) What is the only bird with two toes on each foot?
5) What name is given to a female mouse?
6) What country has the lone sub-species of horse that is still entirely wild, having never been domesticated by humans?
7) Male giraffes determine whether a female is fertile and ready to mate by getting the female to do what?
8) What is the largest rat free populated area in the world?
9) What country has the most reptile species?
10) What is the name for a male mule?
11) What makes an animal viviparous?

12) What is the name for the short, erect tail of a hare, rabbit, or deer?
13) What is the primary reason a dog's nose is wet?
14) Ravens, crows, jays, and some songbirds lie in anthills and roll around letting the ants swarm on them, or they chew up the ants and rub them on their feathers; what is this behavior called?
15) Camels don't store water in their humps; where do they store it?
16) To what bird family does the roadrunner belong?
17) What animal has the most names?
18) What is the second largest bird in the world and is also considered the most dangerous bird?
19) Lemurs in Madagascar capture what animal to get a narcotic hit and ward off insects?
20) What country has the most horses?

Quiz 11 Answers

1) Snood
2) Koala bear - They have the same loopy, whirling ridges as humans.
3) Eyes - Since they don't have muscles to chew their food, they use their eyes to force food down their throats. Their eyes sink inside their skull to push the food down.
4) Ostrich
5) Doe
6) Mongolia - The endangered Przewalski's horse is native to the steppes of Mongolia; all other wild horses are feral horses that are descendants of domesticated horses.
7) Urinate - The male bumps the female until she urinates and then tastes the urine for hormones indicating she is in heat.
8) Canadian province of Alberta - The government has had very aggressive rat control measures since the 1950s, and only the brown rat can survive in the prairie region.
9) Australia - It has over 860 different reptile species, including lizards, crocodiles, turtles, and snakes. North America only has 280 reptile species.
10) John
11) Viviparous animals are born as live young individuals; they do not lay eggs.
12) Scut
13) They secrete mucus that aids their sense of smell.
14) Anting - It isn't understood why they do it.

15) Bloodstream - They can drink up to 20 gallons at a time; the hump is almost all fat and serves as an alternative energy source and helps regulate body temperature. By concentrating fat in the hump as opposed to being spread over their body, they are better able to handle hot climates.
16) Cuckoo
17) Cougar - It is called puma, mountain lion, panther, catamount, or one of another 40 English, 18 native South American, and 25 native North American names.
18) Cassowary - They are up to 6 feet tall and weigh up to 130 pounds and have a 4-inch, dagger-like claw on each foot that can slice open a predator or threat with a single kick. They are native to the tropical forests of Papua New Guinea, Indonesia, and northeastern Australia.
19) Red millipedes - The lemurs bite the millipede gently and throw it back on the ground; when millipedes are picked up, they secrete a toxic combination of chemicals, including cyanide, as a defense mechanism. The lemurs rub the secretion all over their fur, which functions as a natural pesticide and wards off malaria carrying mosquitoes. The secretion also acts as a narcotic, which causes the lemurs to salivate profusely and enter a state of intoxication.
20) United States

Quiz 12

1) Instead of the five tastes that humans can detect, whales and dolphins only perceive what single taste?
2) What mammal sweats milk?
3) What is a group of pandas called?
4) What is the fastest known running insect?
5) What animal does mohair come from?
6) Goldfish are members of what fish family?
7) The wolverine is the largest land member of what animal family?
8) What is the name for a group of locusts?
9) What color are flamingos naturally?
10) What is the longest snake?
11) What is the most abundant wild bird species?
12) What freshwater lake has the most fish species in the world?
13) What kind of animal is a geoduck?
14) What is the only known immortal creature that can transform itself back to a juvenile state?
15) Domestic cats don't seem to have an overall paw preference for right or

left like humans do, but they do have a gender-based preference; what paw do male cats favor?
16) What is the most populous large (average of 20 pounds or more) mammal?
17) What is the loudest land animal?
18) What land animal can go the longest without drinking water?
19) What current multi-organ animal has existed the longest?
20) What is the largest species of bee in the world?

Quiz 12 Answers

1) Salty
2) Platypus - They secrete milk from mammary glands, but they don't have nipples, so the milk oozes from the surface of their skin, more like sweat. Because the delivery system is less hygienic, platypus milk contains antibacterial proteins to protect the babies.
3) Embarrassment
4) Australian tiger beetle - 5.6 mph
5) Angora goats
6) Carp
7) Weasel - Wolverines can be up to 70 pounds.
8) Plague
9) White - Their diet of brine shrimp and algae turns them pink.
10) Reticulated python - up to 30 feet long
11) Red-billed quelea – They are sparrow-sized birds found in sub-Saharan Africa; their population is estimated at 1.5 billion.
12) Lake Malawi - It is located between Malawi, Mozambique, and Tanzania and is the fourth-largest freshwater lake by volume in the world. There are more than 1,000 species of cichlid fish alone.
13) Clam - It is a very large, edible saltwater clam native to the coastal waters of western Canada and the northwest United States.
14) Immortal jellyfish (Turritopsis dohrnii) - Once the adult jellyfish have reproduced, they transform themselves back into their juvenile state. Their tentacles retract, their bodies shrink, and they sink to the ocean floor and start their life cycle all over again. They can do it repeatedly, making them essentially immortal unless they are eaten by another animal or struck by disease.
15) Left - Females are significantly more likely to be right paw dominant.
16) Humans
17) Howler monkey – up to 140 decibels and can be heard 3 miles away

18) Kangaroo rat - They can go their whole life of 3-5 years without drinking.
19) Jellyfish - They evolved 550 million years ago and have no brain or nervous system, and their body is 90% water.
20) Wallace's giant bee - It is native to Indonesia and was thought to be extinct for over a century until it was rediscovered in 1981. Females have a 2.5-inch wingspan and a body length of about 1.5 inches.

Quiz 13

1) A jellyfish's mouth also serves as what?
2) Dire wolves, as seen in *Game of Thrones*, existed up to about 10,000 years ago on what continents?
3) What is the technical name for the pouch of a kangaroo or other marsupial?
4) Not including insects and crustaceans, what are the only two animals that can see completely behind themselves without turning their heads?
5) What is Britain's largest native carnivore?
6) As part of its reproductive process, what animal will sting a cockroach twice, first in the thorax to partially immobilize it and then in the head to block its normal escape reflex?
7) What animal's name means "pig fish"?
8) The fennec is the smallest species of what animal?
9) Chameleons don't change color for camouflage purposes; instead, they change to communicate with other chameleons and for what other reason?
10) What is an ungulate?
11) Central America's Lake Nicaragua is one of the very few freshwater lakes in the world with what animal?
12) How does a giraffe clean its ears?
13) What are the tufts of hair in a cat's ear called?
14) A male donkey and a female horse produce what offspring?
15) What is coprophagy?
16) What was the largest known flying animal that ever lived?
17) What is the dung of an otter called?
18) What is the highest level of sociality called where animals like ants and termites have a single female or caste that produces the offspring, and nonreproductive individuals cooperate in caring for the young?
19) Macaroni, gentoo, and chinstrap are species of what animal?
20) What animal gives birth to the largest young?

Quiz 13 Answers

1) Anus
2) North and South America - They were about the same size as the largest modern gray wolves, at about 150 pounds on average, but their teeth were larger with greater shearing ability, and they had the highest bite force of any known Canis species.
3) Marsupium
4) Rabbit and parrot
5) Badger
6) Jewel wasp - The wasp is too small to carry the cockroach, so it leads it back to its burrow by pulling on one of its antennae. Once in the burrow, the wasp lays an egg on the roach's abdomen and exits and fills in the burrow entrance with pebbles. In about three days, the wasp's egg hatches, and the larva begins feeding on the roach for four to five days before chewing its way into the roach's abdomen. Over eight days, it consumes the roach's internal organs in an order to maximize the time the roach is still alive. The larva enters a pupal stage and forms a cocoon inside the roach, and the fully-grown wasp eventually emerges from the roach's body, completing the reproductive cycle.
7) Porpoise - from Latin
8) Fox - They are found mainly in the Sahara and elsewhere in North Africa; they only weigh two to three pounds but have six-inch ears.
9) Regulate their temperature - They change color by stretching and relaxing cells that contain crystals, affecting how light is reflected.
10) Hoofed mammal
11) Sharks - Bull sharks can survive in both fresh and saltwater and make their way back and forth from the Caribbean Sea to Lake Nicaragua via a 120-mile route through the San Juan River.
12) Its tongue
13) Ear furnishings - They help keep out dirt, direct sounds, and insulate the ears.
14) Mule
15) Eating your own poop - Rats and most rodents have simple digestive systems and eat their own poop to recover additional nutrients.
16) Quetzalcoatlus - It was a pterodactyloid pterosaur from the Late Cretaceous period of North America and had a wingspan up to 36 feet and may have weighed as much as 500 pounds.
17) Spraint
18) Eusocial

19) Penguins
20) Blue whale – Calves are about 23 feet long and weigh 5,000 to 6,000 pounds.

Quiz 14

1) What are baby porcupines called?
2) What animal kills the most people in the world?
3) What do scientists believe is the most abundant vertebrate (animal with a backbone) species?
4) What prehistoric animal from about 150 million years ago is considered the first bird?
5) What is the name for animals that are the opposite of albinos and are all black?
6) China owns all the giant pandas in the world except for two pandas in what country?
7) What is the name for a baby beaver?
8) The aardvark is the first animal alphabetically; what's the second?
9) If you include speed on land, in air, or in water, what is the fastest known mammal?
10) A leveret is the young of what animal?
11) Rats don't sweat; what part of their body do they use to regulate their temperature?
12) What dinosaur's name means "roof lizard" in Greek?
13) What are turkeys called in the country of Turkey?
14) What are the three main parts of an insect's body?
15) What do polled cattle not have?
16) What is the most poached (illegally hunted) animal in the world?
17) What horse breed has a greater bone density than other horses, a shorter back with one fewer lumbar vertebrae, and one fewer pair of ribs?
18) Reindeer eyes change color from gold in the summer to what color in winter?
19) What animal has the highest brain to bodyweight ratio?
20) What endangered New Zealand parrot is the heaviest parrot and the only flightless parrot?

Quiz 14 Answers

1) Porcupettes
2) Mosquitoes - They are by far the deadliest animal in the world, killing

over 700,000 people worldwide annually, primarily from malaria. Snakes are the second most deadly animal, killing about 50,000 people; dogs are third at about 25,000 people, mainly through rabies. Crocodiles are the deadliest of the large animals at about 1,000 people; the hippopotamus is the world's deadliest large land mammal, killing an estimated 500 people annually.

3) Bristlemouth - They are small, deep-sea fish that are only about three inches long and usually live at depths exceeding 1,000 feet. They are believed to number in the quadrillions.
4) Archaeopteryx - It was about the size of a common raven and weighed about two pounds.
5) Melanistic - An excess of melanin makes their skin, hair, or fur very dark or black.
6) Mexico - Any panda in a foreign zoo is on loan from China with the agreement that China owns the panda and any offspring, which must be returned to China before they are four years old. The only exceptions are two pandas China gave to Mexico before implementing the current policy.
7) Kit
8) Aardwolf - It is native to eastern and southern Africa; it is a member of the hyena family and looks like a small striped hyena. It feeds on insects, primarily termites.
9) Mexican free-tailed bat – It can achieve speeds of 100 mph in normal flight.
10) Hare
11) Tail - They constrict or expand blood vessels in their tails.
12) Stegosaurus
13) Hindi - meaning from India
14) Head, thorax, and abdomen
15) Horns
16) Pangolin - It is a small mammal covered in large overlapping scales that eats ants and termites and is generally found in Asia and sub-Saharan Africa. It is poached for its scales, which are used in traditional medicine, and for its meat.
17) Arabian
18) Blue - During bright summer light, their eyes reflect most light and look gold; during winter, the tissue behind their retina becomes less reflective, and their eyes appear blue. This increases their light sensitivity and vision in the low winter light.
19) Ant - Some species have 14-15% of their mass in their brain; humans are about 2.5%.

20) Kakapo - It weighs up to nine pounds.

Quiz 15

1) What animal's milk won't curdle?
2) What is a baby spider called?
3) What is the only insect that has both a king and a queen?
4) What is the national animal of the United States?
5) Why can't giraffes cough?
6) What is the largest mollusk in the world?
7) What mammal only poops once a week and can lose one-third of its body weight from pooping?
8) Vulpine relates to what kind of animal?
9) What small shark, reaching only about two feet in length, is named for its unusual feeding method where it gouges out round plugs of flesh from larger animals?
10) Opossums don't play dead; if frightened, what do they do?
11) What is the largest known flying insect to ever exist?
12) Cats, rabbits, and goats all share what breed name?
13) What is the only animal with four forward-facing knees?
14) What is the only bird with a bill longer than its body?
15) What mammal has the longest pregnancy?
16) What was Didus Ineptus better known as?
17) As a defense mechanism when threatened, what sea creature can eviscerate themself and shoot out their internal organs?
18) Are zebras black with white stripes or white with black stripes?
19) What is the largest species of monkey?
20) What animal is featured on the state flag of California?

Quiz 15 Answers

1) Camel - The structure of the protein in camel milk differs from cows, goats, sheep, and other animals; due to its composition, camel milk does not curdle naturally.
2) Spiderling
3) Termite - The king helps found the colony with the queen and will mate with the queen during his life. There may be more than one pair of kings and queens in the termite mound.
4) Bison
5) Their necks are too long, which means their lungs are too far away

from their epiglottis, and coughing is a combination movement of the lungs and epiglottis.

6) Giant clam - They can reach 4 feet in length and weigh more than 500 pounds. They live in the warm waters of the South Pacific and Indian Oceans and can live more than 100 years.
7) Sloth - They do it on the ground, making them an easy target for predators, and it all comes out in one push. They dig a small hole to go in and cover it up when they are done and head back into the trees.
8) Foxes
9) Cookiecutter shark
10) They go into shock, which induces a comatose state that can last from 40 minutes to 4 hours.
11) Meganeura - It existed more than 300 million years ago during the Carboniferous Period and was a dragonfly-like insect, with a wingspan of about 2.5 feet. It was a carnivore and fed on other insects and small amphibians.
12) Angora
13) Elephant - All other four-legged animals have at least one pair of legs with knees that face backward.
14) Sword-billed hummingbird
15) Elephant - up to 22 months
16) Dodo bird
17) Sea cucumbers - They are echinoderms, which also include marine animals like starfish and sea urchins. Depending on the species, they can shoot the organs out their head or butt, but they can regrow the organs.
18) Black with white stripes - Zebra embryos are completely black; the white stripes appear during the last embryonic stage.
19) Mandrill - They are found mostly in tropical rainforests in southern Cameroon, Gabon, Equatorial Guinea, and the Congo and can be up to 120 pounds.
20) Bear - the once common but now extinct California grizzly bear

Quiz 16

1) What country has the most wild elephants?
2) What animals are in the order Chiroptera?
3) What is the fastest known flying insect?
4) What is the second-largest rodent in the world?
5) What animal has the longest tongue?
6) Ophidian refers to what type of animal?

7) As a mosquito sucks your blood, what else do they do to maintain their fluid and salt balance?
8) A male donkey is called a jack; what is a female donkey called?
9) What is the largest amphibian in the world?
10) What is the largest snake ever known to have existed?
11) What animal has more neck vertebrae than any other warm-blooded animal?
12) What animal has the largest size difference between the sexes of any land vertebrate?
13) What color is hippo milk?
14) What species kill its leader when they become too old or unproductive by clustering around them in a tight ball until they overheat and die?
15) What is a young eel called?
16) What is the largest tree-dwelling animal?
17) What is the first animal whose evidence is legally admissible in some U.S. courts?
18) What country has the world's longest earthworms?
19) What is the national animal of Canada?
20) Why do dogs typically stare at you when they poop?

Quiz 16 Answers

1) Botswana
2) Bats
3) Horsefly - 90 mph
4) North American beaver - up to 110 pounds
5) Blue whale - about 18 feet long
6) Snake
7) They pee on you. Mosquitoes need to get rid of excess fluid and salts as they suck blood.
8) Jenny
9) Chinese giant salamander - They can grow to lengths of almost six feet.
10) Titanoboa - It lived about 60 million years ago and was up to 42 feet long and weighed up to 2,500 pounds.
11) Swan - 24 vertebrae
12) Anaconda – On average, females are 4.7 times larger than males.
13) Bright pink - Hippos secrete two unique acids, hipposudoric acid and norhipposudoric acid, that function as a natural sunscreen and antimicrobial agent. The acids are red and orange, and when mixed

with a hippo mother's milk, they turn it bright pink.

14) Bees - In a process known as "cuddle death" or "balling," the worker bees dispose of the queen by clustering around her in a tight ball until she overheats and dies.
15) Elver
16) Orangutan - They are 48-54 inches tall and weigh up to 200 pounds and spend nearly all their time in the forest canopy.
17) Bloodhound
18) South Africa - They can grow as large as 22 feet, with the average length being about 6 feet.
19) Beaver
20) They know they are vulnerable at that time, and they are looking to you, a member of their pack, for protection.

Quiz 17

1) What is the name for a group of leopards?
2) Horses have a single toe like other equines, such as zebras and donkeys, but their ancient ancestors that lived 55 million years ago were the size of dogs and had how many total toes?
3) What is the largest species of flatfish?
4) When male pandas urinate, they perform an unusual move to get their pee higher up the tree, allowing their scent to be carried further and increasing their mating chances; what do they do?
5) Male goats urinate on their own heads for what reason?
6) What crustacean has 10 eyes spread all over their body, including the top of their shell, on their tail, and near their mouth?
7) Lobsters have nozzles right under their eyes that they use to communicate with each other; what is released from the nozzles?
8) What insect lives the longest?
9) The gender of most turtles, alligators, and crocodiles is determined after fertilization by what?
10) Some expensive perfumes still contain poop from what animal?
11) What is the primary food for a koala?
12) What is South Africa's national animal?
13) How many tusks does a warthog have?
14) What is the smallest mammal native to North America?
15) Outside of micro-organisms, what animal has existed the longest?
16) While there are more than 60 species of eagles worldwide, how many species live in North America?

17) By mass, what is the smallest known mammal?
18) Male horses typically have 40 teeth; how many do females have?
19) As part of its mating, what species has two individuals compete to see which one can inject sperm into the other with the winner becoming the father and the loser becoming the mother?
20) Humans have six muscles in each ear; how many muscles do cats have in each ear?

Quiz 17 Answers

1) Leap
2) 14 toes - four toes on their front feet and three on their back
3) Halibut - up to 500 pounds
4) They do a handstand.
5) To smell more attractive to females
6) Horseshoe crab
7) Urine
8) Termite queen - They have been known to live for at least 50 years, and some scientists believe they may live to 100.
9) The temperature of the eggs decides whether the offspring will be male or female. This is called temperature-dependent sex determination.
10) Sperm whale - Ambergris, a waxy substance produced in the intestines of sperm whales, has been incorporated in perfumes for a long time as a binding agent to help the fragrances linger on the skin and intensify the scent of the perfume. It has now been mostly replaced by synthetic alternatives.
11) Eucalyptus leaves
12) Springbok - a type of antelope
13) Four
14) American pygmy shrew - Its body is about two inches long including tail, and it weighs about 0.07 to 0.16 ounces.
15) Sponge - Fossils dating back 760 million years have been found.
16) Two - bald eagle and golden eagle
17) Etruscan shrew - On average, they weigh about 0.06 ounces. It also has the fastest heartbeat of any mammal at 1,500 beats per minute.
18) 36 - Males usually have four canine teeth, which are located between the front incisors and the cheek teeth; females don't usually have canine teeth.
19) Flatworms - They are hermaphroditic, having both male and female reproductive organs.

20) 32 - They can move each ear independently and can swivel and rotate their ears 180 degrees.

Quiz 18

1) What is the smallest animal that represents a year in the Chinese zodiac?
2) Where is the only population of wild monkeys in Europe?
3) What animal has the densest fur?
4) What is the only animal in the world with cube-shaped poop?
5) Crocodiles don't sweat; what body part do they use to keep cool?
6) What is the name for a group of giraffes?
7) How many noses do slugs have?
8) If a giraffe has seven neck vertebrae, how many does a mouse have?
9) What is the larva of a fly called?
10) What is the world's loudest insect?
11) What is the first animal ever discovered that is also part plant?
12) Including tentacles, how many arms does a squid have?
13) What animal's name means "river horse" in Greek?
14) What is the tallest bird in North America?
15) What is an eagle's nest called?
16) What is the name for a baby opossum?
17) What other animals besides humans have chins?
18) What is the name for a group of hummingbirds?
19) What is the name for a group of mosquitoes?
20) A spider's muscles pull its legs inward, but they can't push them out again; what does it do to push them out again?

Quiz 18 Answers

1) Rat
2) Gibraltar (on Spain's southern coast) - Barbary macaque
3) Sea otter - They have up to 1 million hairs per square inch on the densest parts of their bodies.
4) Wombat - It appears to be due to the irregular shape and elasticity of their intestines.
5) Mouth - They open it like panting.
6) Tower
7) Four
8) Seven - With a couple of exceptions (sloth and manatee), all mammals,

regardless of size or neck, have seven neck vertebrae.

9) Maggot
10) Cicada - They can reach about 120 decibels, which is equivalent to sitting in the front row of a loud rock concert.
11) Green sea slug (Elysia Chlorotica) – They live off the east coast of the United States and take chloroplasts into their skin, which turns them emerald green and makes them capable of photosynthesis. They can go without eating for nine months or more, photosynthesizing as they bask in the sun.
12) 10 - two tentacles and eight arms
13) Hippopotamus
14) Whooping crane - over five feet tall
15) Eyrie
16) Joey
17) None - Humans are the only animal with a chin; no one knows why.
18) Charm
19) Scourge
20) It pumps a watery liquid into its legs.

Quiz 19

1) What is the only animal with two kneecaps on each knee?
2) What is the name for a group of porcupines?
3) Why is it illegal in Switzerland to own just one guinea pig?
4) What is the name for a group of rhinoceroses?
5) What are the patterns starlings create when they flock together in the sky in swooping coordinated movements called?
6) What animal has the largest sperm?
7) What is the only animal born with horns?
8) Compared to humans, cats have six to eight times more of what cells in their eye that gives them their superior night vision?
9) What is the name for a castrated rooster?
10) What animal's name translates as "earth pig"?
11) A male horse and a female donkey produce what offspring?
12) What is the largest marsupial?
13) Lobsters don't have blood like vertebrate animals; the liquid in their body is colorless and is called what?
14) What is the name for a male alligator?
15) What is a diadromous fish?
16) Arkansas, Florida, Mississippi, Tennessee, and Texas all share what

official state bird?
17) The creature most people identify as a daddy-longlegs spider is not a spider at all; what is it?
18) What is the only known venomous primate?
19) Queen Alexandra's birdwing is the largest what?
20) A cat is feline; what animal is murine?

Quiz 19 Answers

1) Ostrich
2) Prickle
3) Because they are social animals, and it is considered animal cruelty to deny them companionship.
4) Crash
5) Murmurations
6) Fruit flies - Their sperm is coiled up and unspools to about 2.3 inches, which is 20 times the length of their body and about 1,000 times bigger than human sperm.
7) Giraffe - Both male and female giraffes are born with two horn-like structures on their heads called ossicones, which consist of hard cartilage.
8) Rod cells
9) Capon
10) Aardvark
11) Hinny
12) Red kangaroo - It is up to 5.3 feet from its head to rump, and its tail can be up to 3.6 feet long. It weighs about 200 pounds.
13) Hemolymph - It turns blue when exposed to air; this is due to oxygen reacting with the copper in the fluid.
14) Bull
15) Species that spend part of their lives in freshwater and part in saltwater
16) Mockingbird
17) Long-legged harvestmen - It is an arachnid but not a spider. Harvestmen have one body section instead of the two spiders have, two eyes instead of eight, a segmented body instead of unsegmented in spiders, no silk, no venom, and a different respiratory system than spiders, among other differences.
18) Slow loris - They are nocturnal and live in southeast Asia. If they lick a gland under their arms and combine it with their saliva, they have a toxic bite.

19) Butterfly - Females can have a wingspan over 10 inches; they are native to Papua New Guinea.
20) Mouse or rat

Quiz 20

1) Cats and some dogs have a fold of skin forming an open pouch at the outer base of their ear; what is it called?
2) How many eyes does a honeybee have?
3) What term is given to creatures such as earthworms that are both male and female?
4) What insect did Napoleon use as his official emblem?
5) What is the only cat species that can't retract its claws?
6) What two birds can swim but not fly?
7) What is the more common name for an animal's vibrissae?
8) If an animal is edentulous, what is it lacking?
9) What animal is related to common earthworms but spends its entire life in glaciers and requires below-freezing temperatures to survive?
10) What type of insect is most commonly eaten by humans?
11) A shark's teeth aren't embedded in its jaw; what are they attached to?
12) What is unique about a palmiped animal?
13) What is the largest frog?
14) The term ursine relates to what kind of animals?
15) What animal can snap their specialized claw shut producing a cavitation bubble that releases a sound as loud as 218 decibels, louder than a rocket launch?
16) What is the part of a horse between the fetlock and the hoof called?
17) What are the only two sea creatures with ivory tusks?
18) What is the heaviest member of the weasel family?
19) What is a group of ravens called?
20) About 80% of all plant and animal species found on what very large island are endemic (not found elsewhere)?

Quiz 20 Answers

1) Cutaneous marginal pouch or informally known as Henry's pocket - The reason it exists isn't clear.
2) Five – They have two large compound eyes, one on either side of their head, and three smaller eyes at the top of their head.
3) Hermaphrodite

4) Honeybee
5) Cheetah
6) Penguin and flightless cormorant
7) Whiskers
8) Teeth
9) Ice worms - They are found across the northern United States and Canada and come to the surface of glaciers to feed on snow algae. At temperatures even five degrees above freezing, their internal membranes start to fall apart, and they essentially liquefy and die.
10) Beetles
11) Skin covering the jaw - A shark can have over 30,000 teeth in its lifetime. New teeth are continually being grown in a groove in the shark's mouth, and the skin moves the teeth forward into new positions. If they couldn't quickly replace their teeth, they wouldn't have been able to develop such a strong bite that causes them to lose so many teeth.
12) Web-footed
13) Goliath frog - It can be more than a foot long and weigh more than seven pounds; it lives in Cameroon and Equatorial Guinea.
14) Bears
15) Snapping shrimp - When the cavitation bubble collapses, it can reach temperatures of 4,700 degrees Celsius, almost as hot as the surface of the sun.
16) Pastern
17) Narwhal and walrus
18) Sea otter - up to 100 pounds
19) Unkindness or conspiracy.
20) Madagascar

Quiz 21

1) What is the largest member of the dolphin family?
2) What is the only living animal that has the same common and scientific name?
3) Insects don't flap their wings as birds do; how do they move their wings?
4) Where did the Lhasa Apso dog breed originate?
5) What animal is the source of the Middle East Respiratory Syndrome (MERS) virus and is also likely the source of the common cold?
6) In some circumstances, what female insect fakes death to avoid mating?

7) Due to the color inside its mouth, what is another name for the water moccasin?
8) To minimize the risk of drowning, how are dolphins born?
9) During their lifetime, what animal likely spends the most time standing?
10) What dog breed gets its name from the Russian word for swift?
11) Bee sting venom contains what acid?
12) What is the smallest species of apes?
13) What type of feeding is ophiophagy?
14) If an animal is oviparous, what does it do?
15) When a horse curls their upper lip and raises their head in the air, what are they trying to do?
16) Why can't owls move or roll their eyes?
17) What is the largest species of antelope?
18) What do frogs have in their mouths that toads don't?
19) What is the heaviest web-footed bird?
20) What is a group of hippos called?

Quiz 21 Answers

1) Killer whale
2) Boa constrictor
3) They contract their muscles and force their whole body to vibrate, causing the wings that are attached to their exoskeleton to vibrate.
4) Tibet - They were originally kept exclusively by nobility and holy men of Tibet and lived in the monastery and palace of the Dalai Lama and the surrounding monasteries.
5) Camel
6) Dragonfly - The process is called sexual death feigning; a female dragonfly will drop to the ground as if dead to avoid an overly aggressive male. Scientists found that it worked about 60% of the time.
7) Cottonmouth - The inside of its mouth is white.
8) Tail first
9) Elephant - In the wild, they live up to 70 years and only sleep about two hours a day, and they often sleep standing up, only lying down every few nights.
10) Borzoi
11) Formic acid
12) Gibbon - up to 3 feet tall when standing upright and 12-20 pounds
13) Eating snakes - There are ophiophagous mammals, birds, lizards, and

snakes.

14) Lay eggs - There is no embryonic development inside the mother.
15) Get a better smell - The behavior is called the flehmen response and is used to transfer inhaled scent molecules into the vomeronasal organ (VNO), a specialized chemosensory structure found in many mammals.
16) Their eyes aren't round; they are elongated tubes and held in place by a bony structure in the skull.
17) Giant eland - They can be almost 6 feet at the shoulder and weigh up to 2,200 pounds.
18) Teeth
19) Emperor penguin - up to 100 pounds
20) Bloat

Quiz 22

1) What animal causes 10%-20% of all power outages in the United States?
2) What is the name for a female mule?
3) Relative to its body size, what mammal has the largest eyes?
4) What is a baby owl called?
5) What is the part of an animal's skin that it can't reach to scratch itself, usually the area between the shoulder blades, called?
6) The poodle didn't originate in France; where did it originate?
7) What is the specific name for a female pig less than six months old?
8) What is the name for a young female cow that has not had a calf?
9) The term caprine relates to what kind of animals?
10) What is the only domestic animal not mentioned in the Bible?
11) Without even flapping their wings, what bird can travel 500-600 miles in a single day and maintain speeds higher than 79 mph for more than 8 hours?
12) Puppies have 28 teeth; how many teeth do adult dogs have?
13) Several species of what kind of animal can breathe through their anus?
14) What mites eat, crawl, and reproduce on human faces and are more likely to exist the older you get?
15) What is the name for a male woodchuck?
16) What is the main visual difference between a monkey and an ape?
17) The hominid or great ape family includes humans, gorillas, chimpanzees, and what?
18) What is the heaviest North American flying bird?
19) Alcatraz Island derives its name from the Spanish for what bird?

20) Since 1994, all dogs are banned in Antarctica; why?

Quiz 22 Answers

1) Squirrel - Squirrel outages tend to be more localized and more quickly fixed than those caused by storms.
2) Molly
3) Tarsier - It is a small primate found on various islands in Southeast Asia, including the Philippines. It is known for its extremely large eyes; even though it is about the size of a squirrel, each eye has a diameter of about 0.6 inches, as large as its brain.
4) Owlet
5) Acnestis
6) Germany - It comes from the German "pudel," which means "to splash about."
7) Gilt
8) Heifer
9) Goats
10) Cat
11) Wandering albatross - They do it through a cycle called dynamic soaring that has four major components: a windward climb, a turn from windward to leeward at the flight's peak, a leeward descent, and a curve from leeward to windward at the flight's base.
12) 42
13) Turtle - The Fitzroy River turtle, a species that can only be found in the Fitzroy River in Australia, can breathe through its anus; they are constantly pumping water in and out of their anus collecting as much as 70% of all the oxygen they need to survive. Consequently, they can stay underwater for up to three weeks at a time. They are not the only turtle species that can breathe through its anus, but they can use the function to a greater extent.
14) Demodex mites - They are sausage-shaped with eight legs; the largest are about one-third of a millimeter long. They spend most of their time buried head down in your hair follicles; they're most commonly found in the eyelids, nose, cheeks, forehead, and chin.
15) He-chuck
16) Monkeys have tails.
17) Orangutans
18) Trumpeter swan - up to 38 pounds
19) Pelican
20) Stop them from introducing diseases to native seals

Arts

Quiz 1

1) What did Sheryl Crow do before she became a singer?
2) What drink did Johann Sebastian Bach enjoy so much that he wrote a cantata for it?
3) In the song "My Darling Clementine," how did Clementine die?
4) What modern musical instrument evolved from the sackbut?
5) What painter's work is the most stolen?
6) What group sang "Wild Thing" in 1966?
7) What was the first compact disc recording released in the United States?
8) What painting depicts the sister and dentist of artist Grant Wood?

9) Victor Willis, Felipe Rose, Randy Jones, David Hodo, Glenn Hughes, and Alex Briley are all members of what singing group?
10) What singer did Elvis Presley say was the greatest in the world?
11) Who was the lead singer of Herman's Hermits?
12) What singer was married to Debbie Reynolds, Elizabeth Taylor, and Connie Stevens?
13) How many paintings did Vincent Van Gogh sell while he was alive?
14) What duo had a hit with the song "Islands in the Stream"?
15) What musical features the song "Getting to Know You"?
16) What instrument did Bob Dylan play in his recording debut?
17) What natural landmark was the inspiration for the song "America the Beautiful"?
18) What is the barber of Seville's name?
19) What was Chuck Berry's only number-one hit?
20) What was the biggest hit for The Animals in 1964?

Quiz 1 Answers

1) Teacher
2) Coffee
3) Drowned
4) Trombone
5) Pablo Picasso
6) Troggs
7) *Born in the USA*
8) *American Gothic*
9) The Village People
10) Roy Orbison
11) Peter Noone
12) Eddie Fisher
13) One
14) Kenny Rogers and Dolly Parton
15) *The King and I*
16) Harmonica
17) Pikes Peak
18) Figaro
19) "My Ding-a-ling"
20) "House of the Rising Sun"

Quiz 2

1) How many movements traditionally make up a concerto?
2) Who is the youngest solo singer ever to win a Grammy?
3) What was Buddy Holly's first hit single?
4) John Henry Deutchendorf became famous under what name?
5) What act has the most Billboard Hot 100 entries of all time?
6) In Greek mythology, how many heads did the Hydra have?
7) Who wrote the music for *Showboat*?
8) Who wrote the symphonic fairy tale *Peter and the Wolf*?
9) Who wrote the song "I Will Always Love You"?
10) In what method of singing does the singer alternate between natural voice and falsetto?
11) What is Frank Sinatra's middle name?
12) Whose son flew too close to the sun on waxen wings?
13) What 1958 song was The Coaster's only number-one hit?
14) Who is generally given credit for coining the term "rock and roll"?
15) In Greek mythology, who was the first woman on the earth?
16) The Passion Play is performed every 10 years where?
17) Who recorded "King of the Road" in 1965?
18) In Greek mythology, who solved the riddle of the Sphinx?
19) Who was a founder and first director of the New York City Ballet?
20) Who is Hercules' father?

Quiz 2 Answers

1) Three
2) Leann Rimes – 13
3) "That'll Be the Day"
4) John Denver
5) Glee cast – 207
6) Nine
7) Jerome Kern
8) Sergei Prokofiev
9) Dolly Parton
10) Yodeling
11) Albert
12) Daedalus
13) "Yakety Yak"

14) Alan Freed
15) Pandora
16) Oberammergau, Germany
17) Roger Miller
18) Oedipus
19) George Balanchine
20) Zeus

Quiz 3

1) The Dove Awards are presented annually for what?
2) Who painted *The Water Lilly Pond* in 1899?
3) What are the names of The Three Tenors?
4) What is the world's best-selling musical instrument?
5) In Greek mythology, what did Daedalus construct for Minos?
6) Who was the first woman inducted into the Country Music Hall of Fame in 1973?
7) Who was the first woman inducted into the Rock and Roll Hall of Fame in 1987?
8) In Greek mythology, who gave fire to mankind?
9) What 1960s protest song includes the line "Think of all the hate there is in Red China, then take a look around to Selma, Alabama"?
10) From what musical does the song "On the Street Where You Live" come?
11) Who wrote the opera *Rigoletto*?
12) What are the four sections of an orchestra?
13) What is painting in watercolor on fresh plaster called?
14) What famous religious hymn was composed by Augustus Montague Toplady in the 18th century?
15) In Greek mythology, who ferries the dead across the river Styx?
16) Who composed *Appalachian Spring*?
17) What singer's autobiography is titled *Bound for Glory*?
18) What was the number-one song of the 1970s in the United States?
19) What musical features the song "Old Man River"?
20) In Arthurian legend, who is Lancelot's son?

Quiz 3 Answers

1) Gospel music
2) Claude Monet

3) Jose Carreras, Placido Domingo, Luciano Pavarotti
4) Harmonica
5) Labyrinth
6) Patsy Cline
7) Aretha Franklin
8) Prometheus
9) "Eve of Destruction" - Barry McGuire
10) *My Fair Lady*
11) Giuseppe Verdi
12) Strings, woodwind, brass, percussion
13) Fresco
14) "Rock of Ages"
15) Charon
16) Aaron Copeland
17) Woody Guthrie
18) "You Light Up My Life" – Debby Boone
19) *Showboat*
20) Galahad

Quiz 4

1) What classical composer wrote "Hark the Herald Angels Sing"?
2) Who was Bette Midler's piano player before he went solo?
3) What song was originally "Good Morning to All" before the words were changed, and it was published in 1935?
4) Who was part of the Million Dollar Quartet in an informal 1956 recording?
5) Who was condemned in Hades to forever push a boulder uphill, only for it to come rolling down before it reached the top?
6) Who sang "Monster Mash"?
7) What 6th-century Greek poet is the father of drama?
8) In 1981, who won song of the year with "Sailing"?
9) What band was named after the inventor of the seed drill?
10) What actor was the narrator on Michael Jackson's *Thriller*?
11) What group originally sang "Louie Louie"?
12) Who wrote *La Traviata*?
13) What renaissance artist had the surname Buonarroti?
14) Who wrote *The Flight of the Bumblebee*?
15) In what musical is the song "Hey Big Spender" featured?

16) In music, what is a semihemidemisemiquaver?
17) According to Wurlitzer, what is the most popular jukebox song of all time?
18) What famous artist could write with both his left and right hand simultaneously?
19) What do the initials B.B. stand for in B.B. King's name?
20) "Ebony and Ivory" was a hit for what famous duo?

Quiz 4 Answers

1) Felix Mendelssohn
2) Barry Manilow
3) "Happy Birthday to You"
4) Elvis Presley, Jerry Lee Lewis, Carl Perkins, Johnny Cash
5) Sisyphus
6) Bobby Boris Picket and the Crypt Kickers
7) Thespis
8) Christopher Cross
9) Jethro Tull
10) Vincent Price
11) The Kingsmen
12) Giuseppe Verdi
13) Michelangelo
14) Nicolai Rimsky Korsakov
15) *Sweet Charity*
16) 1/128th note
17) "Hound Dog" - Elvis Presley
18) Leonardo da Vinci
19) Blues Boy
20) Paul McCartney and Stevie Wonder

Quiz 5

1) Who has performed more concerts in Madison Square garden than any other artist?
2) What female singer died of alcohol poisoning in 2011 at the age of 27?
3) Who wrote and recorded "Spirit in the Sky"?
4) What singer wrote and first recorded "Blue Suede Shoes"?
5) In the song "Yankee Doodle," what does the term macaroni mean?
6) How many copies must an album sell to be certified diamond?

7) Who had the number-one song "The Battle of New Orleans"?
8) What is the name of the Greek goddess of victory?
9) Who is the best-selling Canadian singer of all time?
10) What famous musician was fatally shot by his father in 1984?
11) What was the highest-selling album of the 1980s in the United States?
12) What is the Roman name for the goddess Hecate?
13) What Broadway show has the longest run in history?
14) What famous artist was struck in the face by a rival and disfigured for life?
15) Who has the most all-time number-one hits on Billboard's Hot 100?
16) What artist had the first record to sell over 1 million copies?
17) Based on decibels, what is the loudest instrument in a standard orchestra?
18) How many people have won all four major American entertainment awards (Oscar, Emmy, Tony, Grammy)?
19) Who has won the most Grammy Awards?
20) Who is the youngest artist to win an album of the year Grammy?

Quiz 5 Answers

1) Elton John
2) Amy Winehouse
3) Norman Greenbaum
4) Carl Perkins
5) Stylish or fashionable - In late 18th century England, macaroni meant stylish or fashionable; in the song, it is used to mock the Americans who think they can be stylish by simply sticking a feather in their cap.
6) 10 million
7) Johnny Horton
8) Nike
9) Celine Dion
10) Marvin Gaye
11) *Thriller* - Michael Jackson
12) Trivia
13) *Phantom of the Opera*
14) Michelangelo
15) Beatles – 20
16) Enrico Caruso – 1902
17) Trombone – about 115 decibels

18) 15 – Richard Rogers, Helen Hayes, Rita Moreno, John Gielgud, Audrey Hepburn, Marvin Hamlisch, Mel Brooks, Whoopi Goldberg, Jonathan Tunick, Mike Nichols, Scott Rudin, Robert Lopez, John Legend, Tim Rice, Andrew Lloyd Weber
19) George Solti - 31
20) Taylor Swift – 20

Quiz 6

1) Who wrote and sang "Hello Muddah, Hello Fadduh" about Camp Granada?
2) Who composed *Pomp and Circumstance*?
3) In Greek mythology, who gave Midas the power to turn everything to gold?
4) Who wrote the music *Ride of the Valkyries*?
5) What is the lowest female singing voice called?
6) "I Don't Know How to Love Him" is from what musical?
7) Carlos Marin, Urs Buhler, Sebastien Izambard, and David Miller are members of what vocal group?
8) The Greek statue *Discobolus* is better known by what name?
9) Who composed *The Four Seasons*?
10) Who is the oldest artist to have a number-one hit on Billboard's Hot 100?
11) Who is the oldest female artist to have a number-one hit on Billboard's Hot 100?
12) Who is the youngest solo artist to have a number-one hit on Billboard's Hot 100?
13) Who is the oldest living artist to have a song on Billboard's Hot 100?
14) What songwriter has the most number-one singles on Billboard's Hot 100?
15) What artist has the most consecutive number-one singles on Billboard's Hot 100?
16) What song has the most weeks at number one ever for an instrumental?
17) Janis Joplin, Jimi Hendrix, and Kurt Cobain all died at what age?
18) What singing duo started as Caesar and Cleo?
19) What is the name of the last Beatles album recorded before they split up?
20) What is the highest male singing voice called?

Quiz 6 Answers

1) Allan Sherman
2) Edward Elgar
3) Dionysus
4) Richard Wagner
5) Contralto
6) *Jesus Christ Superstar*
7) Il Divo
8) *The Discus Thrower*
9) Antonio Vivaldi
10) Louis Armstrong – age 62 with "Hello Dolly" in 1964
11) Cher – age 52 in 1999
12) Stevie Wonder – age 13 with "Fingertips Part 2" in 1963
13) Tony Bennet – age 85 in 2011
14) Paul McCartney
15) Whitney Houston – seven
16) "Theme from a Summer Place" – nine weeks in 1960
17) 27
18) Sonny and Cher
19) *Abbey Road*
20) Countertenor

Quiz 7

1) What country has the highest number of museums per capita?
2) The blood-red sky in Edvard Munch's famous painting *The Scream* is believed to be due to what rather than the artist's imagination?
3) Where was the largest free rock concert ever held?
4) Early in his career, Picasso was so poor he did what with most of his early work?
5) Who said, "I think, therefore I am"?
6) Who are the only two people ever to win an Oscar, Emmy, Tony, Grammy, and Pulitzer?
7) In 1939, Earl Wild was the first pianist to give a recital on U.S. television; in 1997, he was also the first person to do what?
8) How many of his own songs did Elvis Presley write?
9) What music group used to be called Johnny and the Moondogs?
10) What is the first and only music group to play on all seven continents?

11) Whose music does the British navy play to help scare off Somali pirates?
12) What country has the highest number of heavy metal bands per capita?
13) Who had the only number-one song recorded by a father and daughter?
14) Who is the only person ever to win a Nobel Prize, Pulitzer, Oscar, and Grammy?
15) What does the word ukulele literally mean?
16) What classical composer wrote numerous letters and an entire song focused on poop?
17) What year was the first piano made?
18) Mozart and Beethoven composed music for the glass armonica instrument; who invented it?
19) What kind of paint did Picasso use?
20) Elvis Presley won three Grammy awards; what music category were his three wins?

Quiz 7 Answers

1) Israel
2) Krakatoa eruption in 1883 – The dust and gases from the eruption caused fiery sunrises and sunsets in Norway that Munch witnessed.
3) Rio de Janeiro, Brazil – Rod Stewart played to 4.2 million people on Copacabana Beach on New Year's Eve 1994.
4) He burned them to keep his apartment warm.
5) Rene Descartes – philosopher, mathematician, scientist, father of analytical geometry
6) Richard Rogers and Marvin Hamlisch
7) Stream a piano performance over the internet
8) None
9) Beatles
10) Metallica
11) Britney Spears
12) Finland
13) Frank and Nancy Sinatra – "Something Stupid" in 1967
14) Bob Dylan
15) Jumping flea – likely after the movements of the player's fingers
16) Mozart – No one is sure if it was his odd humor or a mental issue.
17) 1698
18) Benjamin Franklin – It replicated the sound a wet finger makes when rubbed along the rim of a glass and became very popular.

19) House paint
20) Gospel – His earliest work was before the Grammys started in 1958.

Quiz 8

1) Carl and the Passions changed their band name to what?
2) Whose band was the Quarrymen?
3) In the song “Waltzing Matilda,” what is a jumbuck?
4) Who had a hit with the song “Loco-Motion” in 1962?
5) *La Giaconda* is better known as what?
6) Who wrote the opera *Madam Butterfly*?
7) Robert Allen Zimmerman is the real name of what music artist?
8) *The Aphrodite of Melos* has what better-known name?
9) On what is the *Mona Lisa* painted?
10) The band The Detours changed their name to The High Numbers and then what name?
11) What Henry Mancini song won an Oscar and a Grammy?
12) Who are the only two artists to win best new artist and record, album, and song of the year Grammys in the same year?
13) What opera is about a female cigarette factory worker?
14) Composer Vivaldi had what other profession?
15) Tempera paint's primary ingredients are water and what?
16) Beethoven, Brahms, Chopin, Handel, Liszt, and Ravel have what in common in their personal lives?
17) “What I Did for Love” is from what Broadway musical?
18) Who wrote the song “Johnny B. Goode”?
19) What town is the setting for *The Music Man*?
20) What Italian artist painted *Birth of Venus*?

Quiz 8 Answers

1) Beach Boys
2) John Lennon – The band evolved into the Beatles.
3) Sheep
4) Little Eva
5) *Mona Lisa*
6) Giacomo Puccini
7) Bob Dylan
8) *Venus de Milo*
9) Wood – thin poplar panel

10) The Who
11) "Moon River" - *Breakfast at Tiffany's* Oscar
12) Christopher Cross (1981) and Billie Eilish (2020)
13) *Carmen*
14) Priest
15) Egg yolk
16) Bachelors
17) *A Chorus Line*
18) Chuck Berry
19) River City
20) Sandro Botticelli

Quiz 9

1) What had one eye, one horn, and flew in Sheb Wooley's 1958 hit?
2) Who originally sang "Johnny Angel"?
3) Who was the oldest member of the Beatles?
4) What was Rembrandt's last name?
5) Who wrote more than 1,000 songs including "This Land is Your Land"?
6) Who replaced Pete Best?
7) What Broadway show introduced the song "Some Enchanted Evening"?
8) What Broadway musical was inspired by *Don Quixote*?
9) What comedian had the first comedy album ever to hit number one?
10) What Gilbert and Sullivan opera is about the emperor of Japan?
11) Who jumped off the Tallahatchie Bridge?
12) What is the only single by the same artist to go to number one twice?
13) In Greek mythology, what beautiful youth pined for the love of his reflection?
14) What was the last Rogers and Hammerstein musical?
15) Who wrote the song "God Bless America"?
16) Who is the fourth person mentioned in Dion DiMucci's song "Abraham, Martin and John"?
17) Who wrote "Rhapsody in Blue"?
18) What 1966 hit was sung by Sergeant Barry Sadler?
19) Who painted *The Blue Boy*?
20) Who is the principal character in *Fiddler on the Roof*?

Quiz 9 Answers

1) Flying Purple People Eater
2) Shelley Fabares
3) Ringo Starr
4) Van Rijn
5) Woody Guthrie
6) Ringo Starr – He took his place in the Beatles in 1962.
7) *South Pacific*
8) *Man of La Mancha*
9) Bob Newhart – *The Button-Down Mind of Bob Newhart* in 1960
10) *The Mikado*
11) Billy Joe McAllister
12) "The Twist" – Chubby Checker in 1960 and 1961
13) Narcissus
14) *The Sound of Music*
15) Irving Berlin
16) Bobby Kennedy
17) George Gershwin
18) "The Ballad of the Green Berets"
19) Thomas Gainsborough
20) Tevye

Quiz 10

1) What is the only music group where every member has written more than one number-one single?
2) What was classical composer Mussorgsky's first name?
3) In music, what does the term da capo mean?
4) Based on the number of weeks at number one on Billboard's Hot 100, who was the top artist of the 2000s?
5) What martial arts action movie star is also a pop star in Asia?
6) What composer and musician died in 1750 and fathered twenty children, nine of whom survived him, by two wives?
7) What was the name of the airplane Buddy Holly died in?
8) What singer is known as the "Empress of the Blues"?
9) Mozart wrote a six-piece canon titled *Leck mich im Arsch* that translates as what?
10) In what century did Michelangelo paint the Sistine Chapel?

11) Beethoven's third symphony is nicknamed what?
12) Based on concerns that there were obscene lyrics inserted, the FBI investigated what 1963 song?
13) Based on the number of weeks at number one on Billboard's Hot 100, who was the top artist of the 1970s?
14) In music, what is meant by the term pianissimo?
15) What 19th century French painter was known for his pictures of ballet dancers?
16) What is the longest-running play in history?
17) What was Buddy Holly's real first name?
18) What is the oldest surviving musical instrument?
19) In "The Twelve Days of Christmas," my true love sent to me 10 what?
20) What was Elvis Presley's first song to hit number one on Billboard's Hot 100?

Quiz 10 Answers

1) Queen - All four members have been inducted into the Songwriters Hall of Fame.
2) Modest
3) From the beginning - It is a composer or publisher's directive to repeat the previous piece of music.
4) Usher
5) Jackie Chan - He is a classically trained singer and has produced over 20 different albums, including over 100 songs in five languages, and won the Best Foreign Singer Award in Japan in 1984.
6) Johann Sebastian Bach
7) *American Pie* - Don McLean later used it as the title for his number-one song in 1972.
8) Bessie Smith
9) *Kiss My Ass*
10) 16th century - started in 1509
11) *Eroica*
12) "Louie Louie" - They abandoned the investigation after three months; they were unable to discern what the lyrics were.
13) Bee Gees
14) Very softly
15) Edgar Degas
16) *The Mousetrap* - It is an Agatha Christie murder mystery play and has been running in London's West End since 1952, over 27,000

performances.

17) Charles
18) Flute - Flutes as old as 43,000 years have been found.
19) Lords a leaping
20) "Heartbreak Hotel" - 1956

Quiz 11

1) In *Peter and the Wolf*, what instrument represents the duck?
2) What is the name of the Russian triangular guitar?
3) Who was the Roman goddess of wisdom?
4) In Greek mythology, who was the youngest son of Cronos and Rhea?
5) Based on the number of weeks at number one on Billboard's Hot 100, who was the top artist of the 1990s?
6) According to Billboard, what was the best-selling and most-played song in the United States during the 1960s?
7) What was the first rock and roll song to hit number one on Billboard's pop charts?
8) Based on the number of weeks at number one on Billboard's Hot 100, who was the top artist of the 2010s?
9) What mythic character rode horses called Llamrei and Hengroen?
10) What musical term means to play a piece of music lively and fast?
11) Percivale, Lionell, Gareth, Bleoberis, Lucan, Palomedes, Lamorak, and Pelleas were members of what mythic group?
12) Based on the number of weeks at number one on Billboard's Hot 100, who was the top artist of the 1980s?
13) What female voice comes between contralto and soprano?
14) What is the only work of art Michelangelo ever signed?
15) What was the Beatles' first U.S. number-one hit?
16) How many of the Beatles could read or write music?
17) Italian painter Jacopo Robusti was better known under what name?
18) What famous Italian painter spent the last four years of his life on the run from murder charges?
19) In Gustav Holst's *The Planets*, what planet represents old age?
20) Who was the first rock star arrested on stage?

Quiz 11 Answers

1) Oboe
2) Balalaika

3) Minerva
4) Zeus
5) Mariah Carey
6) "The Twist" - Chubby Checker
7) "Rock Around the Clock" – 1955
8) Drake
9) King Arthur
10) Allegro
11) Knights of the Round Table
12) Michael Jackson
13) Mezzo-soprano
14) *The Pieta*
15) "I Want to Hold Your Hand"
16) None - When they needed to write music for others to play, arrangers at sheet music publishing companies would do it.
17) Tintoretto - his middle name
18) Caravaggio (1571-1610)
19) Saturn
20) Jim Morrison - On December 9, 1967, he was arrested as he performed on stage at the New Haven Arena in Connecticut. He was arrested for an incident that took place with a police officer before the show.

History

Quiz 1

1) Alexander the Great was king of what country?
2) What year did Ferdinand Magellan complete the first circumnavigation of the world?
3) In what country were Arabic numerals first used?
4) Who made the first solo round the world flight?
5) What U.S. founding father was carried to the Constitutional Convention in a sedan chair carried by prisoners?
6) Who succeeded Adolf Hitler in 1945 as the leader of Germany?
7) Who was the first honorary U.S. citizen?
8) Who was Temujin better known as?
9) Who was *Time* magazine's 1938 man of the year?
10) What queen married two of her brothers?
11) Good King Wenceslas was king of what country?
12) The spire on the Empire State building was meant to be used for what?
13) What year did the Berlin wall fall?
14) Who was the first African American in space?

15) Who was the first man to set foot on all the continents other than Antarctica?
16) During the War of 1812, British troops invaded and burned what U.S. landmark?
17) What year was the first telephone call made?
18) What year did the Volkswagen Beetle make its first appearance?
19) Who was the first British monarch to visit America?
20) Who taught Alexander the Great?

Quiz 1 Answers

1) Macedonia
2) 1522
3) India
4) Wiley Post – 1933
5) Benjamin Franklin
6) Admiral Karl Donitz
7) Winston Churchill
8) Genghis Khan
9) Adolf Hitler
10) Cleopatra
11) Bohemia - current Czech Republic
12) Airship dock
13) 1989
14) Guion Bluford
15) Captain James Cook
16) White House
17) 1876
18) 1938
19) George VI - 1939
20) Aristotle

Quiz 2

1) What year was the first U.S. minimum wage instituted?
2) What year did India gain independence from British colonial rule?
3) What book was given to all officers in the Confederate army during the American Civil War?
4) What civilization first domesticated guinea pigs and used them for food, sacrifices, and household pets?

5) Through what town did Lady Godiva ride naked?
6) Who was outlaw Harry Longabaugh better known as?
7) What country did Abel Tasman discover in 1642?
8) By what name is Princess Sophia of Anhalt-Zerbst better known?
9) What country invented the crossbow?
10) Who ordered the Russian nobility to become more European by shaving off their beards?
11) What was the profession of serial killer Ted Bundy?
12) What nationality was the first person in space who wasn't American or Russian?
13) What was the name of Alexander the Great's horse?
14) Who was Abraham Lincoln's first choice to lead the Union army?
15) What was Lech Walesa's job before he founded Solidarity?
16) Where was the first U.S. federal penitentiary?
17) British King Edward VIII abdicated his throne to marry who?
18) Who discovered the source of the Nile River?
19) What Roman killed himself after his defeat at Actium?
20) How many years were there between the first female in space and the first American female in space?

Quiz 2 Answers

1) 1938 – 25 cents per hour
2) 1947
3) Les Misérables – Robert E. Lee believed the book symbolized their cause.
4) Incas
5) Coventry, England
6) Sundance Kid
7) New Zealand
8) Catherine the Great
9) China – about 700 BC
10) Peter the Great
11) Attorney
12) Czech – Vladimir Remek in 1978
13) Bucephalus
14) Robert E. Lee
15) Electrician
16) Leavenworth, Kansas

17) Wallis Simpson
18) John Hanning Speke
19) Mark Antony
20) 20 years – A Soviet woman was the first in 1963.

Quiz 3

1) The saying "Don't give up the ship!" comes from the last words of Captain James Lawrence in what war?
2) What is widely considered "The Gun that Won the West"?
3) What explorer visited Australia and New Zealand and surveyed the Pacific coast of North America?
4) What did the Romans call the tenth part of a legion?
5) What is the oldest alcoholic beverage to gain widespread popularity?
6) Why was the Eiffel Tower built?
7) What year did U.S. prohibition come to an end?
8) What explorer's last words were "I have not told half of what I saw"?
9) What year was NASA founded?
10) What famous battle took place from July 1 to July 3, 1863?
11) What was the real name of the Boston Strangler?
12) Who is known as the father of modern economics?
13) How long was Nelson Mandela in prison?
14) Who was King of Mycenae and commander of the Greek forces in the Trojan War?
15) What did Albert Einstein call "the hardest thing in the world to understand"?
16) Who was the first American born child of English settlers?
17) Who is known as the father of medicine?
18) Introduced in 1888, the first vending machine in the United States dispensed what item?
19) Fylfot is a heraldic name for what symbol?
20) The U.S. icon Uncle Sam is based on Samuel Wilson who did what during the War of 1812?

Quiz 3 Answers

1) War of 1812
2) Winchester Model 1873 rifle
3) Captain George Vancouver
4) Cohort - 300 to 600 men

5) Mead – about 2000 BC from fermenting honey
6) Celebrate the 100th anniversary of the French Revolution
7) 1933
8) Marco Polo
9) 1958
10) Gettysburg
11) Albert DeSalvo
12) Adam Smith
13) 27 years
14) Agamemnon
15) Income taxes
16) Virginia Dare
17) Hippocrates
18) Gum
19) Swastika
20) Meat packer – He supplied barrels of beef to the army stamped with "U.S." for United States, but soldiers started referring to it as Uncle Sam's.

Quiz 4

1) What religion was Adolf Hitler?
2) What is the real name of the serial killer known as Son of Sam?
3) When was apartheid introduced in South Africa?
4) What was the family name of the French brothers who were pioneers in hot air ballooning and conducted the first untethered flights?
5) What year did the United States celebrate its sesquicentennial?
6) Who did Adolf Hitler dictate *Mein Kampf* to while in prison?
7) Who was the first Christian emperor of Rome?
8) Who first suggested the idea of daylight saving time in an essay he wrote in 1784?
9) What happened July 15, 1815, on the *HMS Bellerophon*?
10) What was the name given to textile workers who opposed modernization during the 19th century?
11) On December 1, 1917, who opened Boys Town, a farm village for wayward boys, near Omaha, Nebraska?
12) Who assassinated John Lennon?
13) Where did Churchill, Roosevelt, and Stalin meet in 1945?
14) Who was known as the father of the atomic bomb?

15) *Sputnik* 2 was launched into space in 1957; what was the name of the dog that was on board?
16) At the battle of Actium, who defeated Mark Antony and Cleopatra?
17) What country's troops sustained the greatest number of deaths in WWII?
18) In the 15th century, what was the war between the houses of Lancaster and York?
19) What is the most-visited paid monument in the world?
20) *The Ladies' Mercury* in 1693 was the world's first what?

Quiz 4 Answers

1) Roman Catholic
2) David Berkowitz
3) 1948
4) Montgolfier
5) 1926 – 150th anniversary
6) Rudolf Hess
7) Constantine the Great - emperor from 306 to 337
8) Benjamin Franklin
9) Napoleon surrendered
10) Luddites
11) Father Edward Flanagan
12) Mark David Chapman
13) Yalta
14) Robert Oppenheimer
15) Laika
16) Octavian or Emperor Augustus
17) Soviet Union
18) War of the Roses
19) Eiffel Tower
20) Periodical designed and published for women

Quiz 5

1) What was the first lighthouse?
2) Who made the first phone call to the moon?
3) What battle was fought at Senlac Hill?
4) In 1917, Janette Rankin become the first woman in the United States to do what?

5) What is the oldest college in the United States?
6) Who was the last English king to die on the battlefield?
7) What is the most powerful earthbound explosion ever witnessed by humans?
8) What was the name of Robert E. Lee's horse?
9) What disease is believed to have killed more people than any other throughout history?
10) What year did the *Titanic* sink?
11) Who was the first American astronaut who wasn't in the military when they went into space?
12) What political cartoonist popularized the use of the elephant and donkey as symbols of the two main U.S. political parties?
13) What was the first U.S. state to secede from the Union on December 20, 1860?
14) The Statue of Liberty originally also served what functional role?
15) In honor of whose death in 1931 were all non-essential lights in the United States turned off for one minute?
16) What American statesman wrote the collection of essays *Fart Proudly*?
17) Who was the first person to enter space (100 km above the earth) twice?
18) How many states joined the Confederate States of America?
19) In the 16th century, King James IV of Scotland paid people to practice what on them?
20) Who was married to Adolf Hitler for one day?

Quiz 5 Answers

1) Pharos of Alexandria – 280 BC
2) Richard Nixon
3) Battle of Hastings
4) Elected to the U.S. Congress
5) Harvard – 1636
6) Richard III
7) Mount Tambora volcanic eruption in 1815 in Indonesia – The explosion was equivalent to 800 megatons of TNT, 14 times larger than the largest man-made explosion.
8) Traveller
9) Malaria – Over 1 million people still die from malaria annually.
10) 1912
11) Neil Armstrong - He had been a Navy fighter pilot but was a civilian

when he joined NASA.

12) Thomas Nast
13) South Carolina
14) Lighthouse
15) Thomas Edison
16) Benjamin Franklin
17) Joseph A. Walker – X-15 rocket aircraft in 1963
18) 11
19) Dentistry – He was an amateur dentist and very interested in medicine; he established the Royal College of Surgeons in Scotland two centuries before it was established in England.
20) Eva Braun

Quiz 6

1) Opened in 1852, what infamous prison was off the coast of French Guiana?
2) What war did Joan of Arc's inspirational leadership help end?
3) What year did the first manned space flight occur?
4) The New Testament was originally written in what language?
5) What did Russian Valentina Tereshkova become the first woman to do in 1963?
6) In what war did jet fighter planes first battle each other?
7) According to legend, what historical figure died of a nosebleed on his wedding night?
8) The island of Krakatoa was almost entirely destroyed by a volcanic eruption in what year?
9) Who wrote the words that are engraved on the Statue of Liberty?
10) What city became the U.S. federal capital in 1789?
11) What area of London did Jack the Ripper's murders occur in?
12) What famous priest ministered to the Molokai lepers from 1873 until his death?
13) What was the date for D-Day?
14) What was the last Chinese dynasty?
15) What was the predecessor to the United Nations?
16) How many witches were burned at the stake during the Salem witch trials?
17) Who was the first person to reach the South Pole in 1911?
18) What transportation route re-opened in 1975 after an eight-year closure?

19) What was discovered at Qumran in 1947?
20) What was the first ship to reach the *Titanic* after it sank?

Quiz 6 Answers

1) Devil's Island
2) The Hundred Years War
3) 1961
4) Greek
5) Travel in space
6) Korean War
7) Attila the Hun
8) 1883
9) Emma Lazarus – The words were written in 1883 to raise money for the statue's pedestal.
10) New York
11) Whitechapel
12) Father Damien
13) June 6, 1944
14) Manchu
15) League of Nations
16) None - Twenty were executed, but most were hung, and none were burned.
17) Roald Amundsen
18) Suez Canal
19) Dead Sea Scrolls
20) *Carpathia*

Quiz 7

1) What year did Canada become a country?
2) Who was the first person to sail around the Cape of Good Hope?
3) Who was named *Time* magazine's Man of the Century in 1999?
4) How many states are needed to ratify an amendment to the U.S. Constitution?
5) Where was the tallest tsunami wave ever recorded?
6) Who assassinated Robert Kennedy?
7) Who was the first queen of England?
8) What is the only nation that created nuclear weapons and then voluntarily eliminated them?

9) What year did Cuba get its independence from the United States?
10) Who was the oldest person to sign the Declaration of Independence?
11) Less than a year before Abraham Lincoln was assassinated, who saved Lincoln's oldest son Robert from being hit by a train?
12) Tenochtitlan was the capital of what empire?
13) What U.S. Constitutional amendment granted women the right to vote?
14) What year was the Pledge of Allegiance written?
15) In what city did Rosa Parks refuse to give up her seat?
16) Where was the world's first underwater tunnel?
17) What was the first U.S. department store?
18) Who organized the Boston Tea Party?
19) Who is the only person to win two unshared Nobel Prizes?
20) What did Robert Heft design in 1958 as a part of a high school history class project?

Quiz 7 Answers

1) 1867
2) Vasco da Gama
3) Albert Einstein
4) 38 – 75% of the states
5) Lituya Bay, Alaska in 1958 - An 8.0 earthquake dropped 40 to 50 million cubic yards of rock and ice 3,000 feet down into the bay creating a 1,720-foot wave.
6) Sirhan Sirhan
7) Mary I
8) South Africa
9) 1902
10) Benjamin Franklin – 70 at the time
11) Edwin Booth – brother of John Wilkes Booth
12) Aztec
13) 19th
14) 1892
15) Montgomery, Alabama
16) Thames River, London – 1843
17) Macy's – 1858
18) Samuel Adams
19) Linus Pauling
20) Current 50-star United States flag

Quiz 8

1) What was the nickname for the *Hughes H-4 Hercules* aircraft that made a single flight in 1947?
2) What year did Switzerland last go to war with another country?
3) What country landed the first man-made object on the moon?
4) What empire lasted from 1324 to 1922?
5) What country did Adolf Hitler describe as a pimple on the face of Europe?
6) The final link of the first U.S. transcontinental railway was completed in what state?
7) What year did Mexico get its independence from Spain?
8) What country has the oldest parliament in the world?
9) Who was the first *Time* magazine man of the year?
10) Israel was founded in what year?
11) What year did the gunfight at the O.K. Corral take place?
12) What year was the U.S. Constitution written?
13) What year was the last public execution in the United States?
14) What was the first Confederate state to be readmitted to the Union after the American Civil War?
15) What was suffragette Susan B. Anthony talking about when she said, "I think it has done more to emancipate women than anything else in the world. It gives women a feeling of freedom and self-reliance"?
16) How many people have died outside the earth's atmosphere?
17) What newspaper mistakenly ran the infamous "Dewey Defeats Truman" headline?
18) How many people have walked on the moon?
19) Who was the last man to walk on the moon?
20) What country was known to Europeans as Cathay from the 11th to the 16th century?

Quiz 8 Answers

1) *Spruce Goose*
2) 1515
3) Soviet Union – *Luna* 2 in 1959
4) Ottoman or Turkish Empire
5) Switzerland – Hitler hated Switzerland and thought it had no right to exist; he had a planned invasion but never initiated it.
6) Utah

7) 1810
8) Iceland - 930
9) Charles Lindbergh – 1927
10) 1948
11) 1881
12) 1787
13) 1936 – Kentucky
14) Tennessee
15) Bicycling
16) Three – *Soyuz 11* in 1971
17) *Chicago Daily Tribune*
18) 12
19) Eugene Cernan
20) China

Quiz 9

1) What year did the United States complete the Louisiana Purchase?
2) The end of the Pony Express line was in what western city?
3) What state was the first to elect a woman to the U.S. Congress?
4) What is the bloodiest single day of battle in U.S. history?
5) What was the first nation to have a female prime minister?
6) Who was the first woman to win a Nobel Prize?
7) Who is the only person to win *Time* magazine's person of the year three times?
8) In what city was Archduke Ferdinand killed?
9) What year did seat belts become mandatory in U.S. cars?
10) What Spanish explorer is credited with discovering the Mississippi River?
11) What country first tried unsuccessfully to build the Panama Canal?
12) Who was the pilot in the first fatal airplane crash?
13) What African country was settled by Americans?
14) Before devoting his life to philosophy, what was Socrates' profession?
15) What is the world's oldest snack food?
16) What was the first U.S. college to confer degrees on women?
17) Who was the first female candidate for U.S. vice president on a major party ticket?
18) What was the first city to reach a population of 1 million people?
19) What famous general was attacked by rabbits and had to retreat?

20) Who was the first woman appointed to the U.S. Supreme Court?

Quiz 9 Answers

1) 1803
2) Sacramento, California
3) Montana
4) Battle of Antietam in the American Civil War - 22,000 dead, wounded, or missing
5) Sri Lanka – 1960
6) Marie Curie
7) Franklin D. Roosevelt
8) Sarajevo
9) 1968
10) Hernando de Soto
11) France
12) Orville Wright
13) Liberia
14) Mason or stonecutter
15) Pretzels – sixth century
16) Oberlin College – 1841
17) Geraldine Ferraro – 1984
18) Rome – 5 BC
19) Napoleon – In 1807, Napoleon had just signed the Treaty of Tilsit ending his war with Russia; to celebrate, he went on a rabbit hunt. Hundreds of rabbits had been gathered for the hunt in cages, but when they were released, they swarmed toward Napoleon and his men rather than running away. They swarmed Napoleon's legs and started climbing up; he was forced to retreat to his coach and depart. Instead of wild rabbits, they had bought tame rabbits that weren't afraid of people and probably thought it was feeding time.
20) Sandra Day O'Connor – 1981

Quiz 10

1) Who was Germany's first female chancellor?
2) What was the first major war campaign fought entirely by air forces?
3) Who was the first American casualty of the Revolutionary War?
4) What U.S. Constitutional amendment ended slavery?
5) What country gained its independence from Denmark in 1944?

6) Kim Campbell was the first female prime minister of what country?
7) Who was the famous wife of Leofric Earl of Mercia?
8) In what century did Cleopatra rule Egypt?
9) What was the first man-made object to break the sound barrier?
10) Who is the Danish explorer who gave his name to a strait, sea, island, glacier, and land bridge?
11) Who was the first female U.S. Attorney General?
12) Who is the head of state of New Zealand?
13) What world leader had the nickname "The Great Asparagus"?
14) Who reached the summit of Mount Everest with Edmund Hilary in 1953?
15) Who was the first man to hit a golf ball on the moon?
16) What Mediterranean island gained its independence from Britain in 1960?
17) On taking power in 1959, Fidel Castro banned what board game and ordered all sets destroyed?
18) The 1964 Nobel Peace Prize was awarded to its youngest recipient up to that point; who was it?
19) The Statue of Liberty was originally intended for what country?
20) What year did London get back to its pre-WWII population?

Quiz 10 Answers

1) Angela Merkel
2) Battle of Britain
3) Crispus Attucks
4) 13th
5) Iceland
6) Canada – June 25 to November 4, 1993
7) Lady Godiva
8) 1st century BC
9) Whip
10) Vitus Bering
11) Janet Reno
12) Queen Elizabeth II
13) Charles de Gaulle – He got the name in military school because of his looks.
14) Tenzing Norgay – Sherpa
15) Alan Shepard

16) Cyprus
17) Monopoly – He viewed it as the embodiment of capitalism.
18) Martin Luther King Jr. – 35
19) Egypt – They rejected it.
20) 2015

Quiz 11

1) What is the longest war in U.S. history?
2) What is the loudest sound in recorded history?
3) The Egyptian pyramids were built by what kind of workers?
4) Before he assumed office, Pope Pius II wrote one of the most popular books of the 15th century; what kind of book was it?
5) Who had the largest volunteer army in world history?
6) How many times in history has a submerged submarine deliberately sunk a submerged submarine?
7) During 10 days in 2001, Argentina had how many presidents?
8) Elena Cornaro Piscopia was the first woman in the world to receive a PhD degree in what year?
9) Roman gladiator fights started as a part of what ceremony?
10) From the middle ages until 1809, Finland was part of what country?
11) What year was the first magazine launched?
12) In 1917, Germany invited what country to join WWI by attacking the United States to recover lost territories?
13) What was the first country to implement daylight saving time?
14) How long did it take Berlin to get back to its pre-WWII population?
15) What makes Graca Machel unique among first ladies of the world?
16) Who was the first Hispanic to serve on the U.S. Supreme Court?
17) What year was Antarctica first sighted?
18) Sheep grazed in New York's Central Park until what year?
19) How many Americans were killed in the Hiroshima atomic blast?
20) Of all the countries that celebrate an independence day, the largest number gained independence from what country?

Quiz 11 Answers

1) Afghan War – started 2001
2) Eruption of Krakatoa in 1883 – It ruptured people's eardrums 40 miles away and was clearly heard 3,000 miles away.
3) Paid laborers – not slaves

4) Erotic novel – a tale of two lovers
5) India – 2.5 million during WWII
6) Once
7) Five – economic crash combined with defaulting on foreign debt
8) 1678 – Italy
9) Funerals – When wealthy nobles died, they would have bouts at the graveside.
10) Sweden
11) 1663 – German philosophy and literature magazine
12) Mexico
13) Germany – in 1916 to save energy in WWI
14) It still hasn't.
15) First lady of two separate countries – widow of Nelson Mandela (South Africa president) and Samora Machel (Mozambique president)
16) Sonia Sotomayor
17) 1820
18) 1934 – They were moved during the Great Depression for fear they would be eaten.
19) 12 – prisoners of war
20) Great Britain (58) - followed by France (26), Russia (21), Spain (21)

Quiz 12

1) Where were the remains of England's King Richard III found?
2) What is the world's oldest currency still in use?
3) What was the only independent South American country to send troops to fight in WWII?
4) The Eiffel Tower wasn't intended to be permanent; it was scheduled for demolition in 1909 but was saved to be used as what?
5) Before the 20th century in North America, what now popular and expensive food was considered a mark of poverty, used for fertilizer, and fed to slaves?
6) Why are there 60 seconds in a minute and 360 degrees in a circle?
7) Mississippi was the last state to officially ratify the 13th amendment abolishing slavery in what year?
8) Who was the last pharaoh of Egypt?
9) How many sides does the Great Pyramid of Giza have?
10) What year was the last man on the moon?
11) When the Persians were at war with the Egyptians, they rounded up and released as many of what animal as they could on the battlefield?

12) What two countries still haven't officially signed a peace treaty between them ending WWII?
13) Queen Elizabeth II served in what capacity in WWII?
14) Tsutomu Yamaguchi is the only recognized person in the world to survive what?
15) What country lost the greatest percentage of its population in WWII?
16) What was the only U.S. soil Japan occupied during WWII?
17) What year were the last German WWII POWs released from the Soviet Union?
18) Why did so many U.S. police departments adopt navy blue uniforms?
19) In what year was the first African American elected to serve in the U.S. Congress?
20) Louis Bonaparte, Napoleon's brother, was called the "King of Rabbits"; why?

Quiz 12 Answers

1) Buried under a parking lot in Leicester, England in 2013 - He died on the battlefield in 1485.
2) British pound – 1,200 years
3) Brazil
4) Radio tower
5) Lobster – Its reputation changed when modern transportation allowed shipping live lobsters to urban centers.
6) The ancient Babylonians did math in base 60 instead of base 10 and developed the concepts.
7) 2013 – Mississippi ratified the amendment in 1995 but didn't notify the U.S. archivist and didn't officially complete the process until 2013.
8) Cleopatra
9) Eight – Each of the four sides are split from base to tip by slight concave indentations.
10) 1972
11) Cats – Knowing the Egyptians reverence for cats, they knew they would not want to do anything to hurt the cats; the Persians won.
12) Japan and Russia – dispute over the Kuril Islands
13) Mechanic and driver
14) Both Hiroshima and Nagasaki atomic blasts – He was in Hiroshima on business for the first bomb and then returned home to Nagasaki.
15) Poland – 20%
16) Aleutian Islands – two remote islands

17) 1956
18) They were surplus army uniforms from the American Civil War.
19) 1870 – a senator from Mississippi and a representative from South Carolina
20) He mispronounced the Dutch phrase "I am your King," and instead said "I am your rabbit," when he took over the rule of the Netherlands in 1806.

Quiz 13

1) Who is credited as being the first person to put wheels on an office chair?
2) Notre Dame Cathedral was almost demolished in the 19th century; what saved it?
3) How long did the Spanish Inquisition last?
4) Before unifying Italy, what was Giuseppe Garibaldi's occupation?
5) Alexander the Great, Julius Caesar, Genghis Khan, Napoleon, Mussolini, and Hitler all suffered from ailurophobia; what is it?
6) Of the seven wonders of the ancient world, only the Great Pyramid of Giza still exists; which of the other seven wonders disappeared most recently?
7) Who was Europe's only Muslim king?
8) Who was the first person to fly across the English Channel?
9) In what war was "The Charge of the Light Brigade"?
10) Patty Hearst was kidnapped by what organization?
11) In what country were the Guns of Navarone installed?
12) What was discovered in 1922 by Howard Carter?
13) Who supposedly ran through the streets naked crying "Eureka!"?
14) Who sailed in the *Golden Hind*?
15) Where did the mutineers of the *Bounty* settle?
16) What links Brazil, Uruguay, Mozambique, and Angola?
17) In 1911, Hiram Bingham discovered what?
18) What Norwegian politician's name became synonymous with traitor?
19) In 1763, Great Britain traded Havana, Cuba to Spain for what?
20) Who did the United States buy the Virgin Islands from?

Quiz 13 Answers

1) Charles Darwin – 1840
2) Victor Hugo wrote *The Hunchback of Notre Dame* partially to save the

cathedral from demolition.

3) 356 years – 1479 to 1834
4) Spaghetti salesman in Uruguay
5) Fear of cats
6) Lighthouse at Alexandria – It was toppled by earthquakes in the early 14th century, and its ruined stones were carried off by the late 15th century.
7) King Zog of Albania – coronated in 1928
8) Louis Bleriot
9) Crimean War
10) Symbionese Liberation Army (SLA)
11) Turkey
12) Tutankhamun's tomb
13) Archimedes
14) Sir Francis Drake
15) Pitcairn Islands
16) Portuguese colonies
17) Lost city of Machu Picchu
18) Vidkun Quisling
19) Florida
20) Denmark

Quiz 14

1) What country was the first to introduce old-age pensions?
2) What country originated the concentration camp?
3) Other than the war itself, what killed an estimated 43,000 U.S. servicemen mobilized for WWI?
4) Why was Mary Mallon isolated from 1915 to 1938?
5) Who ran the first marathon upon which all others are based?
6) What is the oldest known name for the island of Great Britain?
7) In what month did the Russian October Revolution take place?
8) What country was the first to abolish capital punishment for all crimes?
9) Who was the original Peeping Tom looking at?
10) What did Lucien B. Smith invent in 1867 that had a great impact on the American west?
11) Who was offered the presidency of Israel in 1952 and turned it down?
12) In 1861, *The Times* newspaper of London carried the world's first what?

13) Edward Teach became famous as who?
14) What pet did Florence Nightingale carry with her?
15) Who is known as the father of history?
16) What did the ancient Greeks use instead of soap to clean themselves?
17) What country invented french fried potatoes?
18) What city was the first U.S. national capital?
19) Who was the first elected head of a nation to give birth in office?
20) During WWII when Hitler visited Paris, what did the French do to the Eiffel Tower?

Quiz 14 Answers

1) Germany – 1889
2) Great Britain – during the Boer War
3) Influenza – about half of all U.S. military deaths in Europe
4) Typhoid Mary
5) Pheidippides - He ran 140 miles round trip from Athens to Sparta over mountainous terrain to ask for military aid; marched 26 miles from Athens to Marathon; fought all morning, and then ran 26 miles to Athens with the victory news and died of exhaustion.
6) Albion
7) November - It was October in the old Julian calendar.
8) Venezuela - by constitution in 1863
9) Lady Godiva
10) Barbed wire
11) Albert Einstein
12) Weather forecast
13) Blackbeard the pirate
14) Owl – She carried it in her pocket.
15) Herodotus
16) Olive oil – They rubbed it into their skin and then scraped it off along with dirt and dead skin.
17) Belgium - late 17th century
18) Philadelphia, Pennsylvania
19) Benazir Bhutto – Pakistan in 1990
20) They cut the lift cables, so Hitler would have to climb the steps if he wanted to go to the top.

Quiz 15

1) What was Gandhi's profession?
2) In what country did coffee originate?
3) What nationality was Cleopatra?
4) How tall was Napoleon?
5) What date was V.E. Day?
6) What British prime minister's mother was born in Brooklyn, New York?
7) What two mountain ranges did Hannibal and his elephants march through in 218 BC?
8) What was the D-Day invasion password?
9) Which side did Britain support in the American Civil War?
10) What year followed 1 BC?
11) What pope died 33 days after his election?
12) What country contains the Waterloo battlefield?
13) The rallying cry “Remember the Maine!” came from what war?
14) What was Al Capone finally imprisoned for in 1931?
15) Who reached the South Pole in January 1912 only to find that Amundsen had gotten there first?
16) What cities were the two original endpoints of the Orient Express' run?
17) What ancient marvel did Nebuchadnezzar build?
18) Who invented the automobile in 1885?
19) What war did Florence Nightingale tend troops in?
20) What amendment to the U.S. Constitution ended prohibition?

Quiz 15 Answers

1) Lawyer
2) Ethiopia – 11th century
3) Greek
4) 5’7” - The average adult French male of his time was 5’5”, so he was taller than average; some of the confusion is the units his height was reported in and that his guards, who he was usually seen with, were required to be quite tall.
5) May 8, 1945
6) Winston Churchill
7) Pyrenees and Alps
8) Mickey Mouse
9) Confederacy

10) 1 AD
11) John Paul I
12) Belgium
13) Spanish-American War
14) Income tax evasion
15) Captain Robert Scott
16) Istanbul and Paris
17) Hanging Gardens of Babylon
18) Karl Benz
19) Crimean
20) 21st

Quiz 16

1) How many stars were on the U.S flag in 1913?
2) Who founded the De Beers mining company?
3) Who was the first president of independent Texas?
4) Where did two jumbo jets collide in 1977, killing 579?
5) What were the original seven wonders of the ancient world?
6) What fighting unit is headquartered in Corsica?
7) What war caused the most American deaths?
8) What was the first railroad to cross the United States?
9) Who was the first American in space?
10) Who was Helen Keller's teacher?
11) What two European countries entered the American Revolutionary War on the side of the Americans?
12) Who was the defense lawyer in the Scopes Monkey Trial?
13) Who was the second man on the moon?
14) What country declared war on both Germany and the Allies in WWII?
15) What famous heist did Ronald Biggs mastermind?
16) What is the claim to fame of Chang and Eng Bunker?
17) What caused 20 million deaths in 1918?
18) Who was the Iron Chancellor of Germany?
19) What was American folk hero John Chapman's nickname?
20) What date was Hiroshima bombed?

Quiz 16 Answers

1) 48 – Alaska and Hawaii weren't states yet.

2) Cecil Rhodes
3) Sam Houston
4) Tenerife, Canary Islands
5) Great Pyramid of Giza, Colossus of Rhodes, Lighthouse of Alexandria, Mausoleum at Halicarnassus, Temple of Artemis at Ephesus, Statue of Zeus at Olympia, Hanging Gardens of Babylon
6) French Foreign Legion
7) American Civil War
8) Union Pacific
9) Alan Shepard Jr.
10) Anne Sullivan
11) France and Spain
12) Clarence Darrow
13) Buzz Aldrin
14) Italy – One month after surrendering to the allies, Italy declared war on Germany, its former ally.
15) Great Train Robbery
16) Original Siamese twins
17) Influenza
18) Otto von Bismarck
19) Johnny Appleseed
20) August 6, 1945

Quiz 17

1) Who is the longest-reigning British monarch?
2) How did Socrates commit suicide?
3) Who inherited the throne of Scotland at the age of six days?
4) Who headed the Gestapo?
5) What two countries did Hadrian's wall separate?
6) What was the first country to legalize abortion in 1935?
7) Who did Winston Churchill succeed as British prime minister at the outbreak of WWII?
8) What was the third country to develop an atomic bomb?
9) How many people were executed for Abraham Lincoln's assassination?
10) Who taught the theory of evolution in 1925 contrary to Tennessee law?
11) How many manned *Apollo* flights preceded the moon landing?
12) What Spanish soldier of fortune led the expedition that discovered the Pacific Ocean?

13) What country did the Romans call Hibernia?
14) What was the name of Charles Darwin's survey ship?
15) What car brand was named for the founder of Detroit, Michigan?
16) What river is Pocahontas buried along?
17) What was the name of the B-29 that dropped the bomb on Hiroshima?
18) Who was the most decorated U.S. soldier of WWII?
19) Who was America's first public enemy number one?
20) What ship collided with the Swedish liner *Stockholm* on July 26, 1956?

Quiz 17 Answers

1) Queen Elizabeth II – She surpassed her great-great-grandmother Victoria's reign in 2015.
2) Drank poison hemlock
3) Mary, Queen of Scots or Mary I
4) Heinrich Himmler
5) England and Scotland
6) Iceland
7) Neville Chamberlain
8) Great Britain
9) Four
10) John T. Scopes – Scopes Monkey Trial
11) Four
12) Vasco Balboa
13) Ireland
14) Beagle
15) Cadillac – French explorer Antoine de la Mothe Cadillac founded Detroit in 1701.
16) Thames in England
17) *Enola Gay*
18) Audie Murphy
19) John Dillinger
20) *Andrea Doria*

Quiz 18

1) What year did "In God We Trust" become the official U.S. national motto?
2) What pandemic beginning in 541 AD is believed to be the first significant occurrence of the bubonic plague?

3) In medieval times, a moment was a unit of time equal to what?
4) What general led the Mexican forces at the Battle of the Alamo?
5) What year did Great Britain formally acknowledge American independence?
6) Who was on the first postage stamp ever issued in the world?
7) Where was the peace treaty that ended WWI signed?
8) The Peloponnesian War from 431–404 BC was fought between Athens and who?
9) What year did the United States effectively go off the gold standard?
10) Hannibal's crossing of the Alps in 218 BC was one of the major events of what war?
11) What African country gained its independence from the United Kingdom in 1962?
12) What does "E Pluribus Unum," the motto on the U.S. great seal, mean?
13) What war greatly increased the number of American women wearing bras?
14) Who are the only mother and daughter to both win Nobel Prizes?
15) Since the British Centurion tank was introduced in 1945, all British tanks and most armored fighting vehicles come equipped with a boiling vessel for what purpose?
16) What year were TV dinners first sold?
17) What ancient dome is still the largest unreinforced, concrete dome in the world?
18) Why was New Amsterdam renamed New York in 1664?
19) What historical event involved ships named the Beaver, Dartmouth, and the Eleanor?
20) What year did the last guillotining in France occur?

Quiz 18 Answers

1) 1956
2) Justinian Plague - It is estimated to have killed 25-50 million people over the following two centuries of recurrence.
3) 1/40th of an hour - An hour was defined as 1/12th of the time between sunrise and sunset, so the length of an hour depended on the time of year. Therefore, the length of a moment wasn't fixed either, but on average, it corresponded to 90 seconds.
4) Santa Anna
5) 1783 - The Treaty of Paris officially brought the war to a close.
6) Queen Victoria - 1840

7) Versailles
8) Sparta
9) 1933 - Franklin D. Roosevelt took the United States off the gold standard during the Great Depression.
10) Second Punic War - It was the second of three Punic Wars between Carthage and Rome.
11) Uganda
12) Out of many, one
13) WWI - Before that time, corsets were still the norm, but corset frames were mostly made of metal that was needed for the war effort. In 1917, the U.S. War Industries Board asked American women to stop buying them, accelerating the move to bras.
14) Marie Curie (1903 Physics and 1911 Chemistry) and her daughter Irene Juliot-Curie (1935 Chemistry)
15) Make tea
16) 1954 - Swanson had 260 tons of leftover frozen turkeys from Thanksgiving. Inspired by the food trays on airlines, they created a meal of turkey, cornbread dressing, gravy, peas, and sweet potatoes.
17) Roman Pantheon dome - It is 142 feet in diameter and was built in 125 AD.
18) Change from Dutch to English rule - Dutch Governor Peter Stuyvesant surrendered New Amsterdam to an English naval squadron under Colonel Richard Nicolls.
19) Boston Tea Party (1773) - The tea belonged to the East India Tea Company, but the ships themselves were American.
20) 1977

Quiz 19

1) What two airlines each had two planes hijacked in the 9/11 terrorist attacks on America?
2) Lasting about 38 minutes, what was the shortest war in history fought on August 27, 1896?
3) The *Demologos* was the first steam powered what?
4) Who invented the first mercury thermometer?
5) Who was the first pharaoh of a unified Egypt and was also supposedly killed by a hippopotamus?
6) What date was the Declaration of Independence signed?
7) In what year did the first African American serve as a U.S. state governor?
8) Who was the first female head of state in the Western Hemisphere?

9) Who was the first African American secretary of state?
10) In the 13th century, Pope Gregory IX believed that what animal was an instrument of Satan and condemned them to death across Europe?
11) What country did Panama gain its independence from in 1903?
12) What year was the first man-made object landed on the moon?
13) What is the better-known name of Charles I who was king of the Franks and Lombards, and emperor of the Romans and united the majority of western and central Europe during the Early Middle Ages?
14) What was the first state to adopt the gas chamber as an execution method in 1921?
15) In what war did submarines make their first appearance?
16) Who was the first Windsor to rule the United Kingdom?
17) The oldest surviving photograph in existence was taken in what year?
18) Who is Mount Rushmore named after?
19) Who originally said, "Houston, we've had a problem here"?
20) Who led a band of abolitionists that seized the federal arsenal at Harpers Ferry, Virginia in October 1859?

Quiz 19 Answers

1) American Airlines and United Airlines
2) Anglo-Zanzibar War - It was a military conflict fought between the United Kingdom and the Zanzibar Sultanate.
3) Warship - It was built to defend New York Harbor from the Royal Navy during the War of 1812 and was launched in 1815.
4) Gabriel Fahrenheit - 1714
5) Menes – about 3000 BC
6) August 2, 1776 - It was adopted on July 4, 1776, but wasn't signed until August.
7) 1872 - P.B.S. Pinchback became the first African American state governor. He had been a Louisiana state senator and was serving as lieutenant governor when Governor Henry Clay Warmoth had to step down temporarily while he battled impeachment charges for election tampering. Pinchback served as governor for 36 days; there wouldn't be another African American governor in the United States until 1990.
8) Isabel Peron - Argentina (1974)
9) General Colin Powell - 2000
10) Black cats
11) Colombia
12) 1959 - Soviet Union's *Luna* 2

13) Charlemagne
14) Nevada
15) American Revolutionary War - The *Turtle*, a submersible built by American David Bushnell in 1775, was used in an attempted attack on the British ship *Eagle* on September 6, 1776.
16) George V – He reigned from 1910-1936.
17) 1826 - French photography pioneer Joseph Nicéphore Niépce took a picture of the view from the window of an estate in Burgundy, France; it was taken with an eight-hour exposure and was made on a pewter plate using asphalt.
18) Charles Edward Rushmore - He was a New York attorney who visited the Black Hills area in 1884 on business. He asked a guide what the name of the mountain was, and the guide said they would name it now. The name somehow stuck.
19) Jack Swigert - The quote is sometimes incorrectly attributed to James Lovell, who repeated, "Houston, we've had a problem" after Swigert, and it is not "Houston, we have a problem" as depicted in the movie.
20) John Brown

Quiz 20

1) What did Pope Gregory XIII introduce in 1582?
2) In what century was the practice of using BC and AD for years established?
3) Why was the Pentagon designed with twice the number of bathrooms needed for its anticipated staffing?
4) Who was the first wife of King Henry VIII?
5) What year did the space shuttle *Challenger* explode killing all seven crew members?
6) What was the largest contiguous land area empire in world history?
7) What conqueror may have been responsible for as many as 40 million deaths and may have reduced the entire world population by up to 11%?
8) What state elected the first African American governor?
9) What was Queen Victoria's first name?
10) Who was the first chancellor of the 20th century unified Germany?
11) Who was the first U.S. Supreme Court chief justice?
12) Who invented a rudimentary water thermometer in 1593 that allowed temperature variations to be measured for the first time?
13) What year did the Falklands War between Argentina and the United Kingdom occur?
14) Killing or attempting to kill a U.S. president wasn't a federal offense

until what year?

15) What was the name of John Glenn's first Earth orbital spacecraft in 1962?
16) What year did the first American woman receive a medical degree?
17) What was the largest denomination currency ever printed in the United States?
18) Iosif Vissarionovich Dzhugashvili became famous under what name?
19) What did Alfred Nobel invent to make his money and establish the Nobel Prizes?
20) What was the first U.S. state to legalize assisted suicide?

Quiz 20 Answers

1) Gregorian calendar - our current calendar
2) 6th century
3) Segregation considerations - President Franklin Roosevelt issued an executive order banning segregation in federal buildings before the building was open, so it opened as a desegregated facility and was for a time the only desegregated building in Virginia since state laws required segregation.
4) Catherine of Aragon - She was queen from 1509-1533 until the marriage was declared invalid.
5) 1986
6) Mongol Empire - It spanned 9.27 million square miles in one mass at its peak in 1270.
7) Genghis Khan
8) Virginia - L. Douglas Wilder in 1990
9) Alexandrina
10) Helmut Kohl - Chancellor of Germany from 1982 to 1998
11) John Jay - 1789
12) Galileo Galilei
13) 1982
14) 1965 - two years after John F. Kennedy's death
15) *Friendship* 7
16) 1849 - Elizabeth Blackwell was the first woman to earn a medical degree in America; she graduated first in her class at New York's Geneva College.
17) $100,000 bill - It featured a picture of Woodrow Wilson and was only printed for three weeks in December 1934 and January 1935. It was only used for official transactions between Federal Reserve Banks.

18) Joseph Stalin
19) Dynamite
20) Oregon - 1994

Quiz 21

1) What year was the first woman elected governor of a U.S. state?
2) What Wild West legend was born Henry McCarty in 1859?
3) What year did Egypt gain its independence from the British?
4) Who met at Ujiji, a town on the shore of Lake Tanganyika in western Tanzania, in 1871?
5) Who was the most photographed American of the 19th century?
6) What pioneering American female journalist was widely known for her 1889-1890 record-breaking trip around the world in 72 days?
7) Practiced between the 5th and 16th centuries, what was a poetic exchange of insults called?
8) Who was the first woman to appear on U.S. paper currency?
9) Istanbul was previously called Constantinople; what was it called before Constantinople?
10) What year did the Soviet Union break up into independent republics?
11) What century was the first hot air balloon?
12) Forks were introduced in Italy in what century?
13) Hitler, Stalin, and Mussolini were all nominated for what prize?
14) From what country did Angola gain its independence in 1975?
15) Who was the father of Alexander the Great?
16) Based on his medical records, Adolf Hitler had a huge problem with what common condition and took 28 different drugs to try to control it?
17) Who was the first person who wasn't a head of state depicted on a postage stamp anywhere in the world?
18) Haile Selassie ruled what country?
19) What state was the setting of the Battle of the Little Bighorn?
20) What woman is widely regarded as the greatest pirate ever with control of more than 1,500 ships and 80,000 sailors at her peak?

Quiz 21 Answers

1) 1925 - Nellie Tayloe Ross
2) Billy the Kid
3) 1922
4) Henry Stanley and David Livingstone

5) Frederick Douglass - He wanted to ensure a more accurate depiction of black Americans and sat for upwards of 160 portraits.
6) Elizabeth Cochran Seaman - better known by her pen name Nellie Bly
7) Flyting - The exchange of insults could get quite rude, including accusations of cowardice or sexual perversion.
8) Pocahontas - She appeared on the back of the $20 bill in 1865.
9) Byzantium
10) 1991
11) 18th century - 1783
12) 11th century - They were originally seen as an offense to God since they were considered artificial hands and therefore sacrilegious.
13) Nobel Peace Prize
14) Portugal
15) Philip II of Macedon - He was king of Macedon from 359 BC until his assassination in 336 BC.
16) Flatulence - Some of the anti-gas pills he used contained a base of strychnine that caused further stomach and liver issues.
17) Benjamin Franklin - 1847 U.S. stamp
18) Ethiopia - emperor from 1930 to 1974
19) Montana
20) Ching Shih (1775-1844) - She was a Chinese prostitute and had one of the biggest naval armies in the history of the world. She robbed and taxed towns and plundered ships along the coast of the South China Sea.

Quiz 22

1) Who are the only two people to win two Nobel Prizes in two different categories?
2) Ratified in 1781, the Articles of Confederation was the original constitution of the United States that was replaced by the U.S. Constitution in 1789; it included an open invitation for what country to join the United States without any consent from the other states?
3) What was the first recorded Chinese dynasty?
4) What country effectively banned Christmas from 1647-1660?
5) What iconic New York City landmark was under construction the year of Custer's defeat at the Battle of Little Bighorn in 1876?
6) What city was home to the first official skyscraper in 1884?
7) What year did the Panama Canal open?
8) What year was the Three Mile Island partial nuclear meltdown in

Pennsylvania?

9) What was the name the American pilot shot down in a U-2 spy plane over Russia in 1960?
10) Who replaced Nikita Khrushchev as the leader of the Soviet Union?
11) What oil tanker was the cause of a massive oil spill in Alaska in 1989?
12) In Boston in January 1919, a 50-foot-tall holding tank burst and sent a 15-foot tall wave through the streets; it crushed houses and swallowed everything in its path, killing 21 people and injuring 150; what was in the tank?
13) What was George Armstrong Custer's rank when he was killed at Little Bighorn in 1876?
14) What was the name of the first space shuttle to go into space?
15) The word deadline originated in what war?
16) What two foods were the most popular staples of the ancient Egyptian diet and were consumed by almost everyone every day?
17) When Disneyland opened in 1955, Tomorrowland was designed to look like what year?
18) The Middle Ages is traditionally thought to have started with the fall of what empire?
19) In what century did Pope Urban II call for the initiation of the Crusades?
20) Ancient Rome had 24 hours in a day, but what was different about their hours?

Quiz 22 Answers

1) Marie Curie (1903 Physics and 1911 Chemistry) and Linus Pauling (1954 Chemistry and 1962 Peace)
2) Canada
3) Xia Dynasty (2070–1600 BC)
4) England - Puritans believed that people needed strict rules to be religious and that any kind of merrymaking was sinful.
5) Brooklyn Bridge
6) Chicago - The Home Insurance Building in downtown Chicago was 10 stories and 136 feet tall; it was demolished in 1931.
7) 1914
8) 1979
9) Francis Garry Powers
10) Leonid Brezhnev - He led the Soviet Union from 1964 until he died in 1982.

11) *Exxon Valdez*
12) Molasses
13) Lieutenant Colonel
14) *Columbia* - April 1981
15) American Civil War - In Civil War prison camps, it was the line that prisoners couldn't go beyond, or they would be shot.
16) Bread and beer - Laborers would have a morning meal of bread, beer, and often onions, and a heartier dinner with boiled vegetables, meat, and more bread and beer.
17) 1986
18) Roman Empire - The Middle Ages started in 476 and lasted about 1,000 years.
19) 11th century - 1095
20) The hours varied in length based on the time of year. They ensured that there were 12 hours of daylight and 12 hours of darkness, adjusting the length of the hours accordingly.

Quiz 23

1) Who was the last emperor of France?
2) What mobster offered a $10,000 reward for information leading to the capture of the Lindbergh baby kidnapper and that he and his men would search for the perpetrators if he was released from prison?
3) What civilization was the first to divide the day into 24 hours?
4) What year did the French Revolution begin?
5) Punctuation as we largely know it today did not exist until what century?
6) In ancient Greece, any citizen could be voted out and expelled for 10 years; it was called ostrakismos and led to what English word?
7) Rounded to the nearest 100 years, how long before Christopher Columbus did Leif Erikson arrive in North America?
8) Who was Russia's longest-ruling female leader?
9) Sandwiches didn't appear in American cookbooks until what century?
10) What was the name of the pandemic that killed 50-100 million people starting in 1918?
11) What current candy was part of U.S. soldier rations in WWII?
12) In what century did Martin Luther initiate the Reformation?
13) In what century was the Taj Mahal completed?
14) What country had the first elected female head of state in the Western Hemisphere?

15) What year did Christmas become a U.S. federal holiday?
16) Since 1869, over a million people have been buried on what island that serves as the burial place for unclaimed bodies for New York City?
17) What year was the first human killed by a robot?
18) What year was the modern paper clip designed?
19) Who is the only woman that married the kings of both France and England?
20) What two countries are part of the world's oldest alliance that is still in effect?

Quiz 23 Answers

1) Napoleon III (Charles-Louis Napoléon Bonaparte) - He ruled from 1852-1870 and was the nephew of Napoleon Bonaparte (Napoleon I).
2) Al Capone
3) Egyptian - Ancient Egyptians used a base 12 system instead of our base 10 system; they counted the knuckles of each finger using their thumbs as pointers. They had 12 hours of light and 12 hours of darkness, so the length of the hours varied by time of the year. Fixed length hours were proposed by the Greeks in the 2nd century BC, but they did not become common until mechanical clocks first appeared in Europe during the 14th century.
4) 1789
5) 15th century
6) Ostracism
7) 500 years - Erikson arrived in Newfoundland in about 1000 AD.
8) Catherine the Great - She ruled from 1762-1796.
9) 19th century
10) Spanish flu - It infected an estimated 500 million people worldwide, about one-third of the world's population.
11) Tootsie Rolls - They were durable in all weather conditions and were good for quick energy.
12) 16th century - 1517
13) 17th century - 1643
14) Nicaragua - Violeta Chamorro in 1990
15) 1870
16) Hart Island - The island is at the western end of Long Island Sound and is 1 mile long by 1/3 mile wide.
17) 1979 - On January 25, 1979, Robert Williams died when he was hit in the head by a mechanical arm at a Ford Motor Company casting plant.

18) 1899
19) Eleanor of Aquitaine - She married Louis VII of France and Henry II of England.
20) England and Portugal - Anglo-Portuguese Alliance from 1373

Quiz 24

1) What was the first country in Europe to give women the right to vote?
2) Who was the first leader of the People's Republic of China?
3) What year was the first Ford Model T produced?
4) How old was the youngest signer of the Declaration of Independence?
5) What year did the Korean War start?
6) In April 1933, Eleanor Roosevelt snuck out of a White House event and went on an airplane joyride with what well-known person?
7) Who was the first democratically elected president of Russia?
8) What year was the first text message sent?
9) What century was the earliest woodblock printed paper book?
10) What is the ancient practice of trying to protect yourself against poisoning by taking non-lethal doses of poison to build immunity called?
11) What famous philosopher said, "Children today are tyrants. They contradict their parents, gobble their food, and tyrannize their teachers"?
12) Who was the last Tudor monarch of England?
13) Who was the first person to cross the Antarctic Circle?
14) Who was Israel's first prime minister?
15) What king was offered plans for the first bacteriological weapon?
16) Functional buttons with buttonholes for fastening or closing clothes first appeared in what century?
17) After his defeat at Waterloo, Napoleon spent the last six years of his life under British supervision on what island?
18) At what Ohio university were four students shot dead in 1970?
19) Who was the first woman to appear on a U.S. postage stamp?
20) What conqueror once had a feast with his army while seated on top of Russian army generals and nobility?

Quiz 24 Answers

1) Finland - 1906
2) Mao Zedong

3) 1908
4) 26 - Edward Rutledge was a lawyer from South Carolina.
5) 1950
6) Amelia Earhart
7) Boris Yeltsin - 1991
8) 1992 - It was sent by a Vodafone engineer working on developing SMS.
9) 9th century - The Chinese book *Diamond Sutra* was created in 868, almost 600 years before the Gutenberg Bible was the first book printed on a mechanical press.
10) Mithridatism - From the end of the 1st century AD, Roman emperors adopted the daily habit of taking a small amount of every known poison to gain immunity. It can be effective against some types of poisons, but depending on the poison, it can lead to a lethal accumulation in the body over time.
11) Socrates (470-399 BC)
12) Elizabeth I - She was the daughter of Henry VIII and ruled from 1558-1603.
13) Captain James Cook - 1773
14) David Ben-Gurion - 1948
15) King Louis XIV - He ruled France from 1643-1715 and was offered plans for the first bacteriological weapon by an Italian chemist; he refused instantly and paid the scientist to keep the discovery a secret.
16) 13th century
17) St. Helena - It is 1,162 miles off the west coast of Africa in the South Atlantic.
18) Kent State
19) Martha Washington - 1902
20) Genghis Khan - In Russia in 1223, the Mongolian army had just won the Battle of the Kalka River; the Russian army surrendered, and the Mongols decided to have a feast to celebrate. The Russian army generals and nobility were forced to lie on the ground, and a heavy wooden gate was thrown on top of them. Chairs and tables were set on top of the gate, and the Mongols sat down for a feast on top of the living bodies of their enemies.

Quiz 25

1) What date was the atomic bomb dropped on Hiroshima?
2) In what century did Marco Polo begin his travels to Asia?
3) Who was the last British monarch to ascend to the throne as a teenager?

4) Who was the first woman to appear on the front of U.S. paper currency?
5) After the fall of the Roman Empire, the technology to make what building material was lost for 1,000 years?
6) Recent research suggests that rats are not likely to blame for transmitting the Black Death bubonic plague that wiped out one-third of Europe's population. What animal likely transmitted the lice and fleas that spread the disease?
7) Who was the first African American U.S. Supreme Court justice?
8) Who did the Greeks defeat at the Battle of Marathon in 490 BC?
9) Where did the Pilgrims first land in America?
10) Who was the leader of the Greek forces during the Trojan War?
11) Sideburns are named after what American Civil War general?
12) What year was the People's Republic of China established?
13) In what state were the only U.S. mainland combat deaths in WWII?
14) During what century did Denmark rule England?
15) Who was shot and killed in New Delhi, India on October 31, 1984?
16) Who was the first president to appear on a U.S. postage stamp?
17) In 2000, what was the last U.S. state to overturn its law against interracial marriage?
18) What island was invaded by the United States in 1983?
19) What country had the first openly gay or lesbian prime minister?
20) What year was the word robot first used?

Quiz 25 Answers

1) August 6, 1945
2) 13th century - 1271
3) Queen Victoria - She was 18 when she became queen in 1837.
4) Martha Washington - She appeared on the $1 silver certificate in 1886.
5) Concrete - Roman concrete is still more durable than the concrete we make today, and it gets stronger over time. Their concrete was created with volcanic ash, lime, seawater, and volcanic rock; it created a rock-like concrete we haven't been able to duplicate.
6) Humans - The transmission was more likely due to human fleas and lice.
7) Thurgood Marshall - 1967
8) Persians - It was during the first Persian invasion of Greece.
9) Provincetown, Massachusetts - The Pilgrims didn't first land at Plymouth Rock; they landed in what is now Provincetown, Massachusetts, and signed the Mayflower Compact there. They arrived

at Plymouth Rock five weeks later.

10) Agamemnon
11) Ambrose Burnside - He was known for having an unusual facial hairstyle with a mustache connected to thick sideburns with a clean-shaven chin.
12) 1949
13) Oregon - On May 5, 1945, a Japanese balloon bomb exploded and killed a woman and five children in Oregon. The balloon bombs had a 33-foot diameter balloon with 35 pounds of explosives and were designed to rise to 30,000 feet and ride the jet stream east, making it from Japan to the United States in about three days. An altimeter would trigger a reaction that would jettison the bombs; Japan released about 9,000 of the bombs. A Sunday school teacher and five students happened upon an unexploded balloon bomb on the ground; it exploded while they were investigating it.
14) 11th century - The Danish House of Knýtlinga ruled the Kingdom of England from 1013 to 1014 and from 1016 to 1042.
15) Indira Gandhi - She was India's first female prime minister and was the daughter of Jawaharlal Nehru, the first prime minister of India. She served as prime minister from 1966-1977 and again from 1980 until her assassination in 1984.
16) George Washington - 1847
17) Alabama
18) Grenada
19) Iceland - Jóhanna Sigurðardóttir was prime minister from 2009-2013.
20) 1920 - It was first used in a 1920 play called *Rossum's Universal Robots* by Czech writer Karel Čapek; it comes from the Slavic word "rabota," meaning slave labor.

Quiz 26

1) What year did the first true ATM debut?
2) Who was the first American to win a Nobel Prize?
3) Who was the last tsar of Russia?
4) Who personally saved the United States from financial collapse during the War of 1812 by placing most of his assets at the disposal of the government and underwriting about 95% of the war loans?
5) What year was the first nonstop transatlantic flight?
6) Who was the emperor of Japan during World War II?
7) What year was the Boston Marathon bombing that killed three people?
8) Meaning apple orchard in Spanish, what is the name of the

concentration camp in California where thousands of Japanese Americans were imprisoned during WWII?

9) What is the only Southeast Asian country never colonized by Europeans?
10) Who is the longest-reigning monarch ever?
11) What type of gun did John Wilkes Booth use to assassinate Abraham Lincoln?
12) The U.S. Secret Service was created specifically to battle what type of crime?
13) What year was the first woman elected to the U.S. Congress?
14) Who was the first female Speaker of the U.S. House of Representatives?
15) What were the two cities at the ends of the Pony Express?
16) What Soviet leader plotted to kill actor John Wayne and sent two men to pose as FBI agents to assassinate him?
17) What country was first to introduce emergency three-digit phone numbers?
18) What did English Queen Mary II die of at age 32?
19) "Make Your Wet Dreams Come True" was a U.S. presidential campaign slogan for what candidate?
20) What was the first nation to officially recognize the independence of the United States?

Quiz 26 Answers

1) 1967 at Barclay's Bank in London - They wouldn't become commonplace until the 1990s.
2) Theodore Roosevelt - 1906 Peace Prize
3) Nicholas II
4) Stephen Girard - He was one of the wealthiest men in American history.
5) 1919 - John Alcock and Arthur Whitten Brown made the flight eight years before Charles Lindbergh, who made the first solo flight.
6) Hirohito - He was emperor from 1926 until his death in 1989 and is the longest-reigning monarch in Japanese history.
7) 2013
8) Manzanar
9) Thailand
10) King Sobhuza II of Swaziland - 82 years 253 days (1899-1982)
11) Derringer pistol
12) Counterfeiting - Shortly after the American Civil War, one-third to

one-half of all U.S. currency was counterfeit. This was a major threat to the economy, and the Secret Service was founded in 1865 specifically to reduce counterfeiting.

13) 1916 - It was four years before women were given the right to vote.
14) Nancy Pelosi - 2007
15) St. Joseph, Missouri and Sacramento, California – The Pony Express could transport a letter over 1,800 miles in 10 days but only ran for 18 months, from April 1860 to October 1861.
16) Joseph Stalin - He was a big film fan and considered Wayne a threat to the Soviet Union because of his strong anti-communist beliefs.
17) United Kingdom - They were first introduced in London in 1937 after a fire killed five people, and the person calling for the fire brigade was kept waiting by the operator. The original number was 999.
18) Smallpox
19) Al Smith - In 1928, former New York governor Al Smith ran for president against Herbert Hoover; a major debate was over whether the prohibition alcohol ban should continue. Drys were people who supported prohibition, and Wets were against it. Smith was against prohibition.
20) Morocco - 1777

Quiz 27

1) Who was murdered at Canterbury Cathedral on December 29, 1170?
2) What are the only three crimes mentioned in the U.S. Constitution?
3) Who was the oldest signer of the Declaration of Independence?
4) In what century was the Aztec Empire at its height as the Spanish arrived?
5) What year was the Great Fire of London that burned for five days and destroyed almost 90% of London's homes?
6) Who was the wife of French King Louis XVI?
7) What were the surnames of Bonnie and Clyde?
8) What year did the United States have its first female cabinet member?
9) What year was the first pedestrian killed by a car?
10) In what year were the first free multi-racial elections held in South Africa?
11) Who was the first American woman to win the Nobel Peace Prize?
12) What year was the first color photograph taken?
13) Who did Adolf Hitler succeed as Germany's head of state?
14) As attorney general of the United States, what government organization did Charles Bonaparte, French Emperor Napoleon's great-

nephew, found in 1908?
15) What was the first man-made object to achieve sub-orbital space flight?
16) By land area, what was the largest empire in world history?
17) In what century was Pompeii buried by Mount Vesuvius?
18) In Victorian times, photography subjects were encouraged to say what instead of "cheese"?
19) What was the name of the Italian cruise ship hijacked by Palestinian terrorists in October 1985?
20) What was the first U.S. state to give women the right to vote?

Quiz 27 Answers

1) Thomas Beckett - He was Archbishop of Canterbury and was killed by followers of King Henry II.
2) Treason, piracy, counterfeiting
3) Benjamin Franklin - 70
4) 16th century - 1519
5) 1666
6) Marie Antoinette
7) Clyde Barrow and Bonnie Parker
8) 1933 - Frances Perkins was Secretary of Labor under Franklin D. Roosevelt.
9) 1896 - Bridget Driscoll was struck by a demonstration car that was going 4 mph.
10) 1994
11) Jane Addams - 1931
12) 1861 - While Kodak didn't introduce color film to the masses until 1935, the first color photograph was taken in 1861. Thomas Sutton and James Clerk Maxwell created a picture of a Scottish tartan ribbon of red, white, and green. They created the photo by taking three separate photos using three different filters (red, green, and blue-violet) and superimposing them together. This is the basic three-color method that is used in all color imaging today.
13) Paul von Hindenburg - Hitler assumed leadership in 1934 on Hindenburg's death.
14) FBI - He created the Bureau of Investigation that was renamed the Federal Bureau of Investigation in 1935.
15) German V2 rocket - June 1944
16) British Empire - In 1922, it ruled over about 24% of the world's land.

17) 1st century - 79 AD
18) Prunes - Among other reasons, Victorians thought it was classless to show a big toothy smile.
19) *Achille Lauro*
20) Wyoming - 1890

Quiz 28

1) What century was the first Viking raid on England?
2) What was the first U.S. state to legalize same-sex marriage?
3) Which of the seven wonders of the ancient world was demolished by an earthquake in 226 BC?
4) What are the names of the two supercontinents that the landmass of Pangaea broke up into about 200 million years ago?
5) What automobile manufacturer invented the three-point seat belt used today?
6) The word salary derives from the Latin "salarium" that referred to a soldier's allowance to buy what?
7) What leader once ordered his army to eat every tenth man?
8) Who was the first explorer to reach the Cape of Good Hope?
9) The French village of Domremy was the birthplace of what famous figure of the 15th century?
10) Why is a ship's speed measured in knots?
11) The word computer was first referenced in what century?
12) Duncan Hines (1880–1959) was a real person; what was he known for?
13) What year did Princess Diana die?
14) In what century did Nostradamus live?
15) Who led the Greek forces against the vastly larger Persian army in the Battle of Thermopylae in 480 BC?
16) What year did Joseph Gayetty commercialize toilet paper much as we know it today?
17) Who was the last Roman Catholic king of England?
18) What was the name of the royal house that ruled Russia from 1613 to 1917?
19) What year did the dollar become the U.S. standard currency?
20) What famous poet was San Francisco's first African American female streetcar conductor?

Quiz 28 Answers

1) 8th century - 793 AD

2) Massachusetts - 2004
3) Colossus of Rhodes
4) Laurasia (northern side) and Gondwana (southern side) - These two supercontinents later broke up to form our current continents.
5) Volvo - They gave away the 1962 patent for free to save lives.
6) Salt - In ancient Rome, soldiers were sometimes paid in salt or given an allowance to purchase it.
7) Genghis Khan - In 1214, Khan was battling the Jin empire in China and laid siege to the city of Chengdu, capital of the Jin empire. The siege went on for a long time, and supplies were short; they were also ravaged by plague. Khan ordered that every tenth man should be sacrificed to feed the others. Khan personally abandoned the siege, leaving it to one of his generals, and Chengdu eventually fell in 1215.
8) Bartolomeu Dias - 1488
9) Joan of Arc (1412-1431)
10) Actual knots were used to measure speed. By the late 16th century, sailors measured a ship's speed by throwing out a piece of wood attached to a length of rope with knots tied at regular intervals. They allowed the rope to go out as the ship moved forward, and after a set length of time, they pulled the rope back in counting the knots that had gone out and calculated the speed. A knot eventually came to mean one nautical mile per hour.
11) 17th century - It originally meant a person who did arithmetic calculations. It didn't take on its meaning of being a machine until the late 1800s or an electronic device until the mid-1900s.
12) He was an American pioneer of restaurant ratings for travelers.
13) 1997
14) 16th century - He lived from 1503 to 1566.
15) King Leonidas of Sparta
16) 1857 - Toilet paper traces its origins back to at least 6th century China when it was first referenced in writings. However, most people didn't experience it until at least 1857 when American inventor Joseph Gayetty commercialized the product much as we know it today.
17) James II - He ruled from 1685-1688.
18) Romanov
19) 1792
20) Maya Angelou

Quiz 29

1) What is the oldest English-speaking university in the world?

2) What year did women receive the right to vote in the United States?
3) When the Gregorian calendar replaced the Julian calendar, how many days had to be skipped to get the calendar back on track with the position of the sun?
4) What year did the United States first adopt the 911 emergency phone number?
5) What year were East and West Germany unified?
6) In ancient Greece, certain women wore sandals that left the words "follow me" imprinted on the ground as they walked; who were they?
7) Who was the last king of the Aztecs?
8) Originally, the term third world country did not mean a developing country; it was coined during the Cold War in 1952 by a French demographer and referred to what?
9) What year was the microwave oven patented?
10) In what century were the last chariot races held in Circus Maximus in Rome?
11) What is the only crime defined in the U.S. Constitution?
12) What famous world leader wrote a romance novel called *Clisson et Eugénie* about the doomed romance of a soldier and his lover?
13) Which king of England was executed in 1649 during the English Civil War?
14) Who was the first English monarch to live in Buckingham Palace?
15) In 1958, a B-47 carrying an atomic bomb larger than the one dropped on Nagasaki accidentally dropped it on what state?
16) Where was the Magna Carta signed in 1215?
17) What was the name of the secret German government program from 1935 to 1945 that encouraged racially fit women to bear children for the Third Reich?
18) What famous world leader said, "How can anyone govern a nation that has two hundred and forty-six different kinds of cheese?"
19) What Russian czar was born Pyotr Alekseyevich in 1672?
20) What century did the Incan Empire start?

Quiz 29 Answers

1) Oxford - It existed about 350 years before the start of the Inca and Aztec empires. There was teaching at Oxford as early as 1096, making it the third-oldest university in continuous operation in the world and the oldest English-speaking university.
2) 1920
3) 10 days - October 4, 1582, was followed by October 15, 1582.

4) 1968 - The first call was made in Haleyville, Alabama.
5) 1990
6) Prostitutes - In ancient Greece, prostitution was common, accepted, and regulated.
7) Montezuma II (1466-1520)
8) Countries that weren't aligned with either the United States or the Soviet Union.
9) 1945 - Raytheon Engineer Percy Spencer first discovered the heating powers of microwaves when he accidentally melted a candy bar in his pocket.
10) 6th century
11) Treason - Article III, Section 3
12) Napoleon Bonaparte - It was based on Bonaparte's relationship with Eugenie Desiree Clary.
13) Charles I
14) Queen Victoria - 1837
15) South Carolina - The core of the bomb was still on the plane, so there wasn't a nuclear explosion, but the 6,000 pounds of conventional high explosives detonated. The bomb fell on a garden in a rural area and created a 35-foot-deep by 75-foot-wide crater and destroyed the nearby house and outbuildings. Fortunately, no one was killed, and there were only minor injuries.
16) Runnymede - It is a meadow alongside the River Thames 20 miles west of central London.
17) Lebensborn - Women in the program were required to hand their children over to the SS to be raised. The program originally started in Germany but spread to other occupied European countries during WWII. There were an estimated 20,000 Lebensborn children born.
18) Charles de Gaulle
19) Peter the Great (1672-1725)
20) 15th century - 1438

Quiz 30

1) Who was India's first prime minister?
2) What English king made boiling to death a form of capital punishment?
3) In what year did Johannes Gutenberg's movable-type printing press produce the first Bible?
4) On which island was Napoleon Bonaparte born?
5) The Black Death bubonic plague that wiped out one-third of Europe's population occurred in what century?

6) What year was Jell-O invented?
7) To the nearest year, how many years was Texas an independent country?
8) What year did the *Hindenburg* explode in New Jersey?
9) What is the earliest surviving system of laws?
10) What year was the first digital still camera created?
11) What explorer brought the first pigs to what is now the United States?
12) Who was the first *Time* magazine Woman of the Year in 1936?
13) Who was the first person to sight the Antarctic continent?
14) What country was divided by the 38th parallel after WWII?
15) Why was the Pentagon, the headquarters for the U.S. Department of Defense, designed in the shape of a pentagon?
16) Measured by its share of the world's population, what is the largest empire in history?
17) In what country did Mahatma Gandhi first employ nonviolent civil disobedience to fight for Indian civil rights?
18) What year was the first known selfie taken?
19) What was the last war that Liechtenstein ever participated in?
20) Pirates wore eye patches for what reason other than to cover up a missing or injured eye?

Quiz 30 Answers

1) Jawaharlal Nehru - 1947
2) Henry VIII (1491-1547)
3) 1455
4) Corsica
5) 14th century - It peaked in 1347-1351
6) 1897 - In LeRoy, New York, Pearl Wait added fruit syrup to gelatin, which had been invented in the 1600s.
7) 10 years - The Republic of Texas was a sovereign state from March 2, 1836, to February 19, 1846.
8) 1937
9) The Code of Hammurabi - Hammurabi was a ruler of ancient Babylon from 1792-1750 BC.
10) 1975 – It was created by Kodak and weighed 8 pounds and took 0.01-megapixel black-and-white photos that took 23 seconds to render onto a cassette tape that displayed the image on a television set.
11) Hernando de Soto - He brought 13 pigs to Tampa Bay, Florida, in 1539.
12) Wallis Simpson - Her marriage to British King Edward VIII forced his

abdication.

13) Fabian Gottlieb von Bellingshausen - 1820
14) Korea
15) It was originally designed to fit on a piece of land that was bordered on five sides by roads. It was decided that the original site was too close to Arlington Cemetery, so it was moved to its current location. Since the design was already complete, it was slightly modified but kept its pentagon shape, even though it wasn't essential any longer.
16) Persian Empire - It accounted for approximately 44% of the world's population in 480 BC. In contrast, the British Empire accounted for about 23% of the world's population at its peak.
17) South Africa - Gandhi initially fought for the right of the resident Indian community in South Africa. He went to South Africa to work at age 23 and spent 21 years there before returning to India in 1915.
18) 1839 - While the first usage of the word selfie didn't occur until 2002, the world's first known selfie was taken in 1839. Robert Cornelius took the first selfie inside his family's store in Philadelphia; he had to remove the camera's lens cap, run into frame, and hold his pose for a full minute.
19) Austro-Prussian War - In 1866, Liechtenstein sent out an army of 80 men for the Austro-Prussian War; they came back with 81 men. They had no casualties and picked up an extra soldier along the way.
20) To see in the dark - They were constantly going above and below deck, and it takes the human eye up to 25 minutes to adapt to seeing in the dark. By wearing a patch, they kept one eye dark adjusted, so they could see in the dark immediately by just moving the eye patch.

Literature

Quiz 1

1) Who wrote *Oedipus Rex*?
2) What is the only Shakespeare play that mentions America?
3) In the original book *The Wonderful Wizard of Oz*, what color are the slippers?
4) Where did Winnie the Pooh live?
5) Who wrote *Wuthering Heights*?
6) What writer coined the term "atomic bomb" approximately 30 years before its invention?
7) By what name is the fictional character Duchess of Saint Bridget better known as?
8) Who wrote *Dracula*?
9) In *Treasure Island*, what was Long John Silver's job when on board ship?
10) Where did Clark Kent attend college?

11) What Stephen King novel features a villain who sometimes goes by the alias Bob Gray?
12) What does the J.K. stand for in Harry Potter author J.K. Rowling's name?
13) Edward Nigma is the birth name of what Batman foe?
14) Who wrote *Breakfast at Tiffany's*?
15) How many lines does a sonnet have?
16) In *Charlotte's Web*, what is the name of the gluttonous rat?
17) What Shakespeare play features the line "All the world's a stage, and all the men and women merely players"?
18) What well known Russian author was also a doctor?
19) What are the two family names central to Shakespeare's *Romeo and Juliet*?
20) What poet won the Pulitzer Prize four times?

Quiz 1 Answers

1) Sophocles
2) *The Comedy of Errors*
3) Silver
4) Hundred Acre Wood
5) Emily Bronte
6) H.G. Wells
7) Lara Croft
8) Bram Stoker
9) Quartermaster – handles the ship's food and drink
10) Metropolis University
11) *It*
12) Joanne Kathleen
13) Riddler
14) Truman Capote
15) 14
16) Templeton
17) *As You Like It*
18) Anton Chekov
19) Capulets and Montagues
20) Robert Frost

Quiz 2

1) In Rudyard Kipling's poem "Gunga Din," what is Gunga Din's role for the British army?
2) In *The Canterbury Tales*, what were the pilgrims traveling to visit?
3) Who wrote *Doctor Zhivago*?
4) What was the first fictional novel blessed by the pope?
5) Which Shakespeare play is set in the Forest of Arden?
6) Edgar Allan Poe created mystery fiction's first detective in what 1841 story?
7) Who wrote *The Hitchhikers Guide to the Galaxy*?
8) In *Little Women*, what is the surname of the sisters?
9) What Shakespeare play has the line "Now is the winter of our discontent"?
10) What Is the name of the evil slave owner and villain in *Uncle Tom's Cabin*?
11) What does the J.R.R. stand for in J.R.R. Tolkien?
12) Who wrote the book that the film *Jurassic Park* is based on?
13) Who wrote *The Strange Case of Dr. Jekyll and Mr. Hyde*?
14) In *Gulliver's Travels*, what is Gulliver's profession?
15) What was Shakespeare's last completed play?
16) Who is the author of *All Creatures Great and Small*?
17) In comics, who is the alter ego of Selina Kyle?
18) What is the title of Charles Dickens' unfinished novel?
19) Who wrote *The Chronicles of Narnia*?
20) Who published *Poor Richard's Almanack*?

Quiz 2 Answers

1) Water bearer
2) Thomas Becket's tomb
3) Boris Pasternak
4) *Ben-Hur: A Tale of the Christ*
5) *As You Like It*
6) *The Murders in the Rue Morgue*
7) Douglas Adams
8) March
9) *Richard III*
10) Simon Legree

11) John Ronald Reuel
12) Michael Crichton
13) Robert Louis Stevenson
14) Surgeon
15) *The Tempest*
16) James Herriot
17) Catwoman
18) *The Mystery of Edwin Drood*
19) C.S. Lewis
20) Benjamin Franklin

Quiz 3

1) What award is the mystery writer's equivalent of an Oscar?
2) Who wrote *Valley of the Dolls*?
3) What Ray Bradbury novel is named for the temperature at which paper catches fire?
4) Pip is the hero in what Charles Dickens novel?
5) Edmond Dantes is better known as what literary hero?
6) What novelist sometimes writes under the pseudonym Richard Bachman?
7) Who was born at Daisy Hill Puppy Farm?
8) What author has the most entries on the *New York Times* best-seller list?
9) Who killed Macbeth?
10) What international best-selling author also wrote under the name Mary Westmacott?
11) What Shakespeare character's last words are "Thus with a kiss I die"?
12) What 18th-century writer first penned the line "For fools rush in where angels fear to tread"?
13) Barbara Gordon is better known as what comic book alter ego?
14) *There and Back Again* is an alternative title of what novel?
15) Who wrote a series of novels about CIA analyst Jack Ryan?
16) What author's thrillers include *The Osterman Weekend* and *The Prometheus Deception*?
17) Who wrote *The Rime of the Ancient Mariner*?
18) What private eye hero did Raymond Chandler create?
19) Who told stories about Brer Rabbit and Brer Fox?
20) What is the surname of the family in *The Grapes of Wrath*?

Quiz 3 Answers

1) Edgar – after Edgar Allan Poe
2) Jacqueline Susann
3) *Fahrenheit 451*
4) *Great Expectations*
5) Count of Monte Cristo
6) Stephen King
7) Snoopy
8) James Patterson
9) Macduff
10) Agatha Christie
11) Romeo
12) Alexander Pope
13) Batgirl
14) *The Hobbit*
15) Tom Clancy
16) Robert Ludlum
17) Samuel Taylor Coleridge
18) Philip Marlowe
19) Uncle Remus
20) Joad

Quiz 4

1) Who was the first man to appear on the cover of *Playboy*?
2) Who in literature is told to "Begin at the beginning and go on till you come to the end; then stop"?
3) Who wrote *The Call of the Wild*?
4) Who created Perry Mason?
5) In Sherlock Holmes, what is Professor Moriarty's first name?
6) What country originated the story of Cinderella?
7) What Dr. Seuss tale is set "on the 15th of May, in the jungle of Nool, in the heat of the day, in the cool of the pool"?
8) What famous character did Jean de Brunhoff create in 1931?
9) What was Shakespeare's first play?
10) Who wrote the play *Androcles and the Lion*?
11) What Shakespeare play ends in the marriage of Benedick and Beatrice?
12) Who wrote *Interview with a Vampire*?

13) *My Fair Lady* is based on what George Bernard Shaw play?
14) Who wrote *Charlie and the Chocolate Factory*?
15) What book contains the line "It is a truth universally acknowledged that a single man in possession of a good fortune must be in want of a wife"?
16) In Shakespeare's *The Taming of the Shrew*, what is the name of the shrew?
17) Who wrote the Father Brown crime stories?
18) What is the title of William Golding's book about boys marooned on an island?
19) Who first wrote about the lost civilization of Atlantis?
20) What is the name of Gandalf's horse?

Quiz 4 Answers

1) Peter Sellers
2) Alice - *Alice's Adventures in Wonderland*
3) Jack London
4) Erle Stanley Gardner
5) James
6) China
7) *Horton Hears a Who!*
8) Babar the Elephant
9) *Henry VI*
10) George Bernard Shaw
11) *Much Ado About Nothing*
12) Ann Rice
13) *Pygmalion*
14) Roald Dahl
15) *Pride and Prejudice*
16) Katherine or Kate
17) G.K. Chesterton
18) *Lord of the Flies*
19) Plato
20) Shadowfax

Quiz 5

1) What did Dr. Seuss write after his editor dared him to write a book using fewer than 50 different words?

2) Michael Bond created what children's character?
3) Who was Dr. Zhivago's great love?
4) Miss Felicity Lemon is what fictional detective's confidential secretary?
5) In the Grimm's fairy tale, the *Pied Piper of Hamelin* is described as pied because he does what?
6) The Newbery Medal is given annually for what?
7) Both Katharine Ross and Nicole Kidman have played Joanna Eberhart, the main character from what novel?
8) What London club does Mycroft Holmes belong to?
9) What book begins with the line "When he was nearly thirteen, my brother Jem got his arm badly broken at the elbow"?
10) Who wrote *The Count of Monte Cristo*?
11) According to Ernest Hemmingway, there are only three sports; what are they?
12) Who wrote *Crime and Punishment*?
13) What is the best-selling fiction book of all time?
14) Who wrote *2001: A Space Odyssey*?
15) Who is the most widely translated author in the world?
16) What was the title of Niccolo Machiavelli's book published in 1532?
17) Who does Sherlock Holmes refer to as "The Woman"?
18) Who wrote *To Kill a Mockingbird*?
19) What is the secret identity of Don Diego de la Vega?
20) What writer established the three laws of robotics?

Quiz 5 Answers

1) *Green Eggs and Ham*
2) Paddington Bear
3) Lara
4) Hercule Poirot
5) Wears a two-colored coat – Pied is thought to come from magpies, which are black and white.
6) Best children's book
7) *The Stepford Wives*
8) Diogenes
9) *To Kill a Mockingbird*
10) Alexandre Dumas
11) Bullfighting, motor racing, mountaineering – According to Hemingway, "All the rest are merely games."

12) Fyodor Dostoevsky
13) *Don Quixote* – estimated 500 million copies
14) Arthur C. Clarke
15) Agatha Christie
16) *The Prince*
17) Irene Adler
18) Harper Lee
19) Zorro
20) Isaac Asimov

Quiz 6

1) What is Tarzan's real identity?
2) What crime novelist created the character Mike Hammer?
3) What classic novel is based on the adventures of Alexander Selkirk, an early 18th-century Scottish sailor?
4) P.L. Travers created what famous character?
5) Who took dictation from Perry Mason?
6) What novel has the line "Four legs good, two legs bad"?
7) Who wrote *The Caine Mutiny*?
8) Who is Oscar Zoroaster Phadrig Isaac Norman Henkle Immanuel Ambrose Diggs?
9) Who ate Chicken Little?
10) Who first wrote, "Do not count your chickens before they are hatched"?
11) What children's classic did Johann David Wyss write?
12) What children's book features the adventures of a boy named Milo and a watchdog named Tock?
13) In comics, Linda Lee Danvers is whose alter ego?
14) Who is the alter ego of the Incredible Hulk?
15) What was the first story to feature Sherlock Holmes?
16) British mathematician Charles Lutwidge Dodgson is better known by what pen name?
17) Who declined the 1964 Nobel Prize for literature?
18) According to Ernest Hemmingway, a man must plant a tree, fight a bull, have a son, and what other thing to be a man?
19) What book won the very first Nebula Award for best science fiction or fantasy novel in 1966?
20) Who was the first *Playboy* centerfold?

Quiz 6 Answers

1) Lord Greystoke
2) Mickey Spillane
3) *Robinson Crusoe*
4) Mary Poppins
5) Della Street
6) *Animal Farm*
7) Herman Wouk
8) The Wizard of Oz
9) Foxy Loxy or Foxy Woxy
10) Aesop – *The Milkmaid and Her Pail*
11) *The Swiss Family Robinson*
12) *The Phantom Tollbooth*
13) Supergirl
14) Dr. David Banner
15) *A Study in Scarlet*
16) Lewis Carroll – *Alice's Adventures in Wonderland*
17) Jean-Paul Sartre
18) Write a book
19) *Dune*
20) Marilyn Monroe

Quiz 7

1) What year was the first issue of *National Geographic* published?
2) What was the first U.S. digital media company to win a Pulitzer Prize?
3) Who was the first woman to win both a Pulitzer Prize and Nobel Prize for literature?
4) The Artful Dodger is a character from what novel?
5) What was Tom Clancy's first novel?
6) Who was the first American to win the Nobel Prize for literature?
7) How many books are in *The Chronicles of Narnia* series by C.S. Lewis?
8) Who is the Green Hornet's alter ego?
9) Civil War Union general Lewis Wallace wrote what book that later became a famous movie?
10) Who wrote the *The Hunger Games* book series?
11) Who wrote *The Little Mermaid*?
12) Whose image is engraved on the Pulitzer Prize gold medals?

13) Psychologist William Marston was one of the inventors of the polygraph, and he also created what well-known comics character?
14) What poem by John Milton tells the story of Adam and Eve's temptation and the fall of man?
15) What is Scarlett O'Hara's real first name in *Gone with the Wind*?
16) In *The Jungle Book*, what is the name of the boy?
17) Who was Truman Capote's best friend and next-door neighbor that he first met when he was five years old?
18) What was the first daily comic strip to win a Pulitzer Prize for best editorial cartoon?
19) What is the best-selling science fiction book of all time?
20) According to the *Guinness Book of World Records*, what single author has the most published works?

Quiz 7 Answers

1) 1888
2) *The Huffington Post*
3) Pearl S. Buck
4) *Oliver Twist*
5) *The Hunt for Red October*
6) Sinclair Lewis – 1930
7) Seven
8) Britt Reed
9) *Ben-Hur: A Tale of the Christ*
10) Suzanne Collins
11) Hans Christian Andersen
12) Benjamin Franklin
13) Wonder Woman
14) *Paradise Lost* – 1667
15) Katie – Scarlett is her middle name.
16) Mowgli
17) Harper Lee – author of *To Kill a Mockingbird*
18) *Doonesbury*
19) *Dune*
20) L. Ron Hubbard – 1,084

Quiz 8

1) What news organization has won the most Pulitzer Prizes?

2) Who coined the word tween?
3) What is Shakespeare's longest play?
4) What is Wonder Woman's alter ego?
5) *The Communist Manifesto* was written by what two German philosophers?
6) Who wrote the poem "The Song of Hiawatha"?
7) What was the best-selling American fiction book of the 19th century?
8) Writer Eric Blair went by what pen name?
9) What institution awards the Pulitzer Prizes?
10) Who was the first English language writer to win the Nobel Prize for literature?
11) How old is Juliet in Shakespeare's *Romeo and Juliet*?
12) Who edited Michael Jackson's autobiography *Moonwalk*?
13) Who wrote *Don Quixote*?
14) Crab, the only named dog in any Shakespeare play, appears in what play?
15) Who wrote *Robinson Crusoe*?
16) What was Dr. Frankenstein's first name?
17) What American novel was the first to sell 1 million copies?
18) What is the name of the gypsy girl Quasimodo falls in love with in *The Hunchback of Notre Dame*?
19) Who wrote *Catch-22*?
20) What book opens with the line "It was the best of times, it was the worst of times"?

Quiz 8 Answers

1) New York Times
2) J.R.R. Tolkien – In *The Hobbit*, it is used to describe Hobbits in their reckless age period.
3) Hamlet
4) Diana Prince
5) Karl Marx and Friedrich Engels
6) Henry Wadsworth Longfellow
7) *Uncle Tom's Cabin*
8) George Orwell
9) Columbia University
10) Rudyard Kipling
11) 13

12) Jacqueline Kennedy Onassis
13) Miguel de Cervantes
14) *Two Gentlemen of Verona*
15) Daniel Defoe
16) Victor
17) *Uncle Tom's Cabin*
18) Esmeralda
19) Joseph Heller
20) *A Tale of Two Cities*

Quiz 9

1) What comics character has the maiden name Boopadoop?
2) What book is subtitled *The Boy Who Wouldn't Grow Up*?
3) Who wrote *The Secret Life of Walter Mitty*?
4) What novel is set in a desert with giant sandworms?
5) Who is the only author to publish books in nine of the ten Dewey Decimal categories?
6) What is the last line of Dickens's *A Christmas Carol*?
7) What novel has the subtitle *The Modern Prometheus*?
8) Who wrote the play *Our Town*?
9) What is the name of the pig in *Charlotte's Web*?
10) Who wrote *Black Beauty*?
11) Who wrote the poem "Paul Revere's Ride"?
12) Who wrote, "If God did not exist, it would be necessary to invent him"?
13) What was Charles Dickens's first novel?
14) Who wrote, "How do I love thee? Let me count the ways"?
15) *Just One More Thing* is an autobiography by what actor?
16) What does DC stand for in DC Comics?
17) Holden Caulfield appears in what novel?
18) What is the first name of Gatsby in *The Great Gatsby*?
19) What is Shakespeare's shortest play?
20) Lenny Small and George Milton are the main characters in what novel?

Quiz 9 Answers

1) Blondie Bumstead
2) *Peter Pan*
3) James Thurber

4) *Dune*
5) Isaac Asimov
6) God bless us, everyone!
7) *Frankenstein*
8) Thornton Wilder
9) Wilbur
10) Anna Sewell
11) Henry Wadsworth Longfellow
12) Voltaire – 1770
13) *The Pickwick Papers*
14) Elizabeth Barrett Browning
15) Peter Falk
16) Detective Comics
17) *Catcher in the Rye*
18) Jay
19) *The Comedy of Errors*
20) *Of Mice and Men*

Quiz 10

1) What fictional doctor is the main character in a series of books by Hugh Lofting?
2) Fictional character Sir Percy Blakeney is better known as who?
3) Oliver Mellors is the lover of what fictional character?
4) Who wrote *The Wonderful Wizard of Oz*?
5) Who wrote the *Twilight* series of books?
6) What was the name of Don Quixote's love?
7) In *The Jungle Book*, what is the name of the bear?
8) What are the names of Peter Cottontail's sisters in *The Tale of Peter Rabbit*?
9) What author was the first to use the word nerd in print?
10) What was the first James Bond book?
11) Who wrote *The Man in the Iron Mask*?
12) Whose autobiography was *The Long Walk to Freedom*?
13) Who wrote *Pride and Prejudice*?
14) Who wrote *Gulliver's Travels*?
15) The title of whose book translates as *My Struggle*?
16) Carlo Collodi created what children's character?
17) In what book are there Eloi and Morlocks?

18) In what book would you find the servant Passepartout?
19) Who created Tarzan?
20) What literary character was the Thane of Cawdor?

Quiz 10 Answers

1) Doctor Dolittle
2) The Scarlet Pimpernel
3) Lady Chatterley
4) L. Frank Baum
5) Stephenie Meyer
6) Dulcinea
7) Baloo
8) Flopsy, Mopsy, Cottontail
9) Dr. Seuss – the name of a creature in *If I Ran the Zoo* in 1950
10) *Casino Royale*
11) Alexandre Dumas
12) Nelson Mandela
13) Jane Austen
14) Jonathan Swift
15) Adolf Hitler – *Mein Kampf*
16) Pinocchio
17) *The Time Machine*
18) *Around the World in 80 Days*
19) Edgar Rice Burroughs
20) Macbeth

Quiz 11

1) Who created the characters Sam Spade and Nick and Nora Charles?
2) In *Moby Dick*, what is the name of Captain Ahab's ship?
3) What was writer O. Henry's real name?
4) Ernest Hemmingway's *The Old Man and the Sea* is set in what country?
5) What author has the most films based on their work?
6) Who is generally credited with first saying, “When in doubt tell the truth”?
7) Who wrote *Little Men*?
8) What was Stephen King's first published novel?
9) What links *The Reivers*, *The Grapes of Wrath*, and *Humboldt’s Gift*?

10) Who wrote *The Picture of Dorian Gray*?
11) What author created the character The Saint?
12) When Lord Byron became a student at Cambridge, dogs were prohibited; what did he get as a pet?
13) Who wrote *The Wind in the Willows*?
14) Who wrote *Charlotte's Web*?
15) What novelist is known as the father of science fiction?
16) Who is the only person to have their own Dewey Decimal classification?
17) Who wrote *Jane Eyre*?
18) Who wrote *The Scarlet Letter*?
19) In *A Christmas Carol*, what is the name of the employer that Scrooge works for in his youth?
20) The Caldecott Medal is given for what?

Quiz 11 Answers

1) Dashiell Hammett
2) Pequod
3) William Sydney Porter
4) Cuba
5) William Shakespeare
6) Mark Twain
7) Louisa May Alcott
8) *Carrie*
9) Pulitzer Prize fiction winners
10) Oscar Wilde
11) Leslie Charteris
12) A bear - The bear stayed in his lodgings, and Byron would walk him.
13) Kenneth Grahame
14) E.B. White
15) Jules Verne
16) William Shakespeare
17) Charlotte Bronte
18) Nathaniel Hawthorne
19) Fezziwig
20) Children's book illustration

Quiz 12

1) What playwright choked to death on the cap of a bottle of barbiturates?
2) What famous Spanish and English writers died on the same day – April 23, 1616?
3) Who wrote *The Red Badge of Courage*?
4) Who is Bertie Wooster's butler?
5) Who wrote *Uncle Tom's Cabin*?
6) What Missouri town was Mark Twain's boyhood home?
7) What mountains did Rip Van Winkle nod off in?
8) Who wrote *In Cold Blood*?
9) Who wrote the poem "The Road Not Taken"?
10) What play recounts the last hours of Willy Loman?
11) What is the last name of Lucy and Linus from the Peanuts cartoon?
12) Who said, "The end justifies the means"?
13) What Shakespeare play features Rosencrantz and Guildenstern?
14) What is Richard Bach's best-selling adult fairy tale?
15) Who wrote, "Poems are made by fools like me, but only God can make a tree"?
16) Who was the first novelist to present a typed manuscript to their publisher?
17) Who created Winnie the Pooh?
18) What Pulitzer Prize winning play dramatized the life of African American boxing champ Jack Johnson?
19) Who created British master spy George Smiley?
20) What Richard Adams book includes an account of Bigwig's encounter with a fox?

Quiz 12 Answers

1) Tennessee Williams
2) Miguel de Cervantes and William Shakespeare
3) Stephen Crane
4) Jeeves – from the novels of P.G. Wodehouse
5) Harriet Beecher Stowe
6) Hannibal
7) Catskills
8) Truman Capote
9) Robert Frost

10) *Death of a Salesman*
11) Van Pelt
12) Niccolò Machiavelli
13) *Hamlet*
14) *Jonathon Livingston Seagull*
15) Joyce Kilmer
16) Mark Twain
17) A.A. Milne
18) *The Great White Hope*
19) John le Carre
20) *Watership Down*

Quiz 13

1) Who wrote *Of Mice and Men*?
2) Who wrote *The Exorcist*?
3) In comics, who is the editor of *The Daily Planet*?
4) What epic chronicles events toward the end of the Trojan wars?
5) What James Dickey novel tells the tale of an ill-fated canoe trip?
6) What was the name of the fisherman in Hemingway's *The Old Man and the Sea*?
7) Who wrote *East of Eden*?
8) How many ghosts appear to Scrooge in Dickens' *A Christmas Carol*?
9) As originally written, what nationality was Aladdin?
10) What American poet wrote a four-volume biography of Abraham Lincoln?
11) What American poet wrote, "Good fences make good neighbors"?
12) Who was Don Quixote's sidekick?
13) Who created Peter Rabbit?
14) Who wrote *The Black Stallion*?
15) What nursery rhyme character had arachnophobia?
16) What phenomenon appeared the day Mark Twain was born and the day he died?
17) Who created Billy Pilgrim, a survivor of the Dresden firestorm?
18) What novel features the character First Lieutenant Milo Minderbinder?
19) Who wrote *The Razor's Edge*?
20) What Shakespeare play contains the line "Something is rotten in the state of Denmark"?

Quiz 13 Answers

1) John Steinbeck
2) William Peter Blatty
3) Perry White
4) *The Iliad*
5) *Deliverance*
6) Santiago
7) John Steinbeck
8) Four – Marley, past, present, and yet to come
9) Chinese
10) Carl Sandburg
11) Robert Frost
12) Sancho Panza
13) Beatrix Potter
14) Walter Farley
15) Little Miss Muffet
16) Halley's Comet
17) Kurt Vonnegut Jr. – *Slaughterhouse-Five*
18) *Catch-22*
19) Somerset Maugham
20) *Hamlet*

Quiz 14

1) What poet wrote, "I have promises to keep, and miles to go before I sleep"?
2) What fictional detective retired to become a beekeeper?
3) What is the nationality of Agatha Christie's detective Hercule Poirot?
4) What imaginary island did Sir Thomas More create in a 1516 work?
5) How many known plays did William Shakespeare write?
6) What was H.G. Wells' first novel?
7) Who wrote, "A thing of beauty is a joy for ever"?
8) What were the names of the three Bronte sisters?
9) What book opens with, "Somewhere in la Mancha, in a place whose name I do not care to remember"?
10) Who wrote *The Glass Menagerie*?
11) Who wrote *The Prince and the Pauper*?
12) Who wrote about the lioness Elsa in *Born Free*, *Living Free*, and *Forever*

Free?

13) Who wrote *The Guns of Navarone*?
14) In what Shakespeare play does the character Caliban appear?
15) In what book did the utopia Shangri-La appear?
16) Who wrote the *Jungle Book* series?
17) What Stephen King story is set at Cold Mountain Penitentiary?
18) Who titled the first of her 723 novels *Jigsaw* in 1925?
19) Who wrote *Ivanhoe*?
20) Who created the fictional detective Nero Wolfe?

Quiz 14 Answers

1) Robert Frost
2) Sherlock Holmes
3) Belgian
4) Utopia
5) 37
6) *The Time Machine*
7) John Keats
8) Anne, Charlotte, Emily
9) *Don Quixote*
10) Tennessee Williams
11) Mark Twain
12) Joy Adamson
13) Alistair MacLean
14) *The Tempest*
15) *Lost Horizon*
16) Rudyard Kipling
17) *The Green Mile*
18) Barbara Cartland
19) Sir Walter Scott
20) Rex Stout

Quiz 15

1) Who wrote, "To err is human; to forgive, divine"?
2) "If you really want to hear about it, the first thing you'll probably want to know is where I was born, and what my lousy childhood was like, and how my parents were occupied and all before they had me, and all that David Copperfield kind of crap," is the opening line to what novel?

3) What is the name of the lion in C.S. Lewis' *The Lion, the Witch and the Wardrobe*?
4) In the Humpty Dumpty nursery rhyme, there is no indication that he is an egg; what did early illustrations portray him as?
5) What was the name of the only son of William Shakespeare?
6) The author of *Moll Flanders* wrote what more famous work?
7) What Jane Austen novel was originally titled *First Impressions*?
8) In Frank Herbert's *Dune*, what is the name of the drug commonly referred to as "the spice" that is central to the story?
9) What century were Chaucer's *Canterbury Tales* written?
10) What novel ends with "It is a far better thing I do, than I have ever done; it is a far, far better rest that I go to than I have ever known"?
11) Who said, "Tis better to have loved and lost than never to have loved at all"?
12) What is Eugene O'Neill's autobiographical play?
13) What is the first name of Agatha Christie's character Miss Marple?
14) What was the first book Mark Twain published?
15) In what century was Cervantes's *Don Quixote* first published?
16) Who wrote the short story "Rip Van Winkle"?
17) Who is likely the bestselling author in history?
18) In the novel *The Wonderful Wizard of Oz*, what is the name of the Good Witch of the South?
19) In the Peanuts comic strip, what is the name of Snoopy's sister?
20) What author created more than 1,700 of our common English words, more than any other person?

Quiz 15 Answers

1) Alexander Pope
2) *The Catcher in the Rye* – J.D. Salinger
3) Aslan
4) Young boy
5) Hamnet
6) *Robinson Crusoe* - Daniel Defoe
7) *Pride and Prejudice*
8) Melange
9) 14th century - 1387 to 1400
10) *A Tale of Two Cities*
11) Alfred Lord Tennyson

12) *Long Day's Journey into Night*
13) Jane
14) The *Celebrated Jumping Frog of Calaveras County* - 1867
15) 17th century - 1605
16) Washington Irving
17) Agatha Christie - 2 to 4 billion copies
18) Glinda
19) Belle
20) William Shakespeare - He did it by changing nouns into verbs, changing verbs into adjectives, connecting words never used together, adding prefixes and suffixes, and creating original words; he also created many common phrases. Some examples of his creations include fancy-free, lie low, foregone conclusion, a sorry sight, for goodness sake, good riddance, laughable, rant, new-fangled, wild goose chase.

Quiz 16

1) Who was on the cover of the first *People* magazine in 1974?
2) What famous European writer was captured by Turkish pirates and held as a slave for five years in Algiers?
3) What is the name of the leader of the pigs in George Orwell's *Animal Farm*?
4) Daniel Quilp, an ill-tempered dwarf, is one of the main antagonists in what Charles Dickens novel?
5) In Shakespeare's *Romeo and Juliet*, who is Romeo's love before he meets Juliet?
6) What novel opens with the line "The Mole had been working very hard all the morning, spring-cleaning his little home"?
7) In what century was Milton's *Paradise Lost* published?
8) In the original story of *Pinocchio*, he gets mad at the talking cricket when he gets some advice he doesn't like and does what?
9) In the Anglo-Saxon epic poem, who kills Grendel?
10) According to the nursery rhyme, how many blackbirds were baked in a pie?
11) Which of her characters did Agatha Christie call "a detestable, bombastic, tiresome, egocentric little creep"?
12) Who wrote *Peter Pan*?
13) Who said, "That which does not kill us makes us stronger"?
14) Who wrote "The Gift of the Magi" and is known for his surprise endings?

15) Which of Shakespeare's plays is responsible for starlings being introduced to North America?
16) In the Peanuts comic strip, what is Peppermint Patty's real name?
17) Tashtego, Daggoo, and Fedallah are all characters in what novel?
18) "In my younger and more vulnerable years my father gave me some advice that I've been turning over in my mind ever since. Whenever you feel like criticizing anyone, he told me, just remember that all the people in this world haven't had the advantages that you've had," is the opening line from what book?
19) What well-known author created the character of the Cisco Kid?
20) What was the name of the only brother of the Bronte sisters?

Quiz 16 Answers

1) Mia Farrow
2) Miguel de Cervantes - author of *Don Quixote*
3) Napoleon
4) *The Old Curiosity Shop*
5) Rosaline
6) *The Wind in the Willows* - 1908
7) 17th century - 1667
8) He kills the cricket. The talking cricket returns later as a ghost to give Pinocchio additional advice.
9) Beowulf
10) 24 - four and twenty
11) Hercule Poirot
12) James Matthew Barrie
13) Friedrich Nietzsche
14) O. Henry or William Sydney Porter
15) *Henry IV, Part 1* - The starling is only mentioned in *Henry IV, Part 1*. In 1890, it was purposefully introduced to North America by Eugene Schieffelin, who wanted to import every bird mentioned in Shakespeare's works. He released starlings in New York's Central Park.
16) Patricia Reichardt
17) *Moby Dick* - They are harpooners.
18) *The Great Gatsby* – F. Scott Fitzgerald
19) O. Henry - The Cisco Kid appeared in his 1907 short story "The Caballero's Way."
20) Branwell - He was the fourth of the Bronte children and was a poet and painter; he died at 31.

Miscellaneous

Quiz 1

1) How did the term "piggy bank" originate?
2) What does the word karaoke mean?
3) What is enuresis?
4) What is a digamy?
5) In 1892, Juan Vucetich was the first person to solve a crime using what?
6) Who was the first pilot to fly faster than the speed of sound?
7) The hard piece at the end of a shoelace is called what?
8) What is the only number spelled out in English that has the same number of letters as its value?
9) The U.S. $10,000 bill was last printed in 1945 and is the largest denomination ever in public circulation; whose portrait appeared on it?
10) What is the original name for the pound or number symbol (#)?
11) What country consumes the most coffee per capita?
12) According to the Bible, how long did Methuselah live?
13) What is the name of the dog on the Cracker Jack box?
14) What vegetable did Mark Twain describe as "cabbage with a college

education"?

15) What country eats the most chocolate per capita?
16) If you have a buccula, what have you got?
17) What is the longest railway line in the world?
18) In what country were fortune cookies invented?
19) What country has the highest per capita consumption of turkey?
20) Who was the first person other than royalty to appear on a British stamp?

Quiz 1 Answers

1) Pygg clay – An orange clay called pygg was used to make dishes and jars that were sometimes used to hold spare change. At some point, people decided to use pygg clay to make pig-shaped banks.
2) Empty orchestra
3) Bedwetting
4) A second legal marriage after death or divorce
5) Fingerprints
6) Chuck Yeager
7) Aglet
8) Four
9) Salmon P. Chase – Secretary of the Treasury
10) Octothorpe – It is believed to have been made up by workers at Bell Telephone Labs who needed a name for the symbol on the telephone keypad.
11) Finland
12) 969 years
13) Bingo
14) Cauliflower
15) Switzerland
16) Double chin
17) Trans-Siberian Railway – 5,772 miles
18) United States
19) Israel
20) William Shakespeare

Quiz 2

1) What is the only number spelled out in English that has letters in alphabetical order?

2) What are camel hair brushes typically made from?
3) What game has the most books written about it?
4) The feeling of hitting your funny bone is due to hitting what?
5) What is the most popular crop in U.S. home gardens?
6) Frank Lloyd Wright's son John invented what after watching workers move timber?
7) What kind of condition is protanopia?
8) What was Queen Victoria prescribed for her menstrual cramps?
9) What was the first type of product sold in aerosol spray cans?
10) Before 1938, toothbrushes were made using hairs from what?
11) What well-known economist studied clarinet performance at Juilliard?
12) What familiar word is derived from a Latin word that means "place where three roads meet"?
13) Acmegenesis is better known as what?
14) What globally successful product was created by Dr. John Pemberton?
15) Who was eaten by dogs in the Bible?
16) What was the name of the apostle who replaced Judas Iscariot?
17) Gail Borden invented what food item?
18) Since pigs don't sweat much, where does the expression "sweat like a pig" come from?
19) What is the study of bumps on the head called?
20) What color is an aircraft's black box flight recorder?

Quiz 2 Answers

1) Forty
2) Squirrel hair
3) Chess
4) Ulnar nerve
5) Tomatoes
6) Lincoln Logs
7) Color blindness
8) Marijuana
9) Insecticide
10) Boar
11) Alan Greenspan
12) Trivia
13) Orgasm
14) Coca-Cola

15) Jezebel
16) Matthias
17) Condensed milk
18) It comes from the iron smelting process. Iron ore was smelted into pig iron, which got its name because the mold the iron was poured into had ingots at right angles to a center channel and resembled a litter of piglets suckling on their mother. They knew the pig iron was cool enough to transport when it started to sweat from condensation as it cooled, which originated the term "sweat like a pig."
19) Phrenology
20) Orange

Quiz 3

1) A cluster of 10-20 bananas is called what?
2) Cognac must be at least five years old before it's labeled what?
3) What does a month beginning on a Sunday always have?
4) What carbonated beverage started in the 1890s as Brad's Drink?
5) What was the first nationally distributed beer in the United States?
6) A standard barrel of crude oil holds roughly how many gallons?
7) Who was the first member of the British royal family to graduate from a university?
8) In what country did chocolate originate?
9) The term "slush fund" was originally used by sailors to refer to the side money they made selling what?
10) Orienteering began in what country?
11) According to the Bible, how tall is Goliath?
12) What was the first product to have a barcode?
13) The dot over the letter "i" is called what?
14) "Fidelity, Bravery, and Integrity" is what U.S. organization's motto?
15) A gross is equal to 144 units; how many units are in a great gross?
16) What toy was originally called the Pluto Platter?
17) What country invented cheesecake?
18) In terms of production volume, what is the most popular fruit in the world?
19) What country has the highest per capita tea consumption?
20) What merchandise brand was created by Adolf Dassler?

Quiz 3 Answers

1) A hand
2) Napoleon
3) Friday the 13th
4) Pepsi
5) Budweiser
6) 42
7) Prince Charles
8) Mexico
9) Animal fat – Sailors sold the fat or grease from the meat cooked on board to tallow makers.
10) Sweden
11) Six cubits - about nine feet
12) Wrigley's gum
13) Tittle
14) FBI
15) 1728 – 12 gross
16) Frisbee
17) Greece
18) Tomato – The tomato is technically a fruit.
19) Turkey
20) Adidas

Quiz 4

1) The largest named wine bottle size is Melchizedek; how large is it?
2) Who is the largest toy distributor in the world?
3) What are the ridges on corduroy called?
4) What year did the first canned beer go on sale in the United States?
5) Who or what are taikonauts?
6) What is the cultivation of grapes known as?
7) What is the world's best-selling candy bar?
8) The practice of performing in public places for tips and gratuities is known as what?
9) What country consumes the most Coca-Cola per capita?
10) What causes a jumping bean to jump?
11) What does UNICEF stand for?
12) What country consumes the most meat per capita?

13) What continent has the largest number of Roman Catholics?
14) How many colored dots are on a Twister game mat?
15) What dog has a statue erected in Edinburgh, Scotland?
16) Before taking its current name, what company was originally called Backrub?
17) Why did pirates wear earrings?
18) What is the only miracle mentioned in all four Bible gospels?
19) What language has the most words?
20) How many people have won two Nobel Prizes?

Quiz 4 Answers

1) 30 liters – equivalent to 40 standard 750 ml wine bottles
2) McDonald's – About 20% of its meals are Happy Meals with a toy.
3) Wales
4) 1935 – Krueger's Finest beer went on sale in Richmond, Virginia.
5) Chinese astronauts
6) Viticulture
7) Snickers
8) Busking
9) Mexico
10) Moth grub moving inside the bean
11) United Nations International Children's Emergency Fund
12) Australia
13) South America
14) 24
15) Greyfriars Bobby
16) Google
17) To improve their eyesight – They believed the precious metal in an earring had healing powers.
18) The feeding of the 5,000
19) English
20) Four – Marie Curie, Linus Pauling, John Bardeen, Frederick Sanger

Quiz 5

1) What mode of transport was invented in 1959 by the Armand Bombardier?
2) What is the name of the strong, heavy grating lowered to block the entrance to a castle?

3) What is Barbie the doll’s full name?
4) What species of bird's nest is used to make bird's nest soup?
5) What modern word comes from a knight who was free for hire?
6) If you suffer from oniomania, what are you obsessed with?
7) What was the first group to appear in Madame Tussauds Wax Museum as waxwork models?
8) What cosmetics giant began in 1892 as the California Perfume Company?
9) According to the Old Testament, who planted the first vineyard?
10) What country was Mother Teresa born in?
11) What religion was founded by Lao Tzu?
12) In what country was Greenpeace founded in 1971?
13) What year did Disneyland open?
14) What is unique about the word detartrated?
15) What is the most frequently sold item at Walmart?
16) Alfred Carlton Gilbert, a 1908 Olympic gold medal pole vaulter, invented what popular toy?
17) What is the most commonly used noun in the English language?
18) What country consumes the most fish per capita?
19) Before 1687, clocks didn't have what?
20) What person has the most statues in their honor in the United States?

Quiz 5 Answers

1) Snowmobile
2) Portcullis
3) Barbara Millicent Roberts
4) Swift – The nest is saliva that has dried and hardened.
5) Freelance
6) Shopping
7) Beatles
8) Avon
9) Noah
10) Macedonia
11) Taoism
12) Canada
13) 1955
14) Longest palindrome word in English – same forward and backward
15) Bananas

16) Erector Set
17) Time
18) Iceland
19) Minute hands
20) Sacagawea

Quiz 6

1) What does a polyandric woman have more than one of?
2) In what game would you use a squidger?
3) What two cities represent letters in the phonetic alphabet?
4) As referenced in the Bible, what is myrrh?
5) If you were caught pandiculating, what were you doing?
6) What is the largest inhabited castle in the world?
7) The Clio Awards recognize achievement in what?
8) What was the first universal credit card that could be used at a variety of locations?
9) What is the oldest authenticated age ever for a human?
10) Who was the first person to speak to Jesus after he had risen from the dead?
11) What did the ancient Romans throw at weddings?
12) What flavoring is added to Earl Grey tea?
13) Which of the five senses is less sharp after you eat too much?
14) What is measured on the Gay-Lussac scale?
15) What was the first patented service uniform in the United States?
16) What is the lowest rank of British nobility?
17) A pirate who is yelling, "Avast, ye mateys" is telling his mates to do what?
18) What country eats the most donuts per capita?
19) What country has the most vending machines per capita?
20) What did Simon of Cyrene do in the Bible?

Quiz 6 Answers

1) Husband
2) Tiddlywinks – Squidgers are the larger discs used to shoot the winks.
3) Lima and Quebec
4) Gum resin from trees
5) Stretching and stiffening your trunk and extremities as when fatigued, drowsy, or waking

6) Windsor Castle – 590,000 square feet
7) Advertising
8) Diners Club – 1950
9) 122
10) Mary Magdalene
11) Walnuts – They signified hopes for the fertility of the bride.
12) Oil of bergamot
13) Hearing
14) Alcohol strength
15) Playboy Bunny
16) Baron
17) Stop or cease
18) Canada – The presence of 3,000 Tim Hortons restaurants is a major factor.
19) Japan – one for every 23 people
20) Carried Christ's cross

Quiz 7

1) Hotfoot Teddy was the original name of what American icon?
2) What language (not dialect) has the most characters in its alphabet?
3) What is the Decalogue more commonly known as?
4) What country has the most emigrants (people living in other countries)?
5) What is the study of word origins called?
6) Characters such as those in Chinese where a word is represented by a picture are called what?
7) What body of water is referenced in the Bible as the Great Sea?
8) In psychology, the tendency for people to believe they are above average is an effect named after what fictional town?
9) What U.S. state's constitution is the longest in the world?
10) What poison is found in apple seeds?
11) Who is credited with suggesting the word hello be used when answering a telephone?
12) What country has the world's oldest operating amusement park?
13) What is the button on the top of a baseball cap called?
14) For what purpose was the mouthwash Listerine originally created for?
15) What country has four of the five highest circulation newspapers in the world?

16) What element, previously used in the production of felt, led to the expression "mad as a hatter"?
17) What is coulrophobia?
18) What is the most expensive man-made object ever built?
19) What was the first car model to sell 20 million units?
20) How many possible ways are there to make change for a dollar?

Quiz 7 Answers

1) Smokey the Bear
2) Cambodian (Khmer) – 74 characters
3) Ten Commandments
4) Mexico
5) Etymology
6) Ideograms
7) Mediterranean Sea
8) Lake Wobegon – from Garrison Keillor's *A Prairie Home Companion*
9) Alabama – 310,000 words
10) Cyanide – very small amount via a substance called amygdalin
11) Thomas Edison – Alexander Graham Bell thought ahoy was better.
12) Denmark – 1583
13) Squatchee
14) Surgical disinfectant
15) Japan
16) Mercury – It caused poisoning.
17) Fear of clowns
18) International Space Station - $160 billion
19) Volkswagen Beetle
20) 293

Quiz 8

1) John Montagu is credited with inventing what food item?
2) How many acres in a square mile?
3) Who is the oldest man to win *People* magazine's sexiest man alive?
4) What year did the first enclosed climate-controlled mall open in the United States?
5) What was Play-Doh originally created for?
6) What company has been a continuous part of the Dow Jones Industrial Average stock index the longest?

7) How did the terms "upper case" and "lower case" originate regarding letters?
8) What year was the first automobile speeding ticket issued?
9) How many eyes are there in a deck of 52 cards?
10) What is the pleasant odor after a rain called?
11) What are the dots on dice called?
12) In what two countries is divorce still illegal?
13) What U.S. state has only two escalators in the entire state?
14) What is the most used letter in the English alphabet?
15) What percent alcohol is 80 proof whiskey?
16) What are the only three countries that don't use the metric system?
17) What was the original flavor of the Twinkie filling?
18) How many dots are used in each letter in the Braille system?
19) What was the first U.S. military academy to admit women?
20) What fast food franchise has the most locations worldwide?

Quiz 8 Answers

1) Sandwich – fourth Earl of Sandwich
2) 640
3) Sean Connery – 59
4) 1956 – Edina, Minnesota
5) Wallpaper cleaning putty to remove coal dust in the 1930s
6) Exxon Mobil – since 1928 as its predecessor Standard Oil of New Jersey
7) In early print shops, individual pieces of metal type were kept in boxes called cases; the smaller, more frequently used letters were kept in a lower case that was easier to reach; the less used capital letters were kept in the upper case.
8) 1896 in England - The car was going 8 mph; the speed limit for cars was 2 mph. You could go over 2 mph if you had someone walk in front of the car waving a red flag to alert people.
9) 42 – The jack of hearts, jack of spades, and the king of diamonds are in profile with only one eye showing.
10) Petrichor
11) Pips
12) Philippines and Vatican City
13) Wyoming
14) E
15) 40%

16) United States, Liberia, Myanmar
17) Banana cream
18) Six
19) Coast Guard
20) Subway

Quiz 9

1) What year was the first published use of the word hello?
2) Kopi Luwak is a very expensive type of what?
3) What is the least used letter in the English alphabet?
4) The material that became Kleenex originally was used for what?
5) What do you call a group of unicorns?
6) What did the famous Hollywood sign in Los Angeles originally say?
7) Ferdinand Porsche designed what car launched in 1937?
8) How many witches are in a coven?
9) How did the Snickers candy bar get its name?
10) What popular soda was originally developed as a mixer for whiskey?
11) What is the U.S. national tree?
12) Inspired by burrs, George de Mestral invented what product in the 1940s?
13) Up until 1954, what color were U.S. traffic stop signs?
14) What country has the longest constitution in the world?
15) What is the most common time to wake up in the middle of the night?
16) Why was Ted Kaczynski called the Unabomber?
17) What is rhinotillexomania?
18) What bathroom staple product was originally called Baby Gays?
19) The Vatican bank has the only ATM in the world that allows users to do what?
20) What was sex therapist Dr. Ruth trained for in the Israeli army?

Quiz 9 Answers

1) 1827 – Hello is a relatively recent word and was initially used to attract attention or express surprise; it didn't get its current meaning until the telephone arrived.
2) Coffee – It is derived from partially digested coffee cherries eaten and defecated by civet cats.
3) Q
4) Gas mask filters in WWI

5) A blessing
6) Hollywoodland
7) Volkswagen Beetle
8) 13
9) Named after the creator's horse
10) Mountain Dew – 1940s
11) Oak
12) Velcro
13) Yellow
14) India – 146,000 words
15) 3:44 AM
16) His early targets were universities (un) and airlines (a).
17) Excessive nose picking
18) Q-tips
19) Perform transactions in Latin
20) Sniper – They thought her short stature (4'7") would make her hard to see; she had an affinity for it.

Quiz 10

1) How did the duffel bag get its name?
2) Based on enrollment, what is the largest university in the United States?
3) Who was the first U.S. citizen to be canonized as a saint?
4) In land surveying, how long is the chain used to measure?
5) What is a pangram?
6) In what country was the world's highest surface wind speed ever recorded?
7) What are the monkeys Mizaru, Kikazaru, and Iwazaru better known as?
8) Until the 1770s, what was used to erase lead pencil marks?
9) The United States has the most Nobel Prize winners in history; what country is second?
10) In Finland, the amount you are fined for a speeding ticket is based on what?
11) Since 1863, Norway has done what with all personal tax returns?
12) The United States has the most billionaires; what country has the second most?
13) The headquarters of Greenpeace is in what city?
14) What is the international distress signal one level less serious than

Mayday?

15) In the Bible, who is Noah's grandfather?
16) What is the name for the part of a sundial that casts the shadow?
17) What is the name of the seat for riding on an elephant?
18) What is the technical name for the foam on beer?
19) Hexakosioihexekontahexaphobia is the fear of what number?
20) On a QWERTY keyboard, what two letters have raised marks to assist with touch typing?

Quiz 10 Answers

1) Duffel, Belgium – The thick cloth used to make the bag originated there.
2) University of Central Florida
3) Mother Frances Xavier Cabrini – 1946
4) 66 feet - 10 square chains are an acre.
5) Sentence or verse that contains all letters in the alphabet at least once
6) Australia – 254 mph during Tropical Cyclone Olivia in 1996
7) See No Evil, Hear No Evil, Speak No Evil
8) Bread – decrusted, moistened, and balled up
9) United Kingdom
10) Your annual income – Fines as high as 112,000 euros have been assessed.
11) Published them for everyone to see - You can see total income and total taxes for anyone; in 2014, they added the restriction that the person whose information is being requested will be notified who is looking, which has resulted in far fewer inquiries.
12) China
13) Amsterdam
14) Pan-Pan
15) Methuselah – He fathered Noah's father at age 187.
16) Gnomon – from Greek meaning indicator
17) Howdah
18) Barm
19) 666
20) F and J

Quiz 11

1) If something is napiform, it is shaped like what vegetable?

2) According to the Bible, what are Adam and Eve's three named children?
3) Ahura Mazda is the sole god of what religion?
4) "March of the Volunteers" is what country's national anthem?
5) The Antoinette Perry Award for Excellence is better known as what?
6) What year was the game of Monopoly released in the United States?
7) When a person is micturating, what are they doing?
8) What country has the highest rate of cocaine usage?
9) It is illegal for drug companies to advertise directly to consumers almost everywhere in the world except the United States and what country?
10) What country has the highest number of psychiatrists per capita?
11) U.S. television allows alcohol to be advertised if what?
12) Who manages Sweden's official Twitter account?
13) Chinese checkers originated in what country?
14) There is a cognitive bias called the cheerleader effect; what is it?
15) What is hippopotomonstrosesquippedaliophobia?
16) The word mortgage comes from a French word that means what?
17) In ancient Greece, throwing an apple at someone was a declaration of what?
18) Jesus' name translated directly from Hebrew to English would be what?
19) What is the only country that is exempt from the international rule that a country's name must appear on its postage stamps?
20) What is the most searched tutorial on YouTube?

Quiz 11 Answers

1) Turnip
2) Cain, Abel, Seth
3) Zoroastrianism
4) China
5) Tony Award
6) 1935
7) Urinating
8) Scotland
9) New Zealand
10) Argentina – about six times higher than the United States
11) No alcohol is consumed in the commercial – It isn't a law or FCC regulation, just a broadcasting standard.
12) A random citizen is chosen each week to manage the account.

13) Germany – 1892
14) It is a bias causing people to think that individuals are more attractive when they are in a group likely due to the averaging out of unattractive idiosyncrasies.
15) Fear of long words
16) Death contract
17) Love
18) Joshua – Jesus comes from translating Hebrew to Greek to Latin to English.
19) Great Britain – They were the first country with postage stamps and had no name on them and were exempted when the rule was made.
20) How to kiss

Quiz 12

1) What year was the company Nintendo founded?
2) Petroleum is the most valuable traded commodity; what is the second most valuable commodity?
3) What did Starbucks only sell when it started?
4) How did cappuccino get its name?
5) King Nebuchadnezzar, who built the Hanging Gardens of Babylon, is the best known historical sufferer of the psychological disorder boanthropy; what is boanthropy?
6) If you have a case of pronoia; what is it?
7) In 1997, Pope John Paul II nominated Saint Isidore of Seville to be the patron saint of what?
8) What country has the world's highest gambling rate?
9) Australia's first police force was composed entirely of what?
10) What is the only country in the world where more than 50% of adults have college degrees?
11) What country eats the most macaroni and cheese per capita?
12) All the gold ever mined would fit in how many Olympic size swimming pools?
13) Scatomancy was popular in ancient Egypt; what is it?
14) What defines a blue moon?
15) Of the 12 men who walked on the moon, 11 were what as children?
16) In what country did *Apollo* astronauts train because they felt it most resembled the surface of the moon?
17) After *Apollo 11* landed on the moon and before anyone set foot on the moon, Buzz Aldrin did something that NASA did not want broadcast or

made public, what was it?
18) What single word is the opposite of extinct?
19) How many people in modern recorded history have been struck dead by a meteorite?
20) What country has the most public holidays?

Quiz 12 Answers

1) 1889 – It originally produced handmade playing cards.
2) Coffee - followed by natural gas, gold, wheat
3) Whole roasted coffee beans
4) Similarity of its color to the robes of the Capuchin monks
5) The sufferer believes they are a cow or ox.
6) Opposite of paranoia – feeling that a conspiracy exists to help you
7) Internet
8) Australia – Over 80% of adults gamble in some form.
9) Convicts – The best-behaved convicts were selected.
10) Canada – 51%
11) Canada
12) Four
13) Telling the future using someone's poop
14) The second full moon in a calendar month – It happens about every three years; thus, the expression "once in a blue moon" for something that doesn't occur very often.
15) Boy Scouts
16) Iceland
17) He took communion.
18) Extant
19) One – In 2016 in India, a 40-year-old man was relaxing outside on the grounds of a small engineering college when there was the sound of an explosion; he was found next to a two-foot crater and later succumbed to injuries sustained.
20) Cambodia - 28

Quiz 13

1) Where did German chocolate cake originate?
2) What is Lake Kinneret known as in the Bible?
3) What was the earliest chocolate treat?
4) In Greek mythology, what did they believe happened to redheads when

they died?
5) At what hour of the night are the most Americans sleeping?
6) At what hour of the day are the most Americans awake?
7) What letter starts the most words in the English language?
8) How many letters is the longest English word with one syllable?
9) Until the 19th century, the word hypocrites referred to what profession?
10) What is the shortest complete English sentence?
11) What are the three most commonly used nouns in English?
12) The word muscle comes from the Latin musculus which means what?
13) What does ambisinistrous mean?
14) The word goodbye is a contraction of what phrase?
15) The term sniper originates from what?
16) What does the word poecilonym mean?
17) What was the first country in the world to fully legalize marijuana?
18) What country has the highest percentage of marijuana users?
19) In the 19th century, doctors treated hysteria in women by inducing orgasms; what product came out of this?
20) Who coined the word makeup?

Quiz 13 Answers

1) United States – It is named after American baker Samuel German.
2) Sea of Galilee
3) Hot chocolate – Aztecs
4) They turned into vampires.
5) 3:00 AM – 95.1%
6) 6:00 PM – 97.5%
7) S
8) Nine letters – including words such as scratched, screeched, stretched, straights, strengths
9) Actors
10) Go.
11) Time, person, year
12) Little mouse – A flexed muscle was thought to resemble a mouse.
13) No good with either hand - opposite of ambidextrous
14) God be with ye.
15) How hard it is to shoot the snipe bird
16) It is a synonym for synonym.

17) Uruguay - 2013
18) Nigeria
19) Vibrator
20) Max Factor – 1920

Quiz 14

1) Where did rock paper scissors originate?
2) The word orchid is Greek and literally means what?
3) What is a sapiosexual?
4) Who is the largest retail seller of firearms in the United States?
5) On average, most people have fewer friends than their friends have; this is known as what?
6) What is parthenogenesis?
7) What is Captain Crunch's full name?
8) What is Minnie Mouse's full first name?
9) What does a funambulist do?
10) If you have caries, what do you have?
11) Who was Erich Weiss better known as?
12) What does a cordwainer do?
13) What English word has the most definitions?
14) What name is mentioned most in the Bible?
15) What is the world's most popular first name?
16) What job does a Foley artist do?
17) If you suffer from epistaxis, what is wrong?
18) In 1891, Whitcomb Judson invented what for fastening shoes?
19) What is the world's largest gold depository?
20) In Denmark, what is a svangerskabsforebyggendemiddel?

Quiz 14 Answers

1) China – about 2,000 years ago
2) Testicle
3) Someone who is sexually attracted to intelligence in others
4) Walmart
5) Friendship paradox – You are more likely to be friends with someone who has more friends than someone who has fewer friends.
6) Asexual reproduction – In animals, it equates to virgin birth.
7) Captain Horatio Magellan Crunch

8) Minerva
9) Tightrope walker
10) Tooth decay
11) Harry Houdini
12) Shoemaker – new shoes from new leather
13) Set – 464 definitions in the Oxford English dictionary
14) David – followed by Jesus
15) Mohammed and its variations
16) Sound effects
17) Nosebleed
18) Zipper
19) Manhattan Federal Reserve Bank – about 6,700 tons
20) Condom – Gummimand is the shorter, more common term.

Quiz 15

1) What poker hand is known as the dead man's hand?
2) What was first published in the *New York World* newspaper on December 21, 1913?
3) In what country did checkers originate?
4) In 1969, what category was added to the Nobel Prizes?
5) What European country's orchestra is bigger than its army?
6) Churches in Malta have two of what item to confuse the devil?
7) What Italian tractor maker first tried making cars in the 1960s?
8) What two people appeared separately on the first U.S. postage stamps issued in 1847?
9) What is the most widely used (most countries and dishes) vegetable in the world?
10) What male human feature was taxed in Elizabethan times?
11) In what country did spinach originate?
12) What does ZIP stand for in ZIP Code?
13) What food was invented in a sanitarium in 1894?
14) The United States has more airports than any other country; what country has the second most?
15) In 1829, Walter Hunt invented what common fastening item?
16) What Roman measurement is 1,500 paces?
17) Who gave the United Nations the land to build their New York headquarters?
18) What is the world's oldest monotheistic religion?

19) Dr. Ludwig Zamenhof invented what language in the 19th century?
20) What links Willy Brandt, Lech Walesa, and Yasser Arafat?

Quiz 15 Answers

1) Two black aces and two black eights – This is what Wild Bill Hickok was holding when he was killed.
2) Crossword puzzle
3) Egypt – as early as 200 BC
4) Economics
5) Monaco
6) Clocks - one with the right time and one with the wrong time
7) Ferruccio Lamborghini
8) George Washington and Benjamin Franklin
9) Onion
10) Beards
11) Iran – ancient Persia
12) Zone Improvement Plan
13) Kellogg's Corn Flakes
14) Brazil - about one-third as many as the United States
15) Safety pin
16) League
17) John D. Rockefeller
18) Judaism
19) Esperanto
20) Nobel Peace Prize winners

Quiz 16

1) What is the name of the bridge world championship?
2) In Scrabble, what two letters are worth 10 points?
3) On a pencil, what do the initials HB stand for?
4) What is the first color mentioned in the Bible?
5) What was the first ready to eat breakfast cereal?
6) What are the four railways in the game Monopoly?
7) What is a dactylogram?
8) What are the six murder weapons in the game Clue?
9) What is the world's busiest airport based on passenger traffic?
10) What is the opposite of the Orient?

11) How many times is a Roman numeral's value increased if it has a line over it?
12) What was the first Lifesaver flavor?
13) What is the largest library in the world?
14) What soft drink first appeared in the Old Corner Drug store in Waco, Texas in 1885?
15) Who was the first American world chess champion?
16) What is the singular of graffiti?
17) What is the most widely played card game in the world?
18) What is the name of the piece flipped into the cup in tiddlywinks?
19) What is the most used punctuation mark?
20) What is the most common surname in the world?

Quiz 16 Answers

1) Bermuda Bowl
2) Q and Z
3) Hard black
4) Green
5) Shredded wheat
6) Reading, Pennsylvania, B&O, Short Line
7) Fingerprint
8) Lead pipe, revolver, rope, knife, wrench, candlestick
9) Atlanta, Georgia
10) The Occident
11) 1,000 times
12) Peppermint
13) Library of Congress, Washington, D.C.
14) Dr. Pepper
15) Bobby Fischer
16) Graffito
17) Solitaire
18) Wink
19) Comma
20) Chang

Quiz 17

1) What are the three colors on a roulette wheel?

2) What letter begins the fewest words in the English language?
3) What is the middle day of a non-leap year?
4) What foreign country is visited most by Americans?
5) What was the first instant coffee?
6) What two suits have one-eyed jacks in a deck of cards?
7) What city is home to the Mayo Clinic?
8) What is AM an abbreviation for in time designations?
9) How deep is "mark twain"?
10) How many people took refuge on Noah's ark?
11) What ancient measure is the distance from the elbow to the tip of the middle finger?
12) How many colored squares are there on a Rubik's cube?
13) What Hebrew word means "so be it"?
14) What was the first U.S. consumer product sold in the former Soviet Union?
15) What IQ level is the beginning of genius?
16) What is the last word of the Bible?
17) What number can't be represented in Roman numerals?
18) In terms of pounds consumed, what is the most popular vegetable in the United States?
19) According to the Bible, how many wise men were there?
20) What craft requires you to interlace your warp and weft?

Quiz 17 Answers

1) Black, red, green
2) X
3) July 2
4) Mexico
5) Nescafe
6) Hearts and spades – The other suits have two-eyed jacks.
7) Rochester, Minnesota
8) Ante meridiem – meaning before noon in Latin
9) Two fathoms or twelve feet – The term was used to call out the water depth on riverboats and meant mark number two for two fathoms; Samuel Clemens worked as a steamboat pilot and took his pen name from it.
10) Eight – Noah and his wife and his three sons and their wives
11) Cubit

12) 54
13) Amen
14) Pepsi
15) 140
16) Amen
17) Zero
18) Potato
19) It doesn't say. It says wise men and mentions the gifts; there is no indication of how many wise men.
20) Weaving

Quiz 18

1) What is a string of typographical symbols (e.g. %@$&*!) used in place of an obscenity called?
2) Owyhee is the original English spelling of what?
3) Karl Marx was once a foreign correspondent for what U.S. newspaper?
4) What country created the Smurfs?
5) What year was the first video game console created?
6) What is the fleshy end of your nose that splits your nostrils called?
7) Who was the only apostle of Jesus to die a natural death?
8) What does the Bible say Adam and Eve ate to get expelled from the Garden of Eden?
9) What plant is linen made from?
10) Humans are naturally drawn towards characteristics including a rounded belly, big head, big eyes, loose limbs, etc. Puppies, kittens, and other animals, including human babies, trigger this. What is this set of physical characteristics called?
11) As a description of a person, what is an ultracrepidarian?
12) Nudiustertian is a time reference; what does it mean?
13) What year was wheeled luggage first sold?
14) Written out in English, what is the second number alphabetically no matter how high you go?
15) What is the word for pocket lint?
16) Including fast food, what is the oldest restaurant chain in the United States?
17) Crapulous is the feeling you get from what?
18) Millions of Japanese treat themselves to what fast food chain food each Christmas?
19) What are the only two countries where Coca-Cola isn't sold?

20) What country originated the tradition of exchanging Christmas gifts?

Quiz 18 Answers

1) Grawlix
2) Hawaii
3) *New York Daily Tribune*
4) Belgium
5) 1972 – It was the Magnavox Odyssey and was 5 years before the first Atari and 13 years before the first Nintendo; it had no sound or color.
6) Columella nasi
7) Saint John
8) Forbidden fruit - It never says it was an apple.
9) Flax
10) Kinderschema
11) Person who expresses opinions on matters outside the scope of their knowledge or expertise
12) Day before yesterday
13) 1970 - Macy's department stores in the United States
14) Eight billion
15) Gnurr
16) A&W – founded in Lodi, California, in 1919
17) Eating or drinking too much
18) KFC chicken - In 1974, KFC created a Japanese marketing campaign promoting "Kentucky for Christmas"; it gained hold quickly to the point that Christmas time KFC sales can be 10 times the normal sales volume. Christmas dinner often requires ordering weeks in advance or waiting in line for hours.
19) Cuba and North Korea.
20) Italy - Romans

Quiz 19

1) What is the little paper tail sticking out of a Hershey's Kiss called?
2) In English, what is the shortest three-syllable word?
3) If you started with $0.01 and had a 100% daily return on your money, how long would it take to become a millionaire?
4) What is the unfilled space between a bottle top and the liquid inside called?
5) Dunce caps were originally a sign of what?

6) If something is quotidian, how often does it occur?
7) What is the largest private home ever built in the United States?
8) What is it called when there is a situation in chess and other games where a player must move, but all the moves are bad or put them at a disadvantage?
9) The modern hula hoop idea came from bamboo hoops used by children for exercise and later sold in stores in what country?
10) In the Middle Ages, men who wanted a boy sometimes had what removed to try to ensure having a baby boy?
11) What common clothing item comes from the Persian for "leg garment"?
12) The Motel 6 and Super 8 motel chains both got their names from what?
13) What is the most popular birth month in the United States?
14) What is a mononymous person?
15) How many letters are in the longest English word with one syllable?
16) What is the wave-like gob of toothpaste you put on your toothbrush called?
17) What country uses a 13-month calendar with 12 months of 30 days each and a 13th month of five days for regular years and six days for leap years?
18) What is the oldest hamburger restaurant chain in the United States?
19) Which country spends more time reading per capita than any other?
20) What is probably the closest thing to a universal word because it means the same thing in every language and everybody in almost every language says it?

Quiz 19 Answers

1) Niggly wiggly
2) W - The letters of the alphabet are generally also considered words since they are nouns referring to the letter.
3) 27 days
4) Ulage
5) Intelligence - Thirteenth-century philosopher John Duns Scotus created the idea of the pointy hat as a reverse funnel to spread knowledge into the brain; the hats became popular and a symbol of high intelligence. In the 1500s, Scotus' ideas fell out of favor, and the pointy hat eventually came to mean the opposite.
6) Daily
7) Biltmore Estate in Asheville, North Carolina - It was built for George Washington Vanderbilt II and was completed in 1895; it has 175,856

square feet.

8) Zugzwang
9) Australia - The founders of Wham-O noticed the popularity of the Australian product and began making plastic hoops.
10) Their left testicle - People believed that the right testicle made boy sperm, and the left made girl sperm.
11) Pajamas
12) Their original room rates - Motel 6 charged $6 per night when it started in 1962, and Super 8 charged $8.88 per night when it started in 1974.
13) September - The time between September 9 and September 20 contains a majority of the 10 most popular birthdates. September is popular due to holiday time conceptions nine months earlier.
14) Someone who is known and addressed by one name
15) 10 – scraunched, meaning to crush or crush noisily
16) Nurdle
17) Ethiopia
18) White Castle – It was founded in 1921 in Wichita, Kansas; the original hamburger slider was 5 cents.
19) India
20) Huh

Quiz 20

1) The palm of your hand can be described as glabrous; what does glabrous mean?
2) What is pantheism?
3) In the 15th century, King Louis XI of France ordered Abbot de Beigne to create a musical instrument using the voices of what animal?
4) In British peerage, what is the highest rank?
5) What is the tall, pleated chef's hat called?
6) What is the difference between coffins and caskets?
7) What is the name for traditional Sardinian sheep milk cheese that contains live maggots?
8) What does the distress signal SOS stand for?
9) Why is a second called a second?
10) What does the Spanish snack or appetizer tapas literally mean?
11) What is the largest company in the world based on revenue?
12) The name arctic is from the Greek word "arktos," meaning bear, which is a reference to what?

13) The Bank of Italy, founded in San Francisco, California, in 1904, grew to become what current bank?
14) What is the name of the device they use to measure your foot at a shoe store?
15) What are the only two English words with three consecutive double letters?
16) What is a susurration?
17) What is the word for the third to the last thing?
18) What year was the first automatically sliced commercial bread produced?
19) Coca-Cola didn't entirely remove cocaine as an ingredient until what year?
20) One floor above the U.S. Supreme Court is an area named "The Highest Court in the Land"; what is it?

Quiz 20 Answers

1) Smooth and without hair
2) Belief that the universe is God
3) Pigs - He built a keyboard that jabbed a spike into the rumps of pigs to produce a squeal.
4) Duke
5) Toque - The 100 folds in the toque are said to represent 100 ways to cook an egg.
6) Coffins are typically tapered and six-sided; caskets are rectangular.
7) Casu marzu - The maggots are put into the cheese to promote more fermentation and break down the cheese's fats. Aficionados consider it unsafe to eat the cheese if the maggots have died, so only cheese with living maggots is usually eaten.
8) Nothing - It doesn't stand for "save our ship" or anything else; it was selected as a distress signal because it is easy to transmit: three dots, three dashes, three dots.
9) It was the second division of the hour; the original term was "second minute."
10) Covers or lids
11) Walmart
12) Great and Little Bear constellations of the Northern Hemisphere
13) Bank of America
14) Brannock Device
15) Bookkeeper and bookkeeping

16) A whisper or murmur
17) Antepenultimate
18) 1928 - Missouri
19) 1929 - Most of the cocaine had been eliminated in 1903.
20) Basketball court - It was once a spare room to house journals. In the 1940s, it was converted into a workout area for courthouse workers, and backboards and baskets were installed later to create a smaller than regulation basketball court.

Quiz 21

1) What celebrity inspired the name for the cartoon dog Scooby-Doo?
2) What real-life person is Captain Morgan rum named after?
3) Why do pen caps have a hole in them?
4) What does the brand name WD-40 stand for?
5) What country originated the croissant?
6) If something is natiform, what does it resemble?
7) Hawaiian pizza was invented in what country?
8) What is the line between two numbers in a fraction called?
9) What are the small strips of wood, plastic, or metal between individual panes of glass called?
10) When Colgate started the mass production of its toothpaste in 1873, what was it originally sold in?
11) What is unique about the words facetiously, abstemiously, and arseniously?
12) What are the little bumps on the surface of a table tennis paddle called?
13) In Sweden, blood donors get what each time their blood is used?
14) Cellophane was invented in 1908 for what purpose?
15) What food gets its name from the French word for melted?
16) In what country was Nutella invented?
17) What is the groove in the upper lip that runs from the top of the lip to the nose called?
18) Why are pencils typically yellow?
19) What food dish gets its name from the French meaning "stirred food"?
20) The word avocado derives from the Nahuatl Indian word "āhuacatl" meaning what?

Quiz 21 Answers

1) Frank Sinatra - Fred Silverman suggested naming him Scooby-Doo

based on the refrain "Scooby-dooby-doo" from Sinatra's song "Strangers in the Night."

2) Sir Henry Morgan - He was a 17th-century Welsh privateer. A privateer is essentially a pirate who is sanctioned by the government; he was hired by the British to protect their interests in the Caribbean from the Spanish.
3) Prevent suffocation in case they are swallowed
4) Water displacement, 40th formula - The chemist who developed it was trying to create a product to prevent corrosion, which is done by displacing water.
5) Austria - It started in Vienna as early as the 13th century as a denser crescent-shaped pastry called a kipferl and didn't show up in France in its current form until the early 1800s.
6) A butt
7) Canada - It was first created in 1962 in Ontario, Canada.
8) Vinculum
9) Muntins
10) Jars - They didn't put it in tubes until the 1890s.
11) They each contain all six vowels (including y) in alphabetical order.
12) Pips
13) A text message
14) Liquid repellant cloth - The inventor saw wine spilled on a tablecloth.
15) Fondue
16) Italy - An Italian pastry maker in 1946 was looking for a cheaper alternative to chocolate that was in short supply due to WWII, so he mixed hazelnuts with some cocoa.
17) Philtrum
18) It is the traditional color of Chinese royalty. In the 1890s when pencils started to be mass-produced, the best graphite came from China. Manufacturers wanted people to know they used the best quality graphite, so they painted them yellow, the color of Chinese royalty.
19) Ratatouille
20) Testicle

Quiz 22

1) Cynophobia is fear of what?
2) What was the first country to ban corporal or physical punishment in all forms?
3) What is unique about the word unprosperousness?

4) Who would use a plessor?
5) What is arachibutyrophobia?
6) What is careless handwriting, or a crude or illegible scrawl called?
7) To the nearest percent, how much larger is a British (imperial) pint compared to an American pint?
8) Lexico was the original name for what popular board game?
9) Who has been on the cover of *Time* magazine more times than any other person?
10) What was the first soft drink sold in all aluminum cans?
11) What is the sound from the rustling of silk or similar cloth called?
12) When bubble wrap was invented, it was originally intended to be used for what?
13) What does Crayola (as in the crayon) mean?
14) In the book of Genesis in the Bible, what did God create on the fourth day?
15) What is the most money you can have in change and not be able to make change for a dollar?
16) What is the name for a person with the same name who shows up in results when you Google yourself?
17) On *Sesame Street*, what is the name of Big Bird's teddy bear?
18) David kills Goliath in what book of the Bible?
19) What is the ringing or tinkling sound a bell makes called?
20) With just the current pope, how many popes per square mile are there in Vatican City?

Quiz 22 Answers

1) Dogs - Cyno means dog in Greek.
2) Sweden - Since 1979, corporal or physical punishment in all forms is banned including parental spanking.
3) Longest English word where each letter occurs at least twice - 16 letters
4) Doctor – It is the small hammer with a rubber head used to test reflexes.
5) Fear of peanut butter sticking to the roof of your mouth
6) Griffonage
7) 20% larger
8) Scrabble
9) Richard Nixon - 55 appearances
10) RC Cola or Diet-Rite Cola - 1964

11) Scroop
12) Wallpaper
13) Oily chalk - It combines the French word "craie," meaning chalk with "ola," shortened from the French word "oléagineux," meaning oily.
14) Sun, moon, and stars
15) $1.19 - three quarters, four dimes and four pennies
16) Googleganger
17) Radar - It is a tribute to Gary Burghoff, who played Walter "Radar" O'Reilly on *M*A*S*H*.
18) Samuel
19) Tintinnabulation
20) 5.9

Quiz 23

1) On a building, what is an interfenestration?
2) September's name comes from the Latin "septem," meaning seven, so why is it the ninth month of the year?
3) In human behavior, what is dysania?
4) What is the most popular school name in the United States?
5) Most Japanese schools don't employ janitors or custodians; who cleans the schools?
6) What is it called when you mishear or misinterpret a phrase in a way that gives it a new meaning, such as when you mishear the lyrics of a song and insert words that sound similar and make sense?
7) How many languages are written right to left?
8) What is the name for a word with two opposite meanings, such as "clip" that can mean to fasten or detach?
9) The device that would evolve into the chainsaw was developed for what purpose?
10) If you have a buccula, what do you have?
11) Mr. and Mrs. are abbreviations for what?
12) What was the first pizza chain in the United States?
13) Charles Stratton became famous as what circus act under P.T. Barnum?
14) Junk email is called spam because of what comedy group?
15) What is the only king in a standard card deck of cards that doesn't have a mustache?
16) Before being dropped, what symbol that is still used today was the 27th letter of the English alphabet?
17) In early Greece and Rome, why was it essentially impossible to

understand a text on a first reading?

18) What is the metal part of a pencil that holds the eraser called?
19) What does hors d'oeuvre mean in French?
20) What did the toy company Mattel originally sell?

Quiz 23 Answers

1) Space between two windows
2) It was the seventh month in the old Roman calendar where the year started with March; its name was carried over to the Julian and current Gregorian calendars where it is the ninth month.
3) State of finding it hard to get out of bed in the morning
4) Lincoln Elementary School
5) Students - They believe that requiring students to clean the school teaches respect, responsibility, and promotes equality.
6) Mondegreen
7) 12 - Arabic, Aramaic, Azeri, Divehi, Fula, Hebrew, Kurdish, N'ko, Persian, Rohingya, Syriac, Urdu
8) Contronym
9) Childbirth aid - Around 1780, two doctors were trying to create something to help remove bone and cartilage from the birth canal to widen it during problematic childbirths. At the time, this method was preferred to caesarian sections and was done with a saw and a knife. The early chainsaw developed for this purpose looked like a regular knife with a small chain around it operated by a hand crank.
10) Double chin
11) Master and mistress
12) Pizza Hut - 1958
13) General Tom Thumb
14) Monty Python - The 1970 *Monty Python's Flying Circus* sketch where a waitress is reading out the menu with an endless variety of Spam options and a chorus of Vikings begins singing "Spam, Spam, Spam, Spam" resulted in spam being used generically for something that drowns out or overrides everything else as junk email does.
15) King of hearts
16) Ampersand (&) - It wasn't called an ampersand at that time and was referred to as "and."
17) There was no punctuation or spacing and no distinction between uppercase and lowercase letters; text was just a run-on string of letters.
18) Ferrule

19) Outside the work – It is not part of the normal meal courses.
20) Picture frames and later dollhouse furniture

Quiz 24

1) What is a letter or combination of letters in a word that are not pronounced, such as the "gh" combination in the word night, called?
2) Who was the first woman other than the queen to appear on British currency?
3) What is the Statue of Liberty made of?
4) What is the feeling you get when you experience something you're already very familiar with, but it feels completely new to you like it is your first time called?
5) Written out in English, what is the first number that contains the letter a?
6) In France, most toilet paper sold for home use is what color?
7) What is the only U.S. state that doesn't have an open bottle law prohibiting drivers or passengers from drinking while driving?
8) The S.O.S Soap Pad is a household cleaning product made from steel wool saturated with soap; what does S.O.S stand for in this case?
9) In what country was pepperoni created?
10) What is arithmomania?
11) What common word comes from Greek meaning "drawing with light"?
12) A butt is an actual measurement unit for wine; a buttload of wine is how many U.S. gallons?
13) What is the burnt part of a candlewick called?
14) What is the more common name for serigraphy?
15) What is the loop on a belt that keeps the end in place after it has passed through the buckle called?
16) French filmmaker Albert Lamorisse (1922-1970) is best known for creating award-winning short films, such as *The Red Balloon* (1956) that won the grand prize at Cannes and an Oscar, but he also invented what well-known board game?
17) In the United States, who is the second-largest purchaser of explosive devices behind the U.S. Department of Defense?
18) In the Chinese zodiac, what animal comes last alphabetically?
19) What is unique about the words bulb, angel, and month?
20) What is a word, art form, or other symbolic representation whose elements retain meaning when viewed or interpreted from a different direction, perspective, or orientation (e.g. the word swims reads the same when it is rotated 180 degrees) called?

Quiz 24 Answers

1) Aphthong
2) Florence Nightingale - in circulation from 1975-1994
3) Copper - About 62,000 pounds of copper were used to create it, and it looked like a new penny when it was first created.
4) Jamais vu - It is the opposite of déjà vu.
5) One thousand
6) Pink
7) Mississippi - If the driver maintains a blood alcohol content below the 0.08 legal limit; it is legal to drink and drive.
8) Save our saucepans - The inventor's wife came up with the name; the period after the last "S" is left off, so the name wasn't identical to the distress signal and could be trademarked.
9) United States
10) Compulsion to count things - In traditional vampire lore, it is one of the weaknesses of vampires and can be used to defend against them by putting grains of rice or sand out, which they will be compelled to count.
11) Photography
12) 126 gallons
13) Snaste
14) Silkscreen printing
15) Keeper
16) Risk - 1957
17) Walt Disney Company
18) Tiger
19) They have no rhyming words in the English language.
20) Ambigram

Quiz 25

1) What is the word for the day after tomorrow?
2) What is the longest word in the English language with only one vowel?
3) What is unique about the word "eunoia"?
4) What two books in the Bible list the Ten Commandments?
5) What is the primary difference between our current Gregorian calendar and the prior Julian calendar?
6) What is the piece of cardboard that goes around your hot cup of coffee called?

7) What is the feeling of having already dreamed something that you are now experiencing called?
8) How did the 3 Musketeers candy bar get its name?
9) What is an autological word?
10) Who is the largest employer in the world?
11) The term "pixel" is short for what?
12) What is the name of Rudolph the Red-Nosed Reindeer's girlfriend?
13) What is the name of the mascot depicted as a portly older man with a mustache, suit, bowtie, and top hat in the game Monopoly?
14) Portland cement gets its name from what country?
15) Why are sewer manhole covers always round instead of square or rectangular?
16) If you wrote out every number in English (one, two, three, etc.), you wouldn't use the letter b until what number?
17) What do the words uncopyrightable and dermatoglyphics have in common?
18) In food, what is the cornicione?
19) Written out in English, what is the first number alphabetically no matter how high you go?
20) What was the first food product tested in a microwave oven?

Quiz 25 Answers

1) Overmorrow
2) Strengths – nine letters
3) It is the shortest English word that contains all five vowels. It means goodwill towards an audience, either perceived or real.
4) Exodus and Deuteronomy
5) Years that are evenly divisible by 100 are not leap years unless they are also evenly divisible by 400.
6) Zarf
7) Deja reve
8) It originally came in a package with three pieces with different nougat flavors - vanilla, chocolate, and strawberry.
9) A word that describes itself. Some examples include word, noun, polysyllabic, unhyphenated, suffixed.
10) U.S. Department of Defense
11) Picture element
12) Clarice
13) Rich Uncle Pennybags - He was inspired by tycoon J.P. Morgan.

14) England - It was created in the mid-19th century and is named because of its similarity to Portland stone, which was quarried on the Isle of Portland off the coast of England.
15) A round cover can't fall through the opening. The cover rests on a lip that is smaller than the cover; no matter its dimensions, a square or rectangular cover could always fall through.
16) One billion
17) Longest English words with no repeated letters
18) Outer part of a pizza crust
19) Eight
20) Popcorn

Movies

Quiz 1

1) What well-known actor made his film debut in *Critters 3* in 1991?
2) What well-known actor is listed only as "stud" in the credits for *Myra Breckinridge* in 1970?
3) Who provided the demon's voice for Linda Blair's performance in *The Exorcist*?
4) What is the name of the character Dustin Hoffman plays in *Rain Man*?
5) Who directed *It's a Wonderful Life*?
6) What movie has the line "What we've got here is a failure to communicate"?
7) What was the first full-length color cartoon talking picture?
8) In what movie was Bill Haley's "Rock Around the Clock" first heard?
9) In what classic western does the character Will Kane appear?
10) The song "Raindrops Keep Falling on My Head" was introduced in what movie?

11) Kevin Kline won the Best Supporting Actor Oscar for what film?
12) What 1956 film caused riots in theaters?
13) What year was *The Wizard of Oz* released?
14) What film was Kevin Costner's directorial debut?
15) What is the best-selling movie soundtrack of all time?
16) What is the name of the con that Paul Newman and Robert Redford carry out in *The Sting*?
17) How old was Shirley Temple when she made her last film?
18) What Oscar-winning actress was the Connecticut state golf champion at age 16?
19) Who made her screen debut in Alfred Hitchcock's *The Trouble with Harry* in 1956?
20) What international movie star was born in a bombed-out French village during WWI?

Quiz 1 Answers

1) Leonardo DiCaprio
2) Tom Selleck
3) Mercedes McCambridge
4) Raymond Babbitt
5) Frank Capra
6) *Cool Hand Luke*
7) *Snow White and the Seven Dwarfs*
8) *Blackboard Jungle*
9) *High Noon*
10) *Butch Cassidy and the Sundance Kid*
11) *A Fish Called Wanda*
12) *Rock Around the Clock*
13) 1939
14) *Dances with Wolves*
15) *The Bodyguard*
16) The wire
17) 22
18) Katharine Hepburn
19) Shirley MacLaine
20) Rin Tin Tin

Quiz 2

1) What is the name of the character played by John Wayne in *The Quiet Man*?
2) Who played the ballet teacher in *Billy Elliot*?
3) What is the name of the police character played by Roy Scheider in *Jaws*?
4) For what film did Frank Sinatra win his only acting Oscar?
5) In the James Bond movies, who is the only actress to play Bond's wife?
6) In what film did Alec Guinness play eight parts?
7) What actor had the male lead in Hitchcock's *The Birds*?
8) Who was the actress sister of Olivia de Havilland?
9) What actor died during the filming of *Gladiator*?
10) What actor led *The Dirty Dozen*?
11) In *Star Wars*, what is the name of Princess Leia's home planet?
12) Who won the Best Actor Oscar for *Marty*?
13) Before *Schindler's List* in 1993, what was the last black and white movie to win the Best Picture Oscar?
14) What is the name of Michael Douglas' character in *Wall Street*?
15) For what 1974 film did Art Carney win the Best Actor Oscar?
16) What character has been portrayed by Reginald Owen, Alistair Sim, and Albert Finney?
17) For what film did Burl Ives win the Best Supporting Actor Oscar?
18) Who was the first film star to earn 1 million dollars for a single film?
19) Who made his film debut as Boo Radley in *To Kill a Mockingbird*?
20) What was Marilyn Monroe's last film?

Quiz 2 Answers

1) Sean Thornton
2) Julie Walters
3) Martin Brody
4) *From Here to Eternity*
5) Diana Rigg – *On Her Majesty's Secret Service*
6) *Kind Hearts and Coronets*
7) Rod Taylor
8) Joan Fontaine
9) Oliver Reed
10) Lee Marvin

11) Alderaan
12) Ernest Borgnine
13) *The Apartment* – 1960
14) Gordon Gekko
15) *Harry and Tonto*
16) Ebenezer Scrooge
17) *The Big Country*
18) Elizabeth Taylor - *Cleopatra* in 1963
19) Robert Duvall
20) *The Misfits*

Quiz 3

1) What year was Clint Eastwood's first spaghetti western made?
2) What movie cast included James Garner, Steve McQueen, Charles Bronson, Donald Pleasance, and James Coburn?
3) What musical won the Best Picture Oscar in 1968?
4) What is the name of Audrey Hepburn's character in *Breakfast at Tiffany's*?
5) Who played James Bond in the 1966 film *Casino Royale*?
6) Who was voted the most popular film performer in the United States in 1926?
7) What was Vincent Price's last film?
8) How old was Orson Welles when he co-wrote, produced, directed, and starred in *Citizen Kane*?
9) Who played the two crooks in *Home Alone*?
10) Who did Sergio Leone originally want to play the lead in *A Fistful of Dollars* but couldn't afford his salary?
11) What is the only movie Alfred Hitchcock made twice?
12) Who is Melanie Griffith's mother?
13) What character did Michael J. Fox play in *Back to the Future*?
14) What film followed the career of athletes Eric Henry Liddell and Harold Abrahams?
15) Set in a Los Angeles office building, the 1979 novel *Nothing Lasts Forever* is the basis for what film?
16) In what film does a disturbed romance novel enthusiast gush, "I am your number one fan"?
17) Who was the first choice to play Indiana Jones but missed out due to other commitments?
18) Who is Ben Hur's rival in the great chariot race?

19) What Marlon Brando film was widely banned?
20) What was the last of the five Dirty Harry movies?

Quiz 3 Answers

1) 1964
2) *The Great Escape*
3) *Oliver!*
4) Holly Golightly
5) David Niven
6) Rin Tin Tin
7) *Edward Scissorhands* – 1990
8) 25
9) Daniel Stern and Joe Pesci
10) Henry Fonda – Many actors turned down the role before Clint Eastwood accepted and was paid $15,000 for the role.
11) *The Man Who Knew Too Much* – 1934 and 1956
12) Tippi Hedren – star of Alfred Hitchcock's *The Birds*
13) Marty McFly
14) *Chariots of Fire*
15) *Die Hard*
16) *Misery*
17) Tom Selleck
18) Messala
19) *Last Tango in Paris*
20) *The Dead Pool*

Quiz 4

1) In what movie did Hugh Grant play the role of the British Prime Minister?
2) Who was the first non-British act to perform a James Bond movie theme song?
3) What character sang "When You Wish Upon a Star" in Disney's *Pinocchio*?
4) "The Windmills of Your Mind" is the theme song for what 1968 film?
5) In *Home Alone*, what is the first name of Macaulay Culkin's character?
6) What is the name of Jeff Bridge's character in *The Big Lebowski*?
7) The Olympics depicted in *Chariots of Fire* took place in what year?
8) Who played Freddy Krueger in the *Nightmare on Elm Street* films?

9) Lee Marvin won the Best Actor Oscar for what 1965 film?
10) What actor is stung in *The Sting*?
11) For what movie did Rod Steiger win the Best Actor Oscar?
12) What was the top-grossing U.S. film of the 1960s?
13) What was Spencer Tracey and Katharine Hepburn's first film in 1942?
14) What comedy ended with the line "Hey, can I try on your yellow dress?"
15) What is the name of the dog owned by Nick and Nora Charles in *The Thin Man*?
16) What character did Mel Gibson play in *Braveheart*?
17) Gene Hackman received an Oscar for his portrayal of the sheriff of Big Whiskey in what movie?
18) What book does Forrest Gump keep in his suitcase?
19) What is Joy Adamson's lion cub called in *Born Free*?
20) What is the name of Kurt Russell's character in *Escape from New York*?

Quiz 4 Answers

1) *Love Actually*
2) Nancy Sinatra - *You Only Live Twice*
3) Jiminy Cricket
4) *The Thomas Crown Affair*
5) Kevin
6) The Dude or Jeff Lebowski
7) 1924
8) Robert Englund
9) *Cat Ballou*
10) Robert Shaw
11) *In the Heat of the Night*
12) *The Sound of Music*
13) *Woman of the Year*
14) *Tootsie*
15) Asta
16) William Wallace
17) *Unforgiven*
18) *Curious George*
19) Elsa
20) Snake Plissken

Quiz 5

1) Who played Lois Lane in 1978's *Superman*?
2) What film has the line "I coulda been a contender"?
3) Who played Miss Hannigan in 1982's *Annie*?
4) What is the name of the serial killer in *Halloween*?
5) Who is the youngest actor ever nominated for an Oscar?
6) Who played Anna in 1956's *The King and I*?
7) Who directed *Blade Runner*?
8) Who played Beau Geste in the 1939 film?
9) *Bambi* was the first Disney film without what?
10) What is the only movie character that has won Oscars for two different actors?
11) What 1948 classic film was advertised as "Greed, gold and gunplay on a Mexican mountain of malice"?
12) What is the name of Kevin Costner's character in *Field of Dreams*?
13) Who played the part of Cruella de Vil in 1996's *101 Dalmatians*?
14) What was the sequel to *Going My Way*?
15) Who played Dr. Frankenfurter in *The Rocky Horror Picture Show*?
16) What was Spencer Tracy's last film?
17) What film has the insult "Your mother was a hamster, and your father smelt of elderberries"?
18) In what 1976 film is the lead character asked repeatedly "Is it safe?"
19) Elvis Presley memorized every line from his all-time favorite movie; what was the film?
20) What cartoon duo has won seven Oscars for best animated short film?

Quiz 5 Answers

1) Margot Kidder
2) *On the Waterfront*
3) Carol Burnett
4) Michael Myers
5) Justin Henry – eight years old for *Kramer vs. Kramer*
6) Deborah Kerr
7) Ridley Scott
8) Gary Cooper
9) Human characters
10) Vito Corleone – Marlon Brando and Robert De Niro in *The Godfather* and

The Godfather Part II

11) *The Treasure of the Sierra Madre*
12) Ray Kinsella
13) Glenn Close
14) *The Bells of St. Mary's*
15) Tim Curry
16) *Guess Who's Coming to Dinner*
17) *Monty Python and the Holy Grail*
18) *Marathon Man*
19) *Patton*
20) Tom and Jerry

Quiz 6

1) The character Marion Crane died famously in what film?
2) Marnie Nixon did what for Deborah Kerr, Natalie Wood, and Audrey Hepburn?
3) What is the name of Gene Hackman's character in *The French Connection*?
4) Who played Norman Bates in *Psycho*?
5) What was the first Disney animated film based on the life of a real person?
6) What romantic comedy has the line "I'll have what she's having"?
7) What is the name of the witch in Disney's *Sleeping Beauty*?
8) What film is set in and around 17 Cherry Tree Lane, London in 1910?
9) What was the first Andrew Lloyd Webber musical to be filmed?
10) What is the name of Bill Murray's character in *Ghostbusters*?
11) In what Hitchcock film does Doris Day sing the Oscar-winning song "Que Sera, Sera"?
12) What 1969 western won the best story and best song Oscars?
13) "Somewhere My Love" is the theme song of what movie?
14) What character is the heroine of *The Silence of the Lambs*?
15) What actor is in both *The Magnificent Seven* and *The Dirty Dozen*?
16) Who was the first actor to receive a posthumous Oscar nomination?
17) What movie has the line "You're gonna need a bigger boat"?
18) What 1954 film won eight Oscars?
19) What are James Dean's three films?
20) Who were the first father and son to win Oscars for the same film?

Quiz 6 Answers

1) *Psycho* – shower scene
2) Dubbed their singing voices
3) Popeye Doyle
4) Anthony Perkins
5) *Pocahontas*
6) *When Harry Met Sally*
7) Maleficent
8) *Mary Poppins*
9) *Jesus Christ Superstar*
10) Peter Venkman
11) *The Man Who Knew Too Much*
12) *Butch Cassidy and the Sundance Kid*
13) *Doctor Zhivago*
14) Clarice Starling
15) Charles Bronson
16) James Dean – *East of Eden* in 1956
17) *Jaws*
18) *On the Waterfront*
19) *Rebel Without a Cause*, *East of Eden*, *Giant*
20) Walter and John Huston – *The Treasure of the Sierra Madre*

Quiz 7

1) What actor said, "Love means never having to say you're sorry"?
2) What actor rode the bomb down in *Dr. Strangelove*?
3) Who played Commodious in *Gladiator*?
4) In what movie did Bruce Willis play Korben Dallas?
5) Linda Hunt won an Oscar for *The Year of Living Dangerously*; it was the first Oscar for what?
6) What does the C stand for in George C. Scott?
7) What was the world's first X-rated cartoon?
8) The Oscar-winning 1968 movie *Charly* is based on what novel?
9) What newspaper owner's career inspired *Citizen Kane*?
10) What film produced the first female Best Director Oscar?
11) Who played the role of Mrs. Robinson in *The Graduate*?
12) Who is the oldest Best Actress Oscar winner?
13) Who is the oldest Best Actor Oscar winner?

14) "Well, nobody's perfect!" is the last line of what comedy?
15) What is the name of Dustin Hoffman's character in *The Graduate*?
16) What 1957 film took place in 1943 Burma?
17) In what film did Paul Newman's character eat 50 hard-boiled eggs?
18) For what film did James Cagney win his only Oscar?
19) What was Charles Foster Kane's dying word?
20) For what 1955 film did Jack Lemon win his first Oscar?

Quiz 7 Answers

1) Ryan O'Neil
2) Slim Pickens
3) Joaquin Phoenix
4) *The Fifth Element*
5) Playing the opposite sex
6) Campbell
7) *Fritz the Cat* – 1972
8) *Flowers for Algernon*
9) William Randolph Hearst
10) *The Hurt Locker* – Kathryn Bigelow
11) Anne Bancroft
12) Jessica Tandy – age 80 for *Driving Miss Daisy*
13) Anthony Hopkins – 83 for *The Father* (2020)
14) *Some Like It Hot*
15) Benjamin Braddock
16) *The Bridge on the River Kwai*
17) *Cool Hand Luke*
18) *Yankee Doodle Dandy*
19) Rosebud
20) *Mister Roberts*

Quiz 8

1) Who won the Best Actor Oscar for *Amadeus*?
2) Who played the sleuthing couple in the *Thin Man* series of films?
3) In what film did Orson Welles play the character Harry Lime?
4) What three counties is Eliza Doolittle taught to pronounce in *My Fair Lady*?
5) What is the name of Humphrey Bogart's character in *The African Queen*?

6) What actor starred in both Alfred Hitchcock's *Rope* and *Strangers on a Train*?
7) Packy East, an amateur boxer, became famous as a comedian under what name?
8) What film featured Rosie O'Donnell, Rita Wilson, and Meg Ryan?
9) What is the name of Sigourney Weaver's character in *Alien*?
10) What mythical Scottish town appears for one day every hundred years?
11) *The Wizard of Oz* lost the Best Picture Oscar to what movie?
12) What are the only two Best Picture Oscar-winning films that were based on best musical Tony Award winners?
13) What 1979 film has a spaceship named Nostromo?
14) What movie sold the most tickets of all time in the United States?
15) What movie starred Lee Marvin as twins Kid Shelleen and Tim Strawn?
16) In *Back to the Future*, how fast does the DeLorean have to go to time travel?
17) What was the first comedy to win the Best Picture Oscar?
18) Who was the first actor to direct himself to the Best Actor Oscar?
19) Robin Williams won the Best Supporting Actor Oscar for what film?
20) What famous actor made his film debut in *A Nightmare on Elm Street*?

Quiz 8 Answers

1) F. Murray Abraham
2) William Powell and Myrna Loy
3) *The Third Man*
4) Hertford, Hereford, Hampshire
5) Charlie Allnut
6) Farley Granger
7) Bob Hope
8) *Sleepless in Seattle*
9) Ellen Ripley
10) Brigadoon
11) *Gone with the Wind*
12) *My Fair Lady* and *The Sound of Music*
13) *Alien*
14) *Gone with the Wind* – About 208 million tickets have been sold; the U.S. population in 1939 when it was released was 131 million.
15) *Cat Ballou*
16) 88 mph

17) *It Happened One Night* – 1934
18) Laurence Olivier – *Hamlet* in 1948
19) *Good Will Hunting*
20) Johnny Depp

Quiz 9

1) What three sports-related movies have won the Best Picture Oscar?
2) What is Dorothy's last name in *The Wizard of Oz*?
3) Adjusted for inflation, what is the highest-grossing U.S. movie of all time?
4) What is the lowest-grossing film to ever win the Best Picture Oscar?
5) What was the first animated film nominated for the Best Picture Oscar?
6) What was the first movie from a non-English speaking country to win the Best Picture Oscar?
7) What Best Picture Oscar nominee used the "F" word the most times?
8) What was Elvis Presley's last movie?
9) What was the first foreign film to win the Best Picture Oscar?
10) What is the highest-grossing romantic comedy film of all time?
11) What famous actor competed in the 1953 Mr. Universe bodybuilding competition?
12) What is the first R-rated movie to win the Best Picture Oscar?
13) What is the first horror film nominated for the Best Picture Oscar?
14) Who is the only person to write back to back Best Picture Oscar winners?
15) What male actor has the most Oscar nominations?
16) What is the only X-rated movie to win the Best Picture Oscar?
17) What was the first movie to make $100 million at the box office?
18) Who is the youngest Oscar winner ever?
19) Who played James Bond in *On Her Majesty's Secret Service* in 1969?
20) What was the first western to win the Best Picture Oscar?

Quiz 9 Answers

1) *Rocky*, *Chariots of Fire*, *Million Dollar Baby*
2) Gale
3) *Gone with the Wind* – followed by *Star Wars* and *The Sound of Music*
4) *The Hurt Locker* – 2008
5) *Beauty and the Beast* – 1991
6) *The Artist* – France in 2011

7) *The Wolf of Wall Street* – more than 500 times
8) *Change of Habit* – 1969 with Mary Tyler Moore
9) *Hamlet* – 1948
10) *My Big Fat Greek Wedding*
11) Sean Connery
12) *The French Connection*
13) *The Exorcist* – 1973
14) Paul Haggis – *Million Dollar Baby* and *Crash*
15) Jack Nicholson
16) *Midnight Cowboy* – It was X-rated at the time of the award; in 1971, its rating was changed to R.
17) *Jaws*
18) Tatum O'Neal – 10 years old for *Paper Moon*
19) George Lazenby
20) *Cimarron* – 1931

Quiz 10

1) What country has won the foreign language Oscar the most times?
2) What was Alfred Hitchcock's only Best Picture Oscar winner?
3) What are the only two Pulitzer Prize-winning novels to be made into Best Picture Oscar winners?
4) What is the first and only G-rated movie to win the Best Picture Oscar?
5) What was the first film to win the Oscar for best animated feature?
6) What was the first sports film to win the Best Picture Oscar?
7) What is the longest movie to ever win the Best Picture Oscar?
8) Who is the only author to have his works simultaneously number one in television, film, and books?
9) What actor has the most Oscar nominations without a win?
10) What was John Wayne's last movie?
11) Bruce Willis played a time traveler in what 1995 movie?
12) What is the only film based on a television show to win the Best Picture Oscar?
13) Who are the two actors who get stuck traveling together in *Planes, Trains and Automobiles*?
14) What are the only three films to win all five major Academy Awards (best picture, director, actor, actress, screenplay)?
15) What is the only fantasy film to win the Best Picture Oscar?
16) What was the first U.S. film with a female director to gross over $100

million?
17) What is the name of the giant bird in *Up*?
18) What is the name of the skunk in Disney's *Bambi*?
19) What was the first feature film broadcast on U.S. television?
20) What was the first full-color film to win the Best Picture Oscar?

Quiz 10 Answers

1) Italy
2) *Rebecca* – 1940
3) *Gone with the Wind* and *All the King's Men*
4) *Oliver!*
5) *Shrek*
6) *Rocky* – 1976
7) *Gone with the Wind* - 238 minutes
8) Michael Crichton – *ER* (television), *Jurassic Park* (film), *Disclosure* (book)
9) Peter O'Toole – eight
10) *The Shootist*
11) *12 Monkeys*
12) *Marty* – 1955
13) Steve Martin and John Candy
14) *It Happened One Night* (1934), *One Flew Over the Cuckoo's Nest* (1975), *The Silence of the Lambs* (1991)
15) *The Lord of the Rings: The Return of the King* – 2003
16) *Big* – directed by Penny Marshall in 1988
17) Kevin
18) Flower
19) *The Wizard of Oz* – broadcast in 1956
20) *Gone with the Wind*

Quiz 11

1) What are the only two sequels to win Best Picture Oscars?
2) Who is the only Oscar winner whose parents were both Oscar winners?
3) Who are the only brothers to receive acting Oscar nominations?
4) What two western movies won Best Picture Oscars in the 1990s?
5) Who are the only brother and sister to win acting Oscars?
6) What two families have three generations of Oscar winners?
7) Who is the only person named Oscar to win an Oscar?

8) Who is the only actor to appear in multiple films and have every one nominated for the Best Picture Oscar?
9) What was the screen name of Lee Yuen Kam?
10) For what 1971 film did Jane Fonda win her first Oscar?
11) What was the screen name of Edda Van Heemstra?
12) Who is the only person with four acting Oscars?
13) Who dubbed Miss Piggy's singing voice in *The Muppet Movie*?
14) What was Disney's first live-action feature movie?
15) For what film did Steven Spielberg win his first Oscar?
16) What movie has the line "I love the smell of napalm in the morning"?
17) "I'm mad as hell, and I'm not going to take this anymore!" is a line from what movie?
18) Sterling Holloway was the original voice of what Disney character?
19) What is the name of the character Sidney Poitier played in *Lilies of the Field*?
20) What three films are tied for the most Oscars at 11 each?

Quiz 11 Answers

1) *The Godfather Part II* and *The Lord of the Rings: The Return of the King*
2) Liza Minnelli
3) River and Joaquin Phoenix
4) *Dances with Wolves* and *Unforgiven*
5) Lionel and Ethel Barrymore
6) Huston (Walter, John, and Anjelica) and Coppola (Carmine, Francis Ford, and Sofia)
7) Oscar Hammerstein II
8) John Cazale – He appeared in *The Godfather*, *The Conversation*, *The Godfather Part II*, *Dog Day Afternoon*, and *The Deer Hunter*.
9) Bruce Lee
10) *Klute*
11) Audrey Hepburn
12) Katharine Hepburn
13) Johnny Mathis
14) *Treasure Island*
15) *Schindler's List*
16) *Apocalypse Now*
17) *Network*
18) Winnie the Pooh

19) Homer Smith
20) *Ben-Hur*, *Titanic*, *The Lord of the Rings: The Return of the King*

Quiz 12

1) What woman has won the most Oscars?
2) Who are the only two actresses who have won consecutive Best Actress Oscars?
3) Who are the only two actors who have won consecutive Best Actor Oscars?
4) For what movie did the first woman win the Best Picture Oscar?
5) What actor has appeared in the most Best Picture Oscar-winning movies?
6) What 1985 western starred Kevin Kline, Danny Glover, Kevin Costner, John Cleese, Jeff Goldblum, and Linda Hunt?
7) What is the first name of Dustin Hoffman's female character in *Tootsie*?
8) What is the day job of Jennifer Beale's character in *Flashdance*?
9) In what film did Sean Connery play James Bond after a 12-year absence?
10) Who spoke the only word in Mel Brooks' *Silent Movie*?
11) Who played Elliot Ness in *The Untouchables*?
12) Who played Louise in *Thelma and Louise*?
13) What is the name of Kevin Spacey's character in *The Usual Suspects*?
14) Who played Dr. Strangelove?
15) What is the name of Jack Nicholson's character in *Chinatown*?
16) Who played Mozart in *Amadeus*?
17) What 1953 western starred Alan Ladd, Jean Arthur, and Van Heflin?
18) What was the first feature film with Tom Hanks and Meg Ryan?
19) Who said during their one and only Oscar acceptance speech, "I think they gave it to me because I'm the oldest"?
20) Who directed *The Bridge on the River Kwai*?

Quiz 12 Answers

1) Edith Head – eight for costume design
2) Luise Rainer – *The Great Ziegfeld* (1936) and *The Good Earth* (1937) and Katharine Hepburn – *Guess Who's Coming to Dinner* (1967) and *The Lion in Winter* (1968)
3) Spencer Tracy – *Captains Courageous* (1937) and *Boys Town* (1938) and Tom Hanks – *Philadelphia* (1993) and *Forrest Gump* (1994)

4) *The Sting* – 1973
5) Franklyn Farnum – He was a character actor in 433 films including seven best picture winners: *The Life of Emile Zola* (1937), *Going My Way* (1944), *The Lost Weekend* (1945), *Gentleman's Agreement* (1947), *All About Eve* (1950), *The Greatest Show on Earth* (1952), and *Around the World in 80 Says* (1956).
6) *Silverado*
7) Dorothy
8) Welder
9) *Never Say Never Again*
10) Marcel Marceau – French mime
11) Kevin Costner
12) Susan Sarandon
13) Keyser Soze or Roger "Verbal" Kint
14) Peter Sellers
15) Jake Gittes
16) Tom Hulce
17) *Shane*
18) *Joe Versus the Volcano*
19) Jessica Tandy – age 80 at the time
20) David Lean

Quiz 13

1) What is the real name of the superhero Iron Man?
2) What was the last animated film personally supervised by Walt Disney?
3) What is Carrie's last name in *Carrie*?
4) For what film did Audrey Hepburn win her only Oscar?
5) Who played Rooster Cogburn in the 2010 *True Grit remake*?
6) What is the highest-grossing hand-drawn animated film in history?
7) What character did Louise Fletcher play in *One Flew over the Cuckoo's Nest*?
8) What 1990 movie was the first western to win the Best Picture Oscar in 59 years?
9) Who was the first actress to win an Oscar for a performance entirely in a foreign language?
10) Who played the title roles in 1977's *Fun with Dick and Jane*?
11) What is the title of the sequel to *Romancing the Stone*?
12) *The Magnificent Seven* is based on what 1954 film?

13) Heath Ledger and Jake Gyllenhaal play sheepherders in what film?
14) In what 1968 film did Benny Hill play a toymaker?
15) What song in 1981's *Arthur* won an Oscar?
16) Who is the arch-enemy of Austin Powers?
17) In *The Hunger Games*, what is the name of the futuristic nation?
18) What are the first names of the film making Coen brothers?
19) In the James Bond films, what does the acronym SPECTRE stand for?
20) What science fiction movie was originally made in 1956 and remade in 1978 and 1993?

Quiz 13 Answers

1) Anthony Stark
2) *The Jungle Book* – 1967
3) White
4) *Roman Holiday*
5) Jeff Bridges
6) *The Lion King*
7) Nurse Ratched
8) *Dances with Wolves*
9) Sophia Loren - 1962
10) George Segal and Jane Fonda
11) *The Jewel of the Nile*
12) *Seven Samurai*
13) *Brokeback Mountain*
14) *Chitty Chitty Bang Bang*
15) "Best That You Can Do"
16) Dr. Evil
17) Panem
18) Joel and Ethan
19) Special Executive for Counterintelligence Terror Revenge and Extortion
20) *Invasion of the Body Snatchers*

Quiz 14

1) Meryl Streep and Dustin Hoffman played husband and wife in what movie?
2) In the *Lethal Weapon* movies, what is Mel Gibson's character name?
3) What three actors played *The Good, The Bad, and The Ugly*?

4) What is the name of John Travolta's character in *Grease*?
5) Who is the only person with a star in each of the five categories (movies, television, music, radio, and live performance) on the Hollywood Walk of Fame?
6) In what Alfred Hitchcock film did Julie Andrews star with Paul Newman?
7) What is Bill Murray's character name in *Caddyshack*?
8) In Disney's *Snow White and the Seven Dwarfs*, what do the dwarfs mine?
9) What film is based on the Stephen King novella *The Body*?
10) Timothy Q. Mouse, Mr. Stork, and Jim Crow are characters in what Disney film?
11) Who is the youngest Best Actress Oscar winner?
12) Who is the youngest Best Actor Oscar winner?
13) Who has the most acting Oscar nominations?
14) What actor or actress has the longest time between their first and last Oscars?
15) What two actresses tied for the 1968 Best Actress Oscar?
16) Who is the only person to win the Best Actor Oscar three times?
17) Who played Danny Ocean in 1960's *Ocean's 11*?
18) In *Ben-Hur*, what is the title character's first name?
19) Contractually, who had to be first offered the role of John McClane in *Die Hard*?
20) What is Richard Gere's middle name?

Quiz 14 Answers

1) *Kramer vs Kramer*
2) Martin Riggs
3) Clint Eastwood, Lee Van Cleef, Eli Wallach
4) Danny Zuko
5) Gene Autry
6) *Torn Curtain*
7) Carl Spackler
8) Diamonds
9) *Stand by Me*
10) *Dumbo*
11) Marlee Matlin – age 21 for *Children of a Lesser God*
12) Adrien Brody – age 29 for *The Pianist*
13) Meryl Streep

14) Katharine Hepburn – 48 years from 1933 to 1981
15) Barbra Streisand (*Funny Girl*) and Katharine Hepburn (*The Lion in Winter*)
16) Daniel Day-Lewis – *My Left Foot*, *There Will Be Blood*, *Lincoln*
17) Frank Sinatra
18) Judah
19) Frank Sinatra – He was 73 at the time. The movie is based on the book *Nothing Lasts Forever* that was a sequel to *The Detective*, which had been made into a 1968 movie starring Sinatra; contractually, he had to be offered the role first.
20) Tiffany

Quiz 15

1) In the original script for *Back to the Future*, the time machine wasn't a DeLorean; what was it?
2) The U.S. film industry relocated from New York to Los Angeles in large part because of what man?
3) During the filming of *The Blues Brothers*, they had a special budget for what during night shoots?
4) The "no animals were harmed" statement on movies only applies when?
5) After dropping out 34 years earlier, Steven Spielberg got his Bachelor of Arts degree from Cal State Long Beach; what did he submit for credit for his final project in advanced film making?
6) What movie has the highest number of on-screen deaths of all time?
7) What actor has died the most times on screen?
8) Who was the inspiration for the character of Biff Tannen, the bully in *Back to the Future*?
9) The Tom Hanks movie *The Terminal* was inspired by a man who lived at the departure lounge of what international airport for 18 years?
10) The first Cannes Film Festival was called off after screening only one film; why?
11) In Disney's *Snow White and the Seven Dwarfs*, how old is Snow White?
12) Who is the first person to have the number-one movie and record album in the same week?
13) Michael Jackson wanted to buy Marvel Comics; what was his primary motive?
14) "Badges? We ain't got no badges! We don't need no badges! I don't have to show you any stinking badges!" is from what film?
15) Why wasn't the original *Tron* movie in 1982 considered for a visual

effects Oscar?

16) What year did the first screen kiss between two men occur?
17) Sylvester Stallone was so poor at one point that he sold something he loved for $50 only to buy it back for $3,000 one week later when he sold the script for Rocky; what was it?
18) What was the first Disney animated feature film set in America?
19) What individual has won the most Oscar awards?
20) What was the first film Clint Eastwood directed?

Quiz 15 Answers

1) Refrigerator
2) Thomas Edison – He held many of the patents on the production and showing of movies and controlled the industry; filmmakers escaped to Los Angeles to get away from his control.
3) Cocaine
4) While the film is recording
5) *Schindler's List*
6) *The Lord of the Rings: The Return of the King* – 836 deaths
7) John Hurt – 43 times including *Alien*, *Spaceballs*, *V for Vendetta*, *Hellboy*
8) Donald Trump
9) Charles de Gaulle Airport
10) WWII broke out.
11) 14
12) Jennifer Lopez – 2001
13) He wanted to play Spider Man in his own movie.
14) *The Treasure of the Sierra Madre*
15) The Academy felt the filmmakers had cheated by using computers.
16) 1927 – *Wings*
17) His dog
18) *Dumbo*
19) Walt Disney – 22 competitive and 4 honorary awards
20) *Play Misty for Me*

Quiz 16

1) Who did Michael Caine play in *The Ipcress File*?
2) Who played the scarecrow in *The Wizard of Oz*?
3) What was the first James Bond film?
4) In movie making, what job does the gaffer do?

5) What actor has been portrayed most on the screen by other actors?
6) Who directed *Dr. Strangelove* and *2001: A Space Odyssey*?
7) In what Alfred Hitchcock film does he make his usual appearance in a newspaper weight loss ad?
8) What country made the world's first feature film in 1906?
9) What is Norman Bates' hobby in *Psycho*?
10) What real person has been played most often in films?
11) Humphrey Bogart starred in the first film John Huston directed; what was it?
12) What film star was the first to appear on a postage stamp?
13) Who did Babe the pig work for?
14) Shirley Bassey sang the theme song for which three Bond films?
15) Anthony Daniels played what character in a series of films?
16) Who was the first actor to appear on the cover of *Time* magazine?
17) Who played the title role in *Lawrence of Arabia*?
18) What 1942 Humphrey Bogart film won the Best Picture Oscar?
19) What country makes the most films per year?
20) Who built the world's first film studio?

Quiz 16 Answers

1) Harry Palmer
2) Ray Bolger
3) *Dr. No*
4) Chief electrician
5) Charlie Chaplin
6) Stanley Kubrick
7) *Lifeboat* – Due to the setting in a lifeboat, he couldn't make his usual cameo appearance.
8) Australia
9) Stuffing birds
10) Napoleon Bonaparte
11) *The Maltese Falcon*
12) Grace Kelly
13) Farmer Hoggett
14) *Goldfinger*, *Diamonds Are Forever*, *Moonraker*
15) C-3PO - *Star Wars*
16) Charlie Chaplin
17) Peter O'Toole

18) *Casablanca*
19) India
20) Thomas Edison

Quiz 17

1) What actor played Wyatt Earp, Frank James, and Abraham Lincoln?
2) In 1944's *National Velvet*, what is the name of Velvet Brown's horse?
3) Who played the Cooler King in *The Great Escape*?
4) What two films did Paul Newman play Fast Eddie Felson in?
5) What is the theme song for *The Grapes of Wrath*?
6) How many Oscars did *Gone with the Wind* win?
7) Who played Tarzan in more movies than anyone else?
8) What actors were chained together in 1958's *The Defiant Ones*?
9) What two child actors co-starred in the first Lassie movie?
10) Who did Gregory Peck portray in *The Boys from Brazil*?
11) What is the name of Jimmy Stewart's character in *It's a Wonderful Life*?
12) For what film did Sidney Poitier win the Best Actor Oscar?
13) Who played Christ in *The Greatest Story Ever Told*?
14) What is the name of the island that is King Kong's home?
15) Who played the cowardly lion in *The Wizard of Oz*?
16) What 1941 portrayal won Gary Cooper the Best Actor Oscar?
17) What is the name of Marlon Brando's character in *A Streetcar Named Desire*?
18) What movie has the tiny country of Grand Fenwick declaring war on the United States?
19) What is the name of the Tennessee sheriff played by Joe Don Baker in *Walking Tall*?
20) What is the theme song for *Midnight Cowboy*?

Quiz 17 Answers

1) Henry Fonda
2) The Pie
3) Steve McQueen
4) *The Hustler* and *The Color of Money*
5) "The Red River Valley"
6) Nine
7) Johnny Weissmuller
8) Tony Curtis and Sidney Poitier

9) Roddy McDowall and Elizabeth Taylor
10) Dr. Josef Mengele
11) George Bailey
12) *Lilies of the Field*
13) Max Von Sydow
14) Skull Island
15) Bert Lahr
16) Sergeant Alvin York
17) Stanley Kowalski
18) *The Mouse That Roared*
19) Buford Pusser
20) "Everybody's Talkin'"

Quiz 18

1) What is Dirty Harry's last name?
2) What pool shark did Jackie Gleason play in *The Hustler*?
3) Who played the demolitions expert in *The Guns of Navarone*?
4) Who is Goldfinger's bodyguard?
5) For what film did Louise Fletcher win the Best Actress Oscar?
6) What film made Hattie McDaniel the first African American Oscar winner?
7) What was Judy Garland's real name?
8) Who were the five Marx brothers?
9) What film dramatized the Scopes Monkey Trial?
10) What judge did Walter Brennan, Edgar Buchanan, and Paul Newman all portray?
11) Which of the seven dwarfs comes first alphabetically?
12) What city is the setting for *Chinatown*?
13) Who were the two stars in the original *Sleuth*?
14) What was the first talking motion picture with the sound in the film?
15) Who played Helen Keller in *The Miracle Worker*?
16) Spencer Tracy played the father in *Father of the Bride*; who played the bride?
17) Who won the Best Actor Oscar for *Network*?
18) For what 1960 role did Burt Lancaster win the Best Actor Oscar?
19) What is the name of Sean Penn's character in *Fast Times at Ridgemont High*?
20) What actor provided the voice for Francis the talking mule?

Quiz 18 Answers

1) Callahan
2) Minnesota Fats
3) David Niven
4) Oddjob
5) *One Flew Over the Cuckoo's Nest*
6) *Gone with the Wind*
7) Frances Gumm
8) Groucho, Chico, Harpo, Zeppo, Gummo
9) *Inherit the Wind*
10) Roy Bean
11) Bashful
12) Los Angeles
13) Laurence Olivier and Michael Caine
14) *The Jazz Singer* - 1927
15) Patty Duke
16) Elizabeth Taylor
17) Peter Finch
18) Elmer Gantry
19) Jeff Spicoli
20) Chill Wills

Quiz 19

1) What actor is often credited with saving Warner Brothers Studio from bankruptcy and received the most votes for the Best Actor Oscar at the first Academy Awards in 1929 before being eliminated from the ballot?
2) What 1963 comedy had more than 50 stars in it?
3) Who is the only person to win Oscars for best actress and best song?
4) What did Cool Hand Luke go to jail for?
5) Who played sidekick to Hopalong Cassidy, Gene Autry, Roy Rogers, and John Wayne?
6) Who received the only Oscar made of wood?
7) What is the name of Katharine Hepburn's character in *The African Queen*?
8) What boxer's life is depicted in *Raging Bull*?
9) What film won Rod Steiger the Best Actor Oscar?
10) What movie ends with the line "After all, tomorrow is another day"?

11) Who are the only two people to win both a Nobel Prize and an Oscar?
12) Who appeared in more than 30 Alfred Hitchcock films?
13) Who has won the most Best Director Oscars?
14) What song does Rick ask Sam to play in *Casablanca*?
15) What is the name of Dustin Hoffman's character in *Midnight Cowboy*?
16) Who is the first character to speak in *Star Wars*?
17) Who wrote and directed *American Graffiti*?
18) Who played the tunnel king in *The Great Escape*?
19) In what country is John Wayne's *The Quiet Man* set?
20) What was the second movie to pair Richard Gere and Julia Roberts?

Quiz 19 Answers

1) Rin Tin Tin – The Academy wanted to appear more serious and have a human win, so they removed him from the ballot and voted again.
2) *It's a Mad, Mad, Mad, Mad World*
3) Barbra Streisand
4) Cutting the heads off parking meters
5) Gabby Hayes
6) Edgar Bergen and Charlie McCarthy
7) Rose Sayer
8) Jake LaMotta
9) *In the Heat of the Night*
10) *Gone with the Wind*
11) George Bernard Shaw and Bob Dylan
12) Alfred Hitchcock
13) John Ford - four
14) "As Time Goes By"
15) Ratso Rizzo
16) C-3PO
17) George Lucas
18) Charles Bronson
19) Ireland
20) *Runaway Bride*

Quiz 20

1) In *Jaws*, Quint describes the sinking of a ship during WWII and how the sharks attacked the survivors. His story is based on a real event; what is the name of the ship that sank?

2) What was the number-one U.S. box office film released in the 2000s?
3) What is the name of the computer in *2001: A Space Odyssey*?
4) What was the number-one U.S. box office film released in the 1940s?
5) *The Rose* stars Bette Midler; the film is loosely based on the life of what singer?
6) Who plays the role of Pharaoh Rameses II in *The Ten Commandments*?
7) Who provides the voice for sultry Jessica Rabbit in *Who Framed Roger Rabbit*?
8) In *Mr. Deeds Goes to Town*, what is the title character's first name?
9) What is the name of the town that is the setting for *It's a Wonderful Life*?
10) What is the name of John Travolta's character in *Saturday Night Fever*?
11) What Quentin Tarantino movie is about two mob hitmen, a boxer, a gangster's wife, and a pair of diner bandits?
12) In *Coneheads*, what planet are the Coneheads from?
13) Who does James Cagney portray in *Yankee Doodle Dandy*?
14) In what science fiction movie does Kevin Spacey say, "Every being in the universe knows right from wrong, Mark"?
15) In *Fight Club*, who plays the nameless first-person narrator?
16) Who plays the title role in *The Princess Bride*?
17) What comedy that spawned two sequels is set in 1954 and has a group of Florida high school students trying to lose their virginity?
18) What two actresses play the two women whose lives are dedicated to ballet in *The Turning Point*?
19) What was the number-one U.S. box office film released in the 1960s?
20) What movie has the tagline "The greatest trick the devil ever pulled was to convince the world he didn't exist"?

Quiz 20 Answers

1) *USS Indianapolis* – After four days in the water, only 317 of the original 1,196-man crew were rescued. Estimates of how many died due to shark attacks range from a few dozen to 150; it is the U.S. Navy's single worst loss at sea and the worst shark attack in recorded history.
2) *Avatar* – 2009
3) HAL 9000 – HAL stands for heuristically programmed algorithmic computer.
4) *Bambi* – 1942
5) Janis Joplin
6) Yul Brynner
7) Kathleen Turner

8) Longfellow
9) Bedford Falls
10) Tony Manero
11) *Pulp Fiction* - 1994
12) Remulak
13) George M. Cohan
14) *K-PAX* - 2001
15) Edward Norton
16) Robin Wright
17) *Porky's* - 1981
18) Anne Bancroft and Shirley MacLaine
19) *The Sound of Music* – 1965
20) *The Usual Suspects* - 1995

Quiz 21

1) What science fiction film was loosely based on Shakespeare's *The Tempest* and was the film debut of Leslie Nielsen?
2) In *Ratatouille*, what is the name of the rat who can cook voiced by Patton Oswalt?
3) What actors play the two opposing lawyers in *Inherit the Wind*?
4) Who plays the dual roles of Madeleine Elster and Judy Barton in *Vertigo*?
5) Who plays the title role in *My Man Godfrey*?
6) What was the number-one U.S. box office film released in the 1930s?
7) Who won a Best Original Screenplay Oscar for *Good Will Hunting*?
8) In *300*, the Spartans fight the Persians in 480 BC at what battle?
9) What is the full name of Humphrey Bogart's character in *Casablanca*?
10) What is the only film where cartoon characters from Walt Disney and Warner Brothers appear together?
11) Gregory Peck stars as Jimmy Ringo, a notorious gunman, in what movie?
12) What movie has Lana Turner convincing a drifter to help her murder her husband?
13) Who was the first actor to win the Best Actor Oscar for a musical performance?
14) What is the name of the character Katharine Ross plays in *Butch Cassidy and the Sundance Kid*?
15) Who directed *Ferris Bueller's Day Off*, *Uncle Buck*, *Weird Science*, and *Planes, Trains and Automobiles*?

16) Special Forces operative turned mercenary Wade Wilson is subjected to a rogue experiment that leaves him with new powers; what is the movie?
17) What crime drama stars Michael Douglas, Catherine Zeta-Jones, and Benicio Del Toro in a Best Supporting Actor Oscar-winning performance?
18) What musical film has won the most Oscars?
19) What Best Picture Oscar winner depicts the childhood, adolescence, and young adulthood of an African American gay man growing up in a rough Miami neighborhood?
20) For what film was the first posthumous Oscar of any kind awarded?

Quiz 21 Answers

1) *Forbidden Planet* - 1956
2) Remy
3) Spencer Tracy and Fredric March
4) Kim Novak
5) William Powell
6) *Gone with the Wind* – Inflation adjusted, it is the all-time U.S. box office record holder.
7) Matt Damon and Ben Affleck
8) Thermopylae
9) Rick Blaine
10) *Who Framed Roger Rabbit* – 1988
11) *The Gunfighter* - 1950
12) *The Postman Always Rings Twice* - 1946
13) James Cagney – *Yankee Doodle Dandy* in 1942
14) Etta Place
15) John Hughes
16) *Deadpool* - 2016
17) *Traffic* - 2000
18) *Gigi* (1958) – nine Oscars
19) *Moonlight* - 2016
20) *Gone with the Wind* – screenwriter Sidney Howard

Quiz 22

1) With nine wins, what film holds the British Academy Awards (BAFTAs) record?

2) Who directed *A Room with a View*, *Howards End*, and *The Remains of the Day*?
3) Who plays Julius Caesar in *Cleopatra*?
4) In *The Terminator*, what is the name of the system that became self-aware and tried to wipe out all humans?
5) What is the name of the summer camp in *Meatballs*?
6) In *Yours, Mine and Ours*, who plays the widower with 10 children and the widow with 8 children who marry?
7) In *Planes, Trains, and Automobiles*, John Candy's character Del Griffith sells what for a living?
8) Who is the only person nominated for Oscars for acting, writing, producing, and directing the same film?
9) Who has the longest screen time performance to ever win the Best Actress Oscar?
10) In *Love Actually*, who plays the aging rocker Billy Mack?
11) Adjusted for inflation, what is the highest-grossing western of all time in the United States?
12) Based on actual events from Virginia in 1971, what movie follows a newly appointed high school football coach and his team in their first season as a racially integrated unit?
13) What character did Basil Rathbone play in *The Adventures of Robin Hood*?
14) Who wrote the novel on which *Breakfast at Tiffany's* is based?
15) Who plays the title role in *Gunga Din*?
16) What was the first movie based on a John Grisham novel?
17) What is the former profession of John Wayne's character in *The Quiet Man*?
18) *This Is the End* has celebrities playing themselves stuck in a house as the biblical apocalypse occurs; what celebrity's house are they stuck in?
19) What film has con man Moses Pray taking on nine-year-old Addie Loggins as his partner?
20) What is the first film by a black director to win the Best Picture Oscar?

Quiz 22 Answers

1) *Butch Cassidy and the Sundance Kid* - 1969
2) James Ivory
3) Rex Harrison
4) Skynet
5) Camp North Star
6) Henry Fonda and Lucille Ball

7) Shower curtain rings
8) Warren Beatty – twice for *Heaven Can Wait* (1978) and *Reds* (1981)
9) Vivien Leigh – 2 hours 23 minutes and 32 seconds for *Gone with the Wind* (1939)
10) Bill Nighy
11) *Butch Cassidy and the Sundance Kid* – 1969
12) *Remember the Titans* - 2000
13) Sir Guy of Gisbourne
14) Truman Capote
15) Sam Jaffe
16) *The Firm* - 1993
17) Boxer
18) James Franco
19) *Paper Moon* - 1973
20) *12 Years a Slave* - 2013

Quiz 23

1) In *The Courtship of Eddie's Father*, who plays the young son Eddie who wants to see his father remarry?
2) In *Dances with Wolves*, who plays Stands With A Fist, a white woman who was raised by the Sioux?
3) What film has a mobster named Chili Palmer who goes to Hollywood and gets involved in the movie business?
4) In *Tremors*, what actor and actress play the survivalist couple who help battle the giant wormlike creatures?
5) What film had a 20-year gap between its release and winning an Oscar?
6) Nicolas Cage and Holly Hunter play a childless couple who steal a baby in *Raising Arizona*; who directed the film?
7) Barbra Streisand plays what real-life performer in *Funny Girl*?
8) What cartoon duo won seven Oscars for the best animated short film?
9) In *City Slickers*, three middle-aged friends go on an adventure holiday driving cattle; who won a Best Supporting Actor Oscar for their role as the trail boss Curly?
10) What film stars Paul Newman as a white man raised by Apaches who tries to save the passengers of a stagecoach from bandits?
11) What are the names of the two rival department stores in *Miracle on 34th Street*?
12) What movie beat *Citizen Kane* for the Best Picture Oscar?
13) What was the most expensive Hollywood film made during the 1930s?

14) In *Underworld*, who plays Viktor, the oldest and strongest of the elder vampires?
15) What is the name Tom Hanks gives to the volleyball he talks to in *Cast Away*?
16) Who wrote and directed *The Sixth Sense*?
17) Who plays Buttons the Clown in *The Greatest Show on Earth*?
18) After *Sleeping Beauty* in 1959, what was the next fairy tale produced by Disney?
19) In *Up*, what is the South American destination that Carl wants to travel to in his house lifted by balloons?
20) What actors play the unlikely prospecting partners who also share a wife in the singing western *Paint Your Wagon*?

Quiz 23 Answers

1) Ron Howard
2) Mary McDonnell
3) *Get Shorty* – 1995
4) Michael Gross and Reba McEntire
5) *Limelight* – It was officially released in 1952 but was not released in Los Angeles County and eligible for an Oscar until 1972. It won a Best Original Score Oscar in 1973 and is Charlie Chaplin's only competitive Oscar win.
6) Joel and Ethan Coen
7) Fanny Brice
8) Tom and Jerry
9) Jack Palance
10) *Hombre* – 1967
11) Macy's and Gimbels
12) *How Green Was My Valley* - 1941
13) *Gone with the Wind* - $4 million at the time
14) Bill Nighy
15) Wilson
16) M. Night Shyamalan
17) James Stewart – He plays the entire movie in his clown makeup.
18) *The Little Mermaid* – 1989
19) Paradise Falls
20) Lee Marvin and Clint Eastwood

Quiz 24

1) Who was the first actor or actress to reject their Oscar win?
2) In *Ice Age*, Manny, Sid, and Diego are the three heroes who save the human baby; what three kinds of animals are they?
3) Who are the three singing and dancing stars of *Singin' in the Rain*?
4) What was the most expensive Hollywood film made during the 1980s?
5) In what country is the action-adventure comedy *Romancing the Stone* set?
6) What South African film features a bushman in the Kalahari Desert who discovers a Coke bottle?
7) Who is the first protagonist in a Disney animated feature to have no dialogue?
8) *The Shawshank Redemption* is based on a short story by Stephen King. For the movie, they dropped the first part of the story title that is a major Hollywood star's name; what is the name?
9) What was the word's first computer-animated feature film?
10) Who plays Sister Mary Benedict in *The Bells of St. Mary's*?
11) Who directed *The Lord of the Rings* trilogy?
12) What Oscar-winning comedy features the famous Walls of Jericho scene?
13) What Disney film features Uncle Remus telling tales of Brer Rabbit?
14) What sports-based movie with Keira Knightley has the tagline "Sometimes, to follow your dreams... you've got to bend the rules!"?
15) Susan Sarandon won the Best Actress Oscar for her portrayal of a nun who befriends a convicted killer on death row in what movie?
16) Who is the oldest Best Director Oscar winner?
17) What movie has the Hoover family trying to get to California so that young daughter Olive can compete in a beauty pageant?
18) Who stars as Scrooge in the 1951 version of *A Christmas Carol*?
19) What Hitchcock film has two strangers trading murders?
20) *All the King's Men* is based on the life of what politician?

Quiz 24 Answers

1) George C. Scott – 1971 for *Patton*
2) Woolly mammoth, sloth, saber-toothed tiger
3) Gene Kelly, Donald O'Connor, Debbie Reynolds – Reynolds was only 19 at the time; she had no prior dance experience and commuted to the set by bus from her parent's home where she lived.

4) *Who Framed Roger Rabbit* - $70 million at the time
5) Colombia – Ironically, the story centers around an American kidnapping in Colombia, but an increase in American kidnappings in Colombia caused the filming to be moved to Mexico.
6) *The Gods Must Be Crazy* - 1980
7) Dumbo – 1941
8) Rita Hayworth – The Stephen King short story title is *Rita Hayworth and the Shawshank Redemption.* Rita Hayworth is the first poster Andy has on the wall in his cell; the prisoners are also watching the Rita Hayworth film *Gilda* in one scene.
9) *Toy Story* – 1995
10) Ingrid Bergman
11) Peter Jackson
12) *It Happened One Night* – Clark Gable and Claudette Colbert build a wall with a blanket hanging on a line between their beds when they share a room.
13) *Song of the South* - 1946
14) *Bend It Like Beckham* - 2002
15) *Dead Man Walking* - 1995
16) Clint Eastwood – age 74 at the time for *Million Dollar Baby* in 2005
17) *Little Miss Sunshine* - 2006
18) Alastair Sim
19) *Strangers on a Train* - 1951
20) Huey Long – Louisiana governor

Quiz 25

1) What was the first film to win at least 10 Oscars?
2) In *Gremlins*, the cute, furry creature Gizmo is what kind of animal?
3) What are the names of the four turtles in *Teenage Mutant Ninja Turtles*?
4) In *Life of Pi*, what is the name of the tiger?
5) What is the first name of the possessed girl Linda Blair plays in *The Exorcist*?
6) Where is the resort where Baby and Johnny fall in love in *Dirty Dancing*?
7) What was the most expensive Hollywood film made in the 1990s?
8) What film features the line "Love means never having to say you're sorry"?
9) What was James Dean's last movie?
10) Only three Christmas movies have been nominated for the Best Picture Oscar; what are they?

11) Who plays John Doe's traveling companion in *Meet John Doe*?
12) What town is the setting for *The Music Man*?
13) Who was the first person to win directing, writing, and best picture Oscars for the same film?
14) What 1953 Marlon Brando film was banned in British theaters for 14 years?
15) What Martin Scorsese film set in 1863 stars Leonardo DiCaprio, Daniel Day-Lewis, Cameron Diaz, Jim Broadbent, John C. Reilly, Henry Thomas, Liam Neeson, and Brendan Gleeson?
16) Abbott and Costello's first starring roles were in what movie that also features the Andrews Sisters singing "Boogie Woogie Bugle Boy"?
17) What is Jimmy Stewart's full character name in *Mr. Smith Goes to Washington*?
18) In *Guardians of the Galaxy*, who is Peter Quill's ship named after?
19) Who was the first African American to win the Best Actress Oscar?
20) What movie has disgruntled Korean War veteran Walt Kowalski setting out to reform his neighbor, a Hmong teenager?

Quiz 25 Answers

1) *Ben-Hur* – 1959
2) Mogwai
3) Raphael, Leonardo, Donatello, Michelangelo
4) Richard Parker
5) Regan
6) Catskill Mountains in New York
7) *Titanic* - $200 million at the time
8) *Love Story* - 1970
9) *Giant* (1956) – He died before it was released.
10) *It's a Wonderful Life* (1946), *Miracle on 34th Street* (1947), *The Bishop's Wife* (1947)
11) Walter Brennan
12) River City, Iowa
13) Billy Wilder - *The Apartment* in 1960
14) *The Wild One* (1953)– It was deemed too violent to show.
15) *Gangs of New York* - 2002
16) *Buck Privates* - 1941
17) Jefferson Smith
18) Alyssa Milano – Peter Quill's childhood crush
19) Halle Berry – *Monster's Ball* (2001)

20) *Gran Torino* - 2008

Quiz 26

1) Who plays the psychopathic character Maggott in *The Dirty Dozen*?
2) *Argo* is based on a true story about an unusual plan to rescue Americans from what country?
3) Who wrote and stars in *My Big Fat Greek Wedding*?
4) In *How to Marry a Millionaire*, what three actresses play the lead roles of the young women looking for love?
5) Kevin Smith's *Clerks* is loosely based on what classic piece of 14th-century literature?
6) Adjusted for inflation, what is the highest-grossing R-rated movie of all time in the United States?
7) *The Greatest Game Ever Played* starring Shia LaBeouf is based on a true story about what major sports championship?
8) What character says, "Today, I consider myself the luckiest man on the face of the earth"?
9) Adjusted for inflation, what is the highest-grossing comedy of all time in the United States?
10) "Pay no attention to that man behind the curtain," is from what classic movie?
11) What Hitchcock film features Joan Fontaine and Laurence Olivier?
12) In *The Da Vinci Code*, what is the name of the military group that is charged with protecting the descendants of Jesus?
13) Sally Field won the Best Actress Oscar for her portrayal of a single woman trying to survive on a small farm during the Great Depression; what is the film?
14) In *She Done Him Wrong*, Mae West says the famous line "Why don't you come up sometime and see me?"; what actor does she say it to?
15) What was Elvis Presley's first feature film?
16) Who won the Best Actor Oscar for their portrayal of Winston Churchill in *Darkest Hour*?
17) Who plays the junkyard tycoon Harry Brock in the original *Born Yesterday*?
18) *Erin Brockovich* is based on a true story involving one of the biggest class-action lawsuits in American history; what was the company that was the target of the lawsuit?
19) Two films share the record for most Oscars by a foreign film at four each; what are the movies?
20) Who plays Mrs. Muir in *The Ghost and Mrs. Muir*?

Quiz 26 Answers

1) Telly Savalas
2) Iran
3) Nia Vardalos
4) Marilyn Monroe, Betty Grable, Lauren Bacall
5) *The Divine Comedy* by Dante – The main protagonist, Dante Hicks, gets his name from this, and there are nine breaks in the film to represent the nine rings of hell.
6) *The Exorcist* – 1973
7) U.S. Open – golf
8) Lou Gehrig – played by Gary Cooper in *The Pride of the Yankees* (1942)
9) *Home Alone* – 1990
10) *The Wizard of Oz* – 1939
11) *Rebecca* - 1940
12) Knights Templar
13) *Places in the Heart* - 1984
14) Cary Grant
15) *Love Me Tender* - 1956
16) Gary Oldman
17) Broderick Crawford
18) Pacific Gas & Electric
19) *Fanny and Alexander* (1982) and *Crouching Tiger, Hidden Dragon* (2000)
20) Gene Tierney

Quiz 27

1) What film starring Kathleen Turner and Nicolas Cage has the tagline "Knowing what you know now, what would you do differently?"
2) Who plays the Civil War veteran father in *The Yearling*?
3) In *White Christmas*, what two actresses play the sisters that become romantically involved with Bing Crosby and Danny Kaye?
4) What is the name of Robert De Niro's character in *Taxi Driver*?
5) Who was the conductor for the music in *Fantasia*?
6) What biographical film directed by Sydney Pollack and starring Robert Redford and Meryl Streep won nine Oscars?
7) In *My Fair Lady*, who plays Colonel Pickering who bets Henry Higgins that he can't transform Eliza Doolittle?
8) Who won the only Oscar for *Cool Hand Luke*?

9) Who plays the title role in *Gypsy*?
10) What Quentin Tarantino western was nominated for the Best Picture Oscar and features Christoph Waltz in the longest Best Supporting Actor Oscar-winning performance ever?
11) In *We Are Marshall*, a plane crash claims the lives of most of the Marshall University football team; what state is Marshall University in?
12) In *Animal House*, what is the name of the college?
13) Who plays James Dean's love interest in *Rebel Without a Cause*?
14) What character does Jackie Gleason play in *Smokey and the Bandit*?
15) Who plays the character whose dismembered body is fed into the woodchipper in *Fargo*?
16) What was the Beatles' first movie?
17) In *Edward Scissorhands*, who plays the inventor who creates Edward?
18) Who is the writer and director for both *Sleepless in Seattle* and *You've Got Mail*?
19) In *Stand by Me*, what four child actors, who all went on to significant acting careers, play the 12-year-old friends Gordy, Chris, Teddy, and Vern that go looking for the dead body?
20) In what city is the *Twilight* series of movies set?

Quiz 27 Answers

1) *Peggy Sue Got Married* - 1986
2) Gregory Peck
3) Rosemary Clooney and Vera-Ellen
4) Travis Bickle
5) Leopold Stokowski
6) *Out of Africa* - 1985
7) Wilfrid Hyde-White
8) George Kennedy – Best Supporting Actor Oscar
9) Natalie Wood – portrays stripper Gypsy Rose Lee
10) *Django Unchained* – 2012
11) West Virginia
12) Faber College
13) Natalie Wood
14) Sheriff Buford T. Justice
15) Steve Buscemi
16) *A Hard Day's Night* - 1964
17) Vincent Price

18) Nora Ephron
19) Will Wheaton, River Phoenix, Corey Feldman, Jerry O'Connell
20) Forks, Washington – Stephenie Meyer, the author of the books, chose the city because it has the most rainfall in the contiguous 48 states and is small, out of the way, and surrounded by forest.

Quiz 28

1) For what film did Ray Milland win a Best Actor Oscar?
2) Who was the first person to win Oscars for both acting and writing?
3) What role did Clark Gable play in *Mutiny on the Bounty*?
4) Who plays the title role in *Gigi*?
5) The term blockbuster has meanings going back to large bombs in WWII, but as it is used to describe films, what was the first movie that the term was applied to?
6) What movie stars Bud Cort as a teenager who wants to marry a 79-year-old woman played by Ruth Gordon?
7) What is the longest movie to ever win the Best Picture Oscar?
8) What film has a notorious gunman played by John Wayne being nursed back to health by a Quaker family?
9) *Quiz Show* is based on a true 1950s game show cheating scandal; Ralph Fiennes plays what real person who was a member of one of America's leading literary families and became a national celebrity based on his fraudulent wins?
10) What character does Humphrey Bogart play in *The Maltese Falcon*?
11) Who plays Gene Hackman's love interest in *Hoosiers*?
12) What is the highest-grossing foreign language or subtitled film ever in the United States?
13) The creator of *Beavis and Butthead* directed the work comedy *Office Space*; who is he?
14) In *Night at the Museum*, what is Ben Stiller's character name?
15) What character does Groucho Marx play in *Duck Soup*?
16) What actor holds the record for the most years between Oscar nominations playing the same character?
17) "Bond. James Bond," is first spoken in what film?
18) What is the only remake of a regular television series to be nominated for the Best Picture Oscar?
19) Who are the only two people to direct themselves to the Best Actor or Best Actress Oscar?
20) What is the shortest film to win the Best Picture Oscar?

Quiz 28 Answers

1) *The Lost Weekend* - 1945
2) Emma Thompson – Best Actress Oscar for *Howards End* (1992) and Best Adapted Screenplay Oscar for *Sense and Sensibility* (1995)
3) Fletcher Christian
4) Leslie Caron
5) *Jaws* - 1975
6) *Harold and Maude* - 1971
7) *Gone with the Wind* - 238 minutes
8) *The Angel and the Badman* - 1947
9) Charles Van Doren
10) Sam Spade
11) Barbara Hershey
12) *The Passion of the Christ* – 2004
13) Mike Judge
14) Larry Daley
15) Rufus T. Firefly
16) Sylvester Stallone – 39 years between *Rocky* (1976) and *Creed* (2015)
17) *Dr. No* (1962)– Sean Connery
18) *The Fugitive* (1993) – Oscar winner *Marty* (1955) was a remake of a television movie; Oscar nominated *Traffic* (2000) was adapted from a miniseries.
19) Laurence Olivier for *Hamlet* (1948) and Roberto Benigni for *Life Is Beautiful* (1997)
20) *Marty* (1955) – 90 minutes

Quiz 29

1) What was the very first film to win the Best Picture Oscar?
2) Who wrote and directed *American Graffiti*?
3) Who has won the most best supporting actor or actress Oscars?
4) What Oscar-winning actress plays Tom Hanks' mother in *Philadelphia*?
5) In *Gorillas in the Mist*, Sigourney Weaver stars as what real-life scientist who went to Africa to study the vanishing mountain gorillas and fought to protect them?
6) Who plays the leader of the Russian team that goes ashore in the comedy *The Russians Are Coming! The Russians Are Coming!*?
7) What was the most expensive Hollywood film made in the 2000s?
8) Meryl Streep plays a Holocaust survivor and won her first Best Actress

Oscar for what film?

9) What role did F. Murray Abraham play in *Amadeus*?
10) In *The Man Who Came to Dinner*, acerbic critic Sheridan Whiteside slips on the front steps of a prominent Ohio family's home and insists on recuperating in their home during Christmas; Bette Davis plays the critic's assistant; who plays the title role?
11) Who plays Gary Cooper's much younger wife in *High Noon*?
12) What does China syndrome refer to in *The China Syndrome*?
13) What suspense thriller stars Cary Grant, Audrey Hepburn, Walter Matthau, James Coburn, and George Kennedy?
14) In *The Shining*, novelist Jack Torrance played by Jack Nicholson takes a job as caretaker at a hotel where an evil presence drives him crazy; what is the name of the hotel?
15) Who are the only five performers to win consecutive acting Oscars?
16) What is the classical piece of music that is playing while Dudley Moore and Bo Derek are making love in *10*?
17) What film has Charlie Chaplin playing dual roles including a Jewish barber?
18) Who has the longest screen time performance to ever win the Best Actor Oscar?
19) Who plays Norman Bates in *Psycho*?
20) Marvin Hamlisch created the music for *The Sting*; much of the score is based on the work of what ragtime era composer?

Quiz 29 Answers

1) *Wings* – 1927
2) George Lucas
3) Walter Brennan – three for *Come and Get It* (1936), *Kentucky* (1938), *The Westerner* (1940)
4) Joanne Woodward
5) Dian Fossey
6) Alan Arkin
7) *Pirates of the Caribbean: At World's End* (2007) - $300 million
8) *Sophie's Choice* - 1982
9) Antonio Salieri
10) Monty Woolley
11) Grace Kelly
12) A hypothetical catastrophic failure where a nuclear reactor melts through the floor of its containment system and penetrates the earth's

surface as if traveling through toward China.

13) *Charade* - 1963
14) Overlook Hotel
15) Luise Rainer (1936 and 1937), Spencer Tracy (1937 and 1938), Katharine Hepburn (1967 and 1968), Jason Robards (1976 and 1977), Tom Hanks (1993 and 1994)
16) *Bolero* – by Maurice Ravel
17) *The Great Dictator* (1940)– He also plays the dictator.
18) Charlton Heston – 2 hours 1 minute and 23 seconds for *Ben-Hur* (1959)
19) Anthony Perkins
20) Scott Joplin

Quiz 30

1) What country is *The King and I* set in?
2) What is the only movie to ever have three Best Actor Oscar nominations?
3) What western stars Henry Fonda, Gregory Peck, John Wayne, Richard Widmark, James Stewart, Spencer Tracy, Walter Brennan, Lee J. Cobb, Karl Malden, Eli Wallach, Robert Preston, Carroll Baker, Carolyn Jones, Debbie Reynolds, and Agnes Moorehead?
4) In *WALL-E*, what does WALL-E stand for?
5) What actor plays himself in *Zombieland*?
6) What George Romero zombie flick was released in 1968?
7) Who is the only person to win an Olympic gold medal and an Oscar?
8) What movie is based on the true story of Christy Brown who was born with cerebral palsy and went on to become a writer and painter?
9) In *E.T. the Extra-Terrestrial*, what is E.T.'s candy of choice?
10) In Disney's animated *Frozen*, who provides the voice for the central character Anna?
11) In the original *The Day the Earth Stood Still*, what is the name of the alien?
12) What classic film originated from a Christmas card?
13) What film stars Richard Gere as a young man at a Navy Officer Candidate School and won Louis Gossett Jr. the Best Supporting Actor Oscar?
14) Anne Bancroft won the Best Actress Oscar playing what character?
15) What was the first all-color film nominated for the Best Picture Oscar?
16) What was the first animated film to win a competitive category Oscar?
17) What Alfred Hitchcock film won Joan Fontaine a Best Actress Oscar and

co-stars Cary Grant as her husband she suspects is planning to kill her?

18) What is the name of Zero Mostel's character in *The Producers*?
19) What is the occupation of the title character in *Marty*?
20) What Hitchcock spy movie pairs Cary Grant and Ingrid Bergman?

Quiz 30 Answers

1) Siam – current day Thailand
2) *Mutiny on the Bounty* – Clark Gable, Charles Laughton, and Franchot Tone in 1936
3) *How the West Was Won* - 1962
4) Waste Allocation Load Lifter: Earth-Class
5) Bill Murray
6) *Night of the Living Dead*
7) Kobe Bryant – Olympic basketball gold medals in 2008 and 2012 and Best Animated Short Film for *Dear Basketball* in 2018
8) *My Left Foot* - 1989
9) Reese's Pieces
10) Kristen Bell
11) Klaatu
12) *It's a Wonderful Life* – Philip Van Doren Stern had written a short story, *The Greatest Gift*, and had unsuccessfully tried to get it published. He sent it out as a 21-page Christmas card to his closest friends; a producer at RKO Pictures got hold of it and purchased the movie rights.
13) *An Officer and a Gentleman* - 1982
14) Anne Sullivan – *The Miracle Worker* (1962)
15) *A Star is Born* – 1937
16) *Pinocchio* (1940) - Two years earlier *Snow White and the Seven Dwarfs* had won a special Oscar.
17) *Suspicion* - 1941
18) Max Bialystock
19) Butcher
20) *Notorious* - 1946

Quiz 31

1) What movie has a deranged Glenn Close boiling a bunny?
2) What was Walt Disney's first animated feature film?
3) *Breaking Away* is about a small-town teen obsessed with cycling and the Italian cycling team; in what real town is the movie set?

4) What movie had the first Best Actress Oscar nomination for a science fiction film?
5) Who plays the title role in *Jane Eyre* opposite Orson Welles as Edward Rochester?
6) For what film, did Jean Dujardin become the first French actor ever to win the Best Actor Oscar?
7) Who was the first actress paid $20 million for a film?
8) What was the first non-English language film to win the Best Picture Oscar?
9) *Bye Bye Birdie* starring Dick Van Dyke, Janet Leigh, and Ann-Margret is a parody of what celebrity?
10) What musical comedy features "The Oldest Established Permanent Floating Crap Game in New York"?
11) In *Hello Dolly*, what is the name of Walter Matthau's character?
12) Who plays Vito Corleone's two sons in *The Godfather*?
13) Adjusted for inflation, what was the first film to surpass the budget for *Cleopatra* in 1963?
14) *The Imitation Game* is set during WWII and stars Benedict Cumberbatch as what real-life mathematical genius?
15) Joel and Ethan Coen's *O Brother, Where Art Thou?* is loosely based on what ancient epic poem?
16) What was the most expensive Hollywood film made during the 1940s?
17) For what film did Judy Holliday win her only Best Actress Oscar?
18) For what film did Spencer Tracy win his first Best Actor Oscar?
19) What woman has the most Oscar nominations?
20) In accepting his Best Supporting Actor Oscar, who said, "Now I know there's a Santa Claus"?

Quiz 31 Answers

1) *Fatal Attraction* - 1987
2) *Snow White and the Seven Dwarfs* – 1937
3) Bloomington, Indiana – home of Indiana University
4) *Aliens* (1986)– Sigourney Weaver
5) Joan Fontaine
6) *The Artist* - 2011
7) Julia Roberts – *Erin Brockovich* (2000)
8) *Parasite* (2019) – from South Korea
9) Elvis Presley
10) *Guys and Dolls* – 1955

11) Horace Vandergelder
12) Al Pacino and James Caan
13) *Waterworld* – 1995
14) Alan Turing
15) Homer's *Odyssey*
16) *Duel in the Sun* - $8 million at the time
17) *Born Yesterday* - 1950
18) *Captains Courageous* – 1937
19) Edith Head – 35 for costume design
20) Edmund Gwenn – for his role as Santa Claus in *Miracle on 34th Street*

Quiz 32

1) What is the theme song for *M*A*S*H*?
2) *A Christmas Story* is based on what writer's work?
3) What character said, "I just put one foot in front of the other. When I get tired, I sleep. When I get hungry, I eat. When I have to go to the bathroom, I go"?
4) *The Blind Side* is based on the true story of a family that takes in a homeless African American teen and helps him succeed in school and become an NFL first-round draft pick; what is the name of the player?
5) What actor provides the voice of the lion Aslan in *The Chronicles of Narnia: The Lion, the Witch and the Wardrobe*?
6) In *Independence Day*, what is used to defeat the aliens?
7) Who plays the scarecrow in *The Wizard of Oz*?
8) A mountain climber becomes trapped under a boulder and resorts to desperate measures to survive; what is the movie?
9) What film directed by Jean-Jacques Annaud doesn't contain a single word of any modern language and traces the movements of a tribe of pre-historic humans?
10) What was the first film to feature Humphrey Bogart and Lauren Bacall?
11) In the remake *The Karate Kid*, Jackie Chan plays the kung fu master; who plays the title role?
12) Who has the most Oscar nominations?
13) Who plays the young Amish boy who witnesses a murder and is protected by Harrison Ford in *Witness*?
14) Who plays Wyatt Earp in *Gunfight at the O.K. Corral*?
15) What was the number-one U.S. box office film released in the 1990s?
16) What are the nicknames of flying partners Tom Cruise and Anthony Edwards in *Top Gun*?

17) In *Four Weddings and a Funeral*, who plays the American Carrie that Hugh Grant's character falls in love with?
18) What suspense thriller has Frank Sinatra as a U.S. Army major believing that one of his men may be a brainwashed Chinese agent?
19) What science fiction film has real-life married couple Hume Cronyn and Jessica Tandy playing a married couple and won Don Ameche the Best Supporting Actor Oscar?
20) In *Sister Act*, what is the stage name of Whoopi Goldberg's character?

Quiz 32 Answers

1) "Suicide is Painless"
2) Jean Shepherd
3) Forrest Gump
4) Michael Oher
5) Liam Neeson
6) Computer virus – The idea was taken from H.G. Wells' *The War of the Worlds* where the Martians are killed by bacteria and viruses.
7) Ray Bolger
8) *127 Hours* - 2010
9) *Quest for Fire* - 1981
10) *To Have and Have Not* – 1944
11) Jaden Smith
12) Walt Disney – 59
13) Lukas Haas
14) Burt Lancaster
15) *Titanic* – 1997
16) Maverick and Goose
17) Andie MacDowell
18) *The Manchurian Candidate* - 1962
19) *Cocoon* - 1985
20) Deloris Van Cartier

Quiz 33

1) Joel and Ethan Coen were screenwriters for *Unbroken*; it is the story of Olympian Louis Zamperini who survives a plane crash in WWII and spends 47 days in a raft before he's caught by the Japanese and sent to a prisoner of war camp; what actress directed the movie?
2) In *The Maze Runner*, what are the creatures that live in the maze and

attack the Gladers called?

3) Who was the first African American to win the Best Supporting Actor Oscar?
4) What Ridley Scott film about two female best friends is one of the very few films ever to produce two Best Actress Oscar nominations?
5) What film has John Wayne, Dean Martin, Ricky Nelson, and Walter Brennan trying to keep an accused murderer in jail?
6) In *The Hangover*, the three men searching for the missing groom are played by Bradley Cooper, Ed Helms, and who?
7) Who plays Gandalf in *The Lord of the Rings: The Return of the King*?
8) Who plays Will Smith's son in *The Pursuit of Happyness*?
9) Who won the most Oscars in a single year?
10) What is the only film Henry Fonda and Jane Fonda made together?
11) What Hitchcock film has Henry Fonda playing an innocent man mistakenly arrested for armed robbery?
12) What was the first science fiction film to win the Best Picture Oscar?
13) In *The Shootist*, John Wayne plays a terminally ill gunfighter who gets a room in a boarding house run by a woman and her son; who plays the mother and son?
14) What two actresses share the record with five consecutive Best Actress Oscar nominations?
15) Who plays the grizzled prospector in *The Treasure of the Sierra Madre*?
16) What is the only film where the top two billed actors playing a married couple won the Best Actor and Best Actress Oscars?
17) Michael Clarke Duncan plays a death row inmate who can work miracles in *The Green Mile*; what is the name of his character?
18) Who is the first character to speak in *Star Wars*?
19) In *Duel in the Sun*, Jennifer Jones is torn between two sons, one good and the other bad; who plays the bad younger son?
20) What Woody Allen film has his character becoming president of the country of San Marcos?

Quiz 33 Answers

1) Angelina Jolie
2) Grievers
3) Louis Gossett Jr. – *An Officer and a Gentleman* (1982)
4) *Thelma & Louise* - 1991
5) *Rio Bravo* - 1959
6) Zach Galifianakis

7) Ian McKellen
8) Jaden Smith – his real-life son
9) Walt Disney – four in 1953
10) *On Golden Pond* – 1981
11) *The Wrong Man* - 1956
12) *The Shape of Water* - 2017
13) Lauren Bacall and Ron Howard
14) Bette Davis (1938-1942) and Greer Garson (1941-1945)
15) Walter Huston – His son John Huston directed the movie.
16) *On Golden Pond* – 1981 with Henry Fonda and Katharine Hepburn
17) John Coffey
18) C-3PO
19) Gregory Peck
20) *Bananas* - 1971

Quiz 34

1) In terms of tickets sold, what is the most popular James Bond film of all time?
2) What was the most expensive Hollywood film made during the 1950s?
3) What movie has the famous line "Here's looking at you kid"?
4) Peter Sellers, Alan Arkin, Roger Moore, Roberto Benigni, and Steve Martin have all played what character?
5) In *Goldfinger*, what is Goldfinger's first name?
6) What Walt Disney film has the most Oscar wins with five?
7) In *Matrix*, what is the name of the legendary hacker played by Laurence Fishburne who awakens Neo to the real world?
8) In Hitchcock's *North by Northwest*, who plays Cary Grant's love interest?
9) Who are the only two people to win both a Nobel Prize and an Oscar?
10) Who are the only sisters to win acting Oscars?
11) What is the only Walt Disney animated feature film that runs for two hours or more?
12) What film series has the most Oscar nominations?
13) What character did Spencer Tracy play in the 1938 film that won him his second consecutive Best Actor Oscar?
14) Who is the oldest supporting acting Oscar winner?
15) Dean Jones starred in 11 Disney films over his career; what was the first one?
16) Peter Dinklage stars as a man born with dwarfism who moves to rural

New Jersey to live a life of solitude but ends up making friends anyway; what is the movie?

17) Who plays the mother and father of the family dealing with the accidental death of its oldest son in *Ordinary People*?
18) How many movies did Spencer Tracy and Katharine Hepburn make together?
19) In *Groundhog Day*, each repeating day starts with what song on the radio?
20) Who won the Best Actor Oscar for *Gandhi*?

Quiz 34 Answers

1) *Thunderball* - 1965
2) *Ben-Hur* - $15 million at the time
3) *Casablanca* (1942) – Humphrey Bogart
4) Inspector Clouseau – Pink Panther movies
5) Auric – Auric is an adjective meaning of, related to, or containing gold.
6) *Mary Poppins* – 1964
7) Morpheus
8) Eve Marie Saint
9) George Bernard Shaw won the Nobel Literature Prize in 1925 and the Best Adapted Screenplay Oscar for *Pygmalion* in 1936; Bob Dylan won the Best Original Song Oscar for "Things Have Changed" from *Wonder Boys* in 2000 and the Nobel Literature Prize in 2016.
10) Olivia de Haviland and Joan Fontaine
11) *Fantasia* – 1940
12) *Lord of the Rings* trilogy – 30 nominations
13) Father Flanagan – *Boys Town*
14) Christopher Plummer – age 82 for best supporting actor in *Beginners* (2011)
15) *That Darn Cat!* - 1965
16) *The Station Agent* - 2003
17) Mary Tyler Moore and Donald Sutherland
18) Nine – *Woman of the Year* (1942), *Keeper of the Flame* (1943), *Without Love* (1945), *The Sea of Grass* (1947), *State of the Union* (1948), *Adam's Rib* (1949), *Pat and Mike* (1952), *Desk Set* (1957), *Guess Who's Coming to Dinner* (1967)
19) Sonny and Cher's "I Got You Babe"
20) Ben Kingsley

Quiz 35

1) What Oscar-winning film centers on a runaway princess who falls in love with a newsman?
2) Who plays the gunslinger Jack Wilson brought in to kill the title character in *Shane*?
3) What was the number-one U.S. box office film released in the 1970s?
4) The character of the boy Dill Harris who is visiting for the summer in *To Kill a Mockingbird* is based on what famous person?
5) Who plays Susan Walker, the little girl who doesn't believe in Santa Claus, in *Miracle on 34th Street*?
6) What British comedy has six unemployed steelworkers forming a striptease act?
7) What Best Picture Oscar winner is set in Hawaii around the time of the Japanese attack on Pearl Harbor?
8) In the *National Lampoon* series of vacation movies, what is the full name of Chevy Chase's character?
9) In *Three Billboards Outside Ebbing, Missouri*, a mother challenges the local authorities to solve her daughter's murder; who won the Best Actress Oscar for her portrayal of the mother?
10) In *Black Panther*, what is the name of the fictional African nation where the action takes place?
11) Who plays the man James Stewart's character believes has murdered his wife in *Rear Window*?
12) What was the number-one U.S. box office film released in the 1950s?
13) Who plays Fast Eddie Felson's manager in *The Hustler*?
14) What is the only film ever to have only one Oscar nomination in total and win the Best Picture Oscar?
15) What William Wyler western stars Gregory Peck, Charlton Heston, Jean Simmons, Burl Ives, and Chuck Connors?
16) What was the number-one U.S. box office film released in the 1980s?
17) Based on a true story, what movie follows Carl Brashear as he attempts to become the first African American U.S. Navy diver?
18) What early Quentin Tarantino film has the tagline "Seven total strangers team up for the perfect crime. They don't know each other's name. But they've got each other's color"?
19) In *Thor*, what is the name of the bridge that connects Asgard and Earth?
20) What film stars Burt Lancaster as an aging small-time gangster and was nominated for all five of the major Oscars?

Quiz 35 Answers

1) *Roman Holiday* (1953) – starring Gregory Peck and Audrey Hepburn
2) Jack Palance
3) *Star Wars* – 1977
4) Truman Capote – He was a childhood friend and neighbor of author Harper Lee, and they remained lifelong friends.
5) Natalie Wood
6) *The Full Monty* - 1997
7) *From Here to Eternity* - 1953
8) Clark Griswold
9) Frances McDormand
10) Wakanda
11) Raymond Burr
12) *The Ten Commandments* – 1956
13) George C. Scott
14) *Grand Hotel* - 1932
15) *The Big Country* - 1958
16) *E.T. the Extra-Terrestrial* – 1982
17) *Men of Honor* - 2000
18) *Reservoir Dogs* - 1992
19) Bifrost
20) *Atlantic City* - 1980

Quiz 36

1) In *Ocean's Eleven*, who plays the role originated by Frank Sinatra in the 1960 original?
2) What Best Picture Oscar-winning film has the longest title?
3) In *Willy Wonka and the Chocolate Factory*, what is the last name of the protagonist Charlie?
4) What was the first of 14 Sherlock Holmes films starring Basil Rathbone and Nigel Bruce?
5) Who was the first actor or actress to win a competitive acting Oscar for a Walt Disney film?
6) In *Slumdog Millionaire*, what is the final answer Jamal gives to win the grand prize?
7) In *Good Morning Vietnam*, Robin Williams' character is based on a real-life disc jockey on U.S. Armed Forces Radio in Saigon during the Vietnam War; what is his name?

8) What Francis Ford Coppola film stars Martin Sheen, Marlon Brando, Robert Duvall, Laurence Fishburne, Dennis Hopper, and Harrison Ford?
9) What western features Steve McQueen playing a teen hunting down the killers of his parents?
10) Who won a Best Adapted Screenplay Oscar for *Sense and Sensibility* and was nominated for a Best Actress Oscar for her performance in the film?
11) Adjusted for inflation, what is the earliest movie made that has grossed $1 billion in the United States?
12) What actor holds the record with four consecutive Best Actor Oscar nominations?
13) David Niven has the record for the shortest screen time performance to ever win the Best Actor Oscar; what film was it in?
14) In *Ghost*, what does Sam always say instead of saying "I love you"?
15) What was Bruce Lee's final film?
16) In *The Social Network*, what is the name of the website Mark Zuckerberg initially creates to rate the attractiveness of female Harvard students and in the process gets a six-month academic probation?
17) What movie has Tobie Maguire and Reese Witherspoon zapped back to the 1950s?
18) In *The Lord of the Rings: The Fellowship of the Ring*, how many are in the original fellowship?
19) What movie features Charlie Chaplin struggling in an industrialized world?
20) What is the name of James Stewart's character in *Harvey*?

Quiz 36 Answers

1) George Clooney – plays Danny Ocean
2) *The Lord of the Rings: The Return of the King* - 2003
3) Bucket
4) *The Hound of the Baskervilles* - 1939
5) Julie Andrews – *Mary Poppins* (1964)
6) Aramis – the third musketeer in *The Three Musketeers*
7) Adrian Cronauer
8) *Apocalypse Now* - 1979
9) *Nevada Smith* - 1966
10) Emma Thompson
11) *Snow White and the Seven Dwarfs* – 1937
12) Marlon Brando (1951-1954)

13) *Separate Tables* (1958)– Niven was on screen for 23 minutes and 39 seconds.
14) Ditto
15) *Enter the Dragon* - 1973
16) FaceMash
17) *Pleasantville* - 1998
18) Nine – Frodo, Gandalf, Legolas, Gimli, Aragorn, Boromir, Merry, Pippin, Samwise
19) *Modern Times* - 1936
20) Elwood P. Dowd

Quiz 37

1) Who directed *Mystic River* about three childhood friends whose lives are shattered when one of their daughters is murdered?
2) What movie features Karl Childers, a simple man hospitalized since childhood for murder, who is released to start a new life in a small town?
3) Ma and Pa Kettle first appeared in supporting roles in *The Egg and I* in 1947 and went on to star in nine movies of their own starting with *Ma and Pa Kettle* in 1949; who played Ma and Pa Kettle?
4) What musical stars Emma Watson, Kevin Kline, Ewan McGregor, Emma Thompson, Ian McKellen, and Stanley Tucci?
5) In the film *In the Heat of the Night*, Virgil Tibbs is a homicide detective in what city?
6) Adjusted for inflation, what is the only horror film to gross $1 billion in the United States?
7) Who plays the role of Big Daddy in *Cat on a Hot Tin Roof*?
8) Directed by Gene Kelly, what was the last film starring James Stewart and Henry Fonda?
9) What film set primarily in New Zealand won the Best Supporting Actress Oscar for Anna Paquin and the Best Actress Oscar for Holly Hunter?
10) What movie has the record for the largest Oscar sweep – winning every category it was nominated for?
11) What is the name of the adventurer Stewart Granger plays in *King Solomon's Mines*?
12) What actor says, "You fell victim to one of the classic blunders - the most famous of which is never get involved in a land war in Asia - but only slightly less well-known is this: Never go in against a Sicilian when death is on the line"?

13) What was Clint Eastwood's character called in *The Good, the Bad and the Ugly*?
14) What film stars Warren Beatty, Julie Christie, and Goldie Hawn and was also Carrie Fisher's screen debut?
15) What 1982 movie is based on Philip K. Dick's book *Do Androids Dream of Electric Sheep*?
16) The first film Steven Spielberg produced was a horror film that he also co-wrote starring Craig T. Nelson and JoBeth Williams; what is the movie?
17) Adjusted for inflation, what is the highest-grossing animated movie of all time in the United States?
18) What film has news anchorman Howard Beale threatening to kill himself on live television after learning he is being forced to retire?
19) What is the only Best Picture Oscar winner without any female speaking roles?
20) What is the name of Humphrey Bogart's character in *The Caine Mutiny*?

Quiz 37 Answers

1) Clint Eastwood
2) *Sling Blade* - 1996
3) Marjorie Main and Percy Kilbride
4) *Beauty and the Beast* - 2017
5) Philadelphia
6) *The Exorcist* – 1973
7) Burl Ives
8) *The Cheyenne Social Club* – 1970
9) *The Piano* - 1993
10) *The Lord of the Rings: Return of the King* (2003) – It won all 11 Oscars it was nominated for.
11) Allan Quartermain
12) Wallace Shawn – as Vizzini in *The Princess Bride* (1987)
13) Blondie
14) *Shampoo* - 1975
15) *Blade Runner*
16) *Poltergeist* - 1982
17) *Snow White and the Seven Dwarfs* – 1937
18) *Network* - 1976
19) *Lawrence of Arabia* - 1962
20) Captain Queeg

Quiz 38

1) What film includes the famous scene where Jack Nicholson's character tries to order toast that isn't on the menu?
2) In Best Picture Oscar winner *The King's Speech*, Colin Firth plays what English king who needed a speech therapist to overcome his stammer?
3) What is the name of Cary Grant's character in *Arsenic and Old Lace*?
4) What was the last film John F. Kennedy saw before his assassination?
5) In *Back to the Future*, what year does Marty McFly go back to?
6) In *Close Encounters of the Third Kind*, what is the real location that Richard Dreyfuss' character builds in mashed potatoes and is drawn to?
7) Who plays the title role in *The Buddy Holly Story*?
8) Jessica Tandy plays elderly Ninny Threadgoode who tells stories about people she used to know in what movie?
9) In Monty Python's *Life of Brian*, Brian is born at the same time as Jesus but in a different stable and is constantly being mistaken for him; who plays Brian?
10) Who are the four actors who play the friends on a canoe trip in *Deliverance*?
11) For what movie did Katharine Hepburn win her first Best Actress Oscar?
12) Who plays General Savage who takes over a bomber unit during WWII and whips them into shape in *Twelve O'Clock High*?
13) In *The Sound of Music*, what branch of the military does Captain von Trapp belong to?
14) What is the name of the town where *Bill and Ted's Excellent Adventure* is set?
15) What is the name of Uma Thurman's assassin character in *Kill Bill: Volume 1*?
16) In *Stand and Deliver*, who plays the teacher in a tough high school who inspires his students to learn calculus?
17) Besides the cartoon character, what is *The Pink Panther* in the movie of the same name?
18) In what movie does Marilyn Monroe's iconic scene with her white dress blowing upward while she stands on a subway grate take place?
19) What 1999 independent film had a $60,000 budget and grossed almost $250 million worldwide?
20) In *Stripes*, who plays Bill Murray's best friend that he convinces to enlist in the army?

Quiz 38 Answers

1) *Five Easy Pieces* - 1970
2) King George VI
3) Mortimer Brewster
4) *Tom Jones* - 1963
5) 1955
6) Devils Tower National Monument in Wyoming
7) Gary Busey
8) *Fried Green Tomatoes* - 1991
9) Graham Chapman
10) Burt Reynolds, Jon Voight, Ned Beatty, Ronny Cox
11) *Morning Glory* – 1933
12) Gregory Peck
13) Navy – Even though Austria is landlocked, there was a combined Austro-Hungarian Navy at the time.
14) San Dimas
15) The Bride
16) Edward James Olmos
17) Diamond
18) *The Seven Year Itch* - 1955
19) *The Blair Witch Project*
20) Harold Ramis

Quiz 39

1) What crime drama stars Russell Crowe, Guy Pearce, Kevin Spacey, James Cromwell, and Danny DeVito and won Kim Basinger the Best Supporting Actress Oscar?
2) What are the names of the three tunnels being dug in *The Great Escape*?
3) In *National Velvet*, Velvet's mother provides the entrance fee for the horse race out of her prize money for doing what?
4) Elizabeth Taylor plays a middle-aged wife in an abusive relationship and won her second Best Actress Oscar for what film?
5) A lion, zebra, giraffe, and what animal find themselves unexpectedly in the wild in *Madagascar*?
6) What is the name of the dog owned by Nick and Nora Charles in *The Thin Man*?
7) In *The Jerk*, what is the name of Steve Martin's idiot character?
8) What film won the Best Actress Oscar for Jane Fonda and the Best Actor

Oscar for Jon Voight?
9) What western stars John Wayne as Ethan Edwards looking for his abducted niece?
10) What Alfred Hitchcock film centers on a serial killer strangling women with a necktie?
11) In *Harold & Kumar Go to White Castle*, what actor playing himself steals their car?
12) In *Trading Places*, what two actors play the Duke brothers whose one dollar bet precipitates the trade in places between Eddie Murphy and Dan Aykroyd?
13) What is Eddie Murphy's character name in *Beverly Hills Cop*?
14) What Best Director Oscar winner appears as an actor in *Chinatown*?
15) What Terry Gilliam film is set in a retro-futuristic world and stars Jonathan Pryce and Robert De Niro?
16) What was the first film to lose (nominated but didn't win) at least 10 Academy awards?
17) What was the first James Bond film where M, the head of MI6, is played by a woman?
18) Who plays the investigative reporters Carl Bernstein and Bob Woodward in *All the President's Men*?
19) What Steve McQueen film features some of the most memorable car chase scenes in a Ford Mustang through San Francisco?
20) What actor and actress play the young couple who want to get married in *You Can't Take It with You*?

Quiz 39 Answers

1) *L.A. Confidential* - 1997
2) Tom, Dick, Harry
3) Swimming the English Channel
4) *Who's Afraid of Virginia Woolf?* - 1966
5) Hippopotamus
6) Asta
7) Navin Johnson
8) *Coming Home* - 1978
9) *The Searchers* - 1956
10) *Frenzy* – 1972
11) Neil Patrick Harris
12) Don Ameche and Ralph Bellamy
13) Axel Foley

14) John Huston
15) *Brazil* - 1985
16) *Mr. Smith Goes to Washington* – It was nominated for 11 Oscars and only won one; its competition in 1939 included *Gone with the Wind*, *The Wizard of Oz*, *Wuthering Heights*, and *Stagecoach.*
17) *GoldenEye* (1995)– Judi Dench
18) Dustin Hoffman and Robert Redford
19) *Bullitt* – 1968
20) James Stewart and Jean Arthur

Science and Nature

Quiz 1

1) What is extracted from the ore cinnabar?
2) Who is the Bluetooth wireless technology named after?
3) What medical condition is detected using the Ishihara test?
4) What condition is singultus?
5) In computing, what is half of a byte called?
6) What sense is most closely linked to memory?
7) What are the only two elements that are liquid at room temperature?
8) What is the only rock that floats in water?
9) Hansen's disease is more commonly known as what?
10) What is the second hardest gem after diamond?
11) What scale is used to measure wind speed?
12) What planet is often called the earth's twin because it is nearly the same size and mass and has similar composition?
13) A positive number that equals the sum of its divisors excluding itself is called what?
14) What is saffron made from?
15) What is the second-largest planet in our solar system?
16) The heat of chili peppers is measured in what?
17) The density of what is measured on the Ringelmann Scale?

18) What two planets in our solar system don't have moons?
19) What is the lightest known solid element?
20) The Fields Medal is awarded for achievement in what field?

Quiz 1 Answers

1) Mercury
2) King Harald "Bluetooth" Gormsson – He ruled Denmark in the 10th century.
3) Color blindness
4) Hiccups
5) Nibble
6) Smell
7) Mercury and bromine
8) Pumice
9) Leprosy
10) Sapphire
11) Beaufort
12) Venus
13) Perfect number
14) Crocus flowers – Only the stigma part of the flower is used; it takes 70,000 to 250,000 flowers to make one pound of saffron.
15) Saturn
16) Scoville Heat Units
17) Smoke
18) Mercury and Venus
19) Lithium
20) Mathematics

Quiz 2

1) What number on the Richter scale does an earthquake have to reach to be considered major?
2) What scale is used to measure the hardness of minerals?
3) On what planet other than the earth did a man-made object first land?
4) What color has the longest wavelength in the visible spectrum?
5) Where in the human body is the labyrinth?
6) What is the largest nerve in the human body?
7) What does the human lacrimal gland produce?
8) The Fahrenheit and Celsius temperature scales are the same at what

temperature?

9) What device converts alternating current into direct current?
10) The small intestine is made up of the jejunum, ileum, and what?
11) Who invented carbonated soda water?
12) What is the male part of a flower called?
13) What are the four types of adult human teeth?
14) Where does the earth rank in size among the planets in our solar system?
15) Syncope is the medical name for what condition?
16) What element has the lowest boiling point?
17) What is the heaviest naturally occurring element?
18) Who invented the exploding shell?
19) During hot or dry periods, what is the equivalent of hibernation?
20) The process where food browns during cooking is known as what?

Quiz 2 Answers

1) Seven
2) Mohs scale
3) Mars
4) Red
5) Ear
6) Sciatic
7) Tears
8) 40 degrees below zero
9) Rectifier
10) Duodenum
11) Joseph Priestley – also discovered oxygen
12) Stamen
13) Incisors, canines, premolars, molars
14) Fifth
15) Fainting
16) Helium – negative 452.1 degrees Fahrenheit
17) Uranium
18) Henry Shrapnel
19) Estivation
20) Maillard reaction

Quiz 3

1) Where on the human body are the most sweat glands?
2) The chemical formula H_2O_2 refers to what?
3) What is the point in the moon's orbit that is farthest from the earth called?
4) After nitrogen and oxygen, what is the third most abundant gas in the atmosphere?
5) What species is the oldest living individual tree?
6) What metal is the best conductor of electricity?
7) Who discovered X-rays?
8) What is the only part of the human body that cannot repair itself?
9) Thomas Edison was involved in a rivalry over which form of electricity would be commercialized; Edison supported direct current; who was his rival that supported alternating current?
10) The Big Dipper is part of what constellation?
11) After calcium, what is the second most abundant mineral in the human body?
12) What are the Magellanic Clouds?
13) Lateral epicondylitis is the medical name for what common medical condition?
14) Who is the author of *Coming of Age in Samoa*, the most widely read book in the field of anthropology?
15) From what plant is the poison ricin obtained?
16) What is an apparatus that converts molecules into ions and separates the ions according to their mass-to-charge ratio called?
17) What is rayon made from?
18) On the periodic table, what is the first element alphabetically?
19) What does AM stand for on radios?
20) How much longer is a day on Mars than a day on Earth?

Quiz 3 Answers

1) Bottom of the feet
2) Hydrogen peroxide
3) Apogee
4) Argon
5) Bristlecone pine - 5,000 years
6) Silver – It is slightly more conductive than copper but much more expensive.

7) Wilhelm Roentgen
8) Teeth
9) Nikola Tesla
10) Ursa Major or Great Bear
11) Phosphorus
12) Galaxies
13) Tennis elbow
14) Margaret Mead
15) Castor oil plant
16) Mass spectrometer
17) Wood pulp
18) Actinium
19) Amplitude modulation
20) 40 minutes

Quiz 4

1) What is the most abundant element in the universe?
2) What is the opposite of nocturnal?
3) Stonehenge is made of what two main types of rock?
4) The Saffir-Simpson scale measures the intensity of what?
5) How long is an eon?
6) What is the name for the point in a planet's orbit when it is nearest the sun?
7) What is the name of the process where plants lose water into the atmosphere?
8) What part of the human body is the axilla?
9) In the electromagnetic spectrum, what comes between X-rays and visible light?
10) What is the practice of concealing a file, message, image, or video within another file, message, image, or video called?
11) What standard international unit of power is equal to 1.341 horsepower?
12) Where will you find the Malpighi's pyramids?
13) What is the number 10 to the power of 100 called?
14) What element is named after the Greek word for green?
15) What name is given to the socket in the human skull that holds the eye?
16) How many vertebrae in the human spine?
17) The atomic mass in the periodic table is stated relative to the weight of

what element?
18) What is the standard international unit of force?
19) From what plant is the heart drug digitalis obtained?
20) The phenomenon where hot water may freeze faster than cold is known as what?

Quiz 4 Answers

1) Hydrogen – about 75% of the universe's mass
2) Diurnal
3) Bluestone and sandstone
4) Hurricanes
5) 1 billion years
6) Perihelion
7) Transpiration
8) Armpit
9) Ultraviolet light
10) Steganography
11) Kilowatt
12) Kidneys – cone shaped tissues
13) Googol
14) Chlorine
15) Orbit
16) 33
17) Carbon – more specifically carbon-12
18) Newton – One newton equals the force needed to accelerate one kilogram of mass at the rate of one meter per second squared.
19) Foxglove
20) Mpemba Effect

Quiz 5

1) Most of the world's supply of cork comes from what type of tree?
2) Due to its unique chemical qualities, what natural food can remain in an edible form for centuries?
3) What is the smallest named time interval?
4) What is the effect of the earth's rotation on the wind called?
5) What is the most abundant metal in the earth's crust?
6) What name is given to a chemical reaction that takes in heat?
7) Who formulated the laws that first explained the movements of the

planets properly?
8) What color is at the top of a rainbow?
9) What gives onions their distinctive smell?
10) What is the brightest star in the night sky?
11) What planet in our solar system has the longest day?
12) What are metals not considered precious called?
13) What is the only planet in our solar system less dense than water?
14) An astronomical unit is defined by what distance?
15) Located near the root of human hair follicles, the arrector pili muscles are responsible for what phenomenon?
16) What figure has four sides all the same length but no right angles?
17) What was the name of the first electronic general-purpose computer?
18) What blood type qualifies as a universal donor?
19) What year was the first email sent?
20) What is the only tree that grows in saltwater?

Quiz 5 Answers

1) Oak – cork oak trees predominantly in Portugal and Spain
2) Honey – Three-thousand-year-old edible honey has been found in tombs.
3) Planck time – 5.39×10^{-44} seconds
4) Coriolis
5) Aluminum
6) Endothermic
7) Johannes Kepler
8) Red – Violet is at the bottom.
9) Sulfur – When cut or crushed, a chemical reaction changes an amino acid to a sulfur compound.
10) Sirius – Dog Star
11) Venus – 243 Earth days
12) Base metals
13) Saturn
14) Earth to the sun – 93 million miles
15) Goosebumps
16) Rhombus
17) ENIAC – 1946
18) O negative
19) 1971

20) Mangrove

Quiz 6

1) What are the four states of matter observable in everyday life?
2) What is the largest two-digit prime number?
3) Marble is formed by the metamorphosis of what rock?
4) What is the densest naturally occurring element?
5) In its natural form, aspirin comes from the bark of what tree?
6) What metal has the highest melting point?
7) How many times does the moon revolve around the earth in a year?
8) What is the smallest organ in the human body?
9) What is the largest 3-digit prime number?
10) The European organization for nuclear research is known by what four letters?
11) What is the study of fungi called?
12) Pascal is a measure of what?
13) What is the best-selling personal computer model of all time?
14) What is the longest muscle in the human body?
15) How many orbits has the sun made around the center of the Milky Way Galaxy in its life?
16) Who first proposed the concept of contact lenses?
17) What planet in our solar system has the shortest day?
18) What are the equivalent megapixels of the human eye?
19) Approximately 2% of all people have what eye color?
20) How many constellations are in the night sky?

Quiz 6 Answers

1) Solid, liquid, gas, plasma
2) 97
3) Limestone
4) Osmium – about 25 times denser than water
5) White willow tree
6) Tungsten – 6,192 degrees Fahrenheit
7) 13
8) Pineal gland – in the center of the brain
9) 997
10) CERN – from the French "Conseil Europeen pour la Recherche Nucleaire"

11) Mycology
12) Pressure
13) Commodore 64 – 17 million units with a 1 MHz processor and 64KB RAM
14) Sartorius – from the pelvis to just below the inside of the knee
15) About 20
16) Leonardo da Vinci
17) Jupiter – 10 hours
18) 576 megapixels
19) Green – Brown is 55%; hazel and blue are 8% each.
20) 88

Quiz 7

1) What is the tallest mountain in the known universe?
2) What are the four lobes of the human brain?
3) How many planets in our solar system have moons?
4) What planet in our solar system has the most moons?
5) What is the densest planet in our solar system?
6) What is the most malleable naturally occurring metal?
7) What year was the first Apple computer released?
8) What human organ has the highest percentage of fat?
9) What is the only part of the human body without a blood supply?
10) What is the more common name for an Einstein Rosen Bridge?
11) What year was the first cell phone call made?
12) What is the fastest healing part of the human body?
13) What two planets in our solar system rotate clockwise?
14) What is the name for the dark gray color the eyes see in perfect darkness because of optic nerve signals?
15) What is the smallest muscle in the human body?
16) How many bones do human babies have?
17) The first web site was launched by CERN in what year?
18) What is the hottest planet in our solar system?
19) What is the closest galaxy to our own Milky Way?
20) Where are the Islands of Langerhans?

Quiz 7 Answers

1) Olympus Mons on Mars – 69,459 feet

2) Frontal, occipital, parietal, temporal
3) Six – Earth, Mars, Jupiter, Saturn, Uranus, Neptune
4) Jupiter – 63
5) Earth
6) Gold
7) 1976
8) Brain – up to 60% fat
9) Cornea
10) Wormhole
11) 1973
12) Tongue
13) Venus and Uranus
14) Eigengrau
15) Stapedius – in the middle ear
16) 300 – Some fuse together to form the 206 bones in adults.
17) 1991
18) Venus – 864 degrees Fahrenheit
19) Andromeda – 2.5 million light-years
20) Human pancreas – produce insulin

Quiz 8

1) In what year will Halley's Comet next appear?
2) If you hear thunder about 15 seconds after seeing lightning, how far away was the lightning?
3) What is the largest moon in our solar system?
4) What year was the first internet domain name registered?
5) In communications, what does VOIP stand for?
6) Sphenopalatine ganglioneuralgia is the medical term for what?
7) How many zeroes in a sextillion?
8) Who invented the electric battery in 1800?
9) In the human body, the hallux is more commonly known as what?
10) In 1997, what was the first mammal to be cloned from an adult cell?
11) What is the name for a three-dimensional object that has only one surface and has no orientation?
12) What name is given to atoms with the same number of protons but different numbers of neutrons?
13) A sequence of numbers where each number is the sum of the two prior numbers is called what?

14) How long can a human live unprotected in space?
15) In space, what color would the sun appear to be?
16) What was the first man-made object in space?
17) Astronauts in space are trained to go to the bathroom every two hours; why?
18) While alone in the *Apollo 15* command module orbiting the moon in 1971, astronaut Al Worden set what world record?
19) Why do Russian astronauts take guns into space?
20) Neil Armstrong didn't say, "That's one small step for man, one giant leap for mankind," when he set foot on the moon; what did he say?

Quiz 8 Answers

1) 2061 – last seen in 1986
2) About three miles - Sound travels about one mile in five seconds.
3) Ganymede – moon of Jupiter, about 41% of the size of Earth
4) 1985
5) Voice over internet protocol
6) Brain freeze – ice cream headache
7) 21
8) Alessandro Volta
9) Big toe
10) Dolly the sheep
11) Mobius strip – such as a strip of paper with a half twist joined at the ends
12) Isotopes
13) Fibonacci sequence
14) About 30 seconds – if you don't hold your breath
15) White
16) German V2 rocket – 1942
17) You can't tell if your bladder is full in space.
18) Most isolated human ever – He was 2,235 miles from the nearest human.
19) To protect themselves from bears if they land off course
20) "That's one small step for a man, one giant leap for mankind" – That is what Armstrong insisted he said; the word "a" before man wasn't heard clearly.

Quiz 9

1) What year was the word scientist first used?
2) What was the occupation of the first person to propose the big bang origin of the universe?
3) What planet in our solar system has a longer day than its year?
4) Who is the only person to win Nobel Prizes in two different areas of science?
5) What is the world's most visited website?
6) What is the first part of the human body to form in the womb?
7) What is the speed in miles per hour of the earth's orbit around the sun?
8) In 1991, the world's first webcam was created to do what?
9) How do the moon and sun fit together so perfectly in a solar eclipse?
10) In what century was it first proposed that the sun was the center around which the planets orbit?
11) What is a galactic or cosmic year?
12) The Catholic church made Galileo recant his theory that the earth revolves around the sun; how many years later did the church declare Galileo was right?
13) The most perfectly round natural object known in the universe is star 5,000 light-years away; before that discovery, what was the most perfectly round natural object known?
14) How many people do you need in a group to have a 50% chance that two will have the same birthday?
15) What does WIFI stand for?
16) What was the first item bought and sold across the internet in 1971?
17) What is the layer of the atmosphere closest to the earth's surface called?
18) What is extirpation?
19) The human eye can differentiate more shades of what color than any other?
20) In the human body, what is a limbal dermoid?

Quiz 9 Answers

1) 1833
2) Priest – Georges Lemaitre
3) Venus – 243 days for one rotation (1 day), 225 days for one orbit around the sun (1 year)
4) Marie Curie – physics and chemistry

5) Google
6) Asshole – Every human starts out as an asshole.
7) 66,600 mph
8) Check the status of a coffee pot at Cambridge University
9) By chance, the sun is about 400 times larger than the moon, and it is also about 400 times further away from the earth, so the two appear to be the same size in the sky.
10) 3rd century BC - Aristarchus of Samos proposed it; Copernicus developed a fully predictive model in the 16th century but wasn't the first to propose the concept.
11) The amount of time it takes the sun to orbit once around the center of the Milky Way Galaxy – about 225 million years
12) 359 years – in 1992
13) Sun
14) 23 – It is known as the Birthday Paradox; the probability goes up to 99.9% with just 70 people.
15) Nothing – It doesn't mean wireless fidelity or anything else; it is just a branding name picked by a company hired for the purpose.
16) Marijuana – Stanford students buying from MIT students.
17) Troposphere
18) Local extinction – Species is extinct locally but still exists elsewhere.
19) Green – That is why night vision goggles are green.
20) A cyst in the eye formed in the womb when skin cells get misplaced in the eye. The cyst can grow hair, cartilage, sweat glands, even teeth just like skin can.

Quiz 10

1) Water doesn't conduct electricity well, so why is electricity so dangerous with water?
2) Walnuts, almonds, pecans, and cashews aren't technically nuts; what are they?
3) When you die, what sense is the last to go?
4) Apples, peaches, and raspberries belong to what plant family?
5) In total darkness, most people naturally adjust to how long of a cycle instead of 24 hours?
6) What parts of the human body never stop growing?
7) In terms of how long it takes to process input, what is the fastest human sense?
8) What planet has the strongest winds in our solar system?

9) On average, what is the coldest planet in our solar system?
10) Mohs hardness scale's hardest substance is diamond; what is the softest?
11) What is the only bone in the human body that isn't attached to any other bone?
12) What is mainly extracted from pitchblende?
13) Alphabetically, what is the last element in the periodic table?
14) Ageusia is the loss of what sense?
15) Who performed the first heart transplant?
16) What calculation device was invented by William Oughtred in 1662?
17) In 1971, what U.S. space probe was the first to orbit another planet?
18) The camellia sinensis evergreen shrub produces what?
19) What do you use your zygomaticus muscle for?
20) What is the white trail behind a jet plane comprised of?

Quiz 10 Answers

1) The impurities in water make it a good conductor.
2) Drupes – They also include peaches, plums, and cherries. Drupes are a type of fruit where an outer fleshy part surrounds a shell or pit with a seed inside.
3) Hearing
4) Roses
5) 48 hours – 36 hours of activity and 12 hours of sleep
6) Ears and nose – parts composed of cartilage
7) Hearing – as little as 0.05 seconds
8) Neptune – more than 1,200 mph
9) Neptune – minus 353 degrees Fahrenheit
10) Talc
11) Hyoid bone – in the throat
12) Uranium
13) Zirconium
14) Taste
15) Dr. Christian Barnard
16) Slide rule
17) *Mariner 9*
18) Tea
19) Smiling
20) Ice crystals

Quiz 11

1) What is the world's tallest grass?
2) An alloy of iron, chromium, and nickel makes what?
3) What country grew the first orange?
4) What French philosopher created analytical geometry?
5) What are the world's smallest natural trees?
6) What is the most common infectious disease in the world?
7) Where on the human body is the thinnest skin?
8) The Easter lily is a native plant of what country?
9) Who first noticed that the sun had spots?
10) In science, what can be up, down, strange, charm, top, or bottom?
11) What drug was introduced by Bayer in 1898 and marketed as a non-addicting alternative to morphine and a treatment for cough inducing illnesses like bronchitis?
12) What compound puts the heat in chili peppers?
13) What is the hardest bone in the human body?
14) Who is known as the father of geometry?
15) What wheel did Blaise Pascal invent in search of perpetual motion?
16) Who established the science of genetics in 1866?
17) How many prime numbers are there that are less than 20?
18) How long does it take the moon to revolve around the earth to the nearest day?
19) What are the four major human blood types?
20) What is the common name for the fruit Citrus grandis?

Quiz 11 Answers

1) Bamboo
2) Stainless steel
3) China
4) Rene Descartes
5) Dwarf willows – They grow in Greenland and are only about two inches high.
6) Hepatitis B – More than one-quarter of the world's population is infected.
7) Eyelid (0.05 mm thick) – The palms and soles of the feet are the thickest at 1.5 mm.
8) Japan

9) Galileo
10) quarks – types or flavors
11) Heroin - The AMA approved it for general use in 1906 and recommended it as a morphine replacement; soon, there were 200,000 heroin addicts in New York City alone.
12) Capsaicin
13) Jawbone
14) Euclid
15) Roulette wheel
16) Gregor Mendel
17) Eight numbers - 2, 3, 5, 7, 11, 13, 17, 19
18) 27 days
19) A, B, AB, O
20) Grapefruit

Quiz 12

1) Atoms stop moving at what temperature?
2) What Polish astronomer demonstrated in 1512 that the sun is the center of the solar system?
3) What is the largest gland in the human body?
4) What five tastes can a human distinguish?
5) What is a googolplexian?
6) What planet in our solar system has the shortest year?
7) What is the end cause of every human death?
8) What is the fastest growing plant?
9) What month is the earth closest to the sun?
10) The word laser is an acronym for what?
11) What is the largest muscle in the human body?
12) What is the longest bone in the human body?
13) What is the simplest gem in chemical composition?
14) Who discovered Saturn's rings?
15) What part of the eye continues to grow throughout a person's life?
16) What is the most frequently broken bone in the human body?
17) What are the three major classifications for rocks?
18) What plant does natural vanilla flavoring come from?
19) What tiny vessel connects an artery with a vein?
20) In math, what does a "lemniscate" shape mean?

Quiz 12 Answers

1) Zero degrees Kelvin or absolute zero - equivalent to -459.67 degrees Fahrenheit
2) Nicholas Copernicus
3) Liver
4) Sweet, sour, bitter, salty, umami
5) The largest named number - A googol is 1 followed by 100 zeroes; a googolplex is 1 followed by a googol of zeroes; a googolplexian is 1 followed by a googolplex of zeroes.
6) Mercury – 88 Earth days
7) Cerebral hypoxia – Lack of oxygen to the brain is the final cause of death regardless of what initiates it.
8) Bamboo – Some species can grow three feet in a day.
9) January
10) Light amplification by stimulated emission of radiation
11) Gluteus maximus
12) Femur
13) Diamond – composed only of carbon
14) Galileo
15) Lens
16) Clavicle or collar bone
17) Igneous, metamorphic, sedimentary
18) Orchid
19) Capillary
20) Infinity - Lemniscate is a shape with two loops meeting at a central point.

Quiz 13

1) What is the oldest known vegetable?
2) What is the clotting protein in the blood called?
3) What metal is the major constituent of rubies?
4) What is the hardest substance in the human body?
5) What do astronomers call a giant cloud of gas and dust?
6) About 2,400 years ago, what did Hippocrates describe as “man's best medicine”?
7) What is the process of wave-like muscle contractions that moves food in the digestive tract starting in the esophagus called?
8) What was the first man-made object to leave the solar system?

9) Which isotope of carbon is used for radiocarbon dating?
10) What is the first prime number after 1,000,000?
11) What was the very first animal to go into space?
12) Who is the oldest person ever to go into space?
13) What planet circles the sun every 84 years?
14) Who was the first person to explain why the sky is blue?
15) What is the only country in the world to have a net gain of trees in the last hundred years?
16) The average lightning bolt is about five miles long and how wide?
17) The busiest muscles in the human body are found where?
18) What color are sunsets on Mars?
19) What makes Mars red?
20) What country has the largest permanent scale model of the solar system?

Quiz 13 Answers

1) Pea
2) Fibrin
3) Aluminum
4) Tooth enamel
5) Nebula
6) Walking
7) Peristalsis
8) *Pioneer 10*
9) Carbon-14
10) 1,000,003
11) Fruit flies – They were sent up in 1947 in a captured V2 rocket and were recovered alive.
12) John Glenn – 77
13) Uranus
14) Leonardo da Vinci
15) Israel
16) One inch
17) Eyes – They move 100,000 times a day.
18) Blue
19) It is covered in iron oxide (rust).
20) Sweden – The sun is represented by the largest hemispherical building in the world in Stockholm; the model is on a 1:20 million-scale and

stretches for 950 kilometers.

Quiz 14

1) What is the study of movement in relation to human anatomy called?
2) What year was the drug ecstasy invented?
3) What is the mass in grams of one cubic centimeter of water at 4 degrees Celsius (temperature water is at its maximum density)?
4) What year was the fax machine patented?
5) What country has the highest percentage of natural redheads?
6) What ingredient makes vinegar taste sour or bitter?
7) What are the three types of human twins?
8) What plant produces about one-half of the earth's oxygen?
9) What is the full name of the SARS virus?
10) What year was the first active communications satellite launched?
11) What is the point in the orbit of the moon or a satellite when it is nearest the earth called?
12) Table sugar from sugar cane or beets is what kind of sugar?
13) At normal atmospheric pressure, what is the only element in the universe that can't freeze?
14) Lyme disease gets its name from a small coastal town where several cases were identified in 1975 in what state?
15) What is the southern version of the aurora borealis (northern lights) called?
16) N_2O is more commonly known as what?
17) What element is named after the moon?
18) What plant's name comes from the Turkish word for turban?
19) What type of galaxy is the most common in the universe?
20) Even though it makes up about 2.4% of the earth's crust, what element is never found in its pure form in nature?

Quiz 14 Answers

1) Kinesiology
2) 1912 - Merck wanted to develop something to stop abnormal bleeding, and it synthesized MDMA to avoid a Bayer patent. They didn't have any real interest in it at the time, and it wasn't until 1975 that the psychoactive effects of the drug were seriously considered.
3) One gram
4) 1843 - The original patent for the electric printing telegraph or fax was in 1843 by Scottish inventor Alexander Bain, and the first commercial

use of a fax machine was in France in 1865, 11 years before the telephone was invented and the year the American Civil War ended.

5) Scotland - about 13%
6) Acetic acid - Vinegar typically contains 5-20% acetic acid.
7) Identical, fraternal, and semi-identical - Identical twins result from a single fertilized egg that splits in two and forms two identical boys or two girls who share 100% of their DNA. Fraternal twins form from two eggs that have been fertilized by two of the father's sperm, creating two genetically unique siblings that share 50% of their DNA. Semi-identical twins share between 50% and 100% of their DNA and are formed when a single egg is fertilized by two sperm, and the egg splits the three sets of chromosomes into two separate cell sets.
8) Phytoplankton
9) Severe acute respiratory syndrome
10) 1962 - Telstar 1 was a medium Earth orbit satellite.
11) Perigee
12) Sucrose
13) Helium - Its freezing point is -458 degrees Fahrenheit.
14) Connecticut
15) Aurora australis
16) Laughing gas - nitrous oxide
17) Selenium - Selene means moon in Greek.
18) Tulip
19) Elliptical
20) Potassium - It is so reactive that it is never found in its pure form in nature; it must be isolated artificially by separating it from its compounds.

Quiz 15

1) In humans, which lung (right or left) is always larger?
2) By what common name is calcium oxide (CaO) known?
3) What metal melts in your hand?
4) What is the more common name for red corundum?
5) What is the scientific name for the moon?
6) An aphyllous plant doesn't have what?
7) Humans have a depression in the right atrium of the heart that is a result of our fetal development; what is it called?
8) What celestial object gets its name from a Greek word meaning long-haired?

9) In computers, the smallest unit of data is a bit that has a binary value of 0 or 1; what is the term "bit" short for?
10) Our current North Star is Polaris, it will be replaced by what star in about 13,000 years?
11) What kind of fruit is a pineapple?
12) What tree that is native to tropical southern North America and northern South America is extremely toxic in all forms and can cause blistering even from standing beneath the tree during rain?
13) On the human body, what is the niddick?
14) What is a device used to measure the amount of moisture in the atmosphere called?
15) What year did people first recognize that dinosaurs had existed?
16) In physics, mass multiplied by acceleration gives you what?
17) Where in the human body would you find the round window and the oval window?
18) What psychologist coined the terms introvert and extrovert?
19) What planet in our solar systems rotates the slowest?
20) Scheelite is an important ore of what element?

Quiz 15 Answers

1) Right - The left lung is smaller to leave enough room for your heart.
2) Quicklime - used in cement, making glass, manufacturing steel, etc.
3) Gallium - It melts at 85.6 degrees Fahrenheit.
4) Ruby - Corundum is a very hard mineral composed of aluminum oxide that is the source for both rubies and sapphires. If it is red, it is a ruby; if it is any other color, it is a sapphire although the most popular and valued sapphire color is blue.
5) Moon - Unlike other moons in our solar system, it doesn't have any other official name.
6) Leaves
7) Fossa ovalis - An unborn child receives oxygen from its mother, so blood goes directly from the right to the left atrium through the foramen ovale; after birth, the opening closes, creating the fossa ovalis.
8) Comet - from the Greek kometes
9) Binary digit
10) Vega - The change is due to a change in the direction the earth's axis points due to a motion called precession. If you think of a spinning top given a slight nudge, the top traces out a cone pattern; that is how the earth moves on its axis. The earth bulges out at the equator, and the gravitational attraction of the moon and sun on the bulge cause the

precession that repeats in a 26,000-year cycle that will make Polaris the North Star again in about 26,000 years.

11) Berry - It produces hundreds of flowers within a small space that produce fruits that coalesce into a single larger fruit.
12) Manchineel tree - Burning the tree can cause eye injuries, and the fruit is possibly fatal producing internal bleeding.
13) Nape of the neck
14) Hygrometer
15) 1824 - Even though the name dinosaur wasn't applied until 1842, William Buckland, a geology professor at Oxford, was the first person to recognize dinosaurs for what they were in 1824 when he used the name Megalosaurus to describe an extinct carnivorous lizard fossil.
16) Force
17) Ear - The round window is an opening from the middle ear to the inner ear; the oval window is an opening that leads from the middle ear to the inner ear.
18) Carl Jung - 1920s
19) Venus - At the equator, Venus rotates 4 mph; the Earth rotates 1,038 mph at the equator.
20) Tungsten

Quiz 16

1) What is the thickest layer of the earth's four layers?
2) How many sides does an enneadecagon have?
3) In the human body, what is produced by the parotid glands?
4) Who originated the quantum theory and won the 1918 Nobel Prize in Physics for his work?
5) In nature, what are drupelets?
6) Who developed the system we use today for classifying plants and animals?
7) What element is named after a village in Scotland?
8) What is the name for the part of the human ear that receives sound vibrations and converts them into nerve impulses?
9) Brass is an alloy of what two metals?
10) What body part does a cicada use to make their loud sound?
11) What is the second-largest moon in our solar system?
12) What is the smallest thing ever photographed?
13) Who developed the first antibiotic, penicillin?
14) Because of the speed the sun moves at, what is the maximum possible

length for a solar eclipse to the nearest minute?
15) What is the study of life in outer space called?
16) What is the second-largest moon of Jupiter?
17) What is a two-dimensional image of a slice through a three-dimensional object called?
18) Gunpowder is made up of a mixture of sulfur, charcoal, and what?
19) What are the only two non-silvery pure metals in the world?
20) What is the name of the prolific meteor shower that peaks in August each year?

Quiz 16 Answers

1) Mantle - It is about 1,802 miles thick and makes up about 84% of the earth's volume.
2) 19 sides
3) Saliva
4) Max Planck
5) The individual bumps forming a fleshy aggregate fruit such as a blackberry or raspberry
6) Carolus Linnaeus - In the first half of the 18th century, he developed a taxonomy for naming and classifying plants and animals.
7) Strontium - It is named after the village of Strontian, Scotland.
8) Cochlea
9) Copper and zinc
10) Ribs - They flex their muscles to buckle a series of ribs one after another to produce their loud sound. Every time a rib buckles, it produces a click; many clicks produce the buzzing sound. The series of ribs are called a tymbal and can produce a sound over 100 decibels that can be heard over a mile and a half away.
11) Titan - 3,200-mile diameter moon of Saturn
12) The shadow of a single atom - In 2012, scientists were able to take a picture of the shadow produced by a single atom. Using an electrical field, they suspended the atom in a vacuum chamber and shot a laser beam at it to produce the shadow.
13) Alexander Fleming - 1928
14) Eight minutes - 7 minutes and 58 seconds
15) Exobiology
16) Callisto - 2,996-mile diameter, third-largest moon in our solar system
17) Tomogram - used in radiology, archaeology, biology, geophysics, oceanography, etc.

18) Potassium nitrate
19) Gold and copper
20) Perseids meteor shower

Quiz 17

1) In what century did the practice of quarantine begin?
2) In our solar system, there are three types of planets - terrestrial, gas giants, and what?
3) Glass is neither a liquid nor a solid; what is it called?
4) Who was the first American to orbit the earth in space?
5) What is the largest cell in the human body?
6) For humans, what is the rarest hair and eye color combination?
7) Up to about 10,000 years ago, all humans had what eye color?
8) What brand name is sildenafil citrate marketed under?
9) In trigonometry, what is calculated as adjacent divided by hypotenuse?
10) What element has the symbol Pb?
11) What was the name of the first orbiting space station?
12) In terms of mass, what is the most abundant element in the human body?
13) What is the branch of medicine concerned with disease as it affects a community of people called?
14) Pewter is an alloy of what two metals?
15) What is the longest number of days a human has ever gone without sleep voluntarily without any artificial stimulants?
16) What planet in our solar system is big enough to fit over 1,300 Earths inside it?
17) What periodic table element has the shortest name?
18) What is the name of the chemical process used to harden rubber by treating it with sulfur?
19) What is the international standard unit of work or energy?
20) What is the small bump on the inner corner of your eye called?

Quiz 17 Answers

1) 14th century - Ships arriving in Venice from plague-infected ports were required to sit at anchor for 40 days before landing. The word quarantine derives from the Italian words "quaranta giorni," which means 40 days.
2) Ice giants - Uranus and Neptune

3) Amorphous solid - a state somewhere between liquid and solid
4) John Glenn - 1962
5) Female egg
6) Red hair and blue eyes - Only about 0.17% of the population has the combination because both red hair and blue eyes are recessive traits where both parents must carry the gene for the child to have it.
7) Brown - A genetic mutation at about that time produced blue eyes.
8) Viagra
9) Cosine
10) Lead - Pb comes from the Latin word "plumbum," meaning waterworks; in ancient times, lead was widely used in the construction of water pipes.
11) *Salyut 1* - launched by the Soviet Union in April 1971
12) Oxygen
13) Epidemiology
14) Tin and lead
15) 11 days
16) Jupiter - It has a diameter of about 88,695 miles and is the largest planet in our solar system.
17) Tin
18) Vulcanization - invented by Charles Goodyear
19) Joule
20) Caruncula

Quiz 18

1) What is the rarest hair color in the world?
2) What does an ichthyologist study?
3) About 1 in every 200 people is born with an extra rib that forms above the first rib at the base of the neck just above the collarbone; what is it called?
4) What year was the first internet search engine created?
5) In astronomy, who coined the term "Big Bang"?
6) In the electromagnetic spectrum, what comes between microwaves and visible light?
7) What astronomy unit of measure is about 93 million miles?
8) Who was the marine biologist and author of *Silent Spring* who was one of the first people to warn of the dangers of pesticides like DDT?
9) Under daylight conditions, the human eye is most sensitive to what color?

10) What is H_2SO_4 the chemical formula for?
11) Harvard didn't offer calculus classes for the first few years; why?
12) What are the most luminous objects in the known universe?
13) In the human body, what is otalgia?
14) What planet is the largest of the terrestrial planets in our solar system?
15) Where on your body would you find rascette lines?
16) In humans, which ear is better at receiving sounds from speech?
17) What is the name for the point in a planet's orbit when it is furthest from the sun?
18) In 1999, NASA estimated that what material cost $28 quadrillion per pound to produce?
19) What was the first Apollo mission to orbit the moon?
20) How many planets in our solar system have rings?

Quiz 18 Answers

1) Red - less than 2% of the population
2) Fish
3) Cervical rib - You can have a cervical rib on either or both sides, and it can be a fully-formed bony rib or a thin strand of tissue fibers.
4) 1990 - It was called Archie and was created by a small group of computer science students at McGill University in Montreal, Quebec, Canada.
5) Fred Hoyle - He was an English astronomer and coined it in 1949 on a BBC radio broadcast.
6) Infrared
7) Astronomical unit - defined by the distance from the earth to the sun
8) Rachel Carson
9) Green - Light at this wavelength produces the impression of the highest brightness compared to light at other wavelengths.
10) Sulfuric acid
11) Calculus hadn't been invented yet. Harvard was established in 1636; calculus wasn't developed until the mid-1600s.
12) Quasars - They are highly luminous radio galaxies with a supermassive black hole; the nearest known quasar is 600 million light-years away.
13) Earache
14) Earth - Terrestrial planets are the inner, rocky planets - Mercury, Venus, Earth, and Mars.
15) Inner wrist creases
16) Right ear - The left ear is more sensitive to the sounds of music.

17) Aphelion
18) Antimatter
19) *Apollo 8* - December 1968
20) Four (Jupiter, Saturn, Uranus, Neptune) - Galileo discovered Saturn's rings in 1610; the rings on the other planets weren't discovered until the 1970s.

Quiz 19

1) Sphalerite is the primary ore of what metal?
2) What synthetic drug was first produced in 1897 by Felix Hoffman, a German chemist for Bayer?
3) What is the medical name for the human butt crack?
4) What type of galaxy is the Milky Way?
5) As a gas, oxygen is odorless and colorless; what color is it in its liquid and solid forms?
6) The surface area of Pluto is only about 3% larger than what country?
7) What is the only human internal organ that can regenerate itself?
8) What common spice can be toxic in a dose of two teaspoons or more inducing hallucinations, convulsions, pain, nausea, and paranoia that can last for several days?
9) What principle states that the position and the velocity of an object cannot both be measured exactly at the same time?
10) What is your pollex?
11) Steel is made by alloying iron with what?
12) What tree native to Africa, Australia, and India can grow to almost 100 feet tall with a trunk diameter up to 36 feet, live for thousands of years, and store up to 32,000 gallons of water in its trunk?
13) What element is named after the earth?
14) What function does the sinoatrial node in the human heart serve?
15) What is the scientific study of trees called?
16) What is the standard international unit of electrical current?
17) What element is named after a U.S. university?
18) What is the heaviest element produced by fusion in a star?
19) The physiological sense called equilibrioception is known by what more common term?
20) What is the study of freshwater environments, particularly lakes, called?

Quiz 19 Answers

1) Zinc
2) Aspirin
3) Intergluteal cleft
4) Spiral
5) Pale blue
6) Russia
7) Liver - You can lose up to 75 percent of your liver, and the remaining portion can regenerate into a whole liver.
8) Nutmeg - It comes from the seed of a tropical evergreen.
9) Heisenberg uncertainty principle
10) Thumb
11) Carbon - usually less than 1%
12) Baobab - Because it stores such large volumes of water in its trunk, elephants, eland, and other animals chew the bark during dry seasons.
13) Tellurium - Tellus is Latin for earth.
14) Pacemaker - It is specialized muscle tissue in the wall of the right atrium that produces a contracting signal at regular intervals.
15) Dendrology
16) Ampere - named after the French mathematician and physicist André-Marie Ampère
17) Berkelium - It was first made in 1950 at the University of California, Berkeley.
18) Iron
19) Sense of balance
20) Limnology

Quiz 20

1) According to research by Johns Hopkins, where do medical errors rank as a cause of death in the United States?
2) What planet in our solar system has a diameter just 397 miles smaller than the earth?
3) What was the first man-made element?
4) The Big Dipper isn't a constellation; what is it?
5) What was the first Apollo mission to use a lunar rover?
6) What is the second most common element in the universe?
7) What creates the sound you hear when you hold a seashell to your ear?
8) In humans, what is the stage before frostbite called?

9) Linseed oil comes from what plant?
10) What plants did Gregor Mendel use for his genetics experiments?
11) What unit of measure is equal to about 3.26 light-years?
12) What does outer space smell most like?
13) Who is widely credited with saving more lives than any other medical scientist of the 20th century?
14) In March 1965, Alexei Leonov was the first person to do what?
15) In the human body, what tube connects the kidney to the bladder?
16) On your body, where would you find your lunula?
17) What was the first country to adopt the metric system?
18) What is the farthest object visible to the naked human eye?
19) What is the study of plants called?
20) In physics, mass multiplied by velocity gives you what?

Quiz 20 Answers

1) Third - behind heart disease and cancer.
2) Venus
3) Technetium - 1937
4) Asterism - There are 88 official constellations in the night sky; any other grouping of stars that isn't one of the 88 is an asterism. In the Big Dipper's case, it is part of the Ursa Major or Great Bear constellation.
5) *Apollo 15* - July 1971
6) Helium - about 25% of the universe by mass
7) Surrounding environmental noise resonating in the seashell cavity - In a soundproof room, you don't hear anything when you hold a seashell to your ear.
8) Frostnip - There is skin irritation causing redness and a cold feeling followed by numbness, but there is no permanent damage.
9) Flax
10) Pea plants
11) Parsec
12) Burning odor of hydrocarbons - like gunpowder, diesel, and barbecue
13) Maurice Ralph Hilleman (1919-2005) - He was an American microbiologist who specialized in developing vaccines and developed over 40 in his career including 8 of the 14 vaccines routinely recommended: measles, mumps, hepatitis A, hepatitis B, chickenpox, meningitis, pneumonia, and Haemophilus influenzae.
14) Spacewalk

15) Ureter
16) White crescent near the base of your fingernail
17) France - 1795
18) Andromeda Galaxy - It is 2.6 million light-years away and is visible as a dim, large gray cloud almost directly overhead in a clear night sky.
19) Botany
20) Momentum

Quiz 21

1) The number zero with its own unique value and properties did not exist until what century?
2) What century was the telescope invented?
3) What kind of organism is the world's largest single living organism?
4) What is the manipulation of matter on an atomic, molecular, and supramolecular scale called?
5) What part of the human brain regulates involuntary functions?
6) If you wrapped a rope around the earth's equator so that it was tightly hugging the ground, how much additional rope would you need for it to hover one foot above the ground all the way around the earth?
7) $C_{10}H_{14}N_2$ is a poisonous alkaloid consumed by millions daily; what is it?
8) What state of matter does the sun largely consist of?
9) How many months after conception do human embryos develop fingerprints?
10) What fibrous protein is the main constituent of hair and nails?
11) Who won the 1922 Nobel Prize in Physics for their research on the structure of the atom and the development of the quantum theory?
12) What did Marie Curie name the first element she discovered?
13) What two physicists first split the atom in 1932 and went on to win a Nobel Prize for their work?
14) What planet was originally called Georgium Sidus or the Georgian Planet in honor of King George III of England?
15) What was the first Apollo mission to get to space and orbit the earth?
16) Based on the arrangement of their molecules, there are two types of solids - crystalline and what?
17) If you yawn and have saliva shoot out of your mouth, what is it called?
18) Even though it is one of the most common elements in the earth's crust, what metal was more valuable than gold in the 1800s?
19) What century did Nicolaus Copernicus develop the heliocentric model?
20) When poured, does hot water have a higher or lower pitch than cold

water?

Quiz 21 Answers

1) 7th century - Early counting systems only saw zero as a placeholder, not a true number.
2) 17th century - 1608
3) Mushroom - It is a honey mushroom in Malheur National Forest in Oregon that covers more than three square miles, weighs at least 7,500 tons, and is at least 2,000 years old. DNA testing has confirmed it is the same organism that has spread from a single location thousands of years ago.
4) Nanotechnology
5) Medulla oblongata
6) 6.3 feet - circumference = 2 x Pi x radius = 2 x Pi x (1 additional foot of radius) = 6.3 feet
7) Nicotine
8) Plasma
9) Three months
10) Keratin
11) Niels Bohr
12) Polonium - after her native country of Poland
13) John Cockcroft and Ernest Walton
14) Uranus
15) *Apollo* 7 - October 1968
16) Amorphous - Crystalline solids have an orderly molecule structure; amorphous solids like glass have a random structure.
17) Gleeking - The salivary glands underneath your tongue become stimulated and shoot a concentrated jet of pure saliva; it typically happens when yawning.
18) Aluminum - It is rarely found in its pure form and is difficult to extract from ores, so before more efficient processes were developed to extract it, aluminum was quite rare. In the 1850s, aluminum was priced at $1,200 per kilogram, and gold was priced at about half that at $664 per kilogram.
19) 16th century - published in 1543
20) Higher - Water changes viscosity with temperature, which affects the sound when poured.

Quiz 22

1) The atomic bomb dropped on Nagasaki used what kind of nuclear material?
2) What year was the world's first artificial satellite, *Sputnik 1*, launched?
3) What gas makes up most of the earth's atmosphere?
4) What planet's moons are named after characters created by William Shakespeare and Alexander Pope?
5) What is the common name for Fe_2O_3?
6) After the sun, what is the closest star to the earth?
7) Bananas, along with foods like spinach, apricots, salmon, avocados, and mushrooms, are very mildly radioactive; what element makes them radioactive?
8) Where does the moon rank in size among all the moons in our solar system?
9) An angle that is more than 90 degrees and less than 180 degrees is called what?
10) The word scuba is an acronym for what?
11) What piece of computer equipment was invented by Douglas Engelbart at Stanford Research Institute in the early 1960s?
12) What two elements make up most of the earth's core?
13) The uppermost region of the sun is called what?
14) What part of the human brain is most responsible for motor functions?
15) What famous actress was one of the inventors of spread spectrum and frequency hopping technology that is the basis for current cellular communications?
16) What is the only human organ that can float in water?
17) The point at which a liquid can exist simultaneously as a liquid, solid, and gas is called its what?
18) What is the fastest spinning planet in our solar system?
19) Why don't people sneeze in their sleep?
20) What is the third-largest planet in our solar system?

Quiz 22 Answers

1) Plutonium - The Hiroshima bomb used uranium-235; Nagasaki used plutonium-239.
2) 1957
3) Nitrogen - about 78%
4) Uranus – It has 27 moons: Cordelia, Ophelia, Bianca, Cressida,

Desdemona, Juliet, Portia, Rosalind, Cupid, Belinda, Perdita, Puck, Mab, Miranda, Ariel, Umbriel, Titania, Oberon, Francisco, Caliban, Stephano, Trinculo, Sycorax, Margaret, Prospero, Setebos, and Ferdinand.

5) Rust- iron oxide
6) Proxima Centauri - 4.22 light-years away
7) Potassium K-40 - A very small fraction of potassium atoms are K-40 radioactive atoms that spontaneously decay releasing beta radiation and gamma rays, which are both capable of tissue damage. However, K-40 is not very radioactive with a half-life of 1.3 billion years, so you would have to eat about 10 million bananas to die of radiation poisoning.
8) Fifth - behind Ganymede, Titan, Callisto, and Io
9) Obtuse
10) Self-contained underwater breathing apparatus
11) Mouse
12) Iron and nickel
13) Corona - It is 1 to 2 million degrees Kelvin
14) Cerebellum
15) Hedy Lamarr - at the beginning of WWII
16) Lungs - They contain about 300 million balloon-like structures called alveoli that replace the carbon dioxide waste in your blood with oxygen.
17) Triple point - It is the temperature and pressure that puts the three states of matter into thermodynamic equilibrium where no one state is trying to change into any other state. For water, the triple point is at 32.02 degrees Fahrenheit and 0.006 atmospheres (normal pressure is one atmosphere).
18) Jupiter - 28,273 mph at the equator compared to 1,038 mph for the Earth
19) The brain shuts down the reflexes that would result in a sneeze through a process called REM atonia.
20) Uranus - It has a diameter of 31,765 miles; its volume is about 63 times larger than the Earth.

Quiz 23

1) What is the standard international unit of capacitance?
2) How many playing cards would you need to have in a deck to have more possible unique sequences than there are stars in the observable universe?
3) What law states that equal volumes of all gases at the same temperature and pressure have the same number of molecules?

4) Only one side of the moon is visible from the earth because the moon rotates on its axis at the same rate that it orbits the earth; what is this known as?
5) Copper gets its name from what island country?
6) What disease was called the white plague in the 1700s due to the paleness of the patients and was commonly called consumption in the 1800s?
7) In physics, force multiplied by velocity gives you what?
8) The ability of litmus paper to change color when exposed to an acid or base is a result of it being infused with what organisms?
9) What periodic table element has the longest name?
10) The first telescope used for astronomy purposes by Galileo Galilei was what kind of telescope?
11) What is the division sign (short horizontal line with a dot above and below) in math called?
12) What part of the human body produces more than 90% of your serotonin, the neurotransmitter that contributes to feelings of well-being and happiness?
13) What European country has two elements on the periodic table named after it?
14) Magnetite, hematite, limonite, and siderite are the primary ores of what metal?
15) The atomic number for an element is determined by what?
16) When you read to yourself, your tongue and vocal cords still get movement signals from the brain in a process called what?
17) Why do human testicles hang outside the body?
18) Who developed the 1869 Periodic Law that forms the basis for the periodic table?
19) What are the three main types of galaxies?
20) Although it had been proposed in some form for over 50 years, the scientific community didn't agree on plate tectonics until what year?

Quiz 23 Answers

1) Farad - named after English physicist Michael Faraday
2) 25 - There are 1.55 x 10^{25} possible sequences for 25 cards; there are only about 10^{24} stars in the observable universe. A full deck of 52 cards has 8.07 x 10^{67} possible sequences.
3) Avogadro's law - developed by Amedeo Avogadro in 1811
4) Synchronous rotation or tidal locking
5) Cyprus - The name comes from the Latin word "cuprum," meaning

"from the island of Cyprus." In ancient Rome, most copper was mined in Cyprus.

6) Tuberculosis
7) Power
8) Lichens
9) Rutherfordium
10) Refractor
11) Obelus
12) Digestive tract
13) France - Francium (Fr) and gallium (Ga) are named for France; gallium comes from the Latin Gallia, the region we now know as France.
14) Iron
15) Number of protons in the atom's nucleus
16) Subvocal speech - It is characterized by minuscule movements in the larynx and other muscles involved in the articulation of speech; the movements are undetectable without the aid of machines.
17) Sperm dies at body temperature.
18) Dmitry Mendeleev
19) Elliptical, spiral, irregular
20) 1967

Quiz 24

1) Lettuce is a member of what plant family?
2) In humans, what prevents the stomach acids from dissolving the stomach?
3) Most members of the nightshade family that includes tomatoes, potatoes, eggplants, and green peppers contain small quantities of what stimulant?
4) What element is named after a U.S. state?
5) When you peel a banana, what are the strings that come off called?
6) If you are locked in a completely sealed room, what will kill you first?
7) What is the smallest cell in the human body?
8) What is the name of the process where a solid turns directly into a gas without passing through the liquid phase?
9) About 90% of the coal we burn today comes from what historical period before wood-eating bacteria evolved?
10) After going deaf, what method did Beethoven use to hear almost perfectly?
11) What is the better-known name for the poison prussic acid?

12) What Swedish scientist has a temperature scale named after him?
13) If a scuba diver suffers from the bends, what gas is being rapidly released from the blood and tissues?
14) How many muscles are in your fingers?
15) Galvanizing is the process of applying a protective coating of what metal to steel or iron to prevent rusting?
16) What element is named after the seventh planet from the sun?
17) What unit of measure is equal to about 5.88 trillion miles?
18) On what two planets in our solar system do scientists believe it rains diamonds?
19) What is the name for the second-lowest layer of the earth's atmosphere from about 7-31 miles altitude?
20) What is the largest living structure in the world?

Quiz 24 Answers

1) Sunflower
2) Mucus lining
3) Nicotine
4) Californium
5) Phloem bundles - They distribute nutrients up and down the banana as it grows.
6) Carbon dioxide poisoning - It will kill you before you die from lack of oxygen.
7) Male sperm
8) Sublimation
9) Carboniferous Period - This era from 359 to 299 million years ago is known as the Carboniferous Period because of the large amounts of coal formed during the time.
10) Bone conduction - He discovered that if he bit on a metal pole connected to the piano he was playing; he could hear almost perfectly. Vibrations are transferred into our bones, and our ears pick up the signal with no sound distortion, bypassing the eardrums.
11) Cyanide or hydrogen cyanide
12) Anders Celsius
13) Nitrogen
14) None - The muscles that bend the finger joints are in the palm and the mid-forearm and are connected to the finger bones by tendons that pull on and move the fingers.
15) Zinc

16) Uranium
17) Light year
18) Jupiter and Saturn - Lightning storms turn methane into soot that under pressure hardens into chunks of graphite and then diamond as it falls. The largest diamonds would likely be about a centimeter in diameter and would eventually melt in the hot planet core.
19) Stratosphere
20) Great Barrier Reef - Situated off the northeastern coast of Australia, it stretches for 1,429 miles and covers an area of approximately 133,000 square miles.

Quiz 25

1) Two angles that add up to 180 degrees are called what?
2) What century was the idea of the atom first introduced?
3) What is the only major nut tree indigenous to North America?
4) In terms of the number of atoms, what is the most abundant element in the human body?
5) What is the three-line symbol you typically find in the upper corner of a screen that you click or tap to get to a menu called?
6) Beriberi disease is caused by a deficiency of what vitamin?
7) In 2009, what famous scientist threw a champagne party for time travelers?
8) Albert Einstein's 1921 Nobel Prize in Physics wasn't for his work on relativity; what was if for?
9) What English scientist is credited with inventing the World Wide Web in 1989?
10) What is the most common radioactive element in the human body?
11) What is the term for the tendency of an object in motion to remain in motion, or an object at rest to remain at rest unless acted upon by a force?
12) The Julian calendar that was used before the current calendar had 365.25 days per year; to the nearest minute, how much longer was that than the actual year as measured by the time from one vernal equinox to the next?
13) If you average out the colors of all the different stars we can see, what color is the universe?
14) What is the second most abundant element in the earth's crust?
15) In humans, what is the only muscle not attached on both ends?
16) What NASA space flight was the last manned mission to the moon?
17) What is the largest herb plant?

18) What is the name for the third major layer of the earth's atmosphere from about 31-50 miles altitude?
19) What four planets in our solar system are Jovian planets?
20) What is the lightest metallic element?

Quiz 25 Answers

1) Supplementary
2) 5th century BC – Around 450 BC, the Greek philosopher Democritus introduced the idea of the atom as the point where matter could not be cut into still smaller pieces. Atom comes from the Greek word "atomos," meaning uncuttable.
3) Pecan - They have not been found growing naturally anywhere else in the world.
4) Hydrogen
5) Hamburger button - It looks like a hamburger.
6) B1 - thiamine
7) Stephen Hawking - He didn't put out invitations until after the party hypothesizing that if someone showed up it would be proof of time travel. No one came.
8) Photoelectric effect - He suggested for the first time that light is both a wave and a particle and established the existence of photons.
9) Tim Berners-Lee
10) Potassium-40 (K-40) - It makes up about 0.012% of the potassium found in nature, and we ingest it in foods containing potassium.
11) Inertia
12) 11 minutes - 11 minutes and 14 seconds to be more exact, one day every 128 years
13) Beige
14) Silicon - 27.7%
15) Tongue
16) *Apollo 17*
17) Banana - Some species grow up to 100 feet; it doesn't have a true woody trunk like a tree and behaves like a perennial.
18) Mesosphere
19) Jupiter, Saturn, Uranus, Neptune - The term is derived from Jupiter; planets are considered Jovian if they are like Jupiter.
20) Lithium - It floats in water.

Quiz 26

1) What two scientists discovered the double-helix structure of DNA in 1953?
2) What was the first planet discovered by telescope?
3) What science deals with the structure of the universe and its origin?
4) Morton's toe is what condition?
5) Who discovered that there is an increase (or decrease) in the frequency of sound, light, or other waves as the source and observer move toward (or away from) each other?
6) The commonly stated low end for human hearing is 20 hertz; what is the upper end?
7) Who discovered the law that the volume of a given mass of gas at a constant temperature is inversely proportional to its pressure?
8) In 1898, who created the first remote control that could control mechanical devices at a distance with radio waves?
9) What gas is the second most common in the earth's atmosphere?
10) What is the most abundant element in the earth's crust?
11) What standard international unit for measuring area is equal to 2.471 acres?
12) What is the most abundant element in Mar's atmosphere?
13) In the human body, what is the common name for the laryngeal prominence?
14) The asteroid belt is a region that contains most of the asteroids in our solar system; it is located between the orbits of what two planets?
15) What are the only two letters that don't appear in any official element names on the periodic table?
16) What element is named after the creator of dynamite?
17) What is the largest part of the human brain?
18) Fluorine, chlorine, bromine, and iodine belong to what group of elements?
19) What is the property called where two particles are inextricably linked together no matter their physical separation?
20) What is an atom or molecule with a net electric charge due to the loss or gain of one or more electrons called?

Quiz 26 Answers

1) James Watson and Francis Crick
2) Uranus - Sir William Herschel in 1781
3) Cosmology

4) Your second toe is longer than your big toe - It occurs in 10-20% of the population.
5) Christian Doppler - Doppler effect
6) 20,000 hertz
7) Robert Boyle - 17th century
8) Nikola Tesla - The first electronic television wasn't invented until 29 years later in 1927, and the first wireless television remote wasn't created until 1956.
9) Oxygen - about 21%
10) Oxygen - 46.6%
11) Hectare - It is equal to the area of a square with 100-meter sides (10,000 square meters).
12) Carbon dioxide - about 96%
13) Adam's apple - The thyroid cartilage that surrounds the larynx tends to protrude outward.
14) Mars and Jupiter
15) J and Q
16) Nobelium - named after Alfred Nobel
17) Cerebrum - It makes up about 85% of the brain's weight.
18) Halogens - They are reactive nonmetallic elements.
19) Quantum entanglement - Although entangled particles are not physically connected, they are still able to share information instantaneously, breaking the rule that no information can be transmitted faster than the speed of light.
20) Ion

Sports

Quiz 1

1) Who was the first woman to swim the English Channel?
2) How many disciplines are there in men's gymnastics?
3) Who has won the most heavyweight boxing title fights in history?
4) Who is the only starting pitcher in a World Series game to bat other than ninth?
5) What do Indianapolis 500 winners traditionally drink in the winner's circle?
6) What sport features a series of bouts known as a barrage?
7) Who was *Sports Illustrated's* first female sportsperson of the year?
8) How many players are there on a water polo team?
9) How many furlongs are there in a mile?
10) Famous pediatrician and author Benjamin Spock won an Olympic gold medal in what sport?
11) What was Mildred Didrikson Zaharias's nickname?
12) What title has been won by the rider who wears the polka dot jersey in the Tour de France?
13) Who was the first unseeded man to win Wimbledon?
14) Who was the last amateur tennis player to win the U.S. Open?
15) Cathy Rigby was the first woman to do what for *Sports Illustrated*?
16) Who is credited with inventing basketball?

17) What former Olympian lit the flame at the 1996 Atlanta Olympic games?
18) Who is the only Major League Baseball player to win MVP in both leagues?
19) Who is Edson Arantes do Nascimento better known as?
20) What sport are Torvill and Dean famous for?

Quiz 1 Answers

1) Gertrude Ederle – 1926
2) Six - vault, rings, floor, high bar, parallel bars, horse
3) Joe Louis
4) Babe Ruth
5) Milk
6) Fencing
7) Billie Jean King - 1972
8) Seven
9) Eight
10) Rowing
11) Babe – one of the greatest female athletes of all time
12) King of the Mountains
13) Boris Becker - 1985
14) Arthur Ashe – 1968
15) Pose nude
16) James Naismith
17) Muhammad Ali
18) Frank Robinson
19) Pele – Brazilian soccer player
20) Ice dancing

Quiz 2

1) The coldest NFL game in history was played where?
2) Who was the first tennis player to achieve the calendar year grand slam?
3) Who was the first thoroughbred horse to win 1 million dollars?
4) Over what distance is a human steeplechase run?
5) Who is the youngest man to win the Wimbledon tennis singles title?
6) Who is the only person to ever play in the Super Bowl and World Series?

7) What is the longest track and field race in the Olympics?
8) What is the first event in the decathlon?
9) What university originated the football huddle?
10) What sport is played 11 on a side on ice with a ball?
11) In a game of horseshoes, how many feet apart are the stakes?
12) What piece of sporting equipment has a maximum length of 42 inches and a maximum diameter of 2.61 inches?
13) Mintonette was the original name of what sport?
14) What is the fastest racquet sport?
15) What sport is played on the largest field?
16) What sports hero wore a cabbage leaf under his cap?
17) In cricket, how many runs are scored if the ball is hit over the boundary without bouncing?
18) What is the only sport where you can see teams defending goals of different sizes?
19) What outdoor game is won by "pegging out"?
20) Who was the first African American after Arthur Ashe to win a Wimbledon singles title?

Quiz 2 Answers

1) Green Bay – 1967 NFL championship
2) Don Budge – 1938
3) Citation – last Triple Crown winner before Secretariat
4) 3,000 meters
5) Boris Becker – 17
6) Deion Sanders
7) 50-kilometer walking race
8) 100 meters
9) Gallaudet University (school for the deaf) in 1892 - They huddled to avoid the other team seeing their sign language.
10) Bandy
11) 40 feet
12) Baseball bat
13) Volleyball
14) Badminton – The shuttlecock can travel over 200 mph.
15) Polo – 300 yards by 160 yards
16) Babe Ruth – He put chilled cabbage leaves under his cap to keep cool.
17) Six

18) Water polo – The goal at the deep end is smaller than the goal at the shallow end.
19) Croquet
20) Venus Williams

Quiz 3

1) Who was the second person to run a sub-four-minute mile?
2) In what year did Eddie the Eagle Edwards leap to stardom at the winter Olympics?
3) In which Olympics did Mark Spitz win seven gold medals?
4) Singer Johnny Mathis was a world-class athlete in what event?
5) The Emperors Cup is awarded in what sport?
6) What was the first U.S. hockey team to win the Stanley Cup?
7) Where is the world's largest bullfighting ring?
8) Who became the oldest rookie in Major League Baseball at age 42?
9) What Wimbledon singles champion had a part in a John Wayne film?
10) Who was the first Major League Baseball player to strike out 4,000 batters?
11) What was the last country to host both the summer and the winter Olympics in the same year?
12) How many throwing events are there in a decathlon?
13) Who is the oldest Olympic swimmer to win a medal?
14) What is the only sports team to play on all seven continents?
15) Who is the only person to win the tennis grand slam (win all four grand slam tournaments in a calendar year) twice?
16) What sport takes place in a 4.55-meter diameter circle?
17) What single sporting event has the most in-person spectators in the world?
18) How many stitches are on a regulation baseball?
19) The Greek god Apollo accidentally killed his friend Hyacinthus while practicing what sporting event?
20) In what year did the last Major League Baseball player bat .400?

Quiz 3 Answers

1) John Landy
2) 1988
3) 1972 – Munich
4) High jump – He was invited to the Olympic trials when he got a

recording contract; his major high jump competitor in the San Francisco Bay area where he grew up was future NBA Hall of Fame star Bill Russell.

5) Sumo wrestling
6) Seattle Metropolitans in 1917 - The Stanley Cup was first awarded in 1893.
7) Mexico City
8) Satchel Paige
9) Althea Gibson - *The Horse Soldiers*
10) Nolan Ryan
11) Germany – 1936
12) Three – discus, shot put, javelin
13) Dara Torres – 41
14) Harlem Globetrotters
15) Rod Laver
16) Sumo wrestling
17) Tour de France bicycle race - 12 to 15 million
18) 108
19) Discus
20) 1941 - Ted Williams

Quiz 4

1) Who was *Sports Illustrated's* first Sportsman of the Year in 1954?
2) How much does a U.S. athlete get for winning an Olympic gold medal?
3) What year were the first Winter Olympics held?
4) What year was the first Kentucky Derby run?
5) How many golf major championships did Jack Nicklaus win?
6) What two Major League Baseball teams share the record for most wins in a season at 116?
7) Where did curling originate?
8) What four horses have won the Triple Crown since Secretariat in 1973?
9) In what country did table tennis originate?
10) How many feet wide is a regulation NFL football field?
11) Who is the only NBA player to score 100 points in a game?
12) Horse racing's Triple Crown has only been won once in consecutive years; what years?
13) What country has won the most Winter Olympics medals?
14) Who was the last Major League Baseball pitcher to win 30 or more

games in a season?
15) What was Babe Ruth's first name?
16) What NFL team was originally called the Senors?
17) How many players are on the field at one time in a men's lacrosse game?
18) How many times have the Olympics been canceled?
19) What is the oldest championship in North American professional sports?
20) Who is the youngest woman to ever win a tennis grand slam singles title?

Quiz 4 Answers

1) Roger Bannister – first sub-four-minute mile
2) $25,000
3) 1924
4) 1875
5) 18
6) Chicago Cubs (1906 in a 154-game season) and Seattle Mariners (2001 in a 162-game season)
7) Scotland
8) Seattle Slew, Affirmed, American Pharoah, Justify
9) England – late 19th century
10) 160
11) Wilt Chamberlain
12) 1977 and 1978 – Seattle Slew and Affirmed
13) Norway
14) Denny McLain – 1968
15) George
16) Oakland Raiders – The original name was the winner of a name the team contest; it was changed to Raiders, the third-place name, after nine days.
17) 20
18) Three – 1916, 1940, 1944
19) Stanley Cup – 1893
20) Martina Hingis – 16 years 3 months

Quiz 5

1) What year were the first modern Olympics held?

2) Who has appeared on the most *Sports Illustrated* covers?
3) In what sport is the Iroquois Cup awarded?
4) Who is the only golfer to complete a calendar-year Grand Slam?
5) How many U.S. cities have hosted the Summer Olympics?
6) Who holds the Major League Baseball record for career strikeouts as a batter?
7) What year did the last undefeated team win the Super Bowl?
8) How many feet long is a regulation NBA basketball court?
9) What country has won the most soccer World Cups?
10) What is the largest population city in the United States that doesn't have an MLB, NFL, NBA, or NHL team?
11) How many feet wide is a regulation volleyball court?
12) How many Olympics have been hosted in Africa?
13) Who was the first American to win the Tour de France bicycle race?
14) What U.S. city was first to host the Olympics?
15) Who holds the NBA record for most career fouls?
16) Who was the first athlete on a Wheaties box?
17) Who was the first American to win the Olympic marathon gold medal?
18) What is the last event in the decathlon?
19) What hockey player has won the most Stanley Cups?
20) What year was the first Indianapolis 500 race?

Quiz 5 Answers

1) 1896 – Athens
2) Michael Jordan
3) Lacrosse
4) Bobby Jones – 1930
5) Three – St. Louis (1904), Los Angeles (1932, 1984), and Atlanta (1996)
6) Reggie Jackson
7) 1972 - Miami
8) 94 feet
9) Brazil
10) Austin, Texas – 11th largest city in the United States
11) 30 feet
12) Zero
13) Greg Lemond – 1986
14) St. Louis – 1904
15) Kareem Abdul-Jabbar

16) Lou Gehrig
17) Frank Shorter – 1972
18) 1500 meters
19) Henri Richard – 11 with the Montreal Canadiens
20) 1911

Quiz 6

1) What year did China make its first appearance in the Summer Olympics?
2) Who is the youngest player inducted to the Hockey Hall of Fame?
3) Of all the players in North American men's professional sports, who has won the most MVP awards?
4) How many games long was Joe DiMaggio's MLB consecutive hit streak record?
5) Who is the only NBA player to win MVP, defensive player of the year, and finals MVP in the same year?
6) According to NBA rules, how long does a player have to shoot a free throw after catching the ball?
7) In what country was the famous Rumble in the Jungle boxing match between Muhammad Ali and George Foreman fought?
8) Who is the only world heavyweight boxing champion to finish his career undefeated?
9) Based on participants, soccer is the most popular sport in the world; what is the second most popular sport?
10) Based on global following, soccer is the most popular sport in the world, what is the second most popular?
11) Who is the youngest ever world heavyweight boxing champion?
12) What were the first two women's sports included in the modern Olympics?
13) Who was the first Olympic boxing gold medalist to also win a boxing world championship?
14) What was the first U.S. college sport to name an All-American team?
15) In 1457, King James II of Scotland banned what two sports because they interfered with archery practice needed for national defense?
16) In horse racing, which of the Triple Crown races is the shortest?
17) At the ancient Olympic games, what did they use as archery targets?
18) In what sport did the word stymie originate?
19) What is the only country to have won medals in the Winter Olympics but never in the Summer Olympics?

20) Who is the only person to win the Heisman Trophy twice?

Quiz 6 Answers

1) 1984
2) Bobby Orr – 31
3) Wayne Gretzky – nine
4) 56
5) Hakeem Olajuwon
6) 10 seconds
7) Zaire
8) Rocky Marciano
9) Badminton – followed by field hockey
10) Cricket – followed by field hockey
11) Mike Tyson – 20
12) Tennis and golf - 1900
13) Floyd Patterson – 1952 Olympics and 1956 world champion
14) Football – 1889
15) Golf and soccer
16) Preakness – 1 3/16 miles
17) Tethered doves
18) Golf – Until 1952 when the rules were changed, balls had to remain in place, so you could be stymied by having another player's ball between your ball and the hole; you had to loft your ball over the other ball.
19) Liechtenstein
20) Archie Griffin – Ohio State in 1974 and 1975

Quiz 7

1) Who pitched the only no-hit game in World Series history?
2) In golf, what do you call a score of four under par on a single hole?
3) Who is the only coach to win both an NCAA Division I basketball championship and an NBA title?
4) What is the only U.S. city to win three of the four major professional sports championships in the same year?
5) Who won the most consecutive Wimbledon singles titles?
6) Who holds the record for most consecutive PGA tour wins?
7) What pitcher holds the Major League Baseball record for most no-hitters?
8) What athlete has appeared on the Wheaties box the most?

9) Who was the first non-American golfer to win the Masters?
10) How many feet wide is a regulation NBA court?
11) In inches, how tall are the hurdles in a men's 110-meter hurdle race?
12) Only three people have won individual gold medals in the same event in four consecutive Olympics, who are they?
13) What is the length of a tennis court in feet?
14) What sport was transferred from the Summer Olympics to the Winter Olympics in 1924?
15) What is the first city to host the Summer Olympics three times?
16) What famous American statesman earned an honorary induction into the International Swimming Hall of Fame?
17) Why did the Russian Olympic team arrive 12 days late for the 1908 London Olympics?
18) Who is the only person to be number one in the world in both table tennis and tennis?
19) What year was the first NFL game televised?
20) What horse has the most Grand National Steeplechase wins?

Quiz 7 Answers

1) Don Larsen – 1956
2) Condor – There have only been four verified; all were hole-in-ones on par-five holes.
3) Larry Brown – Kansas in 1988 and Detroit Pistons in 2004
4) Detroit – 1935, won NFL, NBA, and NHL
5) Martina Navratilova – six
6) Byron Nelson – 11 in 1945
7) Nolan Ryan – seven
8) Michael Jordan
9) Gary Player – 1961
10) 50 feet
11) 42 inches
12) Michael Phelps (swimming 200-meter individual medley), Carl Lewis (long jump), Al Oerter (discus)
13) 78 feet
14) Ice hockey
15) London – 1908, 1948, 2012
16) Benjamin Franklin – He had a lifelong love of swimming and invented some swim fins.
17) Russia was still using the Julian calendar instead of Gregorian.

18) Fred Perry – He won the 1929 world championship in table tennis and was the first player in tennis to win a career grand slam, including three straight Wimbledon titles from 1934-1936.
19) 1939
20) Red Rum – three

Quiz 8

1) Giacomo Agostini won 122 Grand Prix and 15 world titles in what sport?
2) What were table tennis balls originally made from?
3) Barring rain, what is the only track & field event where you get wet?
4) In what sport are you banned from playing left-handed?
5) What husband and wife both won gold medals at the 1952 Helsinki Summer Olympics?
6) Who was the first gymnast to score a perfect 10 in the Olympics?
7) In golf, what device is used to measure the speed of the greens?
8) What horse has the fastest times ever for the Kentucky Derby, Preakness, and Belmont?
9) Who broke the world record over 30 times in the pole vault?
10) What nine-time Olympic champion was known as the Flying Finn?
11) Who is the only coach to win both an NBA and WNBA title?
12) What is the oldest stroke in competitive swimming?
13) What city hosted the first winter Olympics in Asia?
14) What is the world's oldest golf course?
15) What is the highest elevation city to host the Summer Olympics?
16) What year did Roger Maris hit 61 home runs?
17) What is the only host country not to win a gold medal at its own summer Olympics?
18) Who was the first U.S. high school athlete to run a mile in under four minutes?
19) For racing purposes, what is the birthday of all horses in the Northern Hemisphere?
20) How high is a soccer goal?

Quiz 8 Answers

1) Motorcycle racing
2) Cork – from wine bottles
3) Steeplechase
4) Polo - If a left-handed and right-handed player went for the ball, they

would collide.

5) Emil and Dana Zatopek – both in track and field
6) Nadia Comaneci
7) Stimpmeter
8) Secretariat
9) Sergey Bubka
10) Paavo Nurmi
11) Paul Westhead – Los Angeles Lakers and Phoenix Mercury
12) Breaststroke
13) Sapporo, Japan - 1972
14) St. Andrews, Scotland
15) Mexico City
16) 1961
17) Canada – Montreal Olympics in 1976
18) Jim Ryun
19) January 1 – A horse born on December 31 is one year old on January 1.
20) Eight feet

Quiz 9

1) What is the theme song of the Harlem Globetrotters?
2) In what sport does a player use a cesta to hurl a pelota?
3) What two cities usually mark the endpoints of English Channel swims?
4) How many horses are there on a polo team?
5) What is the straightaway opposite the one with the finish line in horse racing called?
6) What is the captain of a curling team called?
7) What race was increased by 385 yards, so Edward VII could see the finish line better?
8) How many points is a ringer worth in horseshoes?
9) What U.S. city has hosted two winter Olympics?
10) How many cities have hosted the Olympics more than once?
11) What is the most common team name for U.S. college football teams?
12) Who was the only female athlete at the 1976 summer Olympics not given a sex test?
13) How many players are there on a cricket side?
14) What year was the first Super Bowl played?
15) In darts, what is the highest score possible with three darts?
16) What American speed skater won five gold medals at the 1980 winter

Olympics?
17) Who was forced to return his Olympic medals after it was learned he had played semi-pro baseball?
18) What sport features the fastest moving ball?
19) What is the diameter of a golf hole?
20) How wide is the home plate in baseball?

Quiz 9 Answers

1) Sweet Georgia Brown
2) Jai-alai
3) Calais and Dover
4) Four
5) Backstretch
6) Skip
7) Marathon at the 1908 London Olympics - 26 miles 385 yards became the standard distance thereafter.
8) Three
9) Lake Placid – 1932 and 1980
10) Seven – Athens, London, Paris, St. Moritz, Lake Placid, Los Angeles, Innsbruck
11) Eagles
12) Princess Anne
13) 11
14) 1967
15) 180 – 3 triple 20s
16) Eric Heiden
17) Jim Thorpe
18) Jai-alai – up to 188 mph
19) 4 ¼ inches
20) 17 inches

Quiz 10

1) Who first flopped to win the 1968 Olympic high jump gold medal?
2) What woman won the only gold medal for the United States at the 1968 winter Olympics?
3) What is the Olympic motto?
4) What did Abebe Bikila go without in winning the 1960 Olympic marathon?

5) What are the two categories of harness racing?
6) How many seconds must a cowboy stay aboard a rodeo bronc?
7) What is the only community-owned franchise in the NFL?
8) What movie Tarzan won the 400-meter freestyle swim in the 1932 Olympics?
9) What team won the inaugural 1950 NBA championship?
10) Who was the first African American to win the Wimbledon men's singles tennis title?
11) How many Major League Baseball teams are named for birds?
12) Who was disqualified for performance enhancing drugs after winning the men's 100 meters at the 1988 Olympic games?
13) What year did the last undefeated team win the NCAA Division I basketball championship?
14) Who held seven American track records from 2,000 to 10,000 meters when he died in a 1975 car crash?
15) What famous U.S. general placed fifth in the pentathlon at the 1912 Olympics?
16) What actor finished runner-up in the Le Mans 24-hour auto race?
17) What are the three weapons used in fencing?
18) The Borg-Warner Trophy is awarded for winning what?
19) Who is the only wild card entrant to win Wimbledon?
20) What is the only country that has played in every soccer World Cup tournament?

Quiz 10 Answers

1) Dick Fosbury – He invented the Fosbury flop that is now the standard for high jumpers.
2) Peggy Fleming
3) Faster, higher, stronger or citius, altius, fortius in Latin
4) Shoes – He ran barefoot.
5) Trotting and pacing
6) Eight
7) Green Bay Packers
8) Buster Crabbe
9) Minneapolis Lakers
10) Arthur Ashe
11) Three – Cardinals, Orioles, Blue Jays
12) Ben Johnson
13) 1976 - Indiana

14) Steve Prefontaine
15) George S. Patton
16) Paul Newman
17) Epee, foil, saber
18) Indianapolis 500
19) Goran Ivanišević – 2001
20) Brazil

Quiz 11

1) Who was the first American NHL player with 50 goals in a season?
2) What sport originated the term southpaw?
3) Who won gold medals in the 5000-meter, 10,000-meter, and marathon races in the 1952 Olympics despite never having run a marathon in competition before?
4) What was the first team to appear in four consecutive Super Bowls?
5) Who has held the MLB season RBI record since 1930?
6) While in college, Jim Brown was an All-American in what other sport besides football?
7) What male or female singles figure skater has won the most U.S. Championships?
8) What was the first NBA team to win 10 championships?
9) At what age did Wayne Gretzky become a professional?
10) Who was the first person to win four consecutive MLB Cy Young Awards?
11) What batter holds the MLB record for being walked the most times in a season?
12) Who holds the NFL career record for most extra points made?
13) Who holds the NBA record for most career free throws made?
14) What was the first team to win three consecutive cricket World Cups?
15) What were the only Olympics where distances were measured in yards?
16) Who has the most career NBA MVP awards?
17) What were golf balls originally made of?
18) What is the NHL record for career goals by a goalie?
19) Where did ice hockey originate?
20) Who was the first quarterback to win Super Bowl MVP without throwing a touchdown?

Quiz 11 Answers

1) Bobby Carpenter - 1984-85 Washington Capitals
2) Boxing - Left-handed fighters were said to use a southpaw stance; no one is quite sure why but hitting someone with a left came to be known as a southpaw punch.
3) Emil Zatopek - Czechoslovakia
4) Buffalo Bills – 1991 to 1994
5) Hack Wilson - 191 in 1930
6) Lacrosse - Syracuse University
7) Dick Button - seven consecutive from 1946-1952
8) Boston Celtics - 10th championship in 1967-68 season
9) 17
10) Gregg Maddux - 1992 to 1995
11) Barry Bonds - 232 in 2004
12) George Blanda - 943 from 1949-1975
13) Karl Malone - 9,787
14) Australia - 1999, 2003, 2007
15) 1904 St. Louis
16) Kareem Abdul-Jabbar - six
17) Wood - In the early 17th century, wood was replaced by a feather ball consisting of boiled feathers compressed inside a stitched leather cover.
18) Two - Ron Hextall and Martin Brodeur
19) United Kingdom - There are references to similar games being played on ice in England, Scotland, and Ireland going back 200 years before the first documented game in Canada.
20) Joe Namath - 1969

Quiz 12

1) What male alpine skier has the most World Cup race wins?
2) Who was the first baseball player to win the ESPY award for the best male athlete?
3) How many Olympic gold medals did Usain Bolt win in the 100 and 200-meter sprints and the 4 x 100-meter relay between 2008 and 2016?
4) What female alpine skier has the most World Cup downhill season titles?
5) Who was the first MLB player to hit 400 home runs and steal 400 bases?
6) Who was the first coach with four Super Bowl wins?

7) What player holds the record for most NHL career penalty minutes?
8) Who was the first MLB pitcher to strike out a side with nine pitches in both leagues?
9) What year did the last undefeated team win the NCAA Division I basketball championship?
10) Who was the first pitcher in MLB history to throw four no-hitters?
11) What NHL team set a record for most consecutive playoff appearances with 25 seasons from 1979-2004?
12) Who is the only person named a first-team high school All-American in football, basketball, and baseball?
13) What metal currently makes up 92.5% of an Olympic gold medal?
14) Where is the Olympic torch originally lit to start its relay to the host site?
15) Who was the last filly to win the Kentucky Derby?
16) How many horses have won racing's Triple Crown?
17) How many fillies have won the Kentucky Derby?
18) What is the longest period any sports trophy has been successfully defended?
19) Who was the first American woman to win three gold medals in a single Olympics?
20) Who was the last woman to win a calendar year tennis Grand Slam?

Quiz 12 Answers

1) Ingemar Stenmark (Sweden) - 86 wins from 1973-1989
2) Barry Bonds - 1994
3) Eight - He initially won all nine events over the three Olympics, but his 2008 4 x 100 gold was taken away due to a doping violation by a teammate.
4) Lindsey Vonn – United States
5) Barry Bonds - 1998
6) Chuck Noll - Pittsburgh Steelers (1975, 1976, 1979,1980)
7) David "Tiger" Williams - 3,971 minutes from 1974-1988
8) Nolan Ryan
9) 1976 - Indiana
10) Sandy Koufax – 1965
11) St. Louis Blues
12) Danny Ainge - He went to high school in Eugene, Oregon.
13) Silver
14) Temple of Hera in Olympia, Greece

15) Winning Colors - 1988
16) 13 - Sir Barton (1919), Gallant Fox (1930), Omaha (1935), War Admiral (1937), Whirlaway (1941), Count Fleet (1943), Assault (1946), Citation (1948), Secretariat (1973), Seattle Slew (1977), Affirmed (1978), American Pharoah (2015), Justify (2018).
17) Three - 1915, 1980, 1988
18) 132 years - America's Cup for sailing was held by the United States from its start in 1851 until Australia won in 1983.
19) Wilma Rudolph - track and field at the 1960 Rome Olympics
20) Steffi Graf - 1988

Quiz 13

1) Who was the first NFL rusher to run for 25 touchdowns in a season?
2) What year was hockey's Stanley Cup first awarded?
3) Who is the only person to win Olympic gold medals in both indoor and beach volleyball?
4) What Olympic sport allowed professionals for the first time in 2016?
5) Who has won the most track and field gold medals in a single Olympics?
6) What international incident prompted the 1980 Moscow Olympics boycott?
7) Who was the first track and field athlete to win four consecutive Olympic gold medals in the same event?
8) Who won the 2018 men's soccer World Cup?
9) In the post-1968 open era, who was the first woman to win a calendar year tennis Grand Slam?
10) Who is the only person to win gold medals in both the winter and summer Olympics?
11) What is the only year in men's or women's NCAA Division I basketball that two undefeated teams have met for the national championship?
12) Who is the first tennis player to win all four Grand Slam tournaments and an Olympic gold medal in tennis in the same calendar year?
13) With a minimum of 3,000 plate appearances, who are the only three MLB players ever with career batting averages over .350?
14) Who holds the NBA record for most seasons leading the league in points?
15) Which Olympics was the first where every participating country had at least one female athlete on their team?
16) The Olympic triathlon consists of a 40-kilometer bike ride, a 10-kilometer run, and how long of a swim?

17) Who was the first college player to be a three-time unanimous, consensus All-American?
18) What driver has the most consecutive NASCAR championships?
19) In 2000, what did the Cincinnati Reds do for the first time in MLB baseball's 162 game season history?
20) How many seasons did Wayne Gretzky win the Art Ross Trophy for leading the NHL in scoring?

Quiz 13 Answers

1) Emmitt Smith - 1995 Dallas Cowboys
2) 1893
3) Karch Kiraly (U.S.) - 1984 and 1988 indoor volleyball gold medals and 1996 beach volleyball gold
4) Boxing
5) Paavo Nurmi (Finland) - five golds in 1924 Paris games
6) Soviet Union's 1979 invasion of Afghanistan
7) Al Oerter - discus from 1956 to 1968
8) France
9) Margaret Court - 1970
10) Eddie Eagan (U.S.) - boxing (1920) and bobsled (1932)
11) 2014 women's tournament - Connecticut beat Notre Dame 79-58.
12) Steffi Graf - 1988
13) Ty Cobb (.366), Rogers Hornsby (.359), Shoeless Joe Jackson (.356)
14) Michael Jordan - 11
15) 2012 London - Saudi Arabia, Qatar, and Brunei sent female athletes for the first time.
16) 1.5 kilometer
17) Herschel Walker - 1980, 1981, 1982 for Georgia
18) Jimmie Johnson - five from 2006-2010
19) They went the entire season without being shutout.
20) 10

Quiz 14

1) Who was the first American woman to win the Olympic women's gymnastics all-around gold medal?
2) What player holds the record for most career points in the men's NCAA Division I basketball tournament?
3) Who was the first person to win a gold medal in three different

Olympics?
4) Who was the first African American Heisman Trophy winner?
5) Who was the first athlete to win the same Olympic running event three times?
6) What is the oldest college football bowl game?
7) Who has the second most career Olympic medals?
8) What bowler has the most career PBA wins?
9) What sport originated the term home run?
10) What is the oldest of horse racing's Triple Crown races?
11) Who was the first professional boxer to win world titles in three weight divisions?
12) What jockey rode Secretariat to his 1973 Triple Crown win?
13) Who was the first pitcher to win an MLB Cy Young Award in both leagues?
14) Who holds the NHL season points record for a defenseman?
15) Ski jumping and cross-country skiing are combined into what Olympic sport?
16) When Mark Spitz won seven swimming gold medals in a single Olympics, in how many of the events did he break the world record?
17) Who has the most career World Series home runs?
18) Who is the only male to win six consecutive Grand Slam singles tennis tournaments?
19) Who is the oldest player ever in an NFL game?
20) What is the only country to win a gold medal at every Summer Olympics?

Quiz 14 Answers

1) Mary Lou Retton - 1984 Los Angeles
2) Christian Laettner - 407 for Duke 1989-1992
3) Sonja Henie - figure skating in 1928, 1932, 1936
4) Ernie Davis - 1961 Syracuse University
5) Usain Bolt - 100 and 200-meter races in 2008, 2012, 2016
6) Rose Bowl - 1902
7) Larisa Latynina (Soviet Union) - 18 medals in gymnastics from 1956-1964
8) Walter Ray Williams Jr. - 47 wins
9) Cricket
10) Belmont Stakes – 1867
11) Bob Fitzsimmons - middleweight (1891), heavyweight (1897), light

heavyweight (1903)

12) Ron Turcotte
13) Gaylord Perry - 1978
14) Bobby Orr - 139 points (102 assists, 37 goals) for 1970-71 Boston Bruins
15) Nordic combined
16) Seven
17) Mickey Mantle - 18
18) Don Budge – 1937 Wimbledon to 1938 U.S. Championships
19) George Blanda - 48
20) Great Britain - Due to boycotts, only Great Britain, France, Australia, Greece, and Switzerland have participated in every Summer Olympics.

Quiz 15

1) Since Joe DiMaggio's record, who has the longest MLB consecutive game streak with at least one hit?
2) Who is the only American who has won an overall cross-country skiing World Cup championship?
3) What country hosted the first Winter Olympics?
4) What female alpine skier has the most overall World Cup titles?
5) At what age did Gordie Howe play his last professional hockey game?
6) What year were women first allowed to compete in the modern Olympics?
7) What golfer has the most PGA tour victories?
8) Who were the second pair of NFL teammates to each rush for 1,000 yards in the same season?
9) Who is the first NBA player ever to average a triple-double over a season twice?
10) Who was the first NHL player to score 100 points in six consecutive seasons?
11) What bowler has won the PBA Player of the Year the most times?
12) Who is the youngest male track and field Olympic gold medalist ever?
13) Who was the first NBA player with more than 3,000 steals?
14) Who was the first NFL player to have 1,000 yards rushing and 1,000 yards receiving in a season?
15) Who is the first driver to ever complete the Triple Crown of Motorsport consisting of winning the Indianapolis 500, 24 Hours of Le Mans, and the Monaco Grand Prix over a career?
16) How old was the youngest Olympic medalist ever in an individual event?

17) Who holds the NBA record for highest season points per game?
18) What woman golfer has the most career LPGA tour wins?
19) What year did Wilt Chamberlain score his 100 points in one NBA game?
20) What will be the first city to host both the summer and winter Olympics?

Quiz 15 Answers

1) Pete Rose - 44 in 1978
2) Bill Koch - 1981-82 season
3) France – Chamonix in 1924
4) Annmarie Moser-Proll (Austria) - six
5) 52
6) 1900
7) Sam Snead - 82 wins from 1936-1965
8) Franco Harris and Rocky Bleier - 1976 Pittsburgh Steelers
9) Russell Westbrook - Oklahoma City Thunder in 2016-17 and 2017-18
10) Bobby Orr - 1969 to 1975
11) Walter Ray Williams Jr. - seven times
12) Bob Mathias (U.S.) - He was 17 years old when he won the 1948 decathlon.
13) John Stockton
14) Roger Craig - 1985 San Francisco 49ers
15) Graham Hill (Great Britain) - 1963 Monaco Grand Prix, 1966 Indianapolis 500, 1972 Le Mans
16) 12 years old - 200-meter women's breaststroke swimming in 1936
17) Wilt Chamberlain - 50.4 ppg in 1961-62 season
18) Kathy Whitworth - 88
19) 1962
20) Beijing - 2008 summer and 2022 winter

Quiz 16

1) What two teammates finished one and two in the NHL scoring race five times?
2) What were the first Olympics held in Asia?
3) Who holds the NBA career record for assists?
4) Who was named MVP of the first Super Bowl in 1967?
5) Who held the MLB record for stolen bases in a season for 47 years?
6) What pitcher has the most career shutouts?

7) What NHL player was the first to win one of the major NHL trophies eight consecutive years?
8) If you include the Canadian Football League, who was the first professional quarterback with 70,000 career passing yards?
9) What Super Bowl-winning NFL head coach also won a NASCAR Cup Series championship as an owner?
10) What year did the first NFL indoor game take place?
11) Who was the first quarterback to lead his team to four Super Bowl titles?
12) Why was Brazil allowed to permanently keep the men's soccer World Cup trophy after their 1970 victory?
13) Who holds the NBA career record for highest rebounds per game average?
14) Who was the first person to swim 100 meters in under one minute?
15) Which NBA team set a record of 33 consecutive regular-season wins in the 1971-72 season?
16) Who won the 2014 men's field hockey World Cup?
17) What year was the famous "Battle of the Sexes" tennis match between Billie Jean King and Bobby Riggs?
18) Who was the first NFL quarterback to throw for 5,000 yards in a season?
19) At the time he retired, how many NHL records did Wayne Gretzky hold?
20) What year was the first Olympic athlete disqualified for drug use?

Quiz 16 Answers

1) Phil Esposito and Bobby Orr
2) Tokyo, Japan - 1964
3) John Stockton - 15,806
4) Bart Starr - Green Bay Packers
5) Ty Cobb – 96 set in 1915
6) Walter Johnson - 110
7) Bobby Orr - won eight Norris Trophies from 1968-1975
8) Warren Moon - 21, 228 yards in the CFL and 49,325 yards in the NFL
9) Joe Gibbs - 2000 NASCAR Cup
10) 1932 - With temperatures of 30 below in Chicago, the Bears played a game indoors against the Portsmouth Spartans in the Chicago Stadium, which was used mainly for horse shows; they played on a modified 80-yard field.
11) Terry Bradshaw - 1975, 1976, 1979, 1980

12) It was Brazil's third win. It was stipulated at the time the tournament was set up that any nation that won the trophy three times would be allowed to keep it permanently.
13) Wilt Chamberlain - 22.9 rebounds per game
14) Johnny Weissmuller - 58.6 seconds in the 100-meter freestyle in 1922
15) Los Angeles Lakers
16) Australia
17) 1973
18) Dan Marino - 1984 Miami Dolphins
19) 61
20) 1968 Mexico City - excessive alcohol

Quiz 17

1) What was the first Summer Olympics to be held entirely during the winter?
2) Who is the only person to hit an MLB home run and score an NFL touchdown in the same week?
3) With a minimum of 3,000 plate appearances, who has the highest MLB career batting average?
4) Who pitched in 1,252 MLB games over 24 years?
5) Who scored the winning goal for the United States in the "Miracle on Ice" hockey game against the Soviet Union in 1980?
6) Who was the first NHL player to use a slapshot?
7) Who was the first NHL goaltender to create and wear a practical mask?
8) The actor who played Jethro on television's *The Beverly Hillbillies* was the son of a famous athlete; who was his father?
9) How long was UCLA's NCAA record men's basketball consecutive game win streak that ended in 1974?
10) Who holds the NBA career record for most triple-doubles?
11) Who was the first person to ever play for 25 years in the NFL?
12) Who won the first women's soccer World Cup?
13) Who was the 20-year-old amateur American golfer who won the U.S. Open in 1913 and started a golf boom in the United States?
14) How many times in NHL history has a goalie been credited with scoring a goal against an opposing goalie (not an empty-net goal)?
15) In what event did Baron Pierre de Coubertin, founder of the modern Olympics, win a gold medal at the 1912 Olympic games?
16) Who is the only MLB player to hit two grand slams in one inning?
17) Who holds the NBA career record for most steals?

18) Who was the first NHL player to score 100 points in a season?
19) Frenchwoman Micheline Ostermeyer won the shot put and discus at the 1948 London Olympics. She also had a demanding day job; what was it?
20) How many times has the United States hosted either the Summer or Winter Olympics?

Quiz 17 Answers

1) Rio de Janeiro (2016) - The other two Summer Olympics in the Southern Hemisphere had taken place at least partly in the spring.
2) Deion Sanders - September 1989
3) Ty Cobb - .366 over 24 seasons
4) Jesse Orosco - He played from 1979-2003 for the Mets, Dodgers, Indians, Brewers, Orioles, Cardinals, Padres, Yankees, and Twins.
5) Mike Eruzione
6) Bernie Geoffrion - 1951
7) Jacques Plante - 1959
8) Max Baer Sr. - world heavyweight boxing champion in 1934
9) 88 games
10) Oscar Robertson – 181
11) George Blanda - He played from 1949-1975 taking off the 1959 season.
12) United States - 1991
13) Francis Ouimet
14) Once - On March 21, 2013, during a game between the New Jersey Devils and Carolina Hurricanes, a delayed penalty was called against New Jersey. Carolina goalie Dan Ellis headed for the bench for the extra attacker, but after he left the crease, the Hurricanes accidentally sent the puck the length of the ice back toward their empty net. Ellis tried to race back but was too late. Because Devils goalie Martin Brodeur had been the last to touch the puck, he was given credit for the goal, and because Ellis was on the ice when the puck went in, the goal went on his record.
15) Mixed literature - Art competition was introduced in 1912 and continued in the Olympics through 1948; Coubertin won for a poem.
16) Fernando Tatis - April 23, 1999
17) John Stockton - 3,265
18) Phil Esposito - 126 points (49 goals, 77 assists) for 1968-69 Boston Bruins
19) Concert pianist - She had never picked up a discus until a few weeks before winning the Olympic title; she also won bronze in the 80-meter

hurdles.

20) Eight (four summer, four winter) - 1904 St. Louis, 1932 Lake Placid, 1932 Los Angeles, 1960 Squaw Valley, 1980 Lake Placid, 1984 Los Angeles, 1996 Atlanta, 2002 Salt Lake City

Quiz 18

1) What are the only two countries that have won consecutive men's soccer World Cups?
2) What NCAA Division I school has the record for most consecutive national championships in any men's or women's sport?
3) Who was the first winner of the women's Olympic marathon?
4) When was the last time the Summer and Winter Olympics were held in the same year?
5) Who was the first player to hit 50 or more home runs in four consecutive seasons?
6) What country won the first men's rugby World Cup?
7) Who has won the most gymnastics gold medals at a single Olympics?
8) What golfer holds the record for most PGA tour wins in a season?
9) How many NHL teams did Wayne Gretzky play for?
10) Who is the youngest man to ever win a tennis Grand Slam singles title?
11) What is the only country to win a gold medal at every Winter Olympics?
12) Who was the first pitcher to have 3,000 career strikeouts?
13) Who was the first American driver to win the Formula One World Championship?
14) Who stunned Kentucky to win the NCAA Division I men's basketball championship in one of the greatest tournament upsets ever in 1966?
15) What sport originated the term hat trick?
16) What male alpine skier has the most overall World Cup titles?
17) What are the five events in an alpine skiing World Cup competition?
18) Who are the only two NBA players with more than 50 rebounds in a game?
19) In what was dubbed as "The Match of the Century," Seabiscuit defeated what 1937 Triple Crown winner in 1938?
20) What college has won the most NCAA Division I women's basketball titles?

Quiz 18 Answers

1) Italy (1934, 1938) and Brazil (1958, 1962)
2) Arkansas - 12 straight men's indoor track and field championships from 1984-1995
3) Joan Benoit - Los Angeles Olympics in 1984
4) 1992
5) Mark McGwire - 1996 to 1999
6) New Zealand - 1987
7) Vitaly Scherbo (Unified Team) - 6 golds in 1992 Barcelona games
8) Byron Nelson – 18 wins in 1945
9) Four - Edmonton, Los Angeles, St. Louis, New York Rangers
10) Michael Chang - 17 years, 110 days old when he won the 1989 French Open
11) United States
12) Walter Johnson - 1923
13) Phil Hill - 1961
14) Texas Western – It was the first all African American lineup to win a national championship.
15) Cricket - The term first appeared in 1858 in cricket when H. H. Stephenson took three wickets with three consecutive balls; fans held a collection for him and presented him with a hat bought with the proceeds.
16) Marcel Hirscher - Austria
17) Slalom, giant slalom, super giant slalom, downhill, and combined (downhill and slalom)
18) Bill Russell and Wilt Chamberlain
19) War Admiral
20) Connecticut

Quiz 19

1) What year was the first NFL night game?
2) What MLB pitcher has the career record for most wins?
3) The famous black power salute of Tommie Smith and John Carlos at the 1968 Mexico City Olympic games took place at the medal ceremony for what event?
4) What is the record for the fewest pitches ever for a complete MLB game?
5) What is the record for most gold medals won in a single Olympics?

6) Who are the only two females to win all four tennis Grand Slam singles tournaments during their career plus the Olympic singles gold medal?
7) What driver has won the most Formula One World Championships?
8) What country has won the most cricket World Cups?
9) How many NCAA Division I men's basketball teams have gone undefeated in winning the national championship?
10) Who is the only MLB player who has won an MVP with two different teams at two different positions?
11) What five disciplines make up the modern Olympic pentathlon?
12) What is the lowest score ever recorded for an 18-hole round in a women's LPGA tournament?
13) In the 1908 London Olympics, a team of eight London policemen beat a team of Liverpool policemen for the gold medal, and a third team of British policemen won the bronze in what sport that was discontinued in 1920?
14) Who was the first PGA golfer to shoot their age in a tournament round?
15) In which Winter Olympics team sport is pebbling part of the preparation?
16) Who is the only MLB player to hit a home run in every inning from the 1st to the 16th over their career?
17) Although no woman has completed a four or five major calendar Grand Slam in golf, one woman won all three majors that were contested in a calendar year; who was she?
18) Who has won the most Vezina Trophies as the NHL's best goaltender?
19) Who holds the NBA career record for most blocks?
20) Who has the highest NCAA Division I men's basketball career scoring average?

Quiz 19 Answers

1) 1929
2) Cy Young - 511
3) 200-meter sprint - Tommie Smith won the gold; John Carlos won the bronze.
4) 58 - Charles Barrett in 1944
5) Eight - Michael Phelps in swimming at the 2008 Beijing games
6) Steffi Graf and Serena Williams
7) Michael Schumacher (Germany) - seven from 1994-2004
8) Australia
9) Seven - San Francisco (1956), North Carolina (1957), UCLA (1964),

UCLA (1967), UCLA (1972), UCLA (1973), Indiana (1976)

10) Alex Rodriguez - Rangers at shortstop and Yankees at third base
11) Shooting, swimming, fencing, equestrian show jumping, and running
12) 59 - Annika Sorenstam in 2001
13) Tug of war - There was no limit on the number of teams a nation could enter, which resulted in the British sweep of the medals.
14) Sam Snead - He shot a 67 at the 1979 Quad Cities Open.
15) Curling - Pebbling the ice is done to create friction for the stone to curl; they sprinkle the ice with tiny water droplets that freeze on the surface to create a pebbled texture.
16) Willie Mays
17) Mildred "Babe" Didrikson Zaharias - 1950
18) Jacques Plante - seven in the 1950s and 1960s
19) Hakeem Olajuwon - 3,830
20) Pete Maravich - 44.2 ppg for LSU from 1967-1970

Quiz 20

1) What are the colors of the five rings on the Olympic flag?
2) How many male golfers have completed a double career Grand Slam by winning each of the four major championships at least twice?
3) From 1900 to 1908, Ray Ewry won eight track and field gold medals in what jumping events that were discontinued in 1912?
4) What country did the United States defeat in the men's hockey gold medal game in Lake Placid Olympics in 1980?
5) Who set a long jump world record at the 1968 Mexico City Olympics that would stand for 23 years?
6) What NHL player has the second most career regular season points?
7) What player has the most MLB World Series wins?
8) Who were first pair of NFL teammates to each rush for 1,000 yards in the same season?
9) What are the seven events in the women's track and field heptathlon?
10) What triple Olympic gold medalist had a daughter who became a princess?
11) The Army vs. Navy football game was the first time instant replay was used in any sports broadcast; what year was it?
12) Who has the MLB record for most runs scored in a season?
13) Who was the first woman to win gold medals in two different sports at the same Winter Olympics?
14) How long was the longest consecutive game win streak in U.S. high

school football?

15) Who was the first African American to win a Wimbledon singles title?
16) Who is the only MLB player to hit 60 or more home runs in a season three times?
17) At which Olympics did Jean-Claude Killy win three skiing gold medals?
18) What was the name of the terrorist group responsible for the violence at the 1972 Munich Olympics?
19) Who was the first NFL quarterback to complete 400 passes in a season?
20) How many basketball players have won NCAA, Olympic, and NBA championships?

Quiz 20 Answers

1) Blue, yellow, black, green, red
2) Two - Jack Nicklaus and Tiger Woods
3) Standing long jump, standing high jump, and standing triple jump - They were the same as today's events, but the athlete started in the standing position with no approach run.
4) Finland - They defeated the Soviet Union 4-3 in the semi-final "Miracle on Ice" game.
5) Bob Beamon (U.S.) - His jump of 29'2 ½" was more than 21 inches better than the prior world record.
6) Jaromir Jagr - 1,921 points
7) Yogi Berra - 10
8) Mercury Morris and Larry Csonka - 1972 Miami Dolphins
9) 100-meter hurdles, high jump, shot put, 200 meters, long jump, javelin, 800 meters
10) John B. Kelly Sr. - He won golds in the single and double sculls in 1920 Antwerp and gold in the double sculls in 1924 Paris and was the father of actress Grace Kelly, who became the Princess of Monaco.
11) 1963
12) Babe Ruth - 179 in 1921
13) Ester Ledecka (Czech Republic) - 2018 PyeongChang Olympics in skiing and snowboarding
14) 151 games - De La Salle Spartans from Concord, California from 1991-2004
15) Althea Gibson - 1957
16) Sammy Sosa - in 1998, 1999, 2001
17) 1968 - Grenoble, France
18) Black September

19) Warren Moon - 1991 Houston Oilers
20) Seven - Clyde Lovellette, Bill Russell, K.C. Jones, Jerry Lucas, Quinn Buckner, Michael Jordan, Magic Johnson

Quiz 21

1) What two athletes are tied for the most track and field career Olympic gold medals?
2) What year were the oldest recorded ancient Olympics?
3) What is the only jersey number retired league-wide by the NHL?
4) Who has the most career World Series RBIs?
5) Who was the first athlete to appear on the front of the Wheaties box?
6) How many times did Wayne Gretzky score 50 NHL goals in the first 50 games of the season?
7) In 1931, what female pitcher became the first woman in professional baseball to strike out Babe Ruth and Lou Gehrig in an exhibition game?
8) Who has the NFL career record for most fumbles?
9) Who was the first player in MLB history to steal 100 bases in a season?
10) The United States lost the men's basketball gold medal for the first time at what Olympics?
11) What was the first Olympics ever televised?
12) Who was the first NHL player with 500 career goals?
13) Ichiro Suzuki broke the MLB single-season hits record with 262 in 2004; whose 84-year-old record did he break?
14) Who did Miami beat to win the Super Bowl and retain their perfect undefeated season?
15) What was the first professional hockey team Wayne Gretzky played for?
16) Who is the only MLB player to ever hit a walk-off inside-the-park grand slam?
17) Who was the first goalie with 500 career wins?
18) How old was the youngest player in MLB history?
19) What hall of fame player won the MLB batting Triple Crown with only nine home runs?
20) Who was the first NFL player to score 200 career touchdowns?

Quiz 21 Answers

1) Paavo Nurmi (Finland) - 9 golds from 1920 to 1928 and Carl Lewis (U.S.) - 9 golds from 1984 to 1996
2) 776 BC
3) 99 - Wayne Gretzky

4) Mickey Mantle - 40
5) Bob Richards in 1958 - He was the 1952 and 1956 Olympic pole vault gold medalist.
6) Three - 1981-82, 1983-84, 1984-85
7) Jackie Mitchell - In an exhibition game between the New York Yankees and the Chattanooga Lookouts, a Class AA minor league team, she struck out Ruth and Gehrig in succession; she was 17 years old at the time. Baseball commissioner Kenesaw Mountain Landis banned women from the sport later that year.
8) Brett Favre - 166
9) Maury Wills – 104 steals in 1962
10) 1972 Munich
11) Berlin - 1936
12) Maurice Richard - 500th in 1957
13) George Sisler - 257 hits in 1920
14) Washington Redskins
15) Indianapolis Racers - He only played eight games with the Racers before being traded to the Edmonton Oilers.
16) Roberto Clemente - 1956
17) Patrick Roy
18) 15 - Joe Nuxhall for the 1944 Cincinnati Reds
19) Ty Cobb - 1909
20) Jerry Rice

Quiz 22

1) What Winter Olympics athlete has the most career medals?
2) Who was the first MLB pitcher to reach 20 wins in a season with only 1 loss?
3) Who was the first NBA player to score 20,000 career points?
4) What was the first country to win consecutive women's rugby World Cups?
5) Who won the 2015 cricket World Cup?
6) How many male golfers have held all four major championships at the same time?
7) Who is the career WNBA scoring leader?
8) Who was the second NHL player with 500 career goals?
9) Who was the first NFL quarterback with 6,000 career completions?
10) Who won the 2015 women's soccer World Cup?
11) Who was the first African American to be named Associated Press

female athlete of the year?

12) What is the only team that was part of the ABA for its entire nine years without ever moving or changing its name and joined the NBA and still has not moved or changed its name?
13) Who was the first player with 20,000 receiving yards in their NFL career?
14) Who were the first two NBA teammates to both score 2,000 points in a season?
15) What is the only Olympic sport that still bans professionals?
16) Who was the first NFL player to intercept 80 passes in their career?
17) What was the first U.S. men's professional sport to have female referees for regular season play?
18) What two players share the NBA career record for most consecutive seasons leading the league in points?
19) Who was the first MLB player to hit home runs in his teens and his forties?
20) What American has the most Winter Olympics medals?

Quiz 22 Answers

1) Marit Bjorgen (Norway) - 15 cross country skiing medals from 2002-2018
2) Roger Clemens – He finished the season 20-3 in 2001.
3) Bob Pettit - 1965
4) New Zealand - 1998 and 2002
5) Australia
6) Two - Bobby Jones and Tiger Woods
7) Diana Taurasi
8) Gordie Howe - 500th in 1962
9) Brett Favre - 2009 Minnesota Vikings
10) United States
11) Althea Gibson - tennis in 1957
12) Indiana Pacers
13) Jerry Rice - 2001 Oakland Raiders
14) Jerry West and Elgin Baylor - Los Angeles Lakers 1964-65 season
15) Wrestling
16) Paul Krause - Washington Redskins and Minnesota Vikings from 1964-1979
17) NBA - 1997
18) Wilt Chamberlain and Michael Jordan - seven

19) Ty Cobb - He played form 1905-1928 and started in MLB at age 18.
20) Apolo Anton Ohno - eight medals from 2002 to 2010 in short track speed skating

Quiz 23

1) What were the first Olympics held in the Southern Hemisphere?
2) What Pro Football Hall of Fame player once led the NFL in passing, interceptions, and punting in the same season?
3) What team won the first college football BCS Championship?
4) Who was the first African American to play Major League Baseball?
5) Who is the oldest golfer to win a PGA tour event?
6) In what country did volleyball originate?
7) Who was the first freshman to win the Heisman Trophy?
8) Who was the first person to win the Olympic marathon twice in a row?
9) Who were the first NFL quarterback and running back teammates to each rush for 1,000 yards in the same season?
10) What is the record for the most Olympic games anyone has ever competed in?
11) Who has the highest season batting average ever for a starting pitcher?
12) What was the first team sport added to the Olympics?
13) What Olympics were the first to feature active NBA players on the U.S. team?
14) Who has the most career MLB batting titles?
15) Who holds the record with seven MLB MVP Awards?
16) What is the name of the biennial men's golf competition between teams from Europe and the United States?
17) What MLB player has the highest career on-base percentage?
18) Who won the 2018 women's field hockey World Cup?
19) What boxer won world titles in the largest number of weight divisions?
20) What 10 events make up the decathlon?

Quiz 23 Answers

1) Melbourne, Australia - 1956
2) Sammy Baugh - 1943 Washington Redskins
3) University of Tennessee - 1998
4) Moses Fleetwood Walker - On May 1, 1884, he became the first African American in the major leagues; he played 42 games for the Toledo Blue Stockings before suffering an injury and returning to the minor

leagues. This was 63 years before Jackie Robinson's major league debut.

5) Sam Snead - He was 52 years old when he won the 1965 Greater Greensboro Open.
6) United States
7) Johnny Manziel - 2012
8) Abebe Bikila - 1960 and 1964
9) Michael Vick and Warrick Dunn - 2006 Atlanta Falcons
10) 10 - A Canadian equestrian rider competed in every Olympics from 1972 to 2012 except the boycotted 1980 games; he won a silver medal in 2008.
11) Walter Johnson - .433 in 1925
12) Soccer - 1900
13) 1992 - Barcelona
14) Ty Cobb - 11
15) Barry Bonds
16) Ryder Cup - established in 1927
17) Ted Williams - .482
18) Netherlands
19) Manny Pacquiao - eight divisions: flyweight, super bantamweight, featherweight, super featherweight, lightweight, light welterweight, welterweight, super welterweight
20) 100, 400, and 1500-meter runs, 110 hurdles, long jump, high jump, pole vault, shot put, discus, javelin

Quiz 24

1) Who is the youngest jockey ever to win horse racing's Triple Crown?
2) Who duplicated Jesse Owens' feat by winning four track and field Olympic gold medals in 1984?
3) Who is the first world boxing champion to hold a PhD degree?
4) Who has the most career World Series hits?
5) What was the first sport to be filmed?
6) Who was the first NFL running back to rush for 100 career touchdowns?
7) Who was the first woman to repeat as Olympic champion in the heptathlon?
8) What was the first country to win two consecutive men's rugby World Cups?
9) How many times did Babe Ruth hit four MLB home runs in one game?
10) What was the first city to host the modern Olympics twice?
11) Since Ted Williams' .406 season in 1941, what MLB player has had the

highest season batting average?

12) In the post-1920 era, who has the most consecutive MLB batting titles leading both leagues?
13) Since the start of the Winter Olympics, how many athletes have won medals at both the winter and summer games?
14) How many players have won more than one MLB batting Triple Crown?
15) Who is the only person to have both a reception and an interception in the Super Bowl?
16) In 1930, who won the first Sullivan Award given to the most outstanding U.S. amateur athlete?
17) What team has the most consecutive NBA championships?
18) What is the name of the biennial women's golf competition between teams from Europe and the United States?
19) Who hit a home run from both sides of the plate in the same game 10 times over their MLB career?
20) What year were professionals allowed to compete in the Olympics?

Quiz 24 Answers

1) Steve Cauthen - He was 18 years old when he won the Triple Crown aboard Affirmed in 1978.
2) Carl Lewis – He won the 100, 200, 4 x 100, and long jump
3) Vitali Klitschko - He was a three-time world heavyweight champion starting in 1999 and ending in 2013 and got his PhD in sports science in 2000. He also served as mayor of Kyiv and in the Ukrainian parliament.
4) Yogi Berra - 71
5) Boxing - 1894
6) Jim Brown - Cleveland Browns from 1957-1965
7) Jackie Joyner-Kersee (U.S.) - 1988 Seoul and 1992 Barcelona
8) New Zealand - 2011 and 2015
9) 0
10) Paris – 1900 and 1924
11) Tony Gwynn - .394 with San Diego in 1994
12) Rod Carew - three from 1973-1975
13) Five - Eddie Eagan (U.S.), Jacob Tullin Thams (Norway), Christa Luding-Rothenburger (East Germany), Clara Hughes (Canada), Lauryn Williams (U.S.)
14) Two - Rogers Hornsby and Ted Williams each won two.
15) Deion Sanders – He had an interception in Super Bowl XXIX and a reception in Super Bowl XXX.

16) Bobby Jones - golf
17) Boston Celtics - eight from 1959-1966
18) Solheim Cup – started in 1990
19) Mickey Mantle
20) 1984

Quiz 25

1) Among countries that have won at least one Olympic medal, what country has the lowest number of medals per capita?
2) Who won the 2017 women's rugby World Cup?
3) Who was the first player in the WNBA to dunk?
4) What is the maximum number of dogs a musher can have on their team at the start of the Iditarod Trail Sled Dog Race?
5) Who was the first athlete to win gold medals in five consecutive Olympics?
6) Who is the first person to win a medal in six straight Summer Olympics?
7) What is the name of one of the oldest trophies in college football contested between Minnesota and Michigan?
8) Who was the oldest player to lead the NBA in scoring?
9) What player won 11 NBA championships and 5 MVP awards?
10) What was the first MLB franchise to move to three different states during their history?
11) What MLB pitcher has the most career losses?
12) Professional bowler Walter Ray Williams Jr. is also a nine-time world champion in what other sport?
13) Who was the first woman to have her name engraved on the Stanley Cup?
14) Who was the first NBA player to average a triple-double for a season?
15) Who was the first NFL punter to average over 50 yards a punt for a season?
16) Who was the second NFL player ever to have 1,000 yards rushing and 1,000 yards receiving in a season?
17) What is the world's oldest tennis tournament?
18) What woman golfer has the most career LPGA Majors wins?
19) To allow visitors to travel safely to Olympia, what was put in place before and during each of the ancient Olympic games?
20) Who was the second NBA player ever to average a triple-double over a season?

Quiz 25 Answers

1) India
2) New Zealand
3) Lisa Leslie - 2002
4) 16
5) Steven Redgrave – British rower from 1984-2000
6) Kim Rhode - U.S. skeet shooter from 1996-2016
7) Little Brown Jug – started in 1892
8) Michael Jordan - 35
9) Bill Russell
10) Baltimore Orioles - formerly Milwaukee Brewers (1901), St. Louis Browns (1902), and then Baltimore Orioles (1954)
11) Cy Young – 316 losses
12) Horseshoes
13) Marguerite Norris - In 1952, she became the first female chief executive in NHL history after inheriting the Detroit Red Wings presidency from her father. In 1954, the Red Wings defeated the Montreal Canadiens, making her the first woman to have her name engraved on the Stanley Cup.
14) Oscar Robertson - 30.8 points, 12.5 rebounds, and 11.4 assists in 1961-62
15) Sammy Baugh – He had 51.4 yards per punt for the 1940 Washington Redskins while also playing quarterback.
16) Marshall Faulk - 1999 St. Louis Rams
17) Wimbledon - 1877
18) Patty Berg - 15 from 1937-1958
19) A truce or ekecheiria - Wars were suspended; legal disputes were put on hold, and no death penalties were carried out during this time.
20) Russell Westbrook - Oklahoma City Thunder in 2016-17

Quiz 26

1) Who is the first player ever in both the Pro Football Hall of Fame and the Canadian Football Hall of Fame?
2) Who is the only six-time winner (male or female) of the Associated Press Athlete of the year?
3) In one Olympics, what is the largest number of different sports a single competitor has won medals in?
4) What country won the first women's rugby World Cup?

5) According to USGA rules, how many clubs can a golfer have in their bag?
6) Who was the first woman to win the Sullivan Award given annually to the most outstanding U.S. amateur athlete?
7) Lacrosse was invented in what country?
8) How old was the oldest Summer Olympics medalist?
9) What is the New Zealand rugby team called?
10) In any NCAA division, what is the record for most consecutive team national championships in any men's or women's sport?
11) Who was the first MLB player to hit 500 home runs and steal 500 bases?
12) Who holds the NBA career record for most minutes played?
13) Who is the only male diver to ever sweep the diving events at consecutive Olympic games?
14) Who was the first person to repeat as the Olympic decathlon gold medalist?
15) Who is the only MLB pitcher with three Triple Crowns leading both leagues?
16) What two MLB players hold the record for playing the most consecutive seasons with the same team?
17) In 1965, Satchell Paige pitched three innings for the Kansas City Athletics against the Boston Red Sox; how old was Paige?
18) Who has the most Stanley Cup wins combined as player and non-player?
19) Who was the first MLB player to steal 1,000 bases?
20) What father and son drivers were both Formula One World Champions?

Quiz 26 Answers

1) Warren Moon
2) Babe Didrikson Zaharias - 1932, 1945, 1946, 1947, 1950, 1954
3) Three – American Frank Kugler won medals in freestyle wrestling, weightlifting, and tug of war in the 1904 St. Louis games.
4) United States - 1991
5) 14
6) Ann Curtis - 1944 for swimming
7) United States - Native Americans invented the game.
8) 72 - shooting in 1920
9) All Blacks
10) 31 years - Kenyon College in Division III men's swimming and diving

from 1980-2010

11) Barry Bonds - 2003
12) Kareem Abdul-Jabbar - 57,446 minutes
13) Greg Louganis - 1984 Los Angeles and 1988 Seoul
14) Bob Mathias (U.S.) - 1948 and 1952
15) Sandy Koufax - 1963, 1965, 1966
16) Brooks Robinson (Baltimore Orioles) and Carl Yastrzemski (Boston Red Sox) - 23 seasons
17) 59
18) Jean Beliveau - 17 wins with 10 as player and 7 as non-player with the Montreal Canadiens
19) Rickey Henderson
20) Graham and Damon Hill - Graham in 1962 and 1968 and son Damon in 1996

Quiz 27

1) In the 22 seasons between 1980-81 and 2001-02, three NHL players won 21 of the 22 Art Ross Trophies for scoring; who were they?
2) Who was the lone college player on the 1992 Olympic basketball Dream Team?
3) In what two Olympic sports do men and women compete head to head?
4) Who was the first person to win the *Sports Illustrated* Sportsperson of the Year twice?
5) What are the only two days during the year where there are no MLB, NFL, NHL, or NBA games played?
6) Who was the first NCAA Division I football player to rush for 2,000 yards in a season?
7) Who was the only Olympic medalist to also win a Nobel Prize?
8) Who was the first NFL quarterback to throw 3,000 completions?
9) Who is the only person to win six consecutive tennis Grand Slam singles tournaments and not complete a calendar-year Grand Slam?
10) Who holds the NBA career record for highest points per game?
11) In 1935, what athlete set world records in three different events in 45 minutes?
12) What two teams played in the first college football game?
13) Who was head of the committee that organized the opening day ceremonies for the 1960 Squaw Valley Winter Olympics?
14) What NASCAR driver has the most career victories?
15) Who was the first president of the NFL?

16) Who was the first tennis player ever expelled from a Grand Slam tournament?
17) What year did Roger Bannister run the first sub-four-minute mile?
18) What Australian was the first woman to swim the 100-meter freestyle in under one minute in the Olympics?
19) Who is the only pitcher in MLB history to throw consecutive no-hitters?
20) Who was the first NBA player drafted number one who never played U.S. high school or college basketball?

Quiz 27 Answers

1) Wayne Gretzky (10 times), Jaromir Jagr (5 times), Mario Lemieux (6 times)
2) Christian Laettner
3) Equestrian and sailing
4) Tiger Woods - 1996 and 2000
5) The Monday before and the Wednesday after the MLB All-Star Game - The All-Star Game is always played on a Tuesday in July, and there are no MLB games the day before or after, and MLB is the only professional sport played in July.
6) Marcus Allen - 1981 USC
7) Philip Noel-Baker (Great Britain) - He won a silver medal in the 1500-meter run in 1920 and the Nobel Peace Prize in 1959.
8) Fran Tarkenton - 1976 Minnesota Vikings
9) Martina Navratilova – 1983 Wimbledon to 1984 U.S. Open
10) Michael Jordan - 30.1 ppg
11) Jesse Owens - At a Big Ten track and field meet, he set world records in the long jump, 220-yard sprint, and 220-yard low hurdles and tied the world record for the 100-yard dash.
12) Rutgers and Princeton - In 1869, Rutgers beat Princeton 6-4 in a game that had 25 players on each side and one-point touchdowns; the first team to reach six points was declared the winner.
13) Walt Disney
14) Richard Petty – 200 wins
15) Jim Thorpe
16) John McEnroe - 1990 Australian Open
17) 1954
18) Dawn Fraser - 1964 Tokyo
19) Johnny Vander Meer - 1938 Cincinnati Reds

20) Yao Ming

Quiz 28

1) What famous philosopher was a two-time winner at the ancient Olympics?
2) How many events were there in the first ancient Olympics?
3) Who is the only NBA player with 40 points and 40 rebounds in a game?
4) How many times have the Winter and Summer Olympics been held in the same country in the same year?
5) Who was the first woman to appear in an NHL game?
6) Who was the first NHL player to score 50 goals in a season?
7) Who won the 2015 men's rugby World Cup?
8) What NHL player has the second most career regular-season goals?
9) Who was the first NFL player to score 2,000 points?
10) What country won the first men's soccer World Cup?
11) Who was the first NHL player with 100 assists in a season?
12) Who was the first MLB player with 3,000 hits and 500 home runs in their career?
13) In 1994, Pete Rose broke the MLB most games played record; whose record did he break?
14) Who was the first player to lead the NBA in scoring and assists in the same season?
15) Who was the lightest boxer to ever hold the world heavyweight title?
16) What college was the first to have seven Heisman Trophy winners?
17) Why are MLB umpires required to wear black underwear?
18) What MLB pitcher led his league the most times in strikeouts?
19) Who was the first non-Canadian player to have a 100-point NHL season?
20) Who was the first NBA player to get a quadruple-double in a game?

Quiz 28 Answers

1) Plato - He won in pankration, which was a submission sport combining elements of wrestling and boxing but with very few rules; only eye-gouging and biting were banned.
2) One - a foot race
3) Wilt Chamberlain - 1968
4) Three - 1924 Paris and Chamonix, 1932 Los Angeles and Lake Placid, 1936 Berlin and Garmisch-Partenkirchen

5) Manon Rheaume - She goaltended for the Tampa Bay Lightning in a pre-season game against the St. Louis Blues in September 1992.
6) Maurice Richard
7) New Zealand
8) Gordie Howe - 801 goals
9) George Blanda
10) Uruguay – 1930
11) Bobby Orr - 1970-71 Boston Bruins
12) Willie Mays - 1970
13) Carl Yastrzemski
14) Nate Archibald - 34 ppg and 11.4 assists per game in 1971-72
15) Bob Fitzsimmons - 167 pounds when he won the title in 1897
16) Notre Dame - Angelo Bertelli, John Lujack, Leon Hart, John Lattner, Paul Hornung, John Huarte, Tim Brown
17) In case their pants split
18) Walter Johnson - 12 times
19) Kent Nilsson (Sweden) - 131 points for 1980-81 Calgary Flames
20) Nate Thurmond - 1974

Quiz 29

1) Who holds the career record for most NBA games played?
2) Who was the first female jockey to win a Triple Crown race?
3) What NHL player never missed a regular-season game in his career and holds the record for most consecutive games played at 964?
4) Who is the only person named Associated Press athlete of the year in two different sports?
5) In addition to his Olympic swimming medals, Johnny Weissmuller won an Olympic medal in what other sport?
6) Who has the highest MLB career slugging percentage?
7) Who holds the MLB record reaching base in 84 consecutive games?
8) In which three Olympic games were there boycotts by various teams?
9) What was the first Olympics televised in the United States?
10) Who was the last person to win an MLB batting Triple Crown?
11) What is the lowest score ever recorded for an 18-hole round of golf in a PGA tournament?
12) In the ancient Olympics, women weren't allowed to participate or even be in the stadium, but they could still win the Olympic prize in what event?
13) Who was the first NFL quarterback with 70,000 career passing yards?

14) Who was the first American born NHL player to score 100 points in a season?
15) Who was the last man to win a calendar year tennis Grand Slam?
16) Who has the most career regular-season points for an NHL defenseman?
17) What college has won the most consecutive NCAA Division I women's basketball titles?
18) What coach leads the NFL in career wins?
19) What player has been named to the most MLB All-Star rosters?
20) In 1932, what athlete won the team championship single-handedly at the AAU national track and field meet?

Quiz 29 Answers

1) Robert Parish - 1,611 games
2) Julie Krone - 1993 Belmont Stakes aboard Colonial Affair
3) Doug Jarvis - played from 1975-1987
4) Babe Didrikson Zaharias - track and field in 1932; golf in 1945, 1946, 1947, 1950, 1954
5) Water polo - bronze in 1924
6) Babe Ruth - .690
7) Ted Williams - 1949
8) 1976 Montreal in protest of a New Zealand rugby tour of South Africa, 1980 Moscow in protest of the Soviet Union's invasion of Afghanistan, and 1984 Los Angeles where the Soviet Union withdrew in retaliation for the 1980 boycott
9) 1960 Squaw Valley Winter Olympics
10) Miguel Cabrera – 2012
11) 58 - Jim Furyk in 2016
12) Chariot racing - The prize went to the owner of the chariot and horse, so women could and did win the prize.
13) Brett Favre - 2010 Minnesota Vikings
14) Neal Broten - 105 points with the 1985-86 Minnesota North Stars
15) Rod Laver - 1969
16) Ray Bourque - 1,579 points
17) Connecticut - four consecutive from 2013-2016
18) Don Shula - 347 with Baltimore Colts and Miami Dolphins
19) Hank Aaron - 21 times
20) Mildred "Babe" Didrikson Zaharias - She competed in 8 out of 10 events; she won 5 and tied for first in a sixth event. She won the team

championship despite being the only member of her team.

Quiz 30

1) What country has won the most Summer Olympics medals?
2) What was the first country to win two consecutive women's soccer World Cups?
3) What was the first Olympics to include competitors from all six continents?
4) Who is the only driver to win five consecutive Formula One World Championships?
5) Who was the first American born NHL player to reach 500 career goals?
6) What MLB player has won the most Gold Glove Awards?
7) At the first modern Olympics, what was awarded to winners?
8) Who was the first female to win individual gold medals at four consecutive Olympics?
9) Who holds the NBA career record for most seasons leading the league in rebounds?
10) Who holds the NBA career record for most points?
11) What was the first U.S. city to host the Olympics twice?
12) What woman won three gold medals in the 100-meters, 200-meters, and 4 x 100-meter relay in the 1988 Seoul Olympic games?
13) How many NFL players have at least 10,000 yards rushing and 5,000 yards receiving in their career?
14) What player appears as the silhouette on the NBA's official logo?
15) What is the largest margin of victory in a college football game?
16) What year was the first America's Cup sailing competition?
17) What male athlete has the most career Winter Olympic medals?
18) What was the last all-Canadian-born team to win the Stanley Cup?
19) What MLB player has the career record for the most total bases?
20) Who holds the NBA record for the fewest games needed to reach 20,000 points?

Quiz 30 Answers

1) United States
2) Germany - 2003 and 2007
3) Stockholm - 1912
4) Michael Schumacher (Germany) - 2000 to 2004
5) Joey Mullen - 500th in 1997

6) Gregg Maddux - 18
7) Silver medal - Second place received bronze medals.
8) Kaori Icho - Japanese wrestler from 2004 to 2016
9) Wilt Chamberlain - 11
10) Kareem Abdul-Jabbar - 38,387
11) Lake Placid – 1932 and 1980
12) Florence Griffith Joyner – U.S.
13) Three - Marshall Faulk, Marcus Allen, Tiki Barber
14) Jerry West
15) 222 points - Georgia Tech beat Cumberland College 222-0 in 1916.
16) 1851 - It was originally called the 100 Guinea Cup but was renamed the America's Cup after the boat *America* won the first competition.
17) Ole Einar Bjorndalen (Norway) - 13 biathlon medals from 1998-2014
18) 1974-75 Philadelphia Flyers
19) Hank Aaron - 6,856 bases
20) Wilt Chamberlain - 499 games

Television

Quiz 1

1) In the sitcom *Married with Children*, what is the dog's name?
2) The Daleks from *Doctor Who* come from what planet?
3) In *Star Trek*, what is the name of Spock's father?
4) What is the name of the train on *Petticoat Junction*?
5) What famous bird first appeared on television in September 1957?
6) What is the name of the family featured in *Father Knows Best*?
7) Bamboo Harvester was the real name of the actor who played what character?
8) What was the first animated series to run in U.S. prime time?
9) What are the character first names of the original *Charlie's Angels*?
10) What is the name of the company that the *Taxi* characters work for?
11) What was the Lone Ranger's real name?
12) What show featured the first interracial kiss broadcast in the United States?
13) On *The X-Files*, what is Mulder's nickname?
14) What is the name of George of the Jungle's pet elephant?
15) Who lives at 0001 Cemetery Lane?
16) What is Batman's butler Alfred's last name?
17) What is the name of Dudley Do-Right's horse?

18) What actress played Emma Peel in *The Avengers*?
19) What planet is the space alien Alf from?
20) What 1980s sitcom featured Tom Hanks in drag?

Quiz 1 Answers

1) Buck
2) Skaro
3) Sarek
4) Cannonball
5) NBC peacock
6) Anderson
7) Mr. Ed
8) *The Flintstones* – 1960
9) Sabrina, Kelly, Jill
10) Sunshine Cab
11) John Reid
12) *Star Trek*
13) Spooky
14) Shep
15) *Addams Family*
16) Pennyworth
17) Horse
18) Diana Rigg
19) Melmac
20) *Bosom Buddies*

Quiz 2

1) On *Leave It to Beaver*, what is Wally's best friend's name?
2) At the end of *M*A*S*H*, what character stayed in Korea?
3) Who became a genius whenever he put on the fabulous Kerwood Derby?
4) What cartoon character's catchphrase is "Exit, stage left!"?
5) What character did Patrick Macnee portray in *The Avengers*?
6) What is the name of Mulder and Scully's supervisor on *The X-Files*?
7) Who played Dr. McCoy in the original *Star Trek* series?
8) The Great Gazoo is an alien in what cartoon series?
9) What century is the setting for *Star Trek*?
10) Where did Rocky and Bullwinkle play college football?

11) Who provided the voices of Bugs Bunny, Sylvester, and Tweety Pie?
12) Wile E. Coyote gets all his traps to try to catch the Roadrunner from what company?
13) What show has the catchphrase "And now for something completely different"?
14) Who played detective Frank Cannon?
15) On *The Beverly Hillbillies*, what is the name of the bank manager?
16) What was the first 90-minute U.S. series in 1962?
17) What sitcom character liked to eat cats?
18) What cartoon character's vital statistics are 19-19-19?
19) *Glee* is set at what high school?
20) On *Kung Fu*, what is Master Po's name for young Cain?

Quiz 2 Answers

1) Eddie Haskell
2) Maxwell Klinger
3) Bullwinkle Moose
4) Snagglepuss
5) Jonathan Steed
6) Walter Skinner
7) DeForest Kelley
8) *The Flintstones*
9) 23rd century
10) Wossamotta U
11) Mel Blanc
12) Acme
13) *Monty Python's Flying Circus*
14) William Conrad
15) Milburn Drysdale
16) *The Virginian*
17) Alf
18) Olive Oyl
19) William McKinley
20) Grasshopper

Quiz 3

1) What cartoon character was originally called Egghead?

2) What is the name of Barbara Stanwyck's character on *The Big Valley*?
3) In 1994, what show broke ground depicting a gay marriage between innkeepers Ron and Erick?
4) What is the name of the ranger who is always after Yogi Bear?
5) What is the last name of the family in *Lost in Space*?
6) What prop was used as Dr. McCoy's medical scanner in *Star Trek*?
7) On *The Flintstones*, what fraternal order do Fred and Barney belong to?
8) What is Lucy's maiden name on *I Love Lucy*?
9) The maiden names of what two cartoon characters are Slaghoople and McBricker?
10) Charles Boyer inspired what cartoon character?
11) What character did Hank Ketcham create?
12) *Mork and Mindy* was a spin-off from what sitcom?
13) What children's show had the cartoon *Tom Terrific with Mighty Manfred the Wonder Dog*?
14) What actress played the barmaid Carla on *Cheers*?
15) Who were David Soul and Paul Michael Glaser better known as?
16) Who was the first celebrity to make a guest appearance on *Sesame Street*?
17) On *Mr. Ed*, what is Ed's owner's full name?
18) Who is the fastest mouse in all of Mexico?
19) Victor Buono played what villain in the original *Batman* series?
20) What star's baby appeared on the first cover of *TV Guide*?

Quiz 3 Answers

1) Elmer Fudd
2) Victoria Barkley
3) *Northern Exposure*
4) Ranger Smith
5) Robinson
6) Salt shaker
7) Water Buffaloes
8) McGillicuddy
9) Wilma Flintstone and Betty Rubble
10) Pepe le Pew
11) Dennis the Menace
12) *Happy Days*
13) *Captain Kangaroo*

14) Rhea Perlman
15) *Starsky and Hutch*
16) James Earl Jones – He appeared on the show's second episode.
17) Wilbur Post
18) Speedy Gonzalez
19) King Tut
20) Lucille Ball

Quiz 4

1) Who played Superman in the original series?
2) The theme music for *Monty Python's Flying Circus* was written by what composer?
3) Bugs Bunny often finds himself at the wrong end of a gun usually toted by what two characters?
4) Before starring in *Modern Family*, Ed O'Neill was best known for playing what television dad?
5) On *The Flintstones*, Dino is Fred's pet; what is Barney's pet called?
6) What cartoon character was born in a warren under the Brooklyn Dodgers' stadium?
7) Where does George Jetson work?
8) Who is Dick Dastardly's pet?
9) On *Frazier*, what is the dad's dog's name?
10) Who was the first *Saturday Night Live* cast member to also have their child become a cast member?
11) What is the Cookie Monster's real name on *Sesame Street*?
12) What U.S. show featured the first openly gay character?
13) What year did *American Bandstand* debut?
14) What was the first series filmed before a live audience?
15) What was the first toy advertised on U.S. television?
16) In what city does SpongeBob SquarePants live?
17) Who was the original host of *The Tonight Show*?
18) Besides his moose strength, what is Bullwinkle's great talent?
19) On what sitcom did Frank Sinatra make his final television appearance?
20) Who was the original host of *Jeopardy!*?

Quiz 4 Answers

1) George Reeves
2) John Philip Sousa – "The Liberty Bell March"

3) Elmer Fudd and Yosemite Sam
4) Al Bundy – *Married with Children*
5) Hoppy - a hoparoo
6) Bugs Bunny
7) Spacely Sprockets
8) Muttley
9) Eddie
10) Chris Elliot
11) Sid
12) *Soap* – 1977
13) 1952
14) *I Love Lucy*
15) Mr. Potato Head – 1952
16) Bikini Bottom
17) Steve Allen
18) He could remember everything he ever ate.
19) *Who's the Boss*
20) Art Fleming – 1964 to 1984

Quiz 5

1) What year did *Saturday Night Live* debut?
2) On *Star Trek*, what is Captain Kirk's middle name?
3) In what year is *Lost in Space* set?
4) What are the names of the two characters that heckle the rest of the cast from the balcony on *The Muppet Show*?
5) How many series were spun off from *All in the Family*?
6) What is the name of George Peppard's character on *The A Team*?
7) *The Simpsons* first debuted as a short on what show?
8) What character's real name is Gordon Shumway?
9) On *Seinfeld*, what is Kramer's first name?
10) What long-running science fiction show first aired in November 1963?
11) What was the first U.S. network show without a theme song?
12) What U.S. show had the first toilet heard flushing?
13) Who was the youngest cast member ever of *Saturday Night Live*?
14) Who played the title role in the 1960s cult classic *The Prisoner*?
15) Who was Johnny Carson's final guest on *The Tonight Show*?
16) What year did *Sesame Street* debut?

17) What is the first name of the son on *Sanford and Son*?
18) What is Archie Bunker's son-in-law's full name on *All in the Family*?
19) What is the longest-running scripted primetime show of all time?
20) What is the name of the son on *The Jetsons*?

Quiz 5 Answers

1) 1975
2) Tiberius
3) 1997
4) Statler and Waldorf
5) Seven – *Maude*, *Good Times*, *The Jeffersons*, *Checking In*, *Archie Bunker's Place*, *Gloria*, *704 Hauser*
6) Hannibal Smith
7) *The Tracey Ullman Show*
8) Alf
9) Cosmo
10) *Doctor Who*
11) *60 Minutes*
12) *All in the Family* – 1971
13) Anthony Michael Hall – 17
14) Patrick McGoohan
15) Bette Midler
16) 1969
17) Lamont
18) Michael Stivic
19) *The Simpsons*
20) Elroy

Quiz 6

1) Who is the oldest person to host *Saturday Night Live*?
2) What was the most-watched U.S. series finale of all time?
3) How tall is Big Bird on *Sesame Street*?
4) The character of Sheriff Andy Taylor first appeared on what show?
5) Who is Alex's youngest sibling on *Family Ties*?
6) What was the first U.S. network show to use the "F" word?
7) What was the first U.S. R-rated show?
8) What is the name of Norm's wife on *Cheers*?

9) What is the name of the inn on *Newhart*?
10) What is the name of the car on *Knight Rider*?
11) *Game of Thrones* is based on a series of novels by what author?
12) On the U.S. series *The Office*, what is the name of the company they work for?
13) What series is known for the catchphrase "Missed it by that much"?
14) According to a British Film Institute poll of industry professionals in 2000, what is the greatest British television series of all time?
15) What is the name of John Travolta's character on *Welcome Back Kotter*?
16) What is the name of the time-traveling scientist on *Quantum Leap*?
17) One of Johnny Depp's early starring roles was on what police show?
18) What is the most widely watched PBS show ever worldwide?
19) In its 2002 list of the 50 greatest television shows of all time, *TV Guide* listed two animated shows, what were they?
20) What show's theme song was the first to hit number one on Billboard's Hot 100?

Quiz 6 Answers

1) Betty White – 88
2) *M*A*S*H*
3) 8'2"
4) *The Danny Thomas Show* – later spun off to *The Andy Griffith Show*
5) Andy – He was born during the series run.
6) *Saturday Night Live*
7) *NYPD Blue* – 1993
8) Vera
9) Stratford Inn
10) Kitt – Knight Industries Two Thousand
11) George R.R. Martin
12) Dunder Mifflin Paper Company
13) *Get Smart*
14) *Fawlty Towers* – aired 12 episodes in the 1970s
15) Vinnie Barbarino
16) Samuel Beckett
17) *21 Jump Street*
18) *Cosmos* – with Carl Sagan
19) *The Simpsons* and *Rocky and Bullwinkle*
20) *S.W.A.T.* - 1976

Quiz 7

1) In children's television, who is Lumpy Brannum better known as?
2) What is the number of the mobile hospital unit on *M*A*S*H*?
3) What 1960s sitcom was based on the novel *The Fifteenth Pelican*?
4) Who was the only main cast member to be in both the movie and television versions of *M*A*S*H*?
5) What was advertised in the first U.S. television commercial?
6) What is the name of Fred Flintstone's paperboy?
7) Who is Underdog in love with?
8) On *Rocky and Bullwinkle*, what is Boris and Natasha's homeland?
9) Who is Dudley Do-Right's nemesis?
10) What is the name of Mr. Peabody's time machine?
11) Charles Addams' *New Yorker* cartoons of a spooky husband and wife were the inspiration for *The Addams Family* and what famous cartoon villain duo?
12) In the original pilot for *Gilligan's Island*, who composed the theme song?
13) In the opening credits for the first season of *Gilligan's Island*, the U.S. flag is at half-mast as the *Minnow* pulls out of the harbor; why is the flag at half-mast?
14) What is the name of the Jetson's dog?
15) To capitalize on the popularity of creepy comedies like *The Addams Family* and *The Munsters*, what show introduced Weirdly and Creepella Gruesome as their new neighbors?
16) Fred Flintstone's "Yabba-dabba-doo" was inspired by what well-known advertising slogan?
17) The Aunt Harriet character on *Batman* didn't exist in the comics; why was she added to the television show?
18) What is the name of the character played by Angela Lansbury in *Murder, She Wrote*?
19) The character Roger "Race" Bannon appeared as a boy's bodyguard in what cartoon series?
20) On *The Munsters*, what is Lily's maiden name?

Quiz 7 Answers

1) Mr. Green Jeans on *Captain Kangaroo*
2) 4077
3) *The Flying Nun*
4) Gary Burghoff – Radar O'Reilly

5) Bulova watches
6) Arnold
7) Sweet Polly Purebred
8) Pottsylvania
9) Snidely Whiplash
10) Wayback (or WABAC) machine
11) Boris Badenov and Natasha Fatale – *Rocky and Bullwinkle*
12) John Williams – The original song was replaced.
13) John F. Kennedy's assassination – The scene was filmed in November 1963 in Hawaii; the cast and crew learned of Kennedy's assassination on the last day of filming.
14) Astro
15) *The Flintstones*
16) Brylcreem's "A little dab'll do you" - The mother of the actor who voiced Fred liked to say the Brylcreem slogan, so he suggested it to the creators.
17) To counter rumors that Bruce Wayne and Dick Grayson were gay - They thought adding a female character would round out the household.
18) Jessica Fletcher
19) *Jonny Quest*
20) Dracula

Quiz 8

1) What is Rob and Laura's last name on *The Dick Van Dyke Show*?
2) What is the last name of the family on *Good Times*?
3) On *The Jeffersons*, what is George's business?
4) On *The Wonder Years*, what is Fred Savage's character name?
5) Who played Captain Frank Furillo on *Hill Street Blues*?
6) What is the character name of the Spanish waiter on *Fawlty Towers*?
7) What is the name of the piano-playing dog on *The Muppet Show*?
8) What is Bob and Emily's last name on *The Bob Newhart Show*?
9) What is the name of Andy Kaufman's character on *Taxi*?
10) What is the name of the character Betty White played on *The Mary Tyler Moore Show*?
11) What is Mary's last name on *The Mary Tyler Moore Show*?
12) What is the name of Tina Fey's character on *30 Rock*?
13) Who was the only American in the group on *Monty Python's Flying Circus*?

14) What recurring character on *The Simpsons* is voiced by Kelsey Grammer?
15) Ted Cassidy, who played Lurch on *The Addams Family*, also played what other role on the show?
16) What cartoon character and gang leader lives in Hoagy's Alley?
17) What is the last name of Woody on *Cheers*?
18) On *Doctor Who*, what planet is the Doctor from?
19) What villain has the real name Oswald Chesterfield Cobblepot?
20) Who played the Lone Ranger in the original series?

Quiz 8 Answers

1) Petrie
2) Evans
3) Dry cleaning
4) Kevin Arnold
5) Daniel J. Travanti
6) Manuel
7) Rowlf
8) Hartley
9) Latka Gravas
10) Sue Ann Nivens
11) Richards
12) Liz Lemon
13) Terry Gilliam
14) Sideshow Bob
15) Thing – the hand
16) Top Cat
17) Boyd
18) Gallifrey
19) Penguin
20) Clayton Moore

Quiz 9

1) What did the acronym ESPN originally stand for?
2) What is cartoon cat Garfield's favorite food?
3) Poopdeck Pappy is what character's father?
4) What was the first game show broadcast on commercial television?
5) How many points does Bullwinkle have on his antlers?

6) Who is the voice of Marge on *The Simpsons*?
7) What is Grandpa Simpson's first name on *The Simpsons*?
8) Who is the first woman to win comedy acting Emmys for three different roles?
9) What was the first streaming series to win the best drama Emmy?
10) What long-running children's show had Mr. Do-Bee, a friendly bumblebee who taught children polite behavior, and the Magic Mirror?
11) What 1957-1968 children's show featured a Claymation duo?
12) Who played Maynard G. Krebs on *The Many Loves of Dobie Gillis*?
13) On *The Flying Nun*, what is Sally Field's character's name?
14) On *Bewitched*, what is the name of the character played by Agnes Moorehead?
15) What sitcom features the expression "Well doggies!"?
16) Mr. Peabody was modeled after what actor?
17) What mountain range do the Clampetts of *The Beverly Hillbillies* come from?
18) In what town is *Petticoat Junction* and *Green Acres* set?
19) On *The Munsters*, what is the name of the normal niece?
20) What sportscaster was the host for *ABC's Wide World of Sports*?

Quiz 9 Answers

1) Entertainment and Sports Programming Network
2) Lasagna
3) Popeye
4) *Truth or Consequences* – 1941
5) Six – three on each side
6) Julie Kavner
7) Abraham
8) Julia Louis-Dreyfus – *Seinfeld*, *The New Adventures of Old Christine*, *VEEP*
9) *The Handmaid's Tale* – Hulu in 2017
10) *Romper Room* – 1953 to 1994
11) *The Gumby Show* – with his horse Pokey
12) Bob Denver
13) Sister Betrille
14) Endora
15) *The Beverly Hillbillies*
16) Clifton Webb
17) Ozarks

18) Hooterville
19) Marilyn
20) Jim McKay

Quiz 10

1) On *The Munsters*, what is the name of Eddie's pet dragon that lives under the stairs?
2) On *McHale's Navy*, who played the bumbling Ensign Parker?
3) What 1960s show follows the work of Pete Malloy and Jim Reed?
4) Who played the villain Egghead on *Batman*?
5) What 1960s show features Robert Wagner as cat burglar Alexander Mundy?
6) Who was the creator of *The Dick Van Dyke Show* and appeared on the show in a supporting role?
7) On *The Saint*, what is the real name of the character played by Roger Moore?
8) What long-running show frequently used the word "wunnerful"?
9) On *F-Troop*, what is the name of the fort?
10) Who created *Jeopardy!* and *Wheel of Fortune*?
11) What are the character first names of the original *My Three Sons*?
12) Who played Herman on *The Munsters*?
13) What is the name of the police detective who chases Dr. Richard Kimble on *The Fugitive*?
14) David Soul and Bobby Sherman played logging brothers on *Here Come the Brides*; where was the show set?
15) What 1969-1972 show was based on a movie of the same name and starred Bill Bixby as a single father raising his son?
16) What 1960s reality show was hosted by Allen Funt and Durward Kirby?
17) What future Oscar winner was a bikini-clad go-go dancer on *Rowan & Martin's Laugh-In*?
18) What show features Mike Connors as a Los Angeles private eye?
19) On *Petticoat Junction*, what is the name of the hotel?
20) What future movie star played the role of blacksmith Quint Asper from 1962-1965 on *Gunsmoke*?

Quiz 10 Answers

1) Spot
2) Tim Conway

3) *Adam-12*
4) Vincent Price
5) *It Takes a Thief*
6) Carl Reiner – He appeared as Alan Brady on the show.
7) Simon Templar
8) *The Lawrence Welk Show*
9) Fort Courage
10) Merv Griffin
11) Mike, Robbie, Chip – Ernie joined later after Mike left due to marriage; sister Dodie was added after Steven remarried.
12) Fred Gwynne
13) Lt. Philip Gerard
14) Seattle – based on *Seven Brides for Seven Brothers*
15) *The Courtship of Eddie's Father*
16) *Candid Camera*
17) Goldie Hawn
18) *Mannix*
19) Shady Rest
20) Burt Reynolds

Quiz 11

1) What show opened with "There is nothing wrong with your television set. Do not attempt to adjust the picture"?
2) What 1951-1972 children's show featured science experiments?
3) What is the name of the POW camp on *Hogan Heroes*?
4) What is Wilbur's occupation on *Mr. Ed*?
5) What popular 1957-1963 western was one of the only television shows to spawn a radio show?
6) What is Marlo Thomas' character's name on *That Girl*?
7) Clint Howard appeared with his brother Ron on several episodes of *The Andy Griffith Show* and later starred in what 1960s series?
8) What 1960s show starred Ben Gazzara as a lawyer who is told he only has two years to live?
9) What show featured Clarence, the Cross-Eyed Lion?
10) Who were the actresses who played John Steed's partner on *The Avengers* before and after Diana Rigg?
11) In *The Lucy Show*, what is the name of the banker Lucy worked for played by Gale Gordon?

12) What western took place on the Shiloh ranch in Medicine Bow, Wyoming?
13) Who was the director of the St. Louis Zoo and co-host of *Mutual of Omaha's Wild Kingdom*?
14) What western featured the Cannon family in the 1870s Arizona territory?
15) In *The Man from U.N.C.L.E.*, what does U.N.C.L.E. stand for?
16) Who played Kato in *The Green Hornet*?
17) What long-running show opened with an animated shoe tapping in time to the theme music?
18) What is Mr. Peabody's first name?
19) What are the names of the twins on *Family Affair*?
20) What 1960s British show had the opening line "I am not a number! I am a free man!"?

Quiz 11 Answers

1) *The Outer Limits*
2) *Watch Mr. Wizard*
3) Stalag 13
4) Architect
5) *Have Gun – Will Travel* – The radio show started one year after the television show and reused stories.
6) Ann Marie
7) *Gentle Ben*
8) *Run for Your Life*
9) *Daktari*
10) Honor Blackman (before) and Linda Thorson (after)
11) Mr. Mooney
12) *The Virginian*
13) Marlin Perkins
14) *The High Chaparral*
15) United Network Command for Law and Enforcement
16) Bruce Lee
17) *My Three Sons*
18) Hector
19) Buffy and Jody
20) *The Prisoner*

Quiz 12

1) On *Green Acres*, what is Arnold the pig's last name?
2) What show opened with "The story you are about to see is true. The names have been changed to protect the innocent"?
3) On *The Honeymooners*, what is Ed Norton's occupation?
4) What 1952-1966 sitcom featured a real family?
5) What show starts with "A fiery horse with the speed of light, a cloud of dust"?
6) What was the first American series to feature teenagers as the lead characters?
7) What actors play the father and mother in *Father Knows Best*?
8) What character works for Gateman, Goodbury, and Graves Funeral Parlor?
9) What show's main character has business cards showing a chess piece?
10) What early sitcom featured the misadventures of an English teacher at Madison High?
11) On *Bonanza*, Hoss is a nickname; what is the character's real first name?
12) Twenty-two-year-old Warren Beatty got his start playing Milton Armitage on what sitcom?
13) What is the name of the saloon in *Gunsmoke*?
14) What comedy had a 20-year run with characters like Freddie the Freeloader?
15) What show has the all-time Nielsen season average share rating record?
16) What western features gambling brothers Bret and Bart?
17) Ken Curtis played the deputy on *Gunsmoke* longer than anyone else; what was his full character name?
18) What classic U.S. sitcom was based on the British show *Till Death Us Do Part*?
19) What comedy variety show became a hit with phrases like "The devil made me do it"?
20) What 1970s television family has eight children?

Quiz 12 Answers

1) Ziffel
2) *Dragnet*
3) Sewer worker

4) *The Adventures of Ozzie and Harriet*
5) *The Lone Ranger*
6) *The Many Loves of Dobie Gillis* - 1959
7) Robert Young and Jane Wyatt
8) Herman Munster
9) *Have Gun – Will Travel*
10) *Our Miss Brooks*
11) Eric
12) *The Many Loves of Dobie Gillis*
13) Long Branch
14) *The Red Skelton Show*
15) *I Love Lucy* in 1953 - It had a Nielsen season average share of 67.3 meaning that on average 67.3% of all households viewing television were watching it.
16) *Maverick* – starring James Garner and Jack Kelly
17) Festus Haggen
18) *All in the Family*
19) *The Flip Wilson Show*
20) Bradford – *Eight Is Enough*

Quiz 13

1) What 1970s undercover cop had a cockatoo named Fred?
2) What 1970s show featured Pete, Linc, and Julie solving crimes undercover?
3) Who had the title role in the *All in the Family* spin-off *Maude*?
4) On *Happy Days*, who is the oldest Cunningham child?
5) Before *Three's Company*, John Ritter played a minister on what 1970s drama?
6) What is the name of Ricardo Montalban's character on *Fantasy Island*?
7) What sitcom featured the popular line "Up your nose with a rubber hose"?
8) On *Kojak*, what is Kojak's first name?
9) Where is *The Flying Nun* set?
10) On *The Mary Tyler Moore Show*, what are the call letters of the station where they work?
11) What 1970s show featured the character Sgt. Pepper Anderson?
12) What is the occupation of Steven Douglas on *My Three Sons*?
13) Who played Tonto in *The Lone Ranger*?

14) Cloris Leachman starred in a spin-off from *The Mary Tyler Moore Show*; what is the name of the character she played?
15) What is John Cleese's full character name in *Fawlty Towers*?
16) In the 1970s show *Chico and the Man*, Freddie Prinze played Chico; who played the man?
17) What sitcom featured a never seen character Carlton the doorman?
18) The actor who voiced the title character on the animated series *Jonny Quest* was 17 at the time and went on to a long acting career; who is he?
19) What is the name of Dennis the Menace's dog?
20) Who played *The Fugitive*?

Quiz 13 Answers

1) *Baretta*
2) *The Mod Squad*
3) Bea Arthur
4) Chuck – He was phased out.
5) *The Waltons*
6) Mr. Roarke
7) *Welcome Back Kotter*
8) Theo
9) Puerto Rico
10) WJM-TV
11) *Police Woman* – starring Angie Dickinson
12) Aeronautical engineer
13) Jay Silverheels
14) Phyllis Lindstrom
15) Basil Fawlty
16) Jack Albertson
17) *Rhoda*
18) Tim Matheson
19) Ruff
20) David Janssen

Quiz 14

1) Ringo Starr narrated what children's show?
2) James Drury had the title role in what western series?
3) Benjamin Kubelsky gained fame as what comedian?
4) What fictional character has been played by the most actors on film and

television?
5) On *The Beverly Hillbillies*, who is Mr. Drysdale's secretary?
6) Color television was first successfully transmitted in the United States in what year?
7) On *Star Trek*, who played Ensign Chekov?
8) Where do Rocky and Bullwinkle live?
9) On *M*A*S*H*, what is Radar's favorite drink?
10) Wo Fat is the enemy of what detective?
11) Roy Thinnes played David Vincent in what 1960s science fiction series?
12) How many seconds elapsed before the tape self-destructed on *Mission Impossible*?
13) Who sang the theme song to *Rawhide*?
14) What is Clint Eastwood's character name on *Rawhide*?
15) How long was the original mission of Star Trek's Enterprise supposed to be?
16) Who is the head news writer for WJM-TV?
17) Where does Yogi bear live?
18) What is the name of the Douglas' family dog on *My Three Sons*?
19) What character did Chuck Connors play on *The Rifleman*?
20) Who was the first woman to anchor a U.S. network evening newscast?

Quiz 14 Answers

1) *Thomas the Tank Engine*
2) *The Virginian*
3) Jack Benny
4) Sherlock Holmes
5) Jane Hathaway
6) 1953
7) Walter Koenig
8) Frostbite Falls, Minnesota
9) Grape Nehi
10) Steve McGarrett - *Hawaii Five-O*
11) *The Invaders*
12) Five seconds
13) Frankie Laine
14) Rowdy Yates
15) Five years
16) Murray Slaughter – *The Mary Tyler Moore Show*

17) Jellystone Park
18) Tramp
19) Lucas McCain
20) Barbara Walters

Quiz 15

1) Who made the Rolling Stones sing "Let's spend the night together" as "Let's spend some time together"?
2) What is Beaver Cleaver's real first name?
3) What character did McLean Stevenson play on *M*A*S*H*?
4) Who took dictation from Perry Mason?
5) Who hosted *Night Gallery*?
6) Who is the Ponderosa's Chinese cook?
7) What is Mickey Mouse's dog's name?
8) Where is Bullwinkle Moose originally from?
9) Who used to ask, "Hey, Eddie, kees me goodnight"?
10) Who played Sally Rogers on *The Dick Van Dyke Show*?
11) What character was a knight without armor in a savage land?
12) Who played Captain Kangaroo?
13) What long time *60 Minutes* correspondent hosted seven game shows early in his career?
14) Who was the first woman to host *Saturday Night Live*?
15) Who played Doc Adams on *Gunsmoke*?
16) What sitcom ran the most first-run episodes in the 1990s?
17) What major cable network put on a polka festival as its first attempt at original programming?
18) When danger appeared, Quick Draw McGraw became what superhero?
19) What 1980s series starred Bruce Willis in a detective agency?
20) *Happy Days* was a spin-off from what show?

Quiz 15 Answers

1) Ed Sullivan
2) Theodore
3) Henry Blake
4) Della Street
5) Rod Serling
6) Hop Sing
7) Pluto

8) Moosylvania – It is a small island in Lake of the Woods that neither the United States nor Canada wants to claim.
9) Topo Gigio – Italian mouse puppet who appeared on *The Ed Sullivan Show*
10) Rose Marie
11) Paladin – from *Have Gun - Will Travel*
12) Bob Keeshan
13) Mike Wallace
14) Candace Bergen - 1975
15) Milburn Stone
16) *The Simpsons*
17) HBO
18) El Kabong
19) *Moonlighting*
20) *Love American Style*

Quiz 16

1) What series starred Keri Russell as a girl fresh out of high school who follows her high school crush to college to be near him?
2) Martin Caldin, a U.S. Air Force pilot and NASA public relations person, wrote the novel *Cyborg* that was the source material for what show?
3) What year was the first *Today* broadcast?
4) What line follows "You are traveling through another dimension, a dimension not only of sight and sound but of mind. A journey into a wondrous land of imagination"?
5) Who played the talk show sidekick on *The Larry Sanders Show*?
6) Who played Joey Potter on *Dawson's Creek*?
7) Who played the title role in *Doogie Howser, M.D.*?
8) What year were the first Emmy Awards?
9) What sitcom starred Ricky Gervais as an actor reduced to working as an extra whose attempts to boost his career end in failure and embarrassment?
10) What was the first soap opera to expand to 60 minutes?
11) On *Game of Thrones*, the seven kingdoms are part of what continent?
12) What is the only television show that was made into a Best Picture Oscar winner?
13) What was the first weekly U.S. television series budgeted at over $1 million per episode?
14) What supernatural series had brothers Stefan and Damon Salvatore

returning to their home of Mystic Falls, Virginia?
15) Who played Lois Lane on *Lois & Clark: The New Adventures of Superman?*
16) In *Mad About You*, what was Paul Buchman's occupation?
17) What were the three main competing syndicated newsmagazine shows that all debuted in the late 1980s?
18) What crime drama focuses on Baltimore's inner-city drug scene?
19) Who played the agent Ari Gold on the sitcom *Entourage*?
20) What is the name of the original DCI on the British detective drama *Midsomer Murders*?

Quiz 16 Answers

1) *Felicity* (1998-2002)
2) *The Six Million Dollar Man* (1974-1978)
3) 1951
4) Next stop, the Twilight Zone!
5) Jeffrey Tambor
6) Katie Holmes
7) Neil Patrick Harris
8) 1949
9) *Extras* (2005-2007)
10) *Another World* – 1975
11) Westeros
12) *Marty* - 1955
13) *Battlestar Galactica* - 1978
14) *The Vampire Diaries* (2009-2017)
15) Teri Hatcher
16) Filmmaker
17) *A Current Affair* (1986), *Inside Edition* (1988), *Hard Copy* (1989)
18) *The Wire* (2002-2008)
19) Jeremy Piven
20) Tom Barnaby

Quiz 17

1) What series followed police officers Mike Danko, Willie Gillis, and Terry Webster?
2) Who plays the title character in *Have Gun - Will Travel*?
3) What was the first series set in Hawaii?
4) What drama starred Leo McKern as a portly eccentric London criminal

law barrister?

5) In what city was *Matlock* set?
6) What was the first U.S. dramatic series to feature an African American actor in a lead role?
7) What sitcom centered on a church deacon and his assistant who disagreed on what was best for their congregation?
8) What was the first U.S. show to broadcast 1,000 episodes?
9) What children's series had a family that is thrown back in time and must survive in the age of dinosaurs?
10) What was the make and model of Rockford's car on *The Rockford Files*?
11) What was the name of the hospital on *St. Elsewhere*?
12) What year was cigarette advertising banned from U.S. television?
13) What is the family name on *Everybody Loves Raymond*?
14) Who played the title role in the private eye series *Barnaby Jones*?
15) What show had John Davidson, Fran Tarkenton, and Cathy Lee Crosby as hosts?
16) Who played the title role in *The Life and Legend of Wyatt Earp*?
17) What U.S. show has aired the most episodes?
18) What sitcom character's real name was Exigius 12½?
19) In *77 Sunset Strip*, what was the character name of the restaurant valet played by Edd Byrnes?
20) Who played the title role in the sitcom *Blossom*?

Quiz 17 Answers

1) *The Rookies* (1972-1976)
2) Richard Boone
3) *Hawaiian Eye* (1959-1963) - It wasn't filmed there.
4) *Rumpole of the Bailey* (1978-1992)
5) Atlanta
6) *I Spy* - starring Bill Cosby in 1965
7) *Amen* (1986-1991)
8) *The Howdy Doody Show* (1947-1960)
9) *Land of the Lost* (1974-1977)
10) Pontiac Firebird
11) St. Eligius
12) 1971
13) Barone
14) Buddy Ebsen

15) *That's Incredible!* (1980-1984)
16) Hugh O'Brian
17) *SportsCenter* - over 50,000 unique episodes since 1979
18) Uncle Martin, the Martian on *My Favorite Martian* (1963-1966)
19) Kookie
20) Mayim Bialik

Quiz 18

1) What was the first show to earn Emmys for all its principal cast members?
2) What science fiction series about an extraterrestrial race arriving on Earth was a reboot of a 1980s miniseries and series?
3) What talent show was originally hosted by Ed McMahon?
4) How did the name Muppet originate for the characters on *The Muppet Show*?
5) What show had the last theme song to make it to number one on Billboard's Hot 100?
6) What series starred Lloyd Bridges as scuba diver Mike Nelson?
7) What was Kyra Sedgwick's character name on *The Closer*?
8) What sitcom was based on the childhood experiences of comedian Chris Rock?
9) What sitcom featured a recovering alcoholic who becomes the manager of a big city bus station?
10) What series centered on the lives of three young alien/human hybrids with extraordinary gifts?
11) What state was *Twin Peaks* set in?
12) What quiz show was the center of the 1950s scandal involving Charles Van Doren and Herb Stempel?
13) What police drama features two Oscar winners in its lead roles?
14) What series centered on the members of a dysfunctional California family that runs an independent funeral home?
15) Who was the first African American to win the Outstanding Lead Actress in a Comedy Series Emmy?
16) What was the name of the house where Mrs. Muir lived with her children on *The Ghost & Mrs. Muir*?
17) What was the nickname of the Dwight Schultz character on *The A-Team*?
18) Who played the title role in *Dr. Quinn, Medicine Woman?*
19) What actress won six consecutive Outstanding Lead Actress in a

Comedy Series Emmys from 2012-2017?

20) Who plays President Conrad Dalton on the political drama *Madam Secretary*?

Quiz 18 Answers

1) *All in the Family* (1971-1979)
2) *V* (2009-2011)
3) *Star Search* (1983-2004)
4) It is a combination of the words marionette and puppet.
5) *Miami Vice* - "Theme from Miami Vice" (1985)
6) *Sea Hunt* (1958-1961)
7) Brenda Johnson
8) *Everybody Hates Chris* (2005-2009)
9) *The John Larroquette Show* (1993-1996)
10) *Roswell* (1999-2002)
11) Washington
12) *Twenty-One* (1956-1958)
13) *The Streets of San Francisco* (1972-1977) - starring Karl Malden and Michael Douglas
14) *Six Feet Under* (2001-2005)
15) Isabel Sanford - *The Jeffersons* (1981)
16) Gull Cottage
17) "Howling Mad" Murdock
18) Jane Seymour
19) Julia Louis-Dreyfus - *Veep*
20) Keith Carradine

Quiz 19

1) What sitcom featured Frank Lambert, a construction worker, and Carol Foster, a beautician, who each have three children and must learn to live together after spontaneously getting married?
2) In *The Prisoner*, all the characters are assigned numbers rather than names; what is the number assigned to the title character?
3) What is the only primetime drama to be spun off from two separate shows?
4) What sitcom was known for obliterating the fourth wall to the point of casually chatting with the studio audience and cast members either in or out of character?

5) Who was a co-host and correspondent on *Entertainment Tonight* for 29 years?
6) Who played Balki Bartokomous on *Perfect Strangers*?
7) What was the name of the all-knowing, all-seeing artificial intelligence created by Harold Finch on *Person of Interest*?
8) Who was the original host of the daytime version of *Wheel of Fortune*?
9) What year did Walt Disney have its first series?
10) The series *GLOW* is set in the 1980s and features women in what activity?
11) What was the first hour-long western on U.S. television?
12) What sitcom starred Ricky Schroeder as spoiled rich kid Ricky Stratton?
13) What U.S. live-action sitcom character appeared for the most consecutive years?
14) What drama was based on five siblings who are left to find their own way after their parents are killed by a drunk driver?
15) What award-winning songwriter appeared in the western *Laramie*?
16) Who was the first person to win Emmys for acting, writing, and directing for the same series?
17) What series centered on cases of an FBI unit specializing in missing person investigations and starred Anthony LaPaglia and Poppy Montgomery?
18) What show has the most Emmy wins for a drama?
19) Who starred in the title role of Dr. Sam Waters in the crime drama *Profiler*?
20) On *Richard Diamond, Private Detective*, a future famous actress played the role of Sam, the switchboard operator, who only ever had her legs and hands visible on camera; who played the role?

Quiz 19 Answers

1) *Step by Step* (1991-1998)
2) Six
3) *Law & Order: Special Victims Unit* - It spun off from *Law & Order*, and the character of Detective John Munch came from *Homicide: Life on the Street*.
4) *It's Garry Shandling's Show* (1986-1990)
5) Mary Hart
6) Bronson Pinchot
7) The Machine
8) Chuck Woolery

9) 1954 – *Disneyland*, which later became *Walt Disney's Wonderful World of Color*
10) Professional wrestling
11) *Cheyenne* (1955-1963)
12) *Silver Spoons* (1982-1987)
13) Frasier Crane - Between *Cheers* and *Frasier*, Kelsey Grammer played the character for 20 consecutive years.
14) *Party of Five* (1990-2000)
15) Hoagy Carmichael - composer of "Stardust" and "Georgia on My Mind"
16) Alan Alda - *M*A*S*H*
17) *Without a Trace* (2002-2009)
18) *Game of Thrones* (2011-2019) - 59 wins
19) Ally Walker
20) Mary Tyler Moore

Quiz 20

1) What sitcom had Martin Lawrence playing a total of 10 characters over the series run?
2) What two series are tied for the most consecutive Outstanding Comedy Series Emmys at five?
3) Who co-starred with Michael Landon on *Little House on the Prairie* and *Highway to Heaven*?
4) What was the first nationally televised children's show in the United States?
5) Who starred as firefighter Tommy Gavin who deals with the fears of his job and his personal problems in the comedy-drama *Rescue Me*?
6) Who was the only female comedy regular on *Your Show of Shows*?
7) What show originated the term "jumped the shark" indicating a show has had a sharp drop in quality or has inserted desperate attempts for ratings?
8) Tim Roth starred as Dr. Cal Lightman, the world's leading deception expert who studies facial expressions and involuntary body language, in what series?
9) Who was the first African American to win the Outstanding Lead Actress in a Drama Series Emmy?
10) Who was the first African American to win the Outstanding Lead Actor in a Comedy Series Emmy?
11) What stop motion animation series features voice work by Seth Green who is also one of the creators?

12) What were the names of the two main characters on *The Wild Wild West*?
13) What sitcom featured Mr. Floppy, a boozing, chain-smoking stuffed rabbit voiced by Bobcat Goldthwait, whom the lead character consults for advice?
14) What is the only U.S. primetime series to be on for at least 14 years without winning an Emmy?
15) What was the name of the late-night music show hosted by Wolfman Jack?
16) What was the first primetime series starring a female private eye?
17) What was the name of the housekeeper played by Miyoshi Umeki on *The Courtship of Eddie's Father*?
18) What was the first *Law & Order* spin-off?
19) *Boston Legal* was a spin-off of what series?
20) What was the name of Christopher Lloyd's character on *Taxi*?

Quiz 20 Answers

1) *Martin* (1992-1997)
2) *Frasier* (1994-1998) and *Modern Family* (2010-2014)
3) Victor French
4) *The Howdy Doody Show* (1947-1960)
5) Dennis Leary
6) Imogene Coca
7) *Happy Days* - During the season five opener, Fonzie jumped a shark while water-skiing, which marked the beginning of a sharp decline in the show's quality.
8) *Lie to Me* (2009-2011)
9) Viola Davis - *How to Get Away with Murder* (2015)
10) Robert Guillaume - *Benson* (1985)
11) *Robot Chicken* - debuted in 2005
12) James West and Artemus Gordon
13) *Unhappily Ever After* (1995-1999)
14) *Supernatural* - debuted in 2005
15) *The Midnight Special* (1972-1981)
16) *Honey West* (1965-1966)
17) Mrs. Livingston
18) *Law & Order: Special Victims Unit* (1999)
19) *The Practice* (1997-2004)
20) Jim Ignatowski

Quiz 21

1) What is the longest-running game show in the United States?
2) What sitcom marked the acting debut of Jerry Seinfeld?
3) What was the last U.S. show to have its entire run filmed in black and white?
4) What series is set 97 years after a nuclear war when a spaceship housing humanity's last survivors sends a group of juvenile delinquents back to Earth in hopes of re-populating the planet?
5) Who plays the alcoholic father Frank Gallagher on *Shameless*?
6) Who was the original host of *Candid Camera*?
7) Who played the title roles in *Kate & Allie*?
8) The characters played by Jim Parsons and Johnny Galecki on *The Big Bang Theory* are named after who?
9) What series was a remake of the British show *Steptoe and Son*?
10) For what series did Rachel Brosnahan win the 2018 Outstanding Lead Actress in a Comedy Series Emmy?
11) What series showed the aftermath of a nearby nuclear explosion on a small peaceful town?
12) What star of one of the favorite family dramas of the 1970s played Frank Gaad, a supervisor in the FBI counter-intelligence department, who is dedicated to identifying the Soviet spies in *The Americans*?
13) What game show featured Ben Stein as host and Jimmy Kimmel as co-host?
14) Who is the creator and star of the comedy *Master of None* about the life of a young actor in New York?
15) What series was spun off from *The Carol Burnett Show*?
16) What actor in *The Big Bang Theory* has a real-life neuroscience PhD?
17) On the prison drama *Oz*, what is the name of the experimental unit of the prison?
18) What series had charming con artist Neal Caffrey helping the FBI catch elusive criminals in exchange for his freedom?
19) What four series have won Emmys for all their main cast members?
20) What year did Nielsen start providing television ratings data?

Quiz 21 Answers

1) *The Price is Right* - started in 1972
2) *Benson* - 1980
3) *The Dick Van Dyke Show* (1961-1966)

4) *The 100* - debuted 2014
5) William H. Macy
6) Allen Funt
7) Susan Saint James and Jane Curtin
8) Sheldon Leonard - famous television producer and actor
9) *Sanford and Son* (1972-1977)
10) *The Marvelous Mrs. Maisel* - debuted 2017
11) *Jericho* (2006-2008)
12) Richard Thomas - John Boy of *The Waltons*
13) *Win Ben Stein's Money* (1997-2002)
14) Aziz Ansari
15) *Mama's Family* (1983-1990)
16) Mayim Bialik
17) Emerald City
18) *White Collar* (2009-2014)
19) *All in the Family, The Golden Girls, Will & Grace*, *Schitt's Creek*
20) 1950

Quiz 22

1) What comedy-drama featured Hank Moody, a self-loathing, narcissistic author, drug user, alcoholic, and borderline sex addict?
2) What series was part of the *NBC Wednesday Mystery Movie* rotation and starred George Peppard as a suave, Polish American freelance investigator who solved seemingly impossible thefts?
3) What was the first television family with a computer in their home?
4) On *Bonanza*, what was Ben Cartwright's occupation before becoming a rancher?
5) What long-running series featured movie stars such as Jane Wyman, Cliff Robertson, Lana Turner, and Kim Novak?
6) What science documentary series debuted in 1974?
7) Who played the title role in *Dennis the Menace*?
8) What drama is about politics in New York high finance and features U.S. Attorney Chuck Rhoades and hedge fund king Bobby Axelrod?
9) What was the first show ever to air on Fox primetime?
10) What sitcom starred Thomas Jane as a struggling suburban Detroit high school coach who resorts to male prostitution?
11) Who played the title roles in *McMillan & Wife*?
12) Who played the original Clarabell the Clown on *The Howdy Doody Show*?

13) What well-known disc jockey, radio personality, voice actor and actor provided the voice for Shaggy on *Scooby-Doo, Where Are You*?
14) What is the longest-running variety show in the United States?
15) What reality series has the theme song "Bad Boys"?
16) The characters on *The Honeymooners* first appeared on what show?
17) What Jack Webb series had real-life husband and wife Julie London and Bobby Troup?
18) What anthology crime drama was Jessica Biel's first leading role in a television series?
19) What series was based on the 1970s British show *Man About the House*?
20) What was the longest-running *All in the Family* spin-off?

Quiz 22 Answers

1) *Californication* (2007-2014)
2) *Banacek* (1972-1974)
3) *The Addams Family* (1964-1966) - They had a huge UNIVAC computer.
4) Ship's captain
5) *Falcon Crest* (1981-1990)
6) *Nova*
7) Jay North
8) *Billions* - debuted 2016
9) *Married with Children* - April 15, 1987
10) *Hung* (209-2011)
11) Rock Hudson and Susan Saint James
12) Bob Keeshan - He went on to play Captain Kangaroo.
13) Casey Kasem
14) *Saturday Night Live* - started in 1975
15) *Cops* - debuted in 1989
16) *The Jackie Gleason Show* - It featured sketches with *The Honeymooners*.
17) *Emergency!* (1972-1979)
18) *The Sinner* - debuted 2017
19) *Three's Company* (1976-1984)
20) *The Jeffersons* - 11 seasons from 1975-1985

Quiz 23

1) Gene Barry played a Los Angeles chief of detectives who was also a millionaire and lived a high-wheeling lifestyle on what series?
2) What actor on the sitcom *Superstore* is a former cast member of *The Kids*

in the Hall and *Saturday Night Live*?

3) What sitcom was based on a 1978 Walter Matthau and Glenda Jackson film of the same name?
4) What show has a Guinness World Record for most swearing in an animated series?
5) What series features a brilliant college dropout who finds himself working as a lawyer for one of New York City's top attorneys?
6) Who played detective Virgil Tibbs in the series *In the Heat of the Night*?
7) What dramatic series had the first romantic kiss between two women on primetime U.S. television?
8) What animated show featured the adventures of a cowardly dog who must defend his unknowing farmer owners from all kinds of dangers?
9) What animated science fiction comedy had character Tad Ghostal hosting a late-night talk show filmed in outer space along with his cohost and former villain Zorak interviewing Earth celebrities through their videophone?
10) What was the first western to have all its episodes broadcast in color?
11) Bea Arthur co-starred with what actress for 13 years over two different series?
12) What is the longest-running animated children's show in the United States?
13) What series features Joel the janitor, Tom Servo, and Crow T. Robot watching and commenting on bad movies?
14) What show is generally credited as the inventor of the rerun?
15) What series featured E.G. Marshall and Robert Reed as a father and son tackling challenging legal cases often involving critical issues for the times?
16) The sweaters children's television star Mr. Rogers wore on his show were created by whom?
17) What two male dramatic characters appeared for the most consecutive years in American live-action primetime television?
18) Who was the only cast member to win an award for *Green Acres*?
19) The actors playing what two characters on the U.S. version of *The Office* went to high school together in real life?
20) Who was the first African American woman to win a primetime acting Emmy?

Quiz 23 Answers

1) *Burke's Law* (1963-1966)
2) Mark McKinney - He plays the store manager Glenn and was one of

The Kids in the Hall and on *SNL* from 1995 to 1997.

3) *House Calls* (1979-1982) - starring Wayne Rogers and Lynn Redgrave
4) *South Park* – debuted 1997
5) *Suits* - debuted 2011
6) Howard E. Rollins Jr.
7) *L.A. Law* - In 1991, female characters Abby played by Michele Greene and C.J. played by Amanda Donohoe kissed.
8) *Courage the Cowardly Dog* (1999-2002)
9) *Space Ghost Coast to Coast* (1993-2008)
10) *Bonanza* (1959-1973)
11) Rue McClanahan - *Maude* and *The Golden Girls*
12) *Arthur* - started on PBS in 1996
13) *Mystery Science Theater 3000* (1988-1999)
14) *I Love Lucy* (1951-1957) - during Lucille Ball's pregnancy
15) *The Defenders* (1961-1965)
16) His mother
17) Matt Dillon - played by James Arness on *Gunsmoke* from 1955 to 1975 and Detective John Munch played by Richard Belzer on *Homicide: Life on the Street* from 1993 to 1999 and on *Law & Order: Special Victims Unit* from 1999 to 2013
18) Arnold the pig - He won a Patsy Award for best animal performance in 1967.
19) Jim Halpert and Ryan Howard - John Krasinski and B.J. Novak both went to Newton South High School in Newton, Massachusetts, and both graduated in 1997. They were even on the same little league baseball team.
20) Gail Fisher - *Mannix* (1970) for Outstanding Supporting Actress in a Drama Series

Quiz 24

1) What were the first names of the four *Designing Women*?
2) What show had the first interracial couple on regular primetime U.S. television?
3) *This Is Your Life* surprised a celebrity each week and told the story of their life; who was the host?
4) What was the name of the groundbreaking 26-part documentary series narrated by Laurence Olivier about WWII?
5) After 227 in 1985, what 1990s sitcom was the second ever to feature four African American females as lead characters?

6) Who is generally credited with inventing the television as we know it and giving the world's first public demonstration of a true television set?
7) What sketch comedy starred Dave Foley, Bruce McCulloch, Kevin McDonald, Scott Thompson, and Mark McKinney?
8) Who played the Beast in the original 1980s *Beauty and the Beast*?
9) What year did the United States begin transitioning to color television?
10) In *A Charlie Brown Christmas*, what Christmas carol do all the children sing at the end?
11) What was the first cable series to win the Outstanding Drama Series Emmy?
12) What actress received an Emmy nomination for Best Lead Actress in a Drama Series for each of the 12 seasons her show ran but never won?
13) On *Seinfeld*, what is Kramer's first name?
14) What science fiction series featured former galactic war veteran Malcolm Reynolds as captain of the transport ship *Serenity*?
15) What former movie Superman plays the part of The Atom on *Arrow*?
16) What children's series is based on the books by Marc Brown and features the adventures of an eight-year-old aardvark and his family and friends?
17) On *Longmire*, Walt Longmire is the dedicated sheriff of Absaroka County who is dealing with the death of his wife; what state is the show set in?
18) What was the name of the small town plagued by bizarre and violent crimes in *Picket Fences*?
19) Who was the first detective character that was created specifically for television and had not appeared in any other media?
20) To prevent continuity problems and allow the episodes to be shown in any order, what 1960s sitcom was always set during winter?

Quiz 24 Answers

1) Julia, Suzanne, Mary Jo, Charlene
2) *The Jeffersons* - neighbors Tom and Helen Willis in 1975
3) Ralph Edwards
4) *The World at War* (1973-1976)
5) *Living Single* (1993-1998)
6) John Logie Baird - He demonstrated a television set in 1926.
7) *The Kids in the Hall* (1988-1994)
8) Ron Perlman

9) 1953
10) "Hark! The Herald Angels Sing"
11) *The Sopranos* - 2006
12) Angela Lansbury - *Murder, She Wrote* (1984-1996)
13) Cosmo
14) *Firefly* (2002-2003)
15) Brandon Routh - He starred as Superman in *Superman Returns* (2006).
16) *Arthur* - started in 1996
17) Wyoming
18) Rome, Wisconsin
19) Peter Gunn - 1958
20) *Hogan's Heroes* (1965-1971)

Quiz 25

1) Who took over as the host of *The Price is Right* after Bob Barker's retirement?
2) Who was the original host of Comedy Central's *The Daily Show*?
3) What was the name of the police informant played by Antonio Fargas on *Starsky and Hutch*?
4) What series featured nurses and doctors in a Vietnam War field hospital?
5) The number-one song "Johnny Angel" debuted on a sitcom and was sung by the actress who played the daughter on the show; what was the series?
6) What science fiction series featured two U.S Secret Service agents who must retrieve supernatural objects called artifacts?
7) Who played the ethically challenged attorney Alan Shore on the crime drama *Boston Legal*?
8) In *Buffy the Vampire Slayer*, what is Buffy's last name?
9) What was the name of the evil organization the agents were always battling on *The Man from U.N.C.L.E.*?
10) *This Old House* debuted in 1979; who was the original master carpenter on the show?
11) Who plays Joyce Byers, the mother of the missing boy, on *Stranger Things*?
12) What was the first name of Chuck Norris' title character on *Walker, Texas Ranger*?
13) What mystery crime drama starred a real-life father and son playing father and son?

14) What show has the most Emmy wins for a comedy?
15) What was the name of the Ewing ranch on *Dallas*?
16) What show popularized and may have originated the phrase "Whoa Nelly!"?
17) What is the name of *The Walking Dead* spin-off that follows two families banding together to survive?
18) Who is the only Star Trek character to appear regularly on two different Star Trek series?
19) *The Partridge Family* was based on what real-life musical family?
20) What comedy series holds the record for most acting Emmy wins?

Quiz 25 Answers

1) Drew Carey
2) Craig Kilborn
3) Huggy Bear
4) *China Beach* (1988-1991)
5) *The Donna Reed Show* - Shelley Fabares played the daughter and sang the song.
6) *Warehouse 13* (2009-2014)
7) James Spader
8) Summers
9) Thrush
10) Norm Abram
11) Winona Ryder
12) Cordell
13) *Diagnosis Murder* (1993-2001) - starred Dick and Barry Van Dyke
14) *Frasier* (1993-2004) - 37 wins
15) Southfork
16) *The Roy Rogers Show* (1951-1957) - On nearly every show, Pat Brady would yell the phrase while racing after villains or rushing for help in his Jeep named Nellybelle.
17) *Fear the Walking Dead* - debuted 2015
18) Worf - He was played by Michael Dorn and appeared on both *Star Trek: The Next Generation* and *Star Trek: Deep Space Nine*.
19) The Cowsills - They were considered for the show, but the children were older than the parts written for the series.
20) *The Mary Tyler Moore Show* (1970-1977) - 16 wins

Quiz 26

1) What is the longest-running live-action primetime spin-off series ever on American television?
2) In what city did *The Oprah Winfrey Show* originate?
3) What was the name of the think tank MacGyver worked for in the original *MacGyver*?
4) Donald Glover became only the second African American to win the Outstanding Lead Actor in a Comedy Series Emmy for what show?
5) Who played the title role on *Trapper John, M.D.*?
6) What year was the first paid television advertisement broadcast in the United States?
7) What year did Fox become the first new national television network since the 1950s?
8) Who played the role of Nell Harper in *Gimme a Break!*?
9) Who played Sgt. Morgan O'Rourke on *F Troop*?
10) Who played the two brothers and title characters of the miniseries *Rich Man, Poor Man*?
11) The sitcom *30 Rock* centers around the creation of a sketch comedy show; what is the name of the show they are creating?
12) Who played the boss in the original British series *The Office*?
13) What drama features teenager Clay Jensen as he tries to uncover the reason behind his classmate's suicide?
14) What was the first regularly scheduled broadcast network in the United States?
15) What do the title initials stand for on *JAG*?
16) How many different actors on *The Mary Tyler Moore Show* won Emmys?
17) What office place sitcom was based on a movie of the same name and starred the sister of one of the movie's stars?
18) Who stars in the title role in the series *Sherlock*?
19) What American primetime scripted show has been the longest-running show on the air for the longest time?
20) What anthology series was created by Steven Spielberg and featured many famous actors and had episodes directed by Spielberg, Clint Eastwood, Martin Scorsese, and Robert Zemeckis?

Quiz 26 Answers

1) *Law & Order: Special Victims Unit* - debuted in 1999
2) Chicago
3) Phoenix Foundation

4) *Atlanta* (2017)
5) Pernell Roberts
6) 1941
7) 1993
8) Nell Carter
9) Forrest Tucker
10) Peter Strauss and Nick Nolte
11) *TGS* - It was originally titled *The Girlie Show* before they brought in Tracy Jordan.
12) Ricky Gervais
13) *13 Reasons Why* - debuted 2017
14) NBC - 1945
15) Judge Advocate General
16) Six - Mary Tyler Moore, Ted Knight, Betty White, Cloris Leachman, Ed Asner, Valerie Harper
17) *Nine to Five* (1982-1988) - Rachel Dennison, Dolly Parton's sister, played the role of Doralee that Parton played in the movie.
18) Benedict Cumberbatch
19) *The Simpsons* - It has been the longest-running show since July 1998.
20) *Amazing Stories* (1985-1987)

Quiz 27

1) What was the first U.S. daily soap opera offered in syndication?
2) What series starred Robert Conrad as Gregory "Pappy" Boyington, squadron leader of a group of fighter pilots stationed on a Pacific island during WWII?
3) What character on *Family Guy* is voiced by the show's creator Seth MacFarlane in his natural speaking voice?
4) Who played the Penguin in the original *Batman* series?
5) What year did *The Tonight Show* debut?
6) What British sitcom was about two best friends, Edina Monsoon and Patsy Stone, who are constantly drugged up and outrageously selfish?
7) Who was the original host for *Unsolved Mysteries* that had re-enactments, interviews, and updates about real mysteries?
8) What was the first name of Dr. Niles Crane's wife who was frequently talked about but never seen on *Frasier*?
9) What are the two main non-human races on *Babylon 5*?
10) Who played the title role in the series *Nurse Jackie*?
11) Who was the first woman to run a major television studio?

12) The early career of Dr. Phil McGraw of the *Dr. Phil* show inspired what crime drama series?
13) What series had this opening "He awoke and found himself trapped in the past, facing mirror images that were not his own, and driven by an unknown force to change history for the better"?
14) Who is the youngest person to have a self-titled U.S. television show?
15) What sitcom follows a group of old friends in a fantasy football league?
16) What was George and Louise's only child's name on *The Jeffersons*?
17) What comedy series had Jim Carrey, Jamie Foxx, and Jennifer Lopez?
18) On *Who's the Boss*, what was Tony's occupation before becoming a housekeeper?
19) What action series featured characters Reno Raines, Bobby Sixkiller, and Cheyenne Phillips working as bounty hunters?
20) Who starred as Carl Kolchak, a Chicago reporter who always got into situations involving the supernatural, in *Kolchak: The Night Stalker*?

Quiz 27 Answers

1) *Dark Shadows* (1966-1971)
2) *Black Sheep Squadron* (1976-1978)
3) Brian - the dog
4) Burgess Meredith
5) 1954
6) *Absolutely Fabulous* (1992-2012)
7) Robert Stack
8) Maris
9) Minbari and Centauri
10) Edie Falco
11) Lucille Ball - She ran Desilu Studio starting in 1962; the studio produced many popular shows including *Mission Impossible* and *Star Trek*.
12) *Bull* - McGraw earned his PhD in psychology from the University of North Texas in 1979 and founded Courtroom Sciences, Inc., a trial sciences firm, in 1980.
13) *Quantum Leap* (1989-1993)
14) Patty Duke - She was 16 years old when *The Patty Duke Show* debuted in 1963.
15) *The League* (2009-2015)
16) Lionel
17) *In Living Color* (1990-1994)

18) Baseball player
19) *Renegade* (1992-1997)
20) Darren McGavin

Quiz 28

1) Who was the first African American to win the Outstanding Lead Actor in a Drama Series Emmy?
2) On *Charmed*, what was the name of the book of witchcraft that was passed down to the sisters?
3) Who was the youngest person to ever host *Saturday Night Live*?
4) What drama centers around the exploits of Colombian drug lord Pablo Escobar?
5) What is the first name of the grizzled old cook played by Frank McGrath on *Wagon Train*?
6) *Maude* was a spin-off from *All in the Family*; what was Maude's relationship to the Bunkers?
7) What is the name of the magic school the central characters attend in *The Magicians*?
8) Who hosted *Night Gallery*?
9) Who played the title role in *The Nanny*?
10) Who played head detective Mac Taylor on *CSI: NY*?
11) What anthology horror series was based on the EC Comics books of the 1950s?
12) The office in *The Dick Van Dyke Show* is based on Carl Reiner's experience on *Your Show of Shows* where he worked as a writer. Dick Van Dyke's character is based on Carl Reiner; Morey Amsterdam's character of Buddy Sorrell is based on what famous writer, director, and actor who was also a writer on *Your Show of Shows*?
13) What children's animated series features Tommy Pickles, Chuckie Finster, and Phil and Lil Deville as four babies?
14) What were the names of the Ewing couple who starred on *Knots Landing*?
15) What year did the first television sitcom in the world debut?
16) What series featured Mia Farrow, Ryan O'Neal, Dorothy Malone, and Ed Nelson?
17) What future national television figure was the first person to play Ronald McDonald in three 1963 television advertisements?
18) What sitcom starred identical twins Tia and Tamera Mowry as twins separated at birth who are reunited as teenagers?
19) What was the first television series to feature a final episode where all

plot lines were resolved, and all questions were answered?

20) What action drama starred Jessica Alba as Max Guevera, a genetically enhanced superhuman prototype, searching for others like her and battling corruption in a post-apocalyptic Pacific Northwest?

Quiz 28 Answers

1) Bill Cosby - *I Spy* (1966)
2) *Book of Shadows*
3) Drew Barrymore – age 7 in 1982
4) *Narcos* (2015-2017)
5) Charlie
6) She was Edith's cousin.
7) Brakebills
8) Rod Serling
9) Fran Drescher
10) Gary Sinise
11) *Tales from the Crypt* (1989-1996)
12) Mel Brooks
13) *Rugrats* (1990-2006)
14) Gary and Valene Ewing - played by Ted Shackelford and Joan Van Ark
15) 1946 - *Pinwright's Progress* debuted on November 29, 1946, on the BBC. It featured the adventures of the smallest store in the world and included the store proprietor, his pretty daughter, a nemesis, and helpful staff who end up making things worse.
16) *Peyton Place* (1964-1969)
17) Willard Scott - The future *Today Show* weatherman was a local radio personality in Washington, D.C., and had played Bozo the Clown on television from 1959-1962.
18) *Sister, Sister* (1994-1999)
19) *The Fugitive* - 1967
20) *Dark Angel* (2000-2002)

Quiz 29

1) Who played the title role in *House*?
2) What is the name of the cruise ship on *The Love Boat*?
3) On *Supergirl*, what is the name of Supergirl's alter ego?
4) What year did U.S. commercial networks first broadcast most of their primetime shows in color?

5) What streaming drama is set in a theocratic dictatorship in a dystopian future after a second American civil war?
6) Who played Wonder Woman in the 1970s series?
7) What series has the most Emmy wins in a single year?
8) What are the names of Lucy and Ricky's landlords and friends in *I Love Lucy*?
9) On *The Patty Duke Show*, what was the reason given that Patty and her cousin looked so much alike?
10) U.S. television allows alcohol to be advertised if what?
11) On the superhero drama *Agents of S.H.I.E.L.D.*, what does S.H.I.E.L.D. stand for?
12) What sitcom featured a free-spirited yoga instructor and a conservative lawyer who get married on their first date?
13) What is the name of the town that is the setting for *Parks and Recreation*?
14) What is the longest-running television show of any kind in the United States?
15) What children's animated series featured Lily Tomlin as Ms. Frizzle?
16) What series had the largest number of performers nominated for lead, supporting, or guest actress or actor Emmys over its run?
17) Who was the host of the true-crime series *America's Most Wanted*?
18) What is the name of the character played by two-time Oscar winner Maggie Smith in *Downton Abbey*?
19) What crime drama had a mathematician helping his FBI brother solve crimes?
20) What town is *Father Knows Best* set in?

Quiz 29 Answers

1) Hugh Laurie
2) *Pacific Princess*
3) Kara Danvers
4) 1965
5) *The Handmaid's Tale* - debuted 2017
6) Lynda Carter
7) *Game of Thrones* - 12 wins in 2015, 2016, and 2019
8) Fred and Ethel Mertz
9) Their fathers were identical twins.
10) No alcohol is consumed in the commercial – It isn't a law or FCC regulation, just a broadcasting standard.

11) Strategic Homeland Intervention, Enforcement and Logistics Division
12) *Dharma & Greg* (1997-2002)
13) Pawnee, Indiana
14) *Meet the Press* - started in 1947 and still running
15) *The Magic School Bus* (1994-1997)
16) *ER* (1994-2009)- 31 separate performers
17) John Walsh
18) Violet Crawley - Dowager Countess of Grantham
19) *Numb3rs* (2005-2010)
20) Springfield

Quiz 30

1) What was the first American series shown on British television?
2) Who played the title role on *Julia* about a widowed nurse?
3) What are the first names of the title characters in *2 Broke Girls*?
4) What was the first U.S. primetime soap opera?
5) Who played the title role in the sitcom *Malcolm in the Middle*?
6) Who plays the role of Jackie Harris on *Roseanne*?
7) What action-adventure character's real name is Don Diego de la Vega?
8) Who was the first African American to win the Outstanding Supporting Actress in a Comedy Series Emmy?
9) The British historical drama *Poldark* features a soldier returning home to England after fighting in the American Revolution; what area of England is the series set in?
10) Who was the narrator and voice of the adult Kevin on *The Wonder Years*?
11) Who starred as Captain Dylan Hunt who is frozen in time for 300 years and along with his sentient warship Andromeda sets out to restore peace to the universe on *Andromeda*?
12) What were the names of the trio of angels on *Touched by an Angel*?
13) What was the occupation of Marlo Thomas's boyfriend on *That Girl*?
14) What was the first streaming series to win the Outstanding Comedy Series Emmy?
15) What series has the most-watched episode in U.S. television history?
16) What comedy-adventure starred Greg Evigan as a trucker who travels the highways of America with his pet chimpanzee?
17) What British comedy-drama centers on a socially challenged doctor who moves from London to Cornwall?
18) What author created the character of *The Saint*?
19) What was the name of the hospital on *Scrubs*?

20) What was the name of Groucho Marx's game show?

Quiz 30 Answers

1) *Dragnet*
2) Diahann Carroll
3) Max and Caroline
4) *Peyton Place* (1964-1969)
5) Frankie Muniz
6) Laurie Metcalf
7) Zorro
8) Jackee Harry - 227 (1987)
9) Cornwall
10) Daniel Stern
11) Kevin Sorbo
12) Monica, Tess, Andrew
13) Magazine reporter
14) *The Marvelous Mrs. Maisel* (2018) - Amazon
15) *M*A*S*H* - series finale in 1983 with over 105 million viewers
16) *B.J. and the Bear* (1978-1981)
17) *Doc Martin* - debuted 2004
18) Leslie Charteris - He wrote a series of books and stories starting in the 1930s.
19) Sacred Heart
20) *You Bet Your Life* (1950-1961)

Quiz 31

1) What is the oldest network newscast in the United States?
2) What were the names of the five children on *The Cosby Show*?
3) What series centers on a young surgeon with autism and savant syndrome who joins a prestigious hospital?
4) What was Ted Knight's final series?
5) Who was the first automaker to advertise on network television?
6) What was the first animated series after *The Flintstones* in 1961 to be nominated for the Outstanding Comedy Series Emmy?
7) What action comedy starring David Rasche was a parody of the *Dirty Harry* movies?
8) In *Buck Rogers in the 25th Century*, what was the empire the earth is battling?

9) What series had the host delivering lines such as "I hope you'll join us again next week when we will present you with another story of gripping, spine-tingling suspense, and three boring commercials to take the edge off of it"?
10) What sitcom starred Danny McBride as a burned-out MLB pitcher who goes home to North Carolina to work as a gym teacher at his old middle school?
11) Where was the crime drama *Silk Stockings* set?
12) Who played the title role in *The Farmer's Daughter* that was based on a 1947 Loretta Young movie of the same name?
13) What was the name of the title character on *The Mentalist*?
14) What was the first show to end while it was still at the top of the Nielsen Ratings?
15) What actor played Dr. Jerry Robinson on *The Bob Newhart Show* and went on to become an award-winning director of hundreds of television episodes for a variety of shows?
16) What actor led the WWII commando squad on *Rat Patrol*?
17) Who played the title roles in *Nanny and the Professor*?
18) What series that started in 1999 won the Outstanding Drama Series Emmy each of its first four seasons?
19) At the time they were cast, which of *The Monkees* were musicians?
20) What state was the sitcom *The Middle* set in?

Quiz 31 Answers

1) *CBS Evening News* - started in 1948
2) Sondra, Denise, Vanessa, Rudy, Theo
3) *The Good Doctor* - debuted 2017
4) *Too Close for Comfort* (1980-1987) - He died during the series.
5) Chevrolet - 1946
6) *Family Guy* - 2009
7) *Sledge Hammer!* (1986-1988)
8) Draconian
9) *Alfred Hitchcock Presents* (1955-1962)
10) *Eastbound & Down* (2009-2013)
11) Palm Beach, Florida
12) Inger Stevens
13) Patrick Jane
14) *I Love Lucy* (1951-1957)
15) Peter Bonerz

16) Christopher George
17) Juliet Mills and Richard Long
18) *The West Wing* (1999-2006)
19) Peter Tork and Michael Nesmith
20) Indiana

Quiz 32

1) Who played Myrna Turner, Oscar Madison's secretary, on the original *The Odd Couple*?
2) In *How the Grinch Stole Christmas!*, what is the name of the Grinch's dog?
3) What is the longest-running children's show in the United States?
4) Who plays the brilliant criminal defense professor Annalise Keating on *How to Get Away with Murder*?
5) What is the name of Jane Lynch's cheerleading coach character on *Glee*?
6) The entire series *How I Met Your Mother* is told from the perspective of what character?
7) What actress has played the same role for the longest time in American live-action primetime television?
8) What was the captain's name in *Star Trek: Enterprise*?
9) What was the name of the character Howard Hesseman played in *WKRP in Cincinnati*?
10) On the sitcom *The Good Place*, who plays Michael, the architect of the good place?
11) What character does Sean Hayes play on *Will & Grace*?
12) Who was the first host of *Saturday Night Live* in 1975?
13) Who plays Detective Jake Peralta on the crime comedy *Brooklyn Nine-Nine*?
14) What drama is based on the Israeli series *Prisoners of War*?
15) What is the name of the FBI unit the team works for on *Criminal Minds*?
16) What is the first primetime U.S. series starring an Asian American family since Margaret Cho's *All-American Girl* in 1994?
17) What fantasy drama centers on a homicide detective who discovers he is a descendant of hunters who fight supernatural forces?
18) Who were the original co-hosts of *Good Morning America* when it debuted in 1975?
19) Who is regarded as the first television entertainer to step out of character and break the fourth wall by talking directly to the television audience?
20) What was the original name of the advertising firm at the center of *Mad*

Men?

Quiz 32 Answers

1) Penny Marshall
2) Max
3) *Sesame Street* - started in 1969
4) Viola Davis
5) Sue Sylvester
6) Ted Mosby
7) Mariska Hargitay - She has played Olivia Benson on *Law & Order: Special Victims Unit* since 1999.
8) Jonathan Archer
9) Dr. Johnny Fever
10) Ted Danson
11) Jack McFarland
12) George Carlin
13) Andy Samberg
14) *Homeland* - debuted 2011
15) Behavioral Analysis Unit (BAU)
16) *Fresh Off the Boat* - debuted 2015
17) *Grimm* (2011-2017)
18) David Hartman and Nancy Dussault
19) George Burns - on *The George Burns and Gracie Allen Show* from 1950-1958
20) Sterling Cooper

Quiz 33

1) What series had 25 different actors fill the six regular roles on the show over its run?
2) Who played the title role on the private detective series *Honey West*?
3) What Oscar winner plays the title role in the sitcom *Mom*?
4) How many continuous years was *American Bandstand* on the air?
5) What sports drama series was based on a 2004 movie of the same name?
6) What was the character name of the vampire on the cult soap opera *Dark Shadows*?
7) What crime drama anthology is inspired by a Coen brothers film?
8) Who sang the theme song and was the narrator on *The Dukes of*

Hazzard?

9) Who plays Los Angeles area college professor Mort Pfefferman who decides to transition from being a male to a female in the comedy *Transparent*?
10) What was the name of the space station leader in *Star Trek: Deep Space Nine*?
11) What actor and actress play the mother and father on *Leave It to Beaver*?
12) What animated comedy features Bob Belcher and his wife and three children trying to run a restaurant?
13) On *Castle*, what was the name of the fictional heroine Castle created based on working with Kate?
14) After *Doctor Who*, what is the second longest-running science fiction or fantasy series?
15) What Hollywood legend played Robert Wagner's father in a recurring role on *It Takes a Thief*?
16) Who was the first African American to host a nationwide show?
17) What was the first show in producer Dick Wolf's set of four Chicago based series?
18) What town was the setting for *Little House on the Prairie*?
19) What series at its height aired in 148 countries on every inhabited continent and was called the most-watched television show in the world by *The Guinness Book of World Records*?
20) What was the first sitcom where the theme song was sung by the leading actors?

Quiz 33 Answers

1) *Law & Order* (1990-2010)
2) Anne Francis
3) Allison Janney
4) 37 years
5) *Friday Night Lights* (2006-2011)
6) Barnabas Collins
7) *Fargo* - debuted 2014
8) Waylon Jennings
9) Jeffrey Tambor
10) Benjamin Sisko
11) Hugh Beaumont and Barbara Billingsley
12) *Bob's Burgers* - debuted 2011
13) Nikki Heat

14) *Supernatural* - debuted in 2005
15) Fred Astaire
16) Nat King Cole - 1956
17) *Chicago Fire* - It debuted in 2012 and was followed by *Chicago P.D.*, *Chicago Med*, and *Chicago Justice*.
18) Walnut Grove, Minnesota
19) *Baywatch* (1989-2001)
20) *Green Acres* (1965-1971)- Eddie Albert and Eva Gabor

Quiz 34

1) Who played agent Jim Hardie in *Tales of Wells Fargo*?
2) Who starred in the title role on *The Life and Times of Grizzly Adams* about a falsely accused man who must flee into the mountains?
3) What BBC crime series follows a fish out of water British police inspector working on the Caribbean island of Saint-Marie solving murders?
4) Who played the young Kunta Kinte on the miniseries *Roots*?
5) Who was the first African American to win a primetime Emmy?
6) On the crime comedy *Monk*, what was Monk's first name?
7) What actor on *Night Court* won four consecutive Emmys for their role?
8) Who was the only actor to appear in both the 1970s and 2000s versions of *Battlestar Galactica*?
9) What series starred Burt Reynolds as a homicide detective in his hometown of Santa Luisa, California?
10) What drama focused on three generations of women living together in Hartford, Connecticut with one of them working as a family court judge?
11) In what year did the first television couple share a bed?
12) What western series starred Richard Boone as an ex-gunfighter who uses contemporary methods of solving crimes?
13) What science fiction drama dealt with decades of missing persons returned by a ball of light without any signs of aging and with many of them having heightened abilities?
14) What series is based on a book of the same name and centers on a public relations executive who is sentenced to a minimum-security women's prison in Connecticut?
15) What was the name of the electronics store Chuck works at as a cover while he is a spy on *Chuck*?
16) What year did *Gunsmoke* debut?

17) In what year was the first color television system demonstrated?
18) What was Earl's last name in the sitcom *My Name is Earl*?
19) What drama series was about the reign and marriages of King Henry VIII?
20) Between the two leads, what series had the Outstanding Actress in a Drama Series Emmy winner six straight years?

Quiz 34 Answers

1) Dale Robertson
2) Dan Haggerty
3) *Death in Paradise* - debuted 2010
4) Levar Burton
5) Harry Belafonte - *Tonight with Harry Belafonte* (1960)
6) Adrian
7) John Larroquette
8) Richard Hatch
9) *Dan August* (1970-1971)
10) *Judging Amy* (1999-2006)
11) 1947 - on *Mary Kay and Johnny*, which was the first American sitcom
12) *Hec Ramsey* (1972-1974)
13) The 4400 (2004-2007)
14) *Orange Is the New Black* (2013-2019)
15) Buy More
16) 1955
17) 1928
18) Hickey
19) *The Tudors* (2007-2010)
20) *Cagney & Lacey* (1981-1988) - Sharon Gless and Tyne Daly

Quiz 35

1) What is the longest-running Superman series?
2) What sitcom centers on a young obstetrician-gynecologist trying to balance her personal and professional life?
3) Who was the host of the game show *Password*?
4) What role does *Seinfeld* co-creator Larry David play in *Curb Your Enthusiasm*?
5) What is the name of the coffee shop where the characters in *Friends* hang out?

6) What is the longest-running sitcom in the United States?
7) Who was the musical director on *Late Night with David Letterman*?
8) What sitcom starred Donna Pescow as a middle-class Italian American who marries into a wealthy family?
9) Lucille Ball played a secretary for her brother-in-law in what kind of business in *Here's Lucy*?
10) What is the name of Kerry Washington's former White House staffer and now professional fixer character on *Scandal*?
11) Who played the title roles on *The Ropers*?
12) Who was the first African American to win the Outstanding Supporting Actor in a Comedy Series Emmy?
13) *The Price Is Right* debuted in 1972 with Bob Barker as host; who was the announcer for many years and popularized the "Come on down!" catchphrase?
14) What was the first series to sweep all seven major Emmys in its category?
15) Who was the first regular character on U.S. television who was a divorcee?
16) Which network holds the record for most primetime Emmy wins in a year?
17) Who played police officer Francis Muldoon on *Car 54, Where Are You*?
18) What is the family name of the two brothers on *Supernatural*?
19) *NCIS* is a spin-off of what series?
20) Richard Anderson and Martin E. Brooks were the first actors in U.S. television history to play the same characters on two different series on two different networks at the same time; what were the two series they were on concurrently?

Quiz 35 Answers

1) *Smallville* (2001-2011)
2) *The Mindy Project* (2012-2017)
3) Allen Ludden
4) Larry David - He plays himself.
5) Central Perk
6) *The Simpsons* - started in 1989
7) Paul Shaffer
8) *Angie* (1979-1980)
9) Employment agency
10) Olivia Pope

11) Norman Fell and Audra Lindley
12) Robert Guillaume - *Soap* (1979)
13) Johnny Olson
14) *Schitt's Creek* - 2020
15) Vivian Bagley - *The Lucy Show* (1962)
16) CBS - 44 wins in 1974
17) Fred Gwynne
18) Winchester
19) *JAG*
20) *The Six Million Dollar Man* and *The Bionic Woman* - They played Oscar Goldman and Dr. Rudy Wells on both shows that were originally both on ABC. *The Bionic Woman* moved to NBC in 1978 for its last season, and they continued their roles on both shows.

U.S. Geography

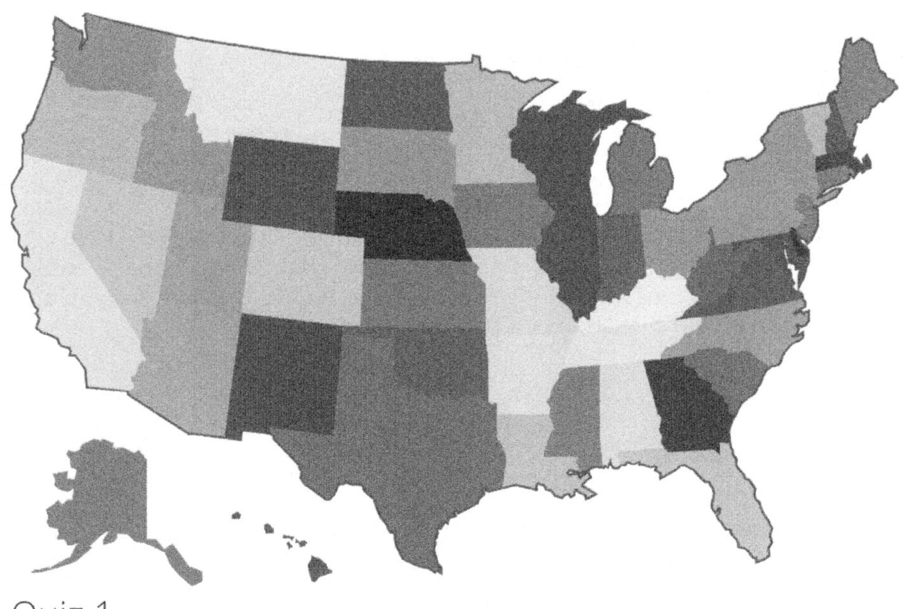

Quiz 1

1) What is the largest city on the Mississippi River?
2) What is the oldest city in the United States?
3) What is the name of the island between the two waterfalls at Niagara Falls?
4) What is the highest waterfall in the United States?
5) What is the least populous state capital?
6) What major city is named after a U.S. vice president of the 1840s?
7) What state has the largest area of inland water?
8) Which of the 48 contiguous states extends farthest north?
9) What state's three most populous cities all have names beginning with the letter C?
10) What is the least accessible state capital?
11) The Statue of Liberty stands on what island?
12) What is the largest island in the contiguous 48 states?
13) How many miles separate the United States and Cuba?
14) What state has a Union Jack on its flag?
15) What is the only borough of New York City that is not mainly on an

island?
16) What state capital is named after a famous German statesman?
17) What state is the geographic center of North America?
18) What state is closest to Bermuda?
19) In the 48 contiguous states, what is the largest city based on land area?
20) What is the second-largest wine-producing state?

Quiz 1 Answers

1) Memphis, Tennessee
2) St. Augustine, Florida – 1565
3) Goat Island
4) Yosemite Falls – 2,425 feet
5) Montpelier, Vermont
6) Dallas – George Mifflin Dallas was vice president for James K. Polk.
7) Alaska
8) Minnesota
9) Ohio – Columbus, Cleveland, Cincinnati
10) Juneau Alaska – You must fly or take a boat.
11) Liberty Island
12) Long Island
13) 90
14) Hawaii
15) Bronx
16) Bismarck, North Dakota – after Otto von Bismarck
17) North Dakota
18) North Carolina
19) Jacksonville, Florida – 758 square miles
20) Washington

Quiz 2

1) What national park has the nickname “Crown of the Continent”?
2) What is the only state with a one-syllable name?
3) By area, what is the third-largest state?
4) What is the only state with the same name as a country?
5) How many state capitals are named after presidents?
6) What state capital has the largest population?
7) What is the highest peak east of the Mississippi River?

8) What two state capitals include the name of the state?
9) What is the only state flag that has an image of a president?
10) What is the most densely populated state?
11) In the 48 contiguous states, what is the most northern state capital?
12) What is the deepest gorge in the United States?
13) How many states border the Gulf of Mexico?
14) What are the five boroughs of New York City?
15) What state has the most counties?
16) What is the tallest volcano in the contiguous 48 states?
17) What is the only non-rectangular state flag?
18) How many states border the Atlantic Ocean (excluding the Gulf of Mexico)?
19) What is the oldest city west of the Rocky Mountains?
20) What state has the fewest counties?

Quiz 2 Answers

1) Glacier National Park
2) Maine
3) California
4) Georgia
5) Four – Lincoln, Jefferson City, Jackson, Madison
6) Phoenix, Arizona
7) Mount Mitchell – 6,684 feet in North Carolina
8) Oklahoma City and Indianapolis
9) Washington
10) New Jersey
11) Olympia, Washington
12) Hells Canyon – 7,993 feet deep on the Snake River on the Oregon and Idaho border
13) Five – Florida, Alabama, Mississippi, Louisiana, Texas
14) Bronx, Queens, Staten Island, Manhattan, Brooklyn
15) Texas – 254
16) Mount Rainier – 14,411 feet in Washington
17) Ohio – swallowtail design
18) 14 – Maine, New Hampshire, Massachusetts, Rhode Island, Connecticut, New York, New Jersey, Delaware, Maryland, Virginia, North Carolina, South Carolina, Georgia, Florida
19) Astoria, Oregon - 1811

20) Delaware – three

Quiz 3

1) What is the most visited U.S. national park?
2) What state is the geographic center of the 48 contiguous states?
3) What is the only state that ends with a "K"?
4) By area, what is the largest U.S. city?
5) What is the highest elevation state capital?
6) Fort Knox is in what state?
7) What is the only state that borders just one other state?
8) What two state capitals are named for royalty?
9) What is the only two-sided state flag (different designs on each side)?
10) How many states share a land or water border with Canada?
11) How many states don't border either the ocean or one of the Great Lakes?
12) What three rivers meet in Pittsburgh?
13) What is the flattest state?
14) What is the only two-word state capital in a two-word state?
15) The Mississippi River runs through or along how many states?
16) What two state capitals sit on the borders of other states?
17) What is the only state name that doesn't share any letters with its capital city?
18) What is the only state capital without a McDonald's?
19) What two state capitals are located on the Mississippi River?
20) In the 48 contiguous states, what is the most southern state capital?

Quiz 3 Answers

1) Great Smoky Mountains
2) Kansas
3) New York
4) Yakutat, Alaska – 9,459 square miles
5) Santa Fe, New Mexico – 7,000 feet
6) Kentucky
7) Maine
8) Annapolis, Maryland, and Albany, New York – They were named for Princess Anne of Denmark and Norway, who became Queen of England, and for the Duke of York and Albany, who became King James II of England.

9) Oregon
10) 13 - Alaska, Washington, Idaho, Montana, North Dakota, Minnesota, Michigan, Ohio, Pennsylvania, New York, Vermont, New Hampshire, Maine
11) 20 - Arizona, Arkansas, Colorado, Idaho, Iowa, Kansas, Kentucky, Missouri, Montana, Nebraska, Nevada, New Mexico, North Dakota, Oklahoma, South Dakota, Tennessee, Utah, Vermont, West Virginia, Wyoming
12) Allegheny, Monongahela, Ohio
13) Florida – 345 feet between its highest and lowest points
14) Santa Fe, New Mexico
15) 10 – Arkansas, Illinois, Iowa, Kentucky, Louisiana, Minnesota, Mississippi, Missouri, Tennessee, Wisconsin
16) Carson City, Nevada (California border) and Trenton, New Jersey (Pennsylvania border)
17) South Dakota – Pierre
18) Montpelier, Vermont
19) St. Paul and Baton Rouge
20) Austin, Texas

Quiz 4

1) What is the only state name that can be typed on one row of a standard keyboard?
2) What is the largest island in the United States?
3) What is the most visited U.S. city?
4) What is the only state on the east coast to fall partly in the Central Time Zone?
5) What state has the highest per capita income?
6) What state has the highest percentage of foreign-born population?
7) What state has the lowest median age?
8) What state has the highest median age?
9) What state has the largest number of active volcanoes?
10) What is the westernmost state?
11) What state has the most miles of rivers?
12) What state has the most national parks?
13) What state has the highest percentage of federal land?
14) What two states share the longest border?
15) How many states refer to themselves as commonwealths in their names?

16) What state capital was once the national capital?
17) What U.S. state is closest to Africa?
18) What is the only letter that doesn't appear in any state name?
19) What is the longest state from north to south?
20) At its closest point, what is the distance between the United States and Russia?

Quiz 4 Answers

1) Alaska
2) Hawaii
3) Orlando, Florida - New York City is second.
4) Florida
5) Connecticut
6) California
7) Utah
8) Maine
9) Alaska – 130 out of the 169 active volcanoes in the United States
10) Alaska
11) Alaska – It has about 365,000 miles of rivers.
12) California – nine
13) Nevada – 81%
14) Texas and Oklahoma – 700 miles
15) Four (Kentucky, Massachusetts, Pennsylvania, Virginia) - There is no legal distinction just a naming difference from earlier times.
16) Annapolis, Maryland
17) Maine – Quoddy Head peninsula is 3,154 miles from Morocco.
18) Q
19) Alaska – 1,479 miles
20) 2.4 miles

Quiz 5

1) How many U.S. states are larger than the United Kingdom?
2) How many states have land farther south than the most northern point of Mexico?
3) At one point in the year, it is the same local time for parts of Oregon and Florida; how is this possible?
4) What is the official language of the United States?
5) What was the original name for the island where the Statue of Liberty

stands?

6) New York City has a larger population than how many states?
7) What is the only major U.S. city founded by a woman?
8) How many states are at least partly north of the southernmost point of Canada?
9) What is the second-largest island in the United States?
10) What Canadian province borders the most states?
11) In the 48 contiguous states, what is the most western state capital?
12) How many states does the Canadian province of Alberta border?
13) What state has the highest lowest elevation point?
14) By area, what is the largest lake in the United States?
15) By area, what is the largest lake that only borders one state?
16) What state has the lowest highest elevation point?
17) What two states have a lowest elevation point below sea level?
18) By area, what is the fourth largest state?
19) Which of the contiguous 48 states has the longest border with Canada?
20) What were the last four states to join the United States?

Quiz 5 Answers

1) 11 – Alaska, Texas, California, Montana, New Mexico, Arizona, Nevada, Colorado, Oregon, Wyoming, Michigan
2) 11 – Alabama, Arizona, California, Florida, Georgia, Hawaii, Louisiana, Mississippi, New Mexico, South Carolina, Texas
3) A small part of eastern Oregon is in the Mountain Time Zone, and a small part of western Florida is in the Central Time Zone. When the change from daylight saving time to standard time is made, these two areas share the same time for one hour after the Central Time Zone has fallen back to standard time and before the Mountain Time Zone has.
4) There isn't one.
5) Bedloe's Island
6) 39
7) Miami – Julia Tuttle
8) 27 – Alaska, California, Connecticut, Idaho, Illinois, Indiana, Iowa, Maine, Massachusetts, Michigan, Minnesota, Montana, Nebraska, Nevada, New Hampshire, New York, North Dakota, Ohio, Oregon, Pennsylvania, Rhode Island, South Dakota, Utah, Vermont, Washington, Wisconsin, Wyoming
9) Kodiak Island, Alaska – 3,672 square miles
10) Ontario – borders Minnesota, Michigan, Ohio, Pennsylvania, New York

11) Olympia, Washington
12) One – Montana
13) Colorado – 3,315 feet
14) Lake Superior – 31,700 square miles
15) Lake Huron – 23,012 square miles
16) Florida – 345 feet
17) California and Louisiana
18) Montana
19) Michigan
20) New Mexico, Arizona, Alaska, Hawaii

Quiz 6

1) What is the most commonly occurring place name in the United States?
2) By area, what is the largest state east of the Mississippi River?
3) What is the source of the Mississippi River?
4) What New Mexico resort town was named after a radio game show?
5) By area, what is the smallest state?
6) How many states border the Great Lakes?
7) What is the highest mountain in the United States?
8) What is the highest mountain in the contiguous 48 states?
9) What state capital is 10 miles from Princeton University?
10) What is the only state name that ends in three vowels?
11) What state receives the least sunshine?
12) What is the southernmost state?
13) After Canada and Mexico, what country is closest to the United States?
14) How many states border California?
15) What two states share the most borders with other states?
16) What state has the lowest average elevation?
17) How many states are at least partially north of the southernmost part of Canada and at least partially south of the northernmost point of Mexico?
18) What state has the longest border with Canada?
19) How many states border the Pacific Ocean?
20) What was the first state with a woman governor?

Quiz 6 Answers

1) Washington

2) Georgia
3) Lake Itasca, Minnesota
4) Truth or Consequences
5) Rhode Island
6) Eight - Illinois, Indiana, Michigan, Minnesota, New York, Ohio, Pennsylvania, Wisconsin
7) Denali or Mount McKinley, Alaska – 20,310 feet
8) Mount Whitney, California – 14,505 feet
9) Trenton, New Jersey
10) Hawaii
11) Alaska
12) Hawaii
13) Russia – 2.4 miles
14) Three – Oregon, Nevada, Arizona
15) Missouri and Tennessee – eight states border each
16) Delaware – 60 feet average elevation
17) One – California
18) Alaska
19) Five – Washington, Oregon, California, Alaska, Hawaii
20) Wyoming

Quiz 7

1) What state has the least rainfall?
2) What landmark became 1,313 feet shorter in 1980?
3) What is the only state that borders a Canadian territory?
4) How many states border Mexico?
5) What state has the second-longest coastline?
6) What four states have active volcanoes?
7) What city has the only royal palace in the United States?
8) What state has the most rainfall?
9) What is the easternmost state capital?
10) What is the easternmost state?
11) What state capital has the largest land area?
12) What state capital has more than 30 Buddhist temples?
13) What state has the highest average elevation?
14) What state has the smallest population?
15) What is the largest U.S. city on the Great Lakes?

16) What is the only state that ends with three consonants?
17) What state has the most tornadoes on average?
18) Where is the lowest elevation land point in the United States?
19) What is the deepest lake in the United States?
20) By area, what is the smallest state west of the Mississippi River?

Quiz 7 Answers

1) Nevada – 9.5 inches mean annual precipitation
2) Mount St. Helens
3) Alaska
4) Four – California, Arizona, New Mexico, and Texas
5) Florida
6) Alaska, California, Hawaii, Washington
7) Honolulu, Hawaii
8) Hawaii – 63.7 inches mean annual precipitation
9) Augusta, Maine
10) Alaska – stretches into the Eastern Hemisphere
11) Juneau, Alaska – 3,255 square miles
12) Honolulu, Hawaii
13) Colorado – 6,800 feet average
14) Wyoming
15) Chicago
16) Massachusetts
17) Texas
18) Death Valley, California – 279 feet below sea level
19) Crater Lake – 1,949 feet
20) Hawaii

Quiz 8

1) What Is the most popular street name in the United States?
2) By volume, what is the largest lake entirely within the United States?
3) Of the 10 tallest mountains in the United States, how many are in Alaska?
4) By volume, what is the largest lake entirely within one state?
5) What state has the highest percentage of its area that is water?
6) What state has the lowest percentage of its area that is water?
7) How many states are entirely north of the southernmost point of

Canada?

8) By area, what state has the largest county?
9) By population, what state has the largest county?
10) What state had the first commercial oil well in the United States?
11) At the start of the 20th century, how many U.S. states were there?
12) What was the first U.S. state?
13) What was the first U.S. national monument?
14) What is the oldest U.S. state capital?
15) What two states donated land to create Washington, D.C.?
16) What is the highest peak between the Rocky Mountains and the Appalachian Mountains?
17) The border between what two states is partially formed by the Continental Divide?
18) What state's southern border is formed by a river of the same name?
19) What two Canadian provinces only border one state?
20) What is the longest interstate highway?

Quiz 8 Answers

1) Park
2) Lake Michigan
3) 10 – Mt. Whitney, the highest peak in the contiguous 48 states, is the 11th highest in the United States.
4) Lake Iliamna, Alaska
5) Michigan – followed by Hawaii and Rhode Island
6) New Mexico – followed by Arizona and Colorado
7) 13 - Alaska, Washington, Oregon, Idaho, Montana, North Dakota, South Dakota, Minnesota, Wisconsin, Michigan, Vermont, New Hampshire, Maine
8) California – San Bernardino county is 20,105 square miles.
9) California – Los Angeles county
10) Pennsylvania
11) 45 – Oklahoma, New Mexico, Arizona, Alaska, and Hawaii weren't states yet.
12) Delaware – December 7, 1787
13) Devils Tower, Wyoming – 1906
14) Santa Fe, New Mexico – 1609
15) Maryland and Virginia
16) Mount Magazine – 2,753 feet in the Ouachita Mountains in Arkansas

17) Idaho and Montana
18) Ohio
19) Alberta and New Brunswick
20) I-90 from Boston to Seattle – 3,111 miles

Quiz 9

1) What state has Lake of the Woods, the 7th largest lake in the United States?
2) The Columbia River enters the United States in what state?
3) What four states border Texas?
4) What state has Crater Lake National Park?
5) What is the second highest mountain in the contiguous 48 states?
6) What state borders Washington to the east?
7) How many states are doubly landlocked (two states or provinces away from the ocean)?
8) How many time zones does Alaska have?
9) What state's highest mountain is Kings Peak?
10) What state has the nickname "The Equality State"?
11) What is the largest desert in the United States?
12) What state has one of the largest pyramids in the world featuring a hotel, indoor swamp, aquarium, bowling alley, and the world's tallest freestanding elevator?
13) What state is Mount Shasta in?
14) What southern state capital is on the Mississippi River?
15) What is the deepest river in the United States?
16) What state borders Missouri to the south?
17) What is the third-longest river in the United States?
18) What was the first state to adopt an official sport?
19) What state is Grand Teton in?
20) The Arkansas River flows into what river?

Quiz 9 Answers

1) Minnesota
2) Washington
3) New Mexico, Oklahoma, Arkansas, Louisiana
4) Oregon
5) Mount Elbert - 14,440 feet in Colorado
6) Idaho

7) 10 - Colorado, Illinois, Indiana, Iowa, Kansas, Missouri, South Dakota, Utah, Wisconsin, Wyoming
8) Two
9) Utah - 13,534 feet
10) Wyoming
11) Great Basin Desert - 200,000 square miles covering most of Nevada and parts of Utah, California, Oregon, and Idaho
12) Tennessee - The Memphis Bass Pro Shops Megastore is 321 feet tall with a 535,000 square foot interior.
13) California - 14,180 feet
14) Baton Rouge, Louisiana
15) St. Lawrence River - maximum depth of 250 feet
16) Arkansas
17) Yukon River - 1,979 miles starting in British Columbia, Canada and flowing through Alaska
18) Maryland - They named jousting as their official sport in 1962.
19) Wyoming - 13,775 feet
20) Mississippi River

Quiz 10

1) If you go north, south, east, or west from Stamford, Connecticut, what is the next state you hit?
2) What state capital is on the Susquehanna River?
3) What is the fourth-longest river in the United States?
4) The Big Island of Hawaii is getting 42 acres larger each year due to what?
5) What is the fourth-longest river entirely in the United States?
6) If you define a mountain as an elevation of 2,000 feet or more, how many states don't have any mountains?
7) What state has the largest cave system in the world?
8) By area, what is the largest lake entirely within the United States?
9) What state had the first motel in the world?
10) What state borders South Dakota to the south?
11) What state's highest mountain is Gannett Peak?
12) What state gets its name from the French for "green mountain"?
13) What is the official state sport of Minnesota?
14) What lake is formed by the Glen Canyon Dam?
15) What is the third most populous state?

16) By area, how many of the five largest lakes in the United States are one of the Great Lakes?
17) What state's name is derived from the Ojibwe word for "great or large lake"?
18) What was the last state to be explored by Europeans or Americans (not Native Americans)?
19) What state has the nickname "The Centennial State"?
20) What is the only state that is at least three states or provinces away from the ocean in every direction?

Quiz 10 Answers

1) New York
2) Harrisburg, Pennsylvania
3) Rio Grande - 1,759 miles
4) Lava flows from Kīlauea volcano
5) Red River - 1,125 miles
6) 13 - Delaware, Florida, Illinois, Indiana, Iowa, Louisiana, Michigan, Mississippi, Missouri, New Jersey, Ohio, Rhode Island, Wisconsin
7) Kentucky - Mammoth Cave, located near Brownsville, Kentucky, is the longest cave in the world, measuring 405 miles.
8) Lake Michigan - 22,300 square miles
9) California - The first motel in the world was opened in 1925 in San Luis Obispo, California; the original room charge was $1.25 per night.
10) Nebraska
11) Wyoming - 13,809 feet
12) Vermont
13) Ice hockey
14) Lake Powell
15) Florida
16) Five
17) Michigan - from the Ojibwe word "mishigamaa"
18) Idaho - It wasn't explored until Lewis and Clark entered Idaho in 1805 on their expedition across America.
19) Colorado
20) Nebraska

Quiz 11

1) How many states don't have any national parks?

2) What state's highest point is Mount Whitney?
3) What state has the nickname "The Gem State"?
4) By area, what is the third-largest lake entirely within the United States?
5) What is the name of Hawaii's time zone?
6) What U.S. state has the world's shortest river?
7) What river flows through three state capitals?
8) What state borders Alabama to the west?
9) What state is named in honor of the wife of King Charles I of England?
10) How many oceans does the United States border?
11) What is the least populated permanently inhabited U.S. territory?
12) What states border Lake Huron?
13) What state capital is on the Willamette River?
14) What state has Isle Royale National Park?
15) What state's name is based on the Spanish term for the Easter season meaning "feast of flowers"?
16) What state capital is on the Hudson River?
17) What state had the first McDonald's drive-thru?
18) What state capital is on the Cumberland River?
19) What is the third highest mountain in the United States?
20) In what state are you never more than six miles from a body of water?

Quiz 11 Answers

1) 23 - Alabama, Connecticut, Delaware, Georgia, Illinois, Indiana, Iowa, Kansas, Louisiana, Maryland, Massachusetts, Mississippi, Missouri, Nebraska, New Hampshire, New Jersey, New York, Oklahoma, Pennsylvania, Rhode Island, Vermont, West Virginia, Wisconsin
2) California - 14,505 feet
3) Idaho
4) Lake Iliamna - 1,012 square miles in Alaska
5) Hawaii-Aleutian Time Zone - It includes Hawaii and Alaska's Aleutian Islands west of 169 degrees 30 minutes west longitude.
6) Montana - The Roe River is recognized as the world's shortest river; it flows for 200 feet between Giant Springs and the Missouri River near Great Falls, Montana.
7) Missouri River - Bismarck, North Dakota; Pierre, South Dakota; Jefferson City, Missouri
8) Mississippi
9) Maryland - in honor of Henrietta Maria

10) Three - Atlantic, Pacific, Arctic (Alaska's northern border in on the Arctic)
11) American Samoa
12) Michigan
13) Salem, Oregon
14) Michigan
15) Florida - It was discovered on Palm Sunday by Juan Ponce de León, and the Spanish term for the Easter season is Pascua Florida.
16) Albany, New York
17) Arizona - The first McDonald's drive-thru was created in 1975 in Sierra Vista, Arizona, near the Fort Huachuca military base. It was designed to serve military personnel who weren't permitted to get out of their cars off base while wearing fatigues.
18) Nashville, Tennessee
19) Mount Foraker - 17,400 feet in Alaska
20) Michigan - It has over 11,000 inland lakes plus four of the five Great Lakes.

Quiz 12

1) What state borders Kansas to the south?
2) What U.S. state experienced the greatest temperature variation ever recorded in 24 hours?
3) What are the only two mobile national monuments in the United States?
4) What state's largest lake is Lake Pontchartrain?
5) How many states are split into two time zones?
6) What state has the second-largest water area?
7) What two states share Lake Champlain?
8) What state has the nickname "The Beehive State"?
9) Of the states that have declared an official state sport, the most popular choice with three states declaring it as their official sport is what?
10) What state gets its name from the Spanish for "ruddy" or "red" referring to the color of one of its primary rivers?
11) What state has the nickname "The Treasure State"?
12) What states border Lake Michigan?
13) By area, what is the sixth largest state?
14) On a per-capita basis, what state produces the most serial killers?
15) What state is the source of the Colorado River?
16) What state gets its name from the Oto Indian word meaning "flat

water" referring to one of its primary rivers?
17) What state's highest point is Mount Hood?
18) What is the second most populous state?
19) By area, what is the fourth-smallest state?
20) What state has the nickname "The Pine Tree State"?

Quiz 12 Answers

1) Oklahoma
2) Montana - On January 23, 1916, Browning, Montana, went from a high of 44 degrees to a low of -56 degrees Fahrenheit in 24 hours.
3) San Francisco's cable cars and the New Orleans Saint Charles streetcar line
4) Louisiana - 631 square miles, 11th largest lake in the United States
5) 14 - Alaska, Florida, Idaho, Indiana, Kansas, Kentucky, Michigan, Nebraska, Nevada, North Dakota, South Dakota, Oregon, Tennessee, Texas
6) Michigan - 40,175 square miles of water
7) New York and Vermont - 490 square miles
8) Utah
9) Rodeo - South Dakota, Texas, Wyoming
10) Colorado - named for the color of the Colorado River
11) Montana
12) Illinois, Indiana, Michigan, Wisconsin
13) Arizona - 113,990 square miles
14) Alaska
15) Colorado
16) Nebraska - The name refers to the Platte River.
17) Oregon - 11,249 feet
18) Texas
19) New Jersey - 8,729 square miles
20) Maine

Quiz 13

1) What state is the source of the Rio Grande River?
2) What state has the nickname "The Peace Garden State"?
3) What state capital is on the Colorado River?
4) What state is the source of the Arkansas River?
5) How many states have more than one national park?

6) What is the third-longest river entirely within the United States?
7) What state is named after Queen Elizabeth I?
8) What is the longest river that flows entirely within one state?
9) Based on discharge volume, what is the largest river in the United States?
10) What state has Guadalupe Mountains National Park?
11) What are the only two U.S. state capitals with rhyming names?
12) What state has Carlsbad Caverns National Park?
13) By land area, what is the largest state capital city?
14) By area, where would Texas rank as a country?
15) What state has the nickname "Land of Enchantment"?
16) What state is the source of the Red River?
17) Including U.S. territories, what two states or territories have the furthest distance between them?
18) What is the largest canyon in the United States?
19) The highest and lowest points in the contiguous United States are in the same county in what state?
20) Which state has more of the 100 largest lakes in the United States than any other?

Quiz 13 Answers

1) Colorado
2) North Dakota
3) Austin, Texas
4) Colorado
5) 13 - Alaska, Arizona, California, Colorado, Florida, Hawaii, Montana, Nevada, South Dakota, Texas, Utah, Washington, Wyoming
6) Arkansas River - The Missouri and Mississippi Rivers are the longest followed by the Arkansas River at 1,443 miles.
7) Virginia - Elizabeth I was the Virgin Queen.
8) Colorado River of Texas - It flows for 970 miles entirely within Texas and is the 11th longest river in the United States.
9) Mississippi River
10) Texas
11) Boston and Austin
12) New Mexico
13) Juneau, Alaska - 2,717 square miles
14) 39th - closest in size to Myanmar

15) New Mexico
16) Oklahoma
17) Guam and U.S. Virgin Islands - 9,514 miles from Point Udall, Guam, to Point Udall, St. Croix, U.S. Virgin Islands
18) Grand Canyon - 277 miles long, up to 18 miles wide, and a maximum depth of 6,093 feet
19) California - Mount Whitney at 14,494 feet and the Badwater Basin in Death Valley at 282 feet below sea level are separated by 85 miles in Inyo county, California.
20) Minnesota - It has eight lakes in the top 100: Lake Superior, Lake of the Woods, Red Lake, Rainy Lake, Mille Lacs Lake, Leech Lake, Lake Winnibigoshish, Lake Vermilion.

Quiz 14

1) By area, what is the third smallest state?
2) What three states share Yellowstone National Park?
3) The furthest distance between any two states is between which two?
4) What river flows through the most states?
5) What two states share the Great Smoky Mountains National Park?
6) What state is the source of the Ohio River?
7) What state gets its name from a Dakota word meaning "sky-tinted water"?
8) What state was named after the future King James II of England?
9) Does Virginia or West Virginia extend further west?
10) What body of water does the Columbia River empty into?
11) What states border Lake Superior?
12) What body of water does the Yukon River empty into?
13) What two states border Illinois to the west?
14) What state borders Ohio to the west?
15) What state's highest point is Humphreys Peak?
16) By area, what is the largest lake entirely within one state?
17) What state has the world's longest continuous bridge over water?
18) What are the two longest mountain ranges in the United States?
19) What is the most populous state?
20) What state has all five of the largest land area cities in the United States?

Quiz 14 Answers

1) Connecticut - 5,543 square miles
2) Wyoming (96%), Montana (3%), Idaho (1%)
3) Hawaii and Florida - 5,859 miles from Log Point, Elliot Key, Florida, and Kure Island, Hawaii
4) Mississippi River - It flows through or along 10 states: Arkansas, Illinois, Iowa, Kentucky, Louisiana, Minnesota, Mississippi, Missouri, Tennessee, Wisconsin.
5) Tennessee and North Carolina
6) Pennsylvania
7) Minnesota
8) New York - He was the Duke of York.
9) Virginia
10) Pacific Ocean
11) Michigan, Minnesota, Wisconsin
12) Bering Sea
13) Iowa and Missouri
14) Indiana
15) Arizona - 12,637 feet
16) Great Salt Lake - 2,117 square miles in Utah
17) Louisiana - The Lake Pontchartrain Causeway is nearly 24 miles in length.
18) Rocky Mountains and Appalachian Mountains
19) California
20) Alaska - Yakutat, Sitka, Juneau, Wrangell, Anchorage.

Quiz 15

1) What state gets its name from a Spanish word meaning "mountain"?
2) What two states share Lake Oahe, the largest man-made lake in the United States?
3) By area, what is the largest U.S. territory?
4) What lake is formed by the Hoover Dam?
5) By area, what is the fifth-largest state?
6) What state's highest point is Borah Peak?
7) There is a chunk of Africa stuck under the United States from when the supercontinent Pangaea broke apart about 250 million years ago. It is located off the coast nearest to what state?
8) What two states share Lake Tahoe?

9) What is the most visited urban park in the United States?
10) What state capital is on the James River?
11) What state has Kings Canyon National Park?
12) What state's highest point is Boundary Peak?
13) What state has Acadia National Park?
14) What state has the smallest national park?
15) By area, what is the second largest lake entirely within the United States?
16) What states border Lake Erie?
17) What state's highest point is Mount Rainier?
18) What two states border Idaho to the west?
19) By discharge volume, what is the second largest river in the United States?
20) On a clear day, how many states can you see from the top of the Empire State Building?

Quiz 15 Answers

1) Montana
2) North and South Dakota - 685 square miles
3) Puerto Rico - 3,515 square miles
4) Lake Mead
5) New Mexico - 121,590 square miles
6) Idaho - 12,668 feet
7) Alabama
8) California and Nevada
9) Central Park - New York City
10) Richmond, Virginia
11) California
12) Nevada - 13,147 feet
13) Maine
14) Arkansas - Hot Springs National Park at 8.7 square miles.
15) Great Salt Lake - 2,117 square miles
16) Michigan, New York, Ohio, Pennsylvania
17) Washington - 14,417 feet
18) Washington and Oregon
19) Ohio River
20) Five - New York, New Jersey, Connecticut, Massachusetts, Pennsylvania

Quiz 16

1) What state is the source of the Missouri River?
2) What state is named after one of the English Channel Islands?
3) How many states border Canada?
4) What state has the third-largest water area?
5) What state has the nickname "The Pelican State"?
6) What is the second highest mountain in the United States?
7) What is the official state sport of California?
8) What city got its name in 1845 when Asa Lovejoy from Massachusetts and Francis Pettygrove from Maine flipped a coin with the winner getting to name the new settlement?
9) What state is Mount St. Helens in?
10) What was the first state to enter the Union after the original 13?
11) What state has the nickname "The Bay State"?
12) What state has the largest number of mountains at least 14,000 feet high?
13) By area, what is the smallest permanently inhabited U.S. territory?
14) What state gets its name from the 1510 book *Las Sergas de Esplandián* by Garci Rodríguez de Montalvo who wrote about a mythical island?
15) What two states share Lake Mead?
16) What two states border Nevada to the north?
17) What state capital is on the Charles River?
18) What two states border Tennessee to the west?
19) What state is Devils Tower National Monument in?
20) What is the only state with no natural lakes?

Quiz 16 Answers

1) Montana
2) New Jersey - named after Jersey
3) 13 - Alaska, Idaho, Maine, Michigan, Minnesota, Montana, New Hampshire, New York, North Dakota, Ohio, Pennsylvania, Vermont, Washington
4) Florida - 12,133 square miles of water
5) Louisiana
6) Mount Saint Elias - 18,009 feet in Alaska
7) Surfing
8) Portland, Oregon - Lovejoy wanted to name the new settlement Boston; Pettygrove wanted to name the new town Portland.

9) Washington - 8,366 feet
10) Vermont – 1791
11) Massachusetts
12) Colorado - 53
13) American Samoa - 76 square miles
14) California - The island in the book was named California.
15) Arizona and Nevada - 247 square mile reservoir on the Colorado River
16) Oregon and Idaho
17) Boston, Massachusetts
18) Missouri and Arkansas
19) Wyoming
20) Maryland

Quiz 17

1) By area, what is the fourth largest state?
2) What state has the nickname "The Silver State"?
3) What state's highest point is Wheeler Peak?
4) What is the only state with a floating post office?
5) What state has the nickname "The Granite State"?
6) What state has the nickname "The Evergreen State"?
7) After Washington, what is the second most common town or city name in the United States?
8) What is the largest national park in the United States?
9) What state has North Cascades National Park?
10) What state capital is on the Chattahoochee River?
11) By area, where would Alaska rank as a country?
12) How many mountains of at least 14,000 feet are there in the United States?
13) What state has Great Basin National Park?
14) What state has Shenandoah National Park?
15) What state has the largest water area?
16) What northern state capital is on the Mississippi River?
17) Wisconsin isn't known as the Badger State because of the animal. Miners in the 1830s lived in temporary caves cut into the hillsides that became known as badger dens, and the miners who lived in them were known as badgers; what were they mining?
18) What is the most populous U.S. territory?
19) What states border Lake Ontario?

20) What is the only state without a straight line in its border?

Quiz 17 Answers

1) Montana - 147,040 square miles
2) Nevada
3) New Mexico - 13,167 feet
4) Michigan – It delivers to ships in Detroit.
5) New Hampshire
6) Washington
7) Springfield
8) Wrangell-St. Elias National Park and Preserve - 20,587 square miles in Alaska
9) Washington
10) Atlanta, Georgia
11) 16th - closest in size to Libya
12) 96
13) Nevada
14) Virginia
15) Alaska - 94,743 square miles of water
16) St. Paul, Minnesota
17) Lead
18) Puerto Rico
19) New York
20) Hawaii - Its borders are entirely defined by natural features.

Quiz 18

1) Which state consumes the most alcohol per capita?
2) By area, what is the second smallest state?
3) What state is named after an English county?
4) What state has Voyageurs National Park?
5) What state produces about 95% of the bourbon in the world?
6) What river has the largest drainage basin in the United States?
7) The Ohio River flows into what river?
8) What state's highest point is Black Elk Peak (formerly Harney Peak)?
9) What state has the most colleges?
10) What state has the nickname "The First State"?
11) What state is the source of the Snake River?

12) What state is the source of the Canadian River, the longest tributary of the Arkansas River?
13) What state borders Colorado to the west?
14) By area, what is the second largest lake entirely within one state?
15) What is the highest mountain east of the Rockies?
16) The Snake River flows into what river?
17) By area, where would the U.S. territory of Puerto Rico rank as a state?
18) What is the deepest canyon in the United States?
19) What state capital is built next to the second largest lake entirely in the United States?
20) What state's highest point is Granite Peak?

Quiz 18 Answers

1) New Hampshire - Its consumption is 103% higher than the national average.
2) Delaware - 2,489 square miles
3) New Hampshire
4) Minnesota
5) Kentucky
6) Mississippi River - It has a drainage basin of 1,245,000 square miles, including all or parts of 31 states.
7) Mississippi River
8) South Dakota - 7,242 feet
9) Texas
10) Delaware
11) Wyoming
12) Colorado – The Canadian River is 906 miles long.
13) Utah
14) Lake Iliamna - 1,012 square miles in Alaska
15) Black Elk Peak (formerly Harney Peak) - 7,242 feet in South Dakota
16) Columbia River
17) 49th
18) Kings Canyon - maximum depth of 8,200 feet in California
19) Salt Lake City, Utah
20) Montana - 12,807 feet

U.S. Presidents

Quiz 1

1) Who is the only president to serve two nonconsecutive terms?
2) Who was the first president to attend Monday night football?
3) Who was the last president with facial hair?
4) Who was the first president born in a hospital?
5) What president twice served as an executioner?
6) Who are the only two first ladies born outside the United States?
7) Who was the first president to live in the White House?
8) Who is the only president born on the Fourth of July?

9) What first lady refused Secret Service coverage and was given her own gun?
10) Who was the first president to have been divorced?
11) Who is the youngest ever president?
12) Who was the first president depicted on a circulating U.S. monetary coin?
13) What president's mother had the first name Stanley?
14) What didn't President James Buchanan have that every other president has had?
15) What president's wife saw him elected but died before his inauguration?
16) What two first lady's husbands and sons both served as U.S. president?
17) Who gave Caroline Kennedy her dog Pushinska while her dad was president?
18) What president had the most children?
19) What president had the shortest term?
20) What president was shot at twice at point-blank range but survived because both guns misfired?

Quiz 1 Answers

1) Grover Cleveland - 22nd and 24th president
2) Jimmy Carter
3) William Howard Taft
4) Jimmy Carter
5) Grover Cleveland – in his duty as sheriff
6) Louisa Adams and Melania Trump
7) John Adams
8) Calvin Coolidge
9) Eleanor Roosevelt
10) Ronald Reagan
11) Theodore Roosevelt – 42
12) Abraham Lincoln
13) Barack Obama
14) A wife – He never married, and many historians speculate that he may have been the first gay president.
15) Andrew Jackson
16) Barbara Bush and Abigail Adams
17) Nikita Khrushchev

18) John Tyler – 15 by two wives
19) William Henry Harrison (31 days) - He caught a cold on inauguration day that turned into a fatal case of pneumonia. His grandson Benjamin would later also be president.
20) Andrew Jackson – first presidential assassination attempt

Quiz 2

1) What does the S stand for in Harry S. Truman?
2) Who was the only president to get married at the White House?
3) Who was the heaviest president?
4) What president remarried his wife three years after their wedding because her first divorce wasn't finalized?
5) What is the most common first name of presidents?
6) Who was the tallest president?
7) Who was the shortest president?
8) Who is the only man to have been both Chief Justice of the U.S. Supreme Court and president?
9) What president is commonly credited with inventing the swivel chair?
10) Who was the first president born outside the original 13 states?
11) At president Andrew Jackson's funeral in 1845, who was removed for swearing?
12) Who was the first president to ride in an automobile while in office?
13) Who was the only president to be held as a prisoner of war?
14) What president was the first to use the Oval Office?
15) Who was the first president to fly on official business?
16) What president enacted the law requiring cigarette manufacturers to put health warnings on their packages?
17) Who are the only two men who have run effectively unopposed for president?
18) What president tried to create the "Great Society"?
19) What president said, "Forgive your enemies, but never forget their names"?
20) What president wrote 37 books?

Quiz 2 Answers

1) Nothing – The S was in honor of both of his grandfathers but didn't stand for a middle name.
2) Grover Cleveland

3) William Howard Taft – about 340 pounds when he left office
4) Andrew Jackson
5) James – six presidents
6) Abraham Lincoln – 6'4"
7) James Madison – 5'4"
8) William Howard Taft
9) Thomas Jefferson
10) Abraham Lincoln
11) His pet parrot
12) Theodore Roosevelt
13) Andrew Jackson – He joined the Revolutionary War at age 13 and was captured by the British.
14) William Howard Taft – He made the West Wing a permanent building and had the Oval Office built.
15) Franklin D. Roosevelt - 1943 secret trip to Casablanca
16) Lyndon B. Johnson
17) George Washington and James Monroe
18) Lyndon B. Johnson – set of domestic programs to eliminate poverty and racial injustice
19) John F. Kennedy
20) Theodore Roosevelt

Quiz 3

1) Who is the only president ever granted a patent?
2) Who was the editor of the magazine *Babies Just Babies* when her husband was elected president?
3) Who was the first president to be photographed at his inauguration?
4) Who was the first vice president to become president upon the death of a president?
5) Three first ladies are tied as the tallest at 5'11"; who are they?
6) What two presidents died on July 4, 1826?
7) What president had a raccoon for a pet while in the White House?
8) Who is the oldest person to win a presidential election?
9) Who was the first Roman Catholic vice president?
10) Who is the youngest ever elected president?
11) Who was the first president to win a Nobel Prize?
12) Which president was a Rhodes Scholar?
13) Which first lady was later elected to public office?

14) Who was the only president not elected president or vice president?
15) What is the most common birth state for presidents?
16) What president signed Father's Day into law?
17) Who was the only Eagle Scout president?
18) Who was the first vice president who didn't go on to become president?
19) What president was born as Leslie Lynch King Jr.?
20) Who was the first president to govern over all 50 states?

Quiz 3 Answers

1) Abraham Lincoln - a device that helped buoy vessels over shoals
2) Eleanor Roosevelt
3) James Buchanan
4) John Tyler – He succeeded William Henry Harrison who died of pneumonia 31 days after his inauguration.
5) Melania Trump, Michelle Obama, Eleanor Roosevelt
6) Thomas Jefferson and John Adams
7) Calvin Coolidge – The raccoon was a gift and was supposed to be served for Thanksgiving dinner; Coolidge made it a pet and even walked it on a leash on the White House grounds.
8) Joseph Biden - 77 at time of election
9) Joseph Biden
10) John F. Kennedy – 43
11) Theodore Roosevelt
12) Bill Clinton
13) Hilary Clinton
14) Gerald Ford
15) Virginia – eight
16) Lyndon B. Johnson
17) Gerald Ford
18) Aaron Burr – third vice president
19) Gerald Ford
20) Dwight D. Eisenhower

Quiz 4

1) What president was a head cheerleader in high school?
2) Who was the first president to declare war?
3) Who was the first president to be impeached?
4) Who was vice president when Abraham Lincoln was assassinated?

5) Who was the youngest first lady ever?
6) Who was the first president to leave the United States while in office?
7) How many presidents were only children?
8) Who was the only president to win a Pulitzer Prize?
9) How many presidents have won the Nobel Peace Prize?
10) What president imposed the first federal income tax?
11) Who was the only president with a PhD?
12) Who was the only president to never sign a bill into law?
13) Who was the first republican president?
14) Who was the first president to appear on television?
15) What two presidents were Quakers?
16) Who was the first president paid a salary of $100,000 or more?
17) Who was president when electricity was installed in the White House?
18) Who was president when running water was installed in the White House?
19) What president had a special bathtub big enough to hold four men installed in the White House?
20) How many presidents never attended college?

Quiz 4 Answers

1) George W. Bush
2) James Madison – War of 1812
3) Andrew Johnson – 1868
4) Andrew Johnson
5) Frances Folsom Cleveland – She was 21 when she married Grover Cleveland in the White House; he was 49.
6) Theodore Roosevelt – He went to Panama to inspect canal construction.
7) Zero
8) John F. Kennedy – for *Profiles in Courage*
9) Four – Theodore Roosevelt, Woodrow Wilson, Jimmy Carter, Barack Obama
10) Abraham Lincoln
11) Woodrow Wilson – history and political science
12) William Henry Harrison – 31 days as president
13) Abraham Lincoln
14) Franklin D. Roosevelt
15) Herbert Hoover and Richard Nixon

16) Harry S. Truman
17) Benjamin Harrison – 1889
18) Andrew Jackson - 1833
19) William Howard Taft
20) Nine – Washington, Jackson, Van Buren, Taylor, Fillmore, Lincoln, Andrew Johnson, Cleveland, Truman

Quiz 5

1) Who was the first president born outside the contiguous 48 states?
2) How many presidents were born as British subjects?
3) What is the most common religious affiliation for presidents?
4) How many presidents have been left-handed?
5) How many presidents served as vice presidents?
6) What president was in office when the term "first lady" was first used?
7) How many presidents were assassinated in office?
8) How many presidents died in office?
9) How many presidential candidates have won the popular vote but lost the election?
10) What president lived the longest?
11) What president died at the youngest age?
12) What first lady lived the longest?
13) Who was the oldest first lady at the time of inauguration?
14) How many first ladies have died while their husband was in office?
15) Who was the only president who had been a union leader?
16) What three presidents have won Grammys for best spoken word album?
17) Who was the first president to appoint a Native American cabinet secretary?
18) How many presidents didn't have a wife when they took office?
19) What president worked as a lifeguard?
20) What president sent Lewis and Clark on their expedition?

Quiz 5 Answers

1) Barack Obama
2) Eight – Washington, John Adams, Jefferson, Madison, Monroe, John Quincy Adams, Jackson, William Henry Harrison
3) Episcopalian
4) Eight – Garfield, Hoover, Truman, Ford, Reagan, G.W. Bush, Clinton,

Obama
5) 14
6) Rutherford B. Hayes – 1877
7) Four – Lincoln, Garfield, McKinley, Kennedy
8) Eight – Harrison, Taylor, Lincoln, Garfield, McKinley, Harding, Franklin D. Roosevelt, Kennedy
9) Four – Andrew Jackson against John Quincy Adams, Samuel Tilden against Rutherford B. Hayes, Al Gore against George W. Bush, and Hilary Clinton against Donald Trump
10) Jimmy Carter
11) John F. Kennedy – 46
12) Bess Truman – 97
13) Jill Biden – 69
14) Three – Tyler, Harrison, Wilson
15) Ronald Reagan – president of the Screen Actors Guild
16) Clinton, Carter, Obama
17) Joe Biden – Secretary of the Interior Deb Haaland
18) Six – Jefferson, Jackson, Van Buren, and Arthur were all widowers; Cleveland married while in office; Buchanan never married.
19) Ronald Reagan
20) Thomas Jefferson

Quiz 6

1) Who was the first president to visit Alaska?
2) What was George Washington's first occupation?
3) Who was the first U.S. senator to serve as president?
4) Who was the first president who had never served in the military?
5) Who won the first presidential election after the 26th amendment gave 18-year-olds the right to vote?
6) What president was known as "The Great Engineer"?
7) What president created the Drug Enforcement Agency?
8) What president was known as "The Trust Buster"?
9) Who was the first sitting president to visit Hiroshima?
10) James Buchanan was morally opposed to slavery but believed it was protected by the constitution, so what did he do?
11) When accused of being two-faced, what president said, "If I had two faces, would I be wearing this one?"
12) Franklin D. Roosevelt was the first president to use an armored car; who did the car previously belong to?

13) What religious holiday was Abraham Lincoln assassinated on?
14) Who was the first president born in the United States?
15) What was Ronald Reagan's pet name for Nancy?
16) Under the original terms of the U.S. Constitution, the president didn't choose his vice president; how was it decided?
17) When President Truman visited Disneyland in 1957, why did he refuse to go on the Dumbo ride?
18) What physical trait did George Washington, Thomas Jefferson, Andrew Jackson, Martin Van Buren, and Dwight Eisenhower have in common?
19) Who was the first president born in the 20th century?
20) What president signed the treaty to purchase Alaska from Russia?

Quiz 6 Answers

1) Warren Harding – 1923
2) Surveyor
3) James Monroe
4) John Adams
5) Richard Nixon
6) Herbert Hoover – He was a mining engineer who worked around the world and had a large engineering consulting company.
7) Richard Nixon
8) Theodore Roosevelt
9) Barack Obama
10) He bought slaves with his own money and freed them.
11) Abraham Lincoln
12) Al Capone
13) Good Friday
14) Martin Van Buren – eighth president
15) Mommy poo pants
16) The candidate with the second most electoral votes was vice president.
17) As a Democrat, he didn't want to be seen riding in the symbol of the Republican party.
18) Redheads
19) John F. Kennedy
20) Andrew Johnson

Quiz 7

1) Walt Whitman's poem "O Captain! My Captain!" was written about

what president?
2) How many future presidents signed the Declaration of Independence?
3) Who was the only president who earned an MBA degree?
4) In what city was President McKinley assassinated?
5) What disease did John F. Kennedy contract as a young child?
6) Who was the first president to campaign by telephone?
7) Who was the first president to call the presidential residence the White House?
8) What U.S. president weighed the least?
9) Who was the first president to ride a railroad while in office?
10) What constitutional amendment limits the president to two terms?
11) Who was the last president who wasn't either a Democrat or Republican?
12) According to his wife, what was Abraham Lincoln's hobby?
13) Who was the first president to run against a woman candidate?
14) Originally, people bowed to the U.S. president; who was the first president to shake hands rather than bowing?
15) Who was the first president to attend a baseball game?
16) George Washington, John Adams, and Thomas Jefferson were all avid collectors and players of what game?
17) Who was the first president to visit all 50 states?
18) Who was the last president to have a beard?
19) What president was once a fashion model?
20) What president collected *Spiderman* and *Conan the Barbarian* comic books?

Quiz 7 Answers

1) Abraham Lincoln – It was written after Lincoln's assassination.
2) Two – John Adams and Thomas Jefferson
3) George W. Bush
4) Buffalo, New York
5) Scarlet fever
6) William McKinley
7) Theodore Roosevelt
8) James Madison – 100 pounds
9) Andrew Jackson
10) 22nd
11) Millard Fillmore – 1850

12) Cats – He loved them and could play with them for hours; he once allowed a cat to eat from the table at a formal White House dinner.
13) Ulysses S. Grant – Virginia Woodhull was a nominee of the Equal Rights Party in 1872.
14) Thomas Jefferson
15) Benjamin Harrison – 1892
16) Marbles
17) Richard Nixon
18) Benjamin Harrison
19) Gerald Ford – *Cosmopolitan* and *Look* magazines in the 1940s
20) Barack Obama

Quiz 8

1) Who was the first president who was a Boy Scout?
2) What president served in the U.S. House of Representatives after he served as president?
3) How many presidents regularly wore beards while in office?
4) What president was the first to have a child born in the White House?
5) Who was the first president born west of the Mississippi River?
6) Who was the only president who made his own clothes?
7) Who was the only president to serve in both the Revolutionary War and the War of 1812?
8) What president had the largest feet?
9) What Christmas item did Theodore Roosevelt ban from the White House?
10) Who was the first Navy veteran to become president?
11) What five surnames have been shared by more than one president?
12) Who was the only president that never lived in Washington, D.C.?
13) What president was the target of two assassination attempts in 17 days?
14) What president had the largest personal book collection in the United States and sold it to become part of the Library of Congress?
15) What play was Abraham Lincoln watching when he was assassinated?
16) Who was the first president to defeat an incumbent president?
17) Who was the first president with no prior elected political experience?
18) Who was the first president to travel in a car, plane, and submarine?
19) Who was president when the first U.S. national park was created?
20) Who was the first president to hold a televised news conference?

Quiz 8 Answers

1) John F. Kennedy
2) John Quincy Adams
3) Five – Lincoln, Grant, Hayes, Garfield, Benjamin Harrison
4) Grover Cleveland – 1893
5) Herbert Hoover – Iowa
6) Andrew Johnson – He had been a tailor's apprentice and opened a tailor shop; he made his own clothes most of his life.
7) Andrew Jackson
8) Warren G. Harding – size 14
9) Christmas trees – He had environmental concerns.
10) John F. Kennedy
11) Adams, Harrison, Johnson, Roosevelt, Bush
12) George Washington
13) Gerald Ford
14) Thomas Jefferson
15) *Our American Cousin*
16) Thomas Jefferson
17) Zachary Taylor – 12th president and Mexican-American War general
18) Theodore Roosevelt
19) Ulysses S. Grant – Yellowstone was the first national park in the world.
20) Dwight D. Eisenhower

Quiz 9

1) Who was the first president to win a Grammy Award?
2) What president helped to make the word OK popular?
3) Who was the only president to serve in the Confederate Congress?
4) What president signed the Civil Rights Act that extended the rights of emancipated slaves?
5) Who is the only president who received a Nobel Peace Prize after leaving office?
6) Who was the first president to appoint a secretary of energy?
7) Who was the first president to live at least 35 years after leaving office?
8) What president played in the first two College World Series baseball tournaments?
9) Who was the first president to send an email?
10) Who was the only president to serve in WWI and WWII?

11) Who was the first president to appear on U.S. coinage while he was still alive?
12) Who was the first president under the age of 50?
13) Who was president when the National Forest Service was established?
14) Which president established the Secret Service?
15) What president was arrested and taken into custody for speeding with a horse and buggy in Washington D.C. while he was in office?
16) Who was the first president to live at least 30 years after leaving office?
17) Who was the first president who was a lawyer?
18) What president was the first American to own a Siamese cat?
19) Who was president when the 18th Amendment establishing prohibition was passed?
20) Who is regarded as the most fashionable president and owned 80 pairs of pants that he liked to change several times a day?

Quiz 9 Answers

1) Bill Clinton
2) Martin Van Buren - One of his nicknames was "Old Kinderhook" based on the town he was from in New York; during his presidential campaign, people held up signs and chanted OK.
3) John Tyler - He served in the Confederate Congress representing Virginia from 1861 until just before he died in 1862; his term as president was 1841-1845.
4) Ulysses S. Grant - 1875
5) Jimmy Carter - 2002
6) Jimmy Carter
7) Jimmy Carter
8) George H.W. Bush
9) Bill Clinton
10) Dwight D. Eisenhower
11) Calvin Coolidge
12) James K. Polk
13) Theodore Roosevelt - 1905
14) Abraham Lincoln - He established the Secret Service on the day he was assassinated, but it was originally only focused on counterfeiting and didn't protect the president until 1902 after McKinley's assassination.
15) Ulysses S. Grant - The police seized his horse and buggy; he paid a fine and walked back to the White House.
16) Herbert Hoover - He left office in 1933 and died in 1964.

17) John Adams
18) Rutherford B. Hayes - The cat was a gift to the president and first lady from the American consul in Bangkok.
19) Woodrow Wilson - ratified on January 29, 1919
20) Chester A. Arthur

Quiz 10

1) How many presidents didn't have a vice president for all or part of their term?
2) Who was the first president to have served in the U.S. House of Representatives?
3) Who was the first president to have a State of the Union broadcast live on the internet?
4) Who was the first president to be elected after losing as vice president on a major party ticket?
5) Who was the first president inaugurated in Washington, D.C.?
6) What two presidents appeared five times on a national ticket for either president or vice president?
7) Who was the first president to be sworn in by another president?
8) Who was the first president to have been widowed?
9) Who was president when Hawaii was annexed?
10) Who was the first president to have two vice presidents?
11) What president was credited with saving 77 people from drowning?
12) What president had a wife who was technically a bigamist since she was still married to her former husband?
13) Who was the first president to be sworn in by a woman?
14) Which first lady was the first who wasn't born a citizen of the United States?
15) Who was the first president to spend part of his time in office without a vice president?
16) Who was the first president to be impeached by the House of Representatives?
17) Who was the first president of the United States under the Articles of Confederation?
18) Which first lady was the first to own and drive a car?
19) Who was the first president to turn 70 while in office?
20) Who was the first president born after the Declaration of Independence?

Quiz 10 Answers

1) 17 - James Madison, Andrew Jackson, John Tyler, Millard Fillmore, Franklin Pierce, Andrew Johnson, Ulysses S. Grant, Chester A. Arthur, Grover Cleveland, William McKinley, Theodore Roosevelt, William H. Taft, Calvin Coolidge, Harry S. Truman, Lyndon B. Johnson, Richard Nixon, Gerald Ford
2) James Madison
3) George W. Bush
4) Franklin D. Roosevelt - He lost as vice president in the 1920 election running along with James M. Cox.
5) Thomas Jefferson - 1801
6) Franklin D. Roosevelt (1920, 1932, 1936, 1940, 1944) and Richard Nixon (1952, 1956, 1960, 1968, 1972)
7) Calvin Coolidge - He was sworn in by William Howard Taft who was U.S. Supreme Court Chief Justice at the time of Coolidge's second inauguration in 1925.
8) John Adams
9) William McKinley - 1898
10) Thomas Jefferson
11) Ronald Reagan - In seven years as a lifeguard at Lowell Park in Dixon, Illinois, Reagan was credited with saving 77 people from drowning in the waters of the Rock River. He started his lifeguard position at the age of 15.
12) Andrew Jackson - His wife Rachel had separated from her first husband, Captain Lewis Robards, in 1790 but never finalized the divorce before marrying Jackson. She remarried Jackson once the divorce was finalized in 1794.
13) Lyndon B. Johnson - Federal Judge Sarah T. Hughes administered the oath of office after John F. Kennedy's assassination on November 22, 1963.
14) Melania Trump - Louisa Adams was also born outside the United States, but her father was American, so she was still a citizen by birthright.
15) James Madison - Both his vice president choices for his first and second terms died partway through their terms, so he finished his terms without a vice president.
16) Andrew Johnson
17) John Hanson - He was chosen by Congress and was in office from 1781-1782. Under the Articles of Confederation, the president was limited to a one-year term during any three-year period.

18) Helen Taft
19) Dwight D. Eisenhower - in 1960
20) Martin Van Buren

Quiz 11

1) Due to the U.S. Electoral College, what is theoretically the smallest percentage of the popular vote you could get and still win the election?
2) Who was the first president to be defeated for a second term in office?
3) What president had a sport invented by his physician to help keep him fit?
4) Who was the first president to be named *Time* magazine's Man of the Year?
5) Who was the first president who attended an Ivy League college?
6) Who was the first president with a beard?
7) What president hated public speaking and only made two speeches that were both inaugural speeches and hardly audible during his entire eight-year presidency?
8) Who was the only president who was a licensed bartender?
9) Who was the first president whose first language wasn't English?
10) Who was the first president with a Medicare card?
11) Who was president when the 14th Amendment was ratified granting citizenship to all persons born or naturalized in the United States including former slaves?
12) Richard Nixon was an accomplished musician and regularly played how many different instruments?
13) Who was the first president to show a motion picture in the White House?
14) Who was the first president to attend a World Series baseball game?
15) Who was the first president widowed in office?
16) Who was the first president to have a secretary of homeland security?
17) What president believed the earth's core was hollow and signed off on an expedition to explore it?
18) What president kept a pair of grizzly bear cubs in a cage on the White House front lawn for a few months?
19) Who was the first president to wear long pants?
20) Who was the first president to live at least 25 years after his presidency?

Quiz 11 Answers

1) 23% - This requires winning the required 270 electoral votes in the smallest electoral vote states by one vote in each state and not getting any votes in the largest electoral vote states.
2) John Adams
3) Herbert Hoover - His physician invented a sport known as Hooverball to help keep the president fit. It is a combination of volleyball and tennis and is played with a six-pound medicine ball.
4) Franklin D. Roosevelt
5) John Adams - Harvard
6) Abraham Lincoln
7) Thomas Jefferson
8) Abraham Lincoln
9) Martin Van Buren - He spoke Dutch as his first language and learned English in school.
10) Harry S. Truman - He received the first Medicare card ever from President Lyndon B. Johnson in 1965 in honor of his work for government healthcare.
11) Andrew Johnson - 1868
12) Five - piano, saxophone, clarinet, accordion, violin
13) Woodrow Wilson - *Birth of a Nation* in 1915
14) Woodrow Wilson - 1915
15) John Tyler
16) George W. Bush
17) John Quincy Adams - The expedition never took place.
18) Thomas Jefferson - They were a gift; he decided they were too dangerous to keep and bequeathed them to a museum.
19) James Madison - Previous presidents wore knee breeches.
20) John Adams

Quiz 12

1) Who was the first president to receive the Purple Heart?
2) Which first lady was the first to enter a combat zone?
3) Who was the first president to die before the age of 50?
4) What president grew hemp on his farm?
5) Who was president when the Civil Rights Act was passed?
6) Who was the first divorcee to be the first lady of the United States?
7) Who was the first president inaugurated with a living grandparent?

8) Which first lady was the first to give birth to a child in the White House?
9) Which first lady was the first to vote?
10) Who was the first president to have a White House chief of staff?
11) What president was reportedly involved in over 100 duels?
12) Who was the first president to visit the Soviet Union?
13) What president survived four plane crashes during WWII?
14) How many people have served as president, vice president, U.S. senator, and U.S. representative?
15) How was Theodore Roosevelt related to Eleanor Roosevelt?
16) Who was president when the United States declared war on Germany in WWI?
17) What president holds the record with over 1,000 rounds of golf played while he was in office?
18) What president could simultaneously write in Greek with one hand and Latin with the other?
19) What president worked as a sports announcer?
20) Who was president when the 1830 Indian Removal Act was passed authorizing the president to grant unsettled lands west of the Mississippi in exchange for Indian lands within existing state borders?

Quiz 12 Answers

1) John F. Kennedy
2) Pat Nixon
3) James A. Garfield
4) George Washington - He grew hemp at Mount Vernon for rope and canvas making.
5) Lyndon B. Johnson - 1964
6) Florence Harding
7) John F. Kennedy
8) Frances Cleveland
9) Florence Harding
10) Harry S. Truman
11) Andrew Jackson
12) Franklin D. Roosevelt
13) George H.W. Bush
14) Four - John Tyler, Andrew Johnson, Lyndon B. Johnson, Richard Nixon
15) Uncle - He was also Franklin D. Roosevelt's fifth cousin.
16) Woodrow Wilson - 1917

17) Woodrow Wilson
18) James A. Garfield - He was ambidextrous and taught both languages while attending college.
19) Ronald Reagan
20) Andrew Jackson

Quiz 13

1) How many presidents were never inaugurated (didn't have a public inauguration and address)?
2) Which first lady was the first to live to see her son become president?
3) Who was president when the first U.S. Census was completed?
4) What president often swam in the Potomac River in the buff?
5) Who was the first president to appear on color television?
6) Who was the first Whig party president?
7) What president banished liquor and wine from the White House?
8) Who was the first president over the age of 65 on taking office?
9) Which president ordered the integration of the U.S. armed forces?
10) What is the only year in which three future presidents were born?
11) Who was president when the Iran Hostage Crisis began?
12) Who was the first president to serve in Congress after his presidency?
13) How many of Abraham Lincoln's children survived him?
14) Who was the first president who went his entire term without a vice president?
15) Who was the first president to name a woman to their cabinet?
16) Who was president when the 19th Amendment giving women the right to vote was ratified?
17) What 20th century president was known as Tommy growing up?
18) Who was the first president who signed the Declaration of Independence?
19) What president kept a journal from the age of 12 until just before his death totaling 51 volumes and 14,000 pages?
20) Who was the first president with a telephone on his desk?

Quiz 13 Answers

1) Five (John Tyler, Millard Fillmore, Andrew Johnson, Chester A. Arthur, Gerald Ford) - All five ascended to the presidency after the death or resignation of a president; they weren't elected president.
2) Barbara Bush

3) George Washington - 1790
4) John Quincy Adams - He wrote of waking at 4 a.m. and taking a nude morning dip.
5) Dwight D. Eisenhower
6) William Henry Harrison
7) Rutherford B. Hayes
8) William Henry Harrison
9) Harry S. Truman - 1948
10) 1946 - Bill Clinton, George W. Bush, Donald Trump
11) Jimmy Carter - 1979
12) John Quincy Adams
13) Two (Robert and Thomas) - He had two other sons who died as children.
14) John Tyler - He became president on the death of William Henry Harrison and never chose a vice president.
15) Franklin D. Roosevelt - In 1933, he named Frances Perkins as secretary of labor.
16) Woodrow Wilson
17) Woodrow Wilson - He was born Thomas Woodrow Wilson but dropped his first name when he was 24.
18) John Adams
19) John Quincy Adams
20) Herbert Hoover

Quiz 14

1) What president was born with the last name Blythe?
2) Who was president when the 22nd Amendment limiting the president to two terms was ratified?
3) Who was president when Florida was acquired from Spain?
4) Who was the first president to have served as director of Central Intelligence?
5) How many vice presidents did Franklin D. Roosevelt have?
6) Who was the only president wounded in the American Civil War?
7) What two Mexican American War generals became president?
8) Who was the first president whose inauguration was streamed on the internet?
9) Who was the first president to live to the age of 90?
10) Who was the first president to leave office on January 20 as the normal ending date for a term?

11) Who was the first Democratic president to die in office?
12) Who was the first president who didn't have any recognized biological children?
13) Which first lady was the first to live in the White House?
14) Who was president when North Dakota, South Dakota, Montana, Washington, Idaho, and Wyoming joined the Union?
15) Who was the first president known to have died of cancer?
16) Who was the first president to complete at least one full term in office and not make a nomination to the U.S. Supreme Court?
17) Who was the first president paid a salary of $200,000?
18) Who was the first president to have previously been a governor?
19) How many American Civil War generals became U.S. president?
20) Who was the first president to have their photo taken while in office?

Quiz 14 Answers

1) Bill Clinton - His biological father died shortly before he was born, and he took the last name of his stepfather when he was 15.
2) Harry S. Truman - 1951
3) James Monroe - 1819
4) George H.W. Bush
5) Three - John Nance Garner, Henry A. Wallace, Harry S. Truman
6) Rutherford B. Hayes
7) Zachary Taylor and Franklin Pierce
8) Bill Clinton
9) John Adams
10) Harry S. Truman - March 4 had been the prior ending date.
11) Franklin D. Roosevelt
12) George Washington
13) Abigail Adams
14) Benjamin Harrison - The states were added from 1889-1890.
15) Ulysses S. Grant - He died of throat cancer after smoking 20 cigars a day for much of his adult life.
16) Jimmy Carter
17) Richard Nixon - 1969
18) Thomas Jefferson - governor of Virginia
19) Six - Andrew Johnson, Ulysses S. Grant, Rutherford B. Hayes, James A. Garfield, Chester A. Arthur, Benjamin Harrison
20) William Henry Harrison

Quiz 15

1) Who was the first president term-limited by the 22nd Amendment?
2) What president wrote a translation of the Bible?
3) What future president was the only southern senator to keep his seat in Congress at the outbreak of the American Civil War?
4) When was the last time there were three presidents in a year?
5) What president was the target of an assassination plot that involved taking over a jet and crashing it into the White House?
6) Who was the first president born in the 19th century?
7) Who was the first president to win the electoral vote but lose the popular vote?
8) Who was the first president born on the west coast?
9) What president was on dollar coins issued from 1971-1978?
10) What president was married the longest?
11) Who was the first president to serve in the U.S. Senate after being president?
12) Who was president when the 16th Amendment allowing the federal government to collect an income tax from all Americans was ratified?
13) Who was the last president who didn't have a vice president for all or part of their term?
14) Which president had a pet hyena named Bill?
15) Which first lady was the first to also be the mother of a president?
16) Who was president when the Interstate Highway System was created?
17) Who is the only president buried in Washington, D.C.?
18) Who was the first president to receive a British monarch during a visit to the United States?
19) What future president delivered an 84-minute campaign speech after being shot just before the event?
20) Who was the first president to be inaugurated on an airplane?

Quiz 15 Answers

1) Dwight D. Eisenhower
2) Thomas Jefferson - He didn't agree with some of the supernatural elements of the Bible and wrote his version eliminating what he didn't agree with.
3) Andrew Johnson - He was pro-slavery but disagreed with secession and stayed loyal to the Union.
4) 1881 - Rutherford B. Hayes started the year as president and was

succeeded by James A. Garfield in March after his election. Chester A. Arthur, Garfield's vice president, became president in September after Garfield's assassination.

5) Richard Nixon - Samuel Byck successfully managed to take over a Delta Airlines plane but didn't get it off the ground; he planned to have the pilots fly close to the White House where he would take over and crash the plane.
6) Franklin Pierce
7) Rutherford B. Hayes
8) Richard Nixon
9) Dwight D. Eisenhower
10) George H.W. Bush - 73 years to Barbara Bush
11) Andrew Johnson
12) William Howard Taft - 1913
13) Gerald Ford - He was without a vice president from August 9 to December 19, 1974.
14) Theodore Roosevelt - It was a present from the Emperor of Ethiopia.
15) Abigail Adams
16) Dwight D. Eisenhower - 1956
17) Woodrow Wilson
18) Franklin D. Roosevelt - George VI in 1939
19) Theodore Roosevelt - He was shot as he stood up in an open-air automobile and waved his hat to the crowd. X-rays taken after the speech showed the bullet lodged against Roosevelt's fourth right rib on an upward path toward his heart.
20) Lyndon B. Johnson - aboard Air Force One in 1963

Quiz 16

1) Before getting married in the White House, which president had his sister perform the duties normally done by the president's wife?
2) Which first lady was the first to earn a college degree?
3) Who was the first president to travel by jet aircraft and helicopter?
4) Which president said, "The ballot is stronger than the bullet"?
5) Who was vice president when the atomic bomb was dropped on Hiroshima?
6) Who is the only president to be the grandson of another president?
7) Who was the first president to have a television installed in the White House?
8) The tradition in the White House Roosevelt Room has been to hang

Franklin Delano Roosevelt's portrait over the mantel during Democratic administrations and hang whose portrait over the mantel during Republican administrations?

9) What president was the target of the first known attempted assassination of a U.S. president?
10) What president had a bowling alley installed in the White House?
11) Who was the first president to be married twice?
12) What president served as a Yellowstone Park Ranger?
13) Who was the last president who didn't have any recognized biological children?
14) Who was the first president to have his voice recorded?
15) Which first lady was the first to have no children?
16) Which first lady was the first who was born in the 20th century?
17) Which first lady was the first to die in the White House?
18) Who was the first president who was a Quaker?
19) Who had the shortest time in office of any president who didn't die in office?
20) Who was the first president to marry a divorced woman?

Quiz 16 Answers

1) Grover Cleveland
2) Lucy Webb Hayes - 1850
3) Dwight D. Eisenhower
4) Abraham Lincoln
5) No one - Harry S. Truman did not have a vice president for the remainder of his first term (1945-1949) after taking over as president on April 12, 1945, after Franklin D. Roosevelt's death.
6) Benjamin Harrison - grandson of William Henry Harrison
7) Harry S. Truman
8) Theodore Roosevelt - Whichever painting is not over the mantel is hung on the south wall of the room.
9) Andrew Jackson - In 1835, he was attending the funeral of South Carolina congressman Warren R. Davis when Richard Lawrence fired two pistols at point-blank range. Both misfired.
10) Harry S. Truman
11) John Tyler
12) Gerald Ford
13) Warren G. Harding
14) Benjamin Harrison

15) Sarah Polk
16) Jacqueline Kennedy
17) Letitia Tyler
18) Herbert Hoover
19) Gerald Ford - 895 days
20) Andrew Jackson

Quiz 17

1) Who was the first president to attend the U.S. Naval Academy?
2) Which first lady was the first to attend an Ivy League college for her undergraduate degree?
3) Who was president when the 15th Amendment was ratified guaranteeing the right of citizens to vote regardless of race, color, or previous condition of servitude?
4) Who was the first president to have both major political parties recruit him for the presidential nomination?
5) How many U.S. presidents got married while in office?
6) Which first lady was the first to earn a postgraduate degree?
7) What president had a nervous breakdown at the age of 24 and spent several weeks in a sanitarium?
8) Who was the first president to appear on U.S. paper currency while in office?
9) Who is the only person in history known to have witnessed the assassination of three U.S. presidents?
10) Who was the first president to have a national security advisor?
11) Which first lady was the first who was not a native speaker of English?
12) What president was the youngest naval aviator in U.S. history at the age of 18?
13) Who was the first president who didn't have any full siblings?
14) Which first lady was the first to hold seances in the White House?
15) Who was president when the Berlin Wall fell?
16) What two War of 1812 generals became presidents?
17) Who was the first president from the state of New York?
18) Who was the first president to have served as vice president?
19) Who was the first president who did not immediately succeed the president he served as vice president?
20) Who was the first president to remarry in office?

Quiz 17 Answers

1) Jimmy Carter
2) Michelle Obama - Princeton University
3) Ulysses S. Grant - 1870
4) Dwight D. Eisenhower - He ran as a Republican.
5) Three - John Tyler and Woodrow Wilson remarried after losing their wives; Grover Cleveland got married for the first time in the White House.
6) Hillary Clinton
7) Warren Harding
8) Abraham Lincoln
9) Robert Lincoln - He was Abraham Lincoln's son and witnessed the assassinations of his father, James A. Garfield, and William McKinley.
10) Dwight D. Eisenhower
11) Melania Trump
12) George H.W. Bush
13) Franklin D. Roosevelt - He had a half-brother.
14) Mary Todd Lincoln
15) Ronald Reagan - 1989
16) Andrew Jackson and William Henry Harrison
17) Martin Van Buren
18) John Adams
19) Richard Nixon - He served from 1953-1961 as Eisenhower's vice president but did not become president until 1969.
20) John Tyler

Quiz 18

1) What president lost the nuclear launch codes for months and nobody found out?
2) What president played football at West Point and was injured trying to tackle Olympic and NFL star Jim Thorpe?
3) Who was president when the Statue of Liberty was presented to the United States by France?
4) Who was president when the 26th Amendment giving 18-year-olds the right to vote was ratified?
5) Who was the first president to own a radio?
6) What president lived for 80 days after being shot?
7) Who was the first president to have served in the U.S. Senate?

8) Who was the first president with a defense secretary?
9) When Thomas Jefferson sent Lewis and Clark on their expedition, what extinct animal did he ask them to look for?
10) Who was the first president to die before the age of 60?
11) Who was president when the 21st Amendment repealing prohibition was ratified?
12) Who was the first president to complete a marathon?
13) Who was the last U.S. president without a college degree?
14) Who was the first president to learn to drive a car?
15) Who was the first president to be filmed?
16) Who was the first president to be physically attacked while in office?
17) Who was the first president to be inaugurated on January 20?
18) Who was president when the Louisiana Purchase was completed?
19) Who was the first president to hold the White House Easter Egg Roll?
20) Who was the first president with facial hair?

Quiz 18 Answers

1) Bill Clinton - The president must keep the launch codes nearby; every 30 days, a Pentagon staffer is required to check the codes to ensure they're correct, and the codes are replaced every four months.
2) Dwight D. Eisenhower
3) Chester A. Arthur - 1884
4) Richard Nixon - 1971
5) Warren G. Harding
6) James A. Garfield
7) James Monroe
8) Harry S. Truman
9) Wooly mammoth - Jefferson believed that there might be wooly mammoths still living in the west.
10) James K. Polk
11) Franklin D. Roosevelt - 1933
12) George W. Bush
13) Harry S. Truman
14) Warren G. Harding
15) Grover Cleveland
16) Andrew Jackson - A man punched him and ran away.
17) Franklin D. Roosevelt
18) Thomas Jefferson - 1803

19) Rutherford B. Hayes
20) John Quincy Adams

Quiz 19

1) What president was the first American to earn a brown belt in judo?
2) What president installed a putting green at the White House and played more than 800 rounds of golf while in office?
3) What president was known for his gambling and once lost a set of priceless White House china on a bet?
4) What president was arrested for running over a woman with his horse while he was in office?
5) Which first lady was the first to give birth to twins?
6) What president's wife was the first to be referred to as the first lady?
7) Who was the first president elected in the 20th century?
8) What president wasn't fond of formal events and often greeted foreign dignitaries in his pajamas?
9) Who was the first president born in Texas?
10) Who is the only president who did not represent a political party when he was elected?
11) Of the first five U.S. presidents, three died on the same day of the year; what day?
12) Which first lady was the first to die the same year as her husband?
13) Who was the first president to speak over the radio?
14) What president married his teacher?
15) What U.S. Constitution amendment moved the beginning and end of the president's term to January 20?
16) Who was the first vice president to become president after the death of the president?
17) How many presidents served their entire term without a vice president?
18) Which first lady was the first to win an Emmy Award?
19) Who was the first Democratic president?
20) Who was the first president to have both parents alive during their presidency?

Quiz 19 Answers

1) Theodore Roosevelt
2) Dwight D. Eisenhower
3) Warren G. Harding

4) Franklin Pierce - The charges were dropped due to a lack of evidence.
5) Laura Bush
6) Rutherford B. Hayes - Lucy Hayes was referred to as the first lady in 1877.
7) Theodore Roosevelt
8) Thomas Jefferson
9) Dwight D. Eisenhower
10) George Washington
11) July 4 - John Adams and Thomas Jefferson both died on July 4, 1826; James Monroe died five years later on July 4, 1831.
12) Barbara Bush
13) Warren G. Harding - 1922
14) Millard Fillmore - Fillmore's first wife, Abigail Powers, was his teacher when he was 19 years old.
15) 20th Amendment
16) John Tyler
17) Four - John Tyler, Millard Fillmore, Andrew Johnson, Chester A. Arthur
18) Jacqueline Kennedy - She won a Trustees Award for a 1962 televised tour of the White House.
19) Andrew Jackson
20) Ulysses S. Grant

Quiz 20

1) Which first lady was the first to outlive her husband?
2) Who was the first president to win election after previously being defeated?
3) Who was the first president to have served as U.S. Senate majority whip?
4) Who was the first elected president to have served as acting president?
5) Woolsey Hall auditorium at Yale University still has an extra-wide seat built specifically for what U.S. president?
6) Who was president when the Soviet Union broke up into independent republics?
7) George Washington had taphephobia; what is it?
8) Who was the first president to serve in the U.S. Army Air Force?
9) What president and first lady were so afraid of being electrocuted when electricity was first installed in the White House that they never touched the light switches and always had staff turn the lights on and off?

10) Who was the first president to be survived by both his parents?
11) What president lost his wife to kidney failure after giving birth to their daughter only 11 hours after losing his mother to typhoid fever in the same house?
12) Who is the only president who served as an ordained minister?
13) Who was the first president elected after women gained the right to vote?
14) Under the Articles of Confederation, how many presidents were there before George Washington?
15) What president had an adopted niece who took over many of the responsibilities that would normally go to the president's wife?
16) What presidential nominee considered Clint Eastwood as his running mate?
17) Who was the first Republican vice president of the United States?
18) Who was the first president to attend and open an Olympics while in office?
19) What president gave the White House its name?
20) What president received a pet alligator as a surprise gift and kept it in the White House East Room bathroom for two months before returning it?

Quiz 20 Answers

1) Martha Washington
2) Thomas Jefferson
3) Lyndon B. Johnson
4) George H.W. Bush - He served as acting president for eight hours when Ronald Reagan was sedated for colon surgery.
5) William Howard Taft - After his presidency, Taft went on to teach at Yale, which installed several special chairs with extra-wide seats to accommodate Taft who was well over 300 pounds. One of the chairs is still in use in Woolsey Hall today; it is balcony seat E-9.
6) George H.W. Bush - 1991
7) Fear of being buried alive
8) Ronald Reagan
9) Benjamin Harrison and his wife
10) John F. Kennedy
11) Theodore Roosevelt
12) James A. Garfield
13) Warren G. Harding

14) Eight - Each served a one-year term.
15) James Buchanan - He is the only president to never marry.
16) George W. Bush
17) Hannibal Hamlin – Lincoln's first vice president
18) Ronald Reagan - 1984 Los Angeles Olympics
19) Theodore Roosevelt - 1901
20) John Quincy Adams

Quiz 21

1) Franklin D. Roosevelt was put on the dime largely for his work for what organization?
2) Who was the first president not of Irish or British descent?
3) What president has an African national capital city named after him?
4) At the time of his death, George Washington was one of the largest U.S. producers of what alcoholic beverage?
5) Who was the first president born after WWII?
6) Who was the first president over the age of 60 when entering office?
7) Which U.S. president was shot by Charles J. Guiteau on July 2, 1881?
8) What president was the first graduate student ever at Princeton University?
9) Which first lady was the first to have a U.S. stamp honoring her?
10) Who was the first president to receive an Emmy Award?
11) What president said, "Not making the baseball team at West Point was one of the greatest disappointments of my life, maybe my greatest"?
12) Who was the first president to die in office?
13) Who was the first president to serve in the Air National Guard?
14) What president was an indentured servant in his early life?
15) Who was the first vice president to serve under two different presidents?
16) What political party has had the most presidents?
17) Who was president when the Peace Corps was created?
18) Who was the first president to leave office with both parents still alive?
19) Which first lady was the first to win a Grammy Award?
20) How many times was Franklin D. Roosevelt elected president?

Quiz 21 Answers

1) March of Dimes - originally called National Foundation for Infantile Paralysis

2) Martin Van Buren - Dutch
3) James Monroe - Monrovia, Liberia
4) Whiskey – In 1799, he had one of the largest whiskey distilleries in America.
5) Bill Clinton
6) John Adams
7) James A. Garfield - He died two months later from infections related to the injury.
8) James Madison
9) Martha Washington
10) Dwight D. Eisenhower - 1956 Governor's Award for his use and encouragement of television
11) Dwight D. Eisenhower
12) William Henry Harrison - 1841
13) George W. Bush
14) Andrew Johnson - He was three years old when his father died, and he and his brother became indentured servants to a tailor.
15) George Clinton - vice president to both Thomas Jefferson and James Madison
16) Republican
17) John F. Kennedy - 1961
18) George W. Bush
19) Hillary Clinton - for best spoken word album for the audio recording of her book *It Takes a Village*
20) Four - He won the 1932, 1936, 1940, and 1944 elections.

World Geography

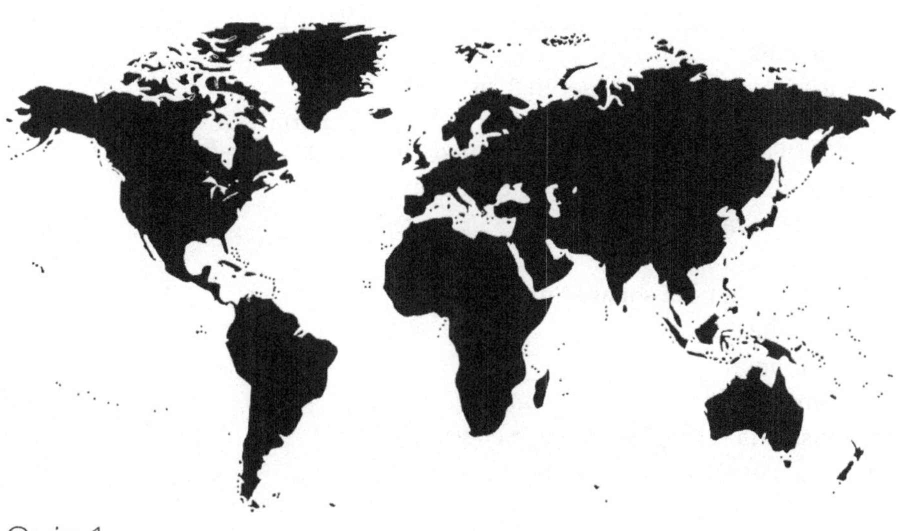

Quiz 1

1) What country are the Galapagos Islands part of?
2) What is the highest mountain in the Western Hemisphere?
3) What kind of animal are the Canary Islands named after?
4) What country has the longest land border?
5) What is the world's third most populous country?
6) Easter Island is a territory of what country?
7) By area, what is the second largest lake in North America?
8) What is the capital of Mongolia?
9) What South American country has Pacific and Atlantic coastlines?
10) What is the most northern African country?
11) What is the lowest average elevation continent?
12) By area, what is the largest of the Canadian provinces and territories?
13) What country has the world's longest road tunnel?
14) What city has the world's busiest McDonald's restaurant?
15) By area, what is the world's fifth largest country?
16) What is the highest active volcano in the world?
17) By area, what is the largest lake in South America?
18) What is the largest island in the Arctic Ocean?

19) What country has the most volcanoes (active and extinct)?
20) What is the smallest ocean?

Quiz 1 Answers

1) Ecuador
2) Aconcagua – 22,841 feet in Argentina
3) Dogs – The name comes from the Latin "canaria" for dog; when the first Europeans arrived, they found large dogs on Gran Canaria.
4) China – 13,743 miles and 14 countries
5) United States
6) Chile
7) Huron – 23,012 square miles
8) Ulaanbaatar
9) Colombia
10) Tunisia
11) Australia – 984 feet average elevation
12) Nunavut – 808,200 square miles
13) Norway – 15.2 miles
14) Moscow, Russia
15) Brazil
16) Ojos Del Salado – 22,595 feet on the Chile and Argentina border
17) Maracaibo – 5,100 square miles
18) Baffin - 195,928 square miles
19) United States – 173
20) Arctic

Quiz 2

1) What Central American country extends the furthest north?
2) What capital city is on the slopes of the volcano Pichincha?
3) How many locks are there on the Suez Canal?
4) What country has the highest average elevation?
5) What two Canadian provinces are landlocked?
6) What two countries have square flags?
7) What is the only river that crosses the equator in both a northerly and southerly direction?
8) What European country has the longest coastline?
9) At over 9,000 miles in length, what country's Highway 1 forms a complete loop along its borders?

10) What is the second-largest island in Europe?
11) What is the least densely populated country in the world?
12) From what South American country does the Orinoco River flow into the Atlantic Ocean?
13) What country does China have its longest land border with?
14) By area, what is the smallest continent?
15) The Canary Islands are part of what country?
16) What is the second-largest city in England?
17) What river is known as China's Sorrow?
18) What is the longest canal in the world?
19) What European country has no single head of state?
20) By area, what is the largest island in Asia?

Quiz 2 Answers

1) Belize
2) Quito, Ecuador
3) Zero
4) Bhutan – 10,760 feet average elevation
5) Alberta and Saskatchewan
6) Switzerland and Vatican City
7) Congo
8) Norway
9) Australia
10) Iceland – 39,702 square miles
11) Mongolia – Areas like Greenland have an even lower density, but they aren't independent countries.
12) Venezuela
13) Mongolia
14) Australia
15) Spain
16) Birmingham
17) Yellow – due to its devastating floods
18) Grand Canal of China – 1,104 miles
19) Switzerland
20) Borneo – 287,000 square miles

Quiz 3

1) What country has the third largest English speaking population?
2) By area, what is the largest Mediterranean island?
3) What country has the fourth largest population?
4) By volume, what is the largest lake in South America?
5) What country took its name from a line of latitude?
6) What country's phone book is alphabetized by first name?
7) What is the most populous country the equator passes through?
8) What is the highest elevation capital city in Europe?
9) What country issued the first Christmas stamp in 1898?
10) What is the world's most northerly national capital city?
11) What was the last province to become part of Canada?
12) What is the longest river in Asia?
13) What is the world's largest gulf?
14) How many oceans are there and what are their names?
15) What is the world's most southerly national capital?
16) What is the second-longest river in North America?
17) What country has the longest coastline?
18) What is the world's highest elevation national capital city?
19) What peninsula does Mexico occupy?
20) Alphabetically, what country comes between Portugal and Romania?

Quiz 3 Answers

1) Pakistan
2) Sicily – 9,927 square miles
3) Indonesia
4) Lake Titicaca
5) Ecuador
6) Iceland – Everyone is referenced by their first name; they don't have surnames in the traditional sense; their surname is their father's first name suffixed with either son or daughter.
7) Indonesia
8) Madrid – 2,188 feet
9) Canada
10) Reykjavik, Iceland – 64 degrees north latitude
11) Newfoundland
12) Yangtze – 3,915 miles

13) Gulf of Mexico – 600,000 square miles
14) Five – Atlantic, Pacific, Indian, Arctic, Southern
15) Wellington, New Zealand – 41 degrees south latitude
16) Mississippi – 2,320 miles
17) Canada
18) La Paz, Bolivia – 11,942 feet
19) Yucatan
20) Qatar

Quiz 4

1) By area, what is the second-largest island in Asia?
2) By area, what is the largest landlocked country?
3) How many countries are there in South America?
4) By area, what is the fourth largest continent?
5) Zanzibar lies off the coast of what country?
6) What is the driest continent?
7) What is the world's widest river?
8) In what location are most of the world's geysers found?
9) What island has the highest maximum elevation?
10) What is the highest mountain in Canada?
11) By area, what is the largest body of freshwater in the world?
12) What percent of the earth's freshwater is in the Antarctic ice sheet?
13) What is the shallowest ocean?
14) What is the driest non-polar desert in the world?
15) What mountain range spans northern Morocco, Algeria, and Tunisia?
16) By area, what is the largest archipelago (chain or group of islands scattered across a body of water)?
17) By area, what is the second-largest country in the world?
18) What is the most populous city south of the equator?
19) What is the capital of Qatar?
20) By area, what is the smallest North American country?

Quiz 4 Answers

1) Sumatra, Indonesia – 164,000 square miles
2) Kazakhstan - the ninth largest country
3) 12
4) South America

5) Tanzania
6) Antarctica – about eight inches of precipitation annually
7) Amazon – from 7-25 miles wide depending on the season
8) Yellowstone National Park, Wyoming
9) New Guinea – 16,024 feet
10) Mt. Logan – 19,551 feet in the Yukon territory
11) Lake Superior – 31,700 square miles
12) 90% - It is equivalent to about 230 feet of water in the world's oceans.
13) Arctic –average depth of 3,407 feet
14) Atacama – Chile
15) Atlas Mountains
16) Malay Archipelago – 25,000 islands making up Indonesia and the Philippines
17) Canada
18) Sao Paulo, Brazil
19) Doha
20) St. Kitts and Nevis – 101 square miles in the Caribbean

Quiz 5

1) How many landlocked countries are there in the world?
2) What is the second-most populous city in Asia?
3) In which country is the Great Victoria Desert?
4) By area, what is the smallest Canadian province?
5) What sea is located between Australia and New Zealand?
6) By area, what is the largest country in Africa?
7) What country would you have to visit to see the ruins of Troy?
8) By area, what is the largest lake that is entirely within Canada?
9) What European country has the lowest population density?
10) What is the deepest lake in North America?
11) What country has the largest number of islands?
12) By area, what is the smallest Central American country?
13) What two South American countries are landlocked?
14) By area, what is the world's largest freshwater island?
15) What is the second-longest river in Africa?
16) What country has the most forest land?
17) What country has the most countries or territories bordering it?
18) What is Europe's second-longest river?

19) What national capital city has views of the volcano Snaefellsjokull?
20) What country has the world's highest railroad?

Quiz 5 Answers

1) 44 - Afghanistan, Andorra, Armenia, Austria, Azerbaijan, Burundi, Burkina Faso, Bhutan, Belarus, Bolivia, Botswana, The Central African Republic, Chad, The Czech Republic, Ethiopia, Hungary, Kazakhstan, Kyrgyzstan, Laos, Lesotho, Liechtenstein, Luxembourg, Malawi, Moldova, Mongolia, Macedonia, Mali, Nepal, Niger, Paraguay, Rwanda, Serbia, San Marino, Switzerland, Slovakia, Swaziland, South Sudan, Tajikistan, Turkmenistan, Uganda, Uzbekistan, Vatican City, Zambia, Zimbabwe
2) Jakarta, Indonesia
3) Australia
4) Prince Edward Island
5) Tasman
6) Algeria
7) Turkey
8) Great Bear Lake – 12,028 square miles
9) Iceland
10) Great Slave Lake in Canada - 2,015 feet deep
11) Finland – over 100,000
12) El Salvador
13) Bolivia and Paraguay
14) Manitoulin – over 1,000 square miles in Lake Huron in Ontario, Canada
15) Congo – 2,922 miles
16) Russia
17) China – 14 countries and 2 territories
18) Danube – 1,777 miles
19) Reykjavik, Iceland
20) China – 16,640 feet

Quiz 6

1) By area, what is the largest country entirely in Europe?
2) How many countries border the Black Sea?
3) By area, what is the largest country with English as an official language?
4) There are only two predominantly Christian countries in Asia; the

smaller is East Timor; what is the other?

5) What is the most populous city in India?
6) The source of the Amazon river is in what country?
7) What is the coldest national capital city in the world?
8) Timbuktu is in what country?
9) What river rises in Tibet and flows through China, Myanmar, Laos, Thailand, Cambodia, and Vietnam?
10) What European country has the highest population density?
11) What desert covers most of southern Mongolia?
12) By volume, what is the largest freshwater lake?
13) What sacred volcano last erupted in 1707?
14) What is the world's warmest sea?
15) In the boot-shaped country of Italy, what region comprises the toe?
16) What is the world's oldest surviving sovereign state?
17) What country has three capital cities?
18) What name is given to a ring-shaped coral reef?
19) What is the only Central American country that has English as its official language?
20) What is the name of the deepest known ocean location?

Quiz 6 Answers

1) Ukraine - 223,000 square miles
2) Six - Turkey, Georgia, Russia, Ukraine, Romania, Bulgaria
3) Canada
4) Philippines – fourth-largest Christian population in the world and third-largest Roman Catholic population
5) Mumbai
6) Peru
7) Ulaanbaatar, Mongolia – Winter temperatures of minus 40 degrees Fahrenheit are not unusual.
8) Mali – West Africa
9) Mekong
10) Monaco – over 47,000 per square mile
11) Gobi
12) Lake Baikal in Russia – It has a maximum depth of 5,387 feet and contains about 20% of the total unfrozen surface freshwater in the world.
13) Mount Fuji

14) Red Sea
15) Calabria
16) San Marino - 301 AD
17) South Africa - Pretoria is the administrative capital; Cape Town is the legislative capital, and Bloemfontein is the judicial capital.
18) Atoll
19) Belize
20) Challenger Deep in the Mariana Trench in the Pacific Ocean – 36,070 feet deep

Quiz 7

1) How many provinces does Canada have?
2) What is the saltiest ocean?
3) What is the only sea without a coastline (no land border)?
4) Mount Kosciuszko is the highest mountain on what continent?
5) What country has the lowest average elevation?
6) What is the longest river in Australia?
7) Which of the Great Lakes doesn't share a border with Canada?
8) What country and its territories cover the most time zones?
9) What percent of the world's population lives in the Northern Hemisphere?
10) What country has the oldest surviving constitution?
11) By area, what is the largest country that the equator passes through?
12) What country has the most pyramids?
13) Where is the lowest dry land point in the world?
14) What is the only continent without an active volcano?
15) What country is Transylvania in?
16) The country of San Marino is completely surrounded by what country?
17) What country has the most official languages?
18) What country has the most lakes?
19) How many countries does the equator pass through?
20) What is the only country that falls in all four hemispheres?

Quiz 7 Answers

1) 10 - Alberta, British Columbia, Manitoba, New Brunswick, Newfoundland and Labrador, Nova Scotia, Ontario, Prince Edward Island, Quebec, Saskatchewan
2) Atlantic

3) Sargasso Sea – It is in the North Atlantic Ocean off the coast of the United States and is defined by currents.
4) Australia
5) Maldives – 1,200 mostly uninhabited islands in the Indian Ocean; average elevation is 6 feet.
6) Murray River – 1,558 miles
7) Lake Michigan
8) France with 12 time zones – The United States and Russia each cover 11 time zones.
9) 88% - About half of the world's population lives north of 27 degrees north latitude.
10) San Marino – 1600
11) Brazil
12) Sudan – almost twice as many as Egypt
13) Dead Sea – 1,411 feet below sea level
14) Australia
15) Romania
16) Italy
17) Zimbabwe – 16
18) Canada – It has more lakes than the rest of the world combined.
19) 13 - Ecuador, Colombia, Brazil, Sao Tome & Principe, Gabon, Republic of the Congo, Democratic Republic of the Congo, Uganda, Kenya, Somalia, Maldives, Indonesia, Kiribati
20) Kiribati - island nation in the Central Pacific Ocean

Quiz 8

1) What is widely regarded as the oldest continuously inhabited city in the world?
2) By discharge volume, what is the largest river in the world?
3) Europe is separated from Asia by what mountain range?
4) Excluding Greenland, what is the easternmost point of the North American continent?
5) What country has the world's deepest cave?
6) How many time zones does Russia have?
7) What is the largest desert in the world?
8) South Africa completely surrounds what other country?
9) What strait separates Europe and Asia?
10) What is the largest country that uses only one time zone?
11) What two countries share the longest land border?

12) What Canadian province or territory is closest to the North Pole?
13) What is the only European national capital not on a river?
14) Valletta is the capital of what country?
15) What color is most common on national flags?
16) What country has the most active volcanoes?
17) By volume, what is the world's largest active volcano?
18) What is the capital of Australia?
19) What is Europe's largest island?
20) What non-landlocked country has the shortest coastline?

Quiz 8 Answers

1) Damascus, Syria – at least 11,000 years
2) Amazon
3) Ural Mountains
4) Cape Spear, Newfoundland, Canada
5) Georgia – Krubera Cave, explored to a depth of 7,208 feet
6) 11
7) Antarctic Polar Desert – 5.5 million square miles
8) Lesotho
9) Bosporus
10) China – Geographically, it has five time zones, but it chooses to use one standard time.
11) United States and Canada – 5,525 miles
12) Nunavut
13) Madrid, Spain
14) Malta
15) Red
16) Indonesia – 76 active volcanoes
17) Mauna Loa, Hawaii
18) Canberra
19) Great Britain
20) Monaco – 2.4 miles

Quiz 9

1) What country has the largest Christian population?
2) What country has the largest Muslim population?
3) What is the second-longest river in South America?

4) By area, what is the second-largest country in South America?
5) By area, what is the largest lake in Africa?
6) What country has the second largest English speaking population?
7) In what country is the highest point that the equator passes through?
8) What country has the largest Spanish speaking population?
9) What is the second-largest landlocked country?
10) What country has the lowest birthrate?
11) The United States and China have the first and second-largest GDP's; what country is third?
12) How many countries have effectively 100% literacy rates?
13) What country has the most international tourists annually?
14) Based on land area, what is the largest airport in the world?
15) What is the most visited city in the world?
16) What is the largest cocoa producing country?
17) Brazil is the largest coffee producing country; what country is second?
18) By area, how many of the 10 largest countries in the world are in Asia?
19) How many of the 10 most populous countries in the world are in Asia?
20) What is the driest place in the world?

Quiz 9 Answers

1) United States
2) Indonesia
3) Parana – 3,032 miles
4) Argentina – 1,073,518 square miles
5) Victoria – 26,564 square miles
6) India
7) Ecuador – 15,387 feet
8) Mexico
9) Mongolia
10) Monaco
11) Japan
12) Five – Andorra, Finland, Liechtenstein, Luxembourg, Norway
13) France
14) King Fahd International, Saudi Arabia - 301 square miles
15) Bangkok, Thailand – followed by London
16) Ivory Coast (Cote d'Ivoire)
17) Vietnam

18) Four – Russia, China, India, Kazakhstan
19) Seven – China, India, Indonesia, Pakistan, Bangladesh, Russia, Japan
20) McMurdo Dry Valleys, Antarctica – a row of snow-free valleys that haven't seen water in millions of years

Quiz 10

1) What are the only three countries that have Atlantic and Mediterranean coasts?
2) How many countries are completely surrounded by one other country?
3) What is the only continent with land in all four hemispheres?
4) What continent has the most freshwater?
5) What ocean has about 75% of the world's volcanoes?
6) What country has the largest city in the world based on land area?
7) What is the only major city located on two continents?
8) What country has the world's longest freshwater beach?
9) What is the most populous city in Europe?
10) What is the most populous city in Asia?
11) What is the most populous city in North America?
12) What two countries have the second-longest shared land border?
13) What city has the most millionaires in the world?
14) What country consumes the most electricity in the world?
15) What city has the most skyscrapers in the world?
16) What is the sunniest city in the world?
17) What two countries produce a majority of the world's vanilla?
18) Astana is the capital of what country?
19) What is the most frequently crossed international border in the world?
20) What country is in the eastern Pyrenees between France and Spain?

Quiz 10 Answers

1) France, Spain, Morocco
2) Three – Lesotho (surrounded by South Africa), Vatican City and San Marino (both surrounded by Italy)
3) Africa
4) Antarctica – The ice sheet contains about 90% of the world's freshwater.
5) Pacific
6) China – The city of Hulunbuir is 102,000 square miles.
7) Istanbul, Turkey

8) Canada – Wasaga Beach on the shores of Lake Huron is 14 miles long.
9) Moscow, Russia
10) Tokyo, Japan
11) Mexico City
12) Russia and Kazakhstan – 4,254 miles
13) Tokyo, Japan
14) China - followed by the United States and Russia
15) Hong Kong - followed by New York City and Dubai
16) Yuma, Arizona – On average, the sun shines 90% of daylight hours.
17) Madagascar and Indonesia
18) Kazakhstan
19) United States and Mexico
20) Andorra

Quiz 11

1) What country has the world's longest fence?
2) What three South American countries does the equator pass through?
3) The Anatolian peninsula makes up most of what country?
4) What place on the earth is closest to the moon?
5) Of the 25 highest mountain peaks in the world, how many are in the Himalayas?
6) What is the only country in the world without an official capital?
7) What country has the world's tallest vertical cliff?
8) What continent has the most countries?
9) What country has the third most countries bordering it?
10) What is the most populous Canadian province?
11) Outside of Warsaw, what city has the largest Polish population in the world?
12) Taumatawhakatangihangakoauauotamateaturipukakapikimaunga-horonukupokaiwhenuakitanatahu has what distinction?
13) How many people have been to the deepest part of the ocean?
14) The word Canada comes from an Indian word meaning what?
15) What is the only continent without a major desert?
16) What is the longest river in Canada?
17) What is different about how the flag of the Philippines is flown?
18) Amman, the capital of Jordan, was previously named what?
19) Russia is the most populous country in Europe; what country is second?
20) What country is the largest wine producer in the world?

Quiz 11 Answers

1) Australia – The dingo fence completed in 1885 is 3,488 miles long.
2) Ecuador, Colombia, Brazil
3) Turkey
4) Mount Chimborazo, Ecuador – It is 20,548 feet high, but it is very close to the equator, so the bulge in the earth makes it 1.5 miles closer than Mount Everest.
5) 19
6) Nauru – It is the third-smallest country in the world in the Central Pacific Ocean.
7) Canada – Mount Thor on Baffin Island with a 4,101 feet vertical drop
8) Africa – 54, Europe – 47, Asia – 44
9) Brazil – 10
10) Ontario
11) New York City
12) Longest place name in the world – a hill in New Zealand
13) Three – Director James Cameron is one of them.
14) Village or settlement
15) Europe
16) Yukon – 1,981 miles
17) It is displayed with the blue side up in times of peace and with the red side up in times of war.
18) Philadelphia – after Philadelphus, the Egyptian king who conquered the area in the third century BC
19) Germany
20) Italy - followed by Spain, France, United States

Quiz 12

1) What is the second largest island in North America?
2) The Eiffel Tower was originally intended for what city?
3) What European national capital city is built on 14 islands?
4) At the closest point, Europe and Africa are separated by what distance?
5) Almost half the gold ever mined has come from what single location?
6) What continent has the most French speakers?
7) What is the only country to lie completely above 1,000 meters elevation?
8) What is the windiest continent?

9) What city has the largest taxi fleet in the world?
10) What country has the highest annual average hours worked in the world?
11) What is the most linguistically diverse (highest number of languages spoken) city in the world?
12) Technically, who is the largest landowner in the world?
13) By area, how many of the 10 largest countries in the world are in South America?
14) The United Kingdom and Great Britain are not the same; what is the difference?
15) Brazil borders all but what two South American countries?
16) What city was the only European capital outside of Europe?
17) What is the most populous democratic country?
18) What country has the largest number of languages spoken?
19) What is the only country in the world named after a woman?
20) What is the smallest population country with at least one Nobel Prize winner?

Quiz 12 Answers

1) Baffin – 195,928 square miles
2) Barcelona – Spain rejected the project.
3) Stockholm, Sweden
4) Nine miles – across the Strait of Gibraltar between Spain and Morocco
5) Witwatersrand, South Africa
6) Africa – 120 million French speakers
7) Lesotho
8) Antarctica
9) Mexico City
10) Mexico
11) New York City – 800 languages
12) Queen Elizabeth II – She technically owns 6.6 billion acres or about 1/6 of the world's land including Canada and Australia.
13) Two – Brazil and Argentina
14) Great Britain includes England, Scotland, and Wales; the United Kingdom includes those countries plus Northern Ireland.
15) Chile and Ecuador
16) Rio de Janeiro, Brazil, was the capital of Portugal from 1808 to 1822. Napoleon was invading Portugal at the time, so the Portuguese royal family moved to Rio de Janeiro, and it became the capital.

17) India
18) Papua New Guinea – about 840 languages or one for every 10,000 citizens
19) St. Lucia – It is named after St. Lucy of Syracuse.
20) Faroe Islands – with 50,000 people located halfway between Norway and Iceland

Quiz 13

1) What national capital city has the smallest percent of the country's population?
2) What continent has the world's largest volcanic region?
3) How many debt-free countries are there in the world?
4) How many countries in the world require their head of state to be a specific religion?
5) What is the only Asian country the equator passes through?
6) Is the Northern or Southern Hemisphere warmer?
7) How many countries don't maintain an army?
8) What location has the most lightning strikes in the world?
9) By population, what is the world's largest island country?
10) What country has on average the tallest people?
11) What country has on average the shortest people?
12) How many landlocked countries are there in North America?
13) What is the largest city in the Caribbean?
14) What is the largest city in Central America?
15) What is the southernmost city in the world with a population of over 1 million?
16) What is the northernmost city in the world with a population of over 1 million?
17) By area, what is the smallest country in South America?
18) By area, what is the smallest country in Africa?
19) By area, what is the largest lake in Europe?
20) By area, what is the smallest country in Asia?

Quiz 13 Answers

1) Washington, D.C., United States – 0.21% of the U.S. population
2) Antarctica – an area of over 100 volcanoes under the ice sheet in western Antarctica
3) Five - Macau, British Virgin Islands, Brunei, Liechtenstein, Palau

4) 30
5) Indonesia
6) Northern – 2.7 degrees Fahrenheit warmer due to ocean circulation
7) 22 – including Andorra, Costa Rica, Panama, Grenada, Haiti, Iceland, Liechtenstein
8) Lake Maracaibo, Venezuela - Lightning storms occur for about 10 hours a night, 140 to 160 nights a year, for a total of about 1.2 million lightning discharges per year.
9) Indonesia
10) Netherlands – an average of 6'½" for men and 5'7" for women
11) Indonesia – an average of 5'2" for men and 4'10" for women
12) Zero
13) Santo Domingo, Dominican Republic
14) Guatemala City, Guatemala
15) Melbourne, Australia – 37.8 degrees south latitude
16) St. Petersburg, Russia – 59.9 degrees north latitude
17) Suriname – 63,252 square miles
18) Seychelles – Group of 115 islands covering 177 square miles and lying 932 miles east of mainland Africa
19) Ladoga – 6,834 square miles in Russia
20) Maldives – 115 square mile group of 26 islands in the Indian Ocean

Quiz 14

1) What is the most populous country in Central America?
2) How many countries are in North America?
3) What is the only continent without glaciers?
4) What is the largest island in the world formed solely by volcanic activity?
5) How many landlocked countries are there in Europe?
6) What is the longest freshwater lake in the world?
7) What continent has the most landlocked countries?
8) What is the longest river in North America?
9) What is the highest mountain outside of Asia?
10) By area, what is the world's smallest mountain range?
11) By area, what is the largest country in the Southern Hemisphere?
12) By volume, what is the second-largest freshwater lake in the world?
13) What country is the fourth largest in the Americas (North and South America)?

14) What is the largest island in North America?
15) What two countries share Victoria Falls in Africa?
16) What African country was divided in two in 2011?
17) What country has the highest asphalt road in the world?
18) What is the highest navigable lake in the world?
19) What city of at least 1 million population is furthest away from another city of at least 1 million population?
20) What is the most remote (furthest from the nearest land) island in the world?

Quiz 14 Answers

1) Guatemala
2) 23 – Antigua and Barbuda, Bahamas, Barbados, Belize, Canada, Costa Rica, Cuba, Dominica, Dominican Republic, El Salvador, Grenada, Guatemala, Haiti, Honduras, Jamaica, Mexico, Nicaragua, Panama, St. Kitts and Nevis, St. Lucia, St. Vincent and the Grenadines, Trinidad and Tobago, United States
3) Australia
4) Iceland – 39,768 square miles
5) 14 - Andorra, Austria, Belarus, Czech Republic, Hungary, Liechtenstein, Luxembourg, Macedonia, Moldova, San Marino, Serbia, Slovakia, Switzerland, Vatican City
6) Tanganyika – 420 miles in Africa
7) Africa – 16
8) Missouri – 2,341 miles
9) Aconcagua – 22,841 feet in Argentina
10) Sutter Buttes in the northern Great Valley of central California - 75 square miles with a maximum elevation of 2,122 feet
11) Brazil – A small portion is in the Northern Hemisphere.
12) Tanganyika – maximum depth of 4,820 feet
13) Argentina
14) Greenland – 836,300 square miles
15) Zambia and Zimbabwe
16) Sudan – now Sudan and South Sudan
17) China (Tibet) – 18,258 feet
18) Lake Titicaca – 12,507 feet elevation in Bolivia and Peru
19) Auckland, New Zealand – 1,347 miles away from Sydney, Australia
20) Bouvet Island in the South Atlantic Ocean - 994 miles to Antarctica

Quiz 15

1) By discharge volume, what is the second-largest river in the world?
2) The point in the oceans furthest from the nearest land is called what?
3) By area, Germany is closest in size to what U.S. state?
4) Greenland is a territory of what country?
5) By area, what is the largest island nation?
6) How many Canadian territories are there?
7) What European country is divided into areas called cantons?
8) By area, what is the largest country with Spanish as an official language?
9) What is the largest lake in Antarctica?
10) What country has the second-largest Spanish speaking population?
11) What is the highest waterfall in the world?
12) The world's largest pyramid by volume is in what country?
13) What is the most common symbol on flags of the world?
14) What country is last alphabetically?
15) What country is first alphabetically?
16) Why is the city of La Paz, Bolivia one of the most fire-safe cities?
17) What river flows through eight countries and four national capitals?
18) What is the deepest lake in the world?
19) What are Africa's four great rivers?
20) The Somers Islands have what more familiar name?

Quiz 15 Answers

1) Congo
2) Point Nemo – It is in the South Pacific Ocean 1,670 miles from the nearest land.
3) Montana – Germany is 137,983 square miles; Montana is 147,040 square miles.
4) Denmark
5) Indonesia – 735,358 square miles
6) Three - Northwest Territories, Nunavut, Yukon
7) Switzerland
8) Argentina
9) Lake Vostok – largest of the subglacial lakes
10) United States
11) Angel Falls, Venezuela – 3,212 feet high

12) Mexico – The Great Pyramid of Cholula has a base of 450 meters each side and a height of 66 meters.
13) Star
14) Zimbabwe
15) Afghanistan
16) At an elevation of 11,800 feet, it is difficult for fires to spread due to the low oxygen level.
17) Danube
18) Lake Baikal, Russia – 5,387 feet deep
19) Nile, Congo, Zambezi, Niger
20) Bermuda

Quiz 16

1) What national capital city is heated by volcanic springs?
2) By area, what is the world's largest island?
3) By area, Vatican City is the world's smallest country; what is the second smallest?
4) What is the world's longest mountain range?
5) What country has the world's second-largest Christian population?
6) What is the most populous African country?
7) What is the only country crossed both by the equator and Tropic of Capricorn?
8) What is the largest desert in the Western Hemisphere?
9) By area, what is the largest island in South America?
10) By area, what is the largest Canadian province?
11) What is the second-longest river in Asia?
12) What country has the highest per capita electricity consumption?
13) What is the oldest national capital city in the Americas?
14) What is the northernmost Scandinavian country?
15) What major city is on an island in the St. Lawrence River?
16) By area, what is the world's largest sea?
17) What is the only Middle Eastern country without a desert?
18) What is the largest enclosed inland body of water in the world?
19) What river goes over Victoria Falls?
20) What is the most populous city in Africa?

Quiz 16 Answers

1) Reykjavik, Iceland

2) Greenland – 836,300 square miles
3) Monaco – 0.78 square miles
4) Andes – 4,300 miles
5) Brazil
6) Nigeria
7) Brazil
8) Patagonian Desert – 258,688 square miles primarily in Argentina
9) Tierra del Fuego – 18,605 square miles
10) Quebec – 595,400 square miles
11) Yellow – 3,395 miles
12) Iceland – more than four times higher than the United States
13) Mexico City – founded in 1521
14) Norway
15) Montreal, Canada
16) Philippine – 2.2 million square miles
17) Lebanon
18) Caspian Sea – It is considered a lake by some, but it has saltwater and has 3.5 times more water than all the Great Lakes combined, covering 143,244 square miles.
19) Zambezi
20) Lagos, Nigeria

Quiz 17

1) What country has the southernmost point in continental Europe?
2) What national capital city does the River Liffey flow through?
3) By area, what is the second-largest continent?
4) What is the only Dutch-speaking country in South America?
5) What is Abyssinia now called?
6) What national capital rises where the Blue Nile and White Nile converge?
7) Of all meteorites ever found, 90% come from what continent?
8) What two cities are at the ends of the Trans-Siberian railroad?
9) What four seas are named for colors?
10) By area, what is the second-largest island in the world?
11) By volume, what is the world's largest volcano (active or extinct)?
12) What continent has the highest population density?
13) What is Europe's longest river?
14) What continent has the highest average elevation?

15) By area, what is the smallest of the Great Lakes?
16) What country has the world's highest elevation city?
17) What peninsula do Spain and Portugal share?
18) What is the longest river in the Americas?
19) By area, what is the largest country in Central America?
20) What country's flag has lasted the longest without change?

Quiz 17 Answers

1) Spain
2) Dublin, Ireland
3) Africa
4) Suriname – former Dutch colony
5) Ethiopia
6) Khartoum, Sudan
7) Antarctica
8) Moscow and Vladivostok
9) Red, Black, Yellow, White
10) New Guinea – 303,476 square miles
11) Tamu Massif – extinct volcano 1,000 miles east of Japan under the Pacific Ocean
12) Asia
13) Volga – 2,294 miles
14) Antarctica – 8,200 feet average elevation
15) Lake Ontario – 7,320 square miles
16) Peru – La Rinconada is a mining town at 16,700 feet in the Andes and has about 30,000 residents.
17) Iberian
18) Amazon – 4,345 miles
19) Nicaragua – 50,338 square miles
20) Denmark – 1370 or earlier

Quiz 18

1) What country has the largest Portuguese speaking population?
2) What country's flag is incorporated most often in other flags?
3) What African capital city is named for a U.S. president?
4) What is the northernmost country in continental South America?
5) What country has the most tornadoes?

6) By area, what is the largest Scandinavian country?
7) What country has the most earthquakes?
8) How many Canadian provinces border the Great Lakes?
9) What country has the world's southernmost city?
10) What is the official language of Nigeria?
11) Which of the Great Lakes do all the others flow into?
12) What continent has the lowest highest point?
13) How many landlocked countries are there in Asia?
14) What is the world's most populous metropolitan area?
15) What is the second most widely spoken language in the world?
16) The land location furthest from any ocean is in what country?
17) How many Australian states are there?
18) What is the capital of Monaco?
19) Switzerland has four official languages; what are they?
20) What river flows through Rome?

Quiz 18 Answers

1) Brazil
2) Great Britain
3) Monrovia, Liberia
4) Colombia
5) United States
6) Sweden
7) Indonesia – followed by Japan
8) One – Ontario
9) Chile
10) English
11) Lake Ontario
12) Australia - Mount Kosciuszko at 7,310 feet
13) 12 - Afghanistan, Armenia, Azerbaijan, Bhutan, Laos, Kazakhstan, Kyrgyzstan, Mongolia, Nepal, Tajikistan, Turkmenistan, Uzbekistan
14) Tokyo, Japan
15) Spanish – Mandarin is first; English is third.
16) China – 1,645 miles from the ocean near the Kazakhstan border in extreme northwestern China
17) Six – New South Wales, Queensland, South Australia, Tasmania, Victoria, Western Australia
18) Monaco – It is both a city and a country.

19) German, French, Italian, and Romanish, a romance language spoken predominantly in one canton
20) Tiber

Quiz 19

1) What two South American countries share the region of Patagonia?
2) What is the smallest population country with two or more Nobel Prize winners?
3) What is Australia's island state?
4) What country contains South America's highest and lowest points?
5) What is the world's highest mountain that isn't part of a range?
6) By area, what is the smallest country in the Australian continent?
7) By area, what is the largest country entirely within the Southern Hemisphere?
8) What two countries have Sierra Nevada mountains?
9) By area, what is the largest Japanese island?
10) What was Canada's first national park?
11) What is the most populous city north of the Arctic Circle?
12) What is the most populous country with English as an official language?
13) Mount Chogori is better known by what name?
14) In what country is the only point on the equator with snow on the ground?
15) If you flew due east from New York City, what is the first foreign country you would reach?
16) What two bodies of water does the Suez Canal connect?
17) What is the most populous city in Canada?
18) What language is the official language of the most countries?
19) What country spans the Pacific Ocean, the Caribbean Sea, Amazon River, and the Andes Mountains?
20) What is the largest island on the Australian continent?

Quiz 19 Answers

1) Chile and Argentina
2) St. Lucia – Caribbean island with 185,000 people and two Nobel Prize winners
3) Tasmania
4) Argentina – 22,841 feet above sea level to 344 feet below

5) Mount Kilimanjaro, Tanzania – 19,341 feet
6) Nauru – eight square miles
7) Australia – A small portion of Brazil is in the Northern Hemisphere.
8) United States and Spain
9) Honshu – 87,182 square miles
10) Banff National Park
11) Murmansk, Russia – over 300,000 people at 69 degrees north latitude
12) India
13) K2 – second highest mountain in the world
14) Ecuador
15) Portugal
16) Red Sea and Mediterranean Sea
17) Toronto
18) English – 54 countries
19) Colombia
20) New Guinea – 303,476 square miles

Quiz 20

1) What river flows through Baghdad, Iraq?
2) What is the easternmost national capital city in South America?
3) What is the main river that flows through Shanghai, China?
4) In 1937, Liechtenstein added a crown to their flag after discovering at the 1936 Summer Olympics that their flag was identical to what country?
5) What is the deepest lake in Asia?
6) What country has the northernmost permanent settlement in the world?
7) What island nation was once one of the wealthiest countries on a GDP per capita basis due to phosphate mining but became one of the poorest after strip mining 80% of the country and depleting the phosphate deposits?
8) What is the capital of the Canadian province of Quebec?
9) What is the smallest landlocked country in the world?
10) What is the largest city in the Southern Hemisphere?
11) The island of Hispaniola is divided into what two countries?
12) What country is bordered by Mexico and Guatemala?
13) What country has the northernmost 18-hole golf course in the world?
14) What is the most populous national capital city in South America?

15) By population, what is the largest country in the European Union?
16) What is the largest desert in Asia?
17) What country has the southernmost point in North America?
18) What is Australia's largest island?
19) What is the major river that flows through Delhi, India?
20) What is the southernmost urban area in the world with a population of over 20 million?

Quiz 20 Answers

1) Tigris
2) Brasilia, Brazil - 47.9 degrees west longitude
3) Huangpu River
4) Haiti
5) Lake Baikal - 5,387 feet in Russia
6) Canada - Alert, Nunavut, Canada, is at 82.5 degrees north latitude, about 508 miles from the North pole
7) Nauru - 8 square miles in the South Pacific. The phosphate deposits were based on the decay of marine microorganisms and thousands of years of seabird droppings.
8) Quebec City
9) Vatican City - 0.17 square miles
10) Sao Paulo, Brazil
11) Haiti and Dominican Republic
12) Belize
13) Norway - Tromsø Golfpark at Breivikeidet near Tromsø, Norway at 69.7 degrees north latitude
14) Lima, Peru
15) Germany
16) Arabian Desert - 900,000 square miles
17) Costa Rica - Cocos Island at 5.5 degrees north latitude
18) Tasmania - 25,105 square miles
19) Yamuna River
20) Sao Paulo, Brazil at 23.9 degrees south latitude

Quiz 21

1) What is the longest tributary river in the world?
2) What country has the easternmost point in Asia?
3) What is the deepest sea in the world?

4) What is the most densely populated European country?
5) What is the second-highest mountain in North America?
6) What country consists of more than 17,500 islands with about 6,000 of them inhabited?
7) What national capital city is closest to the equator?
8) What river flows through Lisbon, Portugal?
9) What country has the most bicycles per capita?
10) What is the capital of the Canadian province of New Brunswick?
11) What is the most popular letter for country names to begin with?
12) What is the westernmost national capital city in Africa?
13) How many rivers in the world are over 3,000 miles long?
14) What country is Mount Kilimanjaro in?
15) What is the largest volume lake in North America?
16) What new country was established in 2011?
17) What African country has the most lakes?
18) What country has the largest area of inland waters?
19) Based on the number of members, what country has the largest legislature in the world?
20) What is the largest island in the Pacific Ocean?

Quiz 21 Answers

1) Irtysh River - 2,640 miles in Russia, China, and Kazakhstan. It is the chief tributary of the Ob River.
2) Russia - Big Diomede at 169.1 degrees west longitude
3) Caribbean Sea - 25,217 feet maximum depth
4) Monaco
5) Mount Logan - 19,551 feet in Yukon province of Canada
6) Indonesia
7) Quito, Ecuador - 15.9 miles south of the equator
8) Tagus River
9) Netherlands - almost one per person
10) Fredericton
11) A - 11 countries - Afghanistan, Albania, Algeria, Andorra, Angola, Antigua and Barbuda, Argentina, Armenia, Australia, Austria, Azerbaijan
12) Praia, Cape Verde - 23.5 degrees west longitude
13) Five - Nile, Amazon, Yangtze, Yellow, Parana
14) Tanzania

15) Lake Superior - United States and Canada
16) South Sudan
17) Uganda
18) Canada
19) China - The National People's Congress is a single house made up of 2,980 members.
20) New Guinea - 303,476 square miles

Quiz 22

1) What is the deepest river in South America?
2) What country has the second-highest average elevation?
3) What mountain range is Mount Kilimanjaro part of?
4) What country is bordered by Russia, Azerbaijan, Armenia, and Turkey?
5) The southern end of the Suez Canal is at Port Tewfik at the city of Suez, Egypt; what port city is at the northern end?
6) What is the longest mountain range in Asia?
7) What country is bordered by Chile, Uruguay, Brazil, Paraguay, and Bolivia?
8) By area, what is the largest Greek island?
9) How many European countries share a name with their capital city?
10) By area, what is the third-largest island in the world?
11) What is the largest volume lake in Africa?
12) What country has the southernmost point in mainland North America?
13) How many federated states does Mexico have?
14) What country's flag has the most stars?
15) How many countries does the Arctic Circle pass through?
16) By population, what is the second-largest city in Australia?
17) What is the deepest river in Africa?
18) How many countries don't have any airports within their boundaries?
19) How many North American countries have a land border with only one other country?
20) What is the second smallest landlocked country in the world?

Quiz 22 Answers

1) Amazon - 328 feet maximum depth
2) Nepal - 10,715 feet average elevation
3) None – At 19,340 feet, it is the highest mountain in the world that isn't part of a range.

4) Georgia
5) Port Said, Egypt
6) Kunlun Mountains - 1,900 miles in China
7) Argentina
8) Crete - 3,219 square miles, 5th largest island in the Mediterranean
9) Five - Vatican City, Monaco, Luxembourg, Andorra, San Marino
10) Borneo - 287,000 square miles
11) Lake Tanganyika - Tanzania, DRC, Burundi, and Zambia
12) Panama - Punta Mariato at 7.2 degrees north latitude
13) 31 - plus the Federal District of Mexico City
14) United States
15) Eight - Norway, Sweden, Finland, Russia, United States, Canada, Denmark (Greenland), Iceland
16) Melbourne
17) Congo – up to 750 feet
18) Five - Vatican City, San Marino, Liechtenstein, Andorra, Monaco
19) Three - Canada, Haiti, Dominican Republic
20) San Marino - 23.6 square miles

Quiz 23

1) What river has the largest drainage basin area in the world?
2) What country has the highest minimum elevation?
3) What mountain range passes through the most countries?
4) What is the smallest population national capital city in the world?
5) What is the only Central American country that doesn't border the Pacific Ocean?
6) What provinces and territories meet at The Four Corners of Canada?
7) What is the highest mountain in China?
8) How many countries border the Gulf of Mexico?
9) What are the only two countries in South America with left-hand driving?
10) What continent has the largest number of individual deserts?
11) What country has the easternmost point in North America?
12) What country has the world's largest rock?
13) What river flows through Prague, Czech Republic?
14) What is the least densely populated Canadian province?
15) What country has the largest area devoted to national parks?
16) What country has the world's highest elevation airport?

17) If you wanted to dig a hole straight through the center of the earth and end up in China, what country would you have to start in?
18) What mountain range is Canada's highest peak a part of?
19) What country is bordered by Germany, Austria, Slovakia, and Poland?
20) What province or territory has the southernmost point in Canada?

Quiz 23 Answers

1) Amazon - 2.7 million square miles drainage basin
2) Lesotho - 4,593 feet minimum elevation
3) Andes - seven countries - Venezuela, Colombia, Ecuador, Peru, Bolivia, Chile, Argentina
4) Ngerulmud, Palau - It has less than 400 residents; Palau is an island nation in the Pacific Ocean.
5) Belize
6) Saskatchewan, Manitoba, Northwest Territories, Nunavut
7) Mount Everest - 29,020 feet
8) Three - Mexico, United States, Cuba
9) Suriname and Guyana
10) Asia
11) Denmark (Greenland) - Nordostrundingen at 11.5 degrees west longitude
12) Australia - Mount Augustus in the Australian Outback is 2,350 feet high and 5 miles long occupying an area of about 18.5 square miles. It is about 2.5 times larger than Ayers Rock.
13) Vltava River
14) Newfoundland and Labrador
15) Canada – It has over 145,000 square miles of national parks, an area larger than Norway.
16) China - Daocheng Yading Airport at 14,472 feet
17) Argentina
18) Saint Elias Mountains – They run through southeastern Alaska, southwestern Yukon, and the very far northwestern part of British Columbia, Canada.
19) Czech Republic
20) Ontario

Quiz 24

1) What country has the southernmost national park in the world?

2) What country has the oldest city in Europe?
3) What country has the longest coastline in Asia?
4) What country is bordered by Honduras and Guatemala?
5) What is the oldest national capital city in South America?
6) How many provinces are there in China?
7) What is the northernmost national capital city in Africa?
8) How many European countries have a land border with only one other country?
9) The largest uninhabited island in the world is part of what country?
10) What continent stretches from the equator to the Arctic Circle?
11) What is the least populous country in Asia?
12) The five smallest landlocked countries in the world are all on what continent?
13) What is the most densely populated North American country?
14) What country has the shortest written constitution?
15) What tiny country of just over 20,000 people is divided into 16 states each with an elected legislature and a tribal chiefdom?
16) What are the names of the two main islands that make up over 98% of New Zealand's area?
17) What province or territory has the westernmost point in Canada?
18) French Sudan is the former name of what country?
19) How many Asian countries does the equator pass through?
20) What river flows through Dublin, Ireland?

Quiz 24 Answers

1) Chile - Cabo de Hornos National Park, Tierra Del Fuego, Chile, at 55.8 degrees south latitude
2) Bulgaria - The city of Plovdiv was founded about 6000 BC.
3) Indonesia - 33,939 miles
4) El Salvador
5) Quito, Ecuador - founded in 980 AD
6) 23
7) Tunis, Tunisia - 36.8 degrees north latitude
8) Seven - Portugal, Ireland, United Kingdom, Denmark, San Marino, Monaco, Vatican City
9) Canada - Devon Island in Nunavut Territory is 21,331 square miles at an elevation of 6,300 feet. It is at 75.2 degrees north latitude and is the 27th largest island in the world.
10) Asia

11) Maldives
12) Europe - Vatican City, San Marino, Liechtenstein, Andorra, Luxembourg
13) Bermuda
14) Monaco – 3,814 words
15) Palau - It is an archipelago of over 500 islands in the western Pacific Ocean occupying 177 square miles in total.
16) North Island is the 14th largest island in the world at 43,082 square miles, and South Island is the 12th largest in the world at 56,308 square miles.
17) Yukon
18) Mali
19) Two - Maldives and Indonesia
20) River Liffey

Quiz 25

1) What river flows through Bangkok, Thailand?
2) What four national capital cities does the Danube River flow through?
3) If you exclude the Vatican as a national capital, what pair of national capital cities are closest together?
4) What country has the easternmost point in mainland South America?
5) What is the capital of the Canadian province of Newfoundland and Labrador?
6) What country is closest to 0 degrees latitude and 0 degrees longitude (the intersection of the equator and the prime meridian)?
7) What is the least populous country in Europe?
8) Based on average depth, what is the deepest of the Great Lakes?
9) The most national capital cities start with what letter?
10) Among countries that share a land border, what pair of national capital cities are the greatest distance apart?
11) What is the northernmost national capital city in Asia?
12) What country has the southernmost international airport in the world?
13) How many country's official currency is the dollar (either U.S. dollar or other dollar)?
14) By population, what is the second-largest city in Africa?
15) What country is bordered by Mexico, Belize, Honduras, and El Salvador?
16) What is the largest desert in Australia?
17) What is the westernmost national capital city in Asia?

18) What is the longest mountain range in Antarctica?
19) By population, what is the second-largest city in Canada?
20) What country has the longest coastline in mainland Africa?

Quiz 25 Answers

1) Chao Phraya River
2) Vienna, Austria; Bratislava, Slovakia; Budapest, Hungary; Belgrade, Serbia
3) Brazzaville, Republic of the Congo, and Kinshasa, Democratic Republic of the Congo - two miles apart
4) Brazil - Ponta do Seixas at 34.8 degrees west longitude
5) St. John's
6) Ghana - The equator and prime meridian intersect 380 miles south of Ghana in the Gulf of Guinea.
7) Vatican City
8) Superior - 483 feet average depth
9) B - Baghdad, Baku, Bamako, Bandar Seri Begawan, Bangkok, Bangui, Banjul, Basseterre, Beijing, Beirut, Belgrade, Belmopan, Berlin, Bern, Bishkek, Bissau, Bogota, Brasilia, Bratislava, Brazzaville, Bridgetown, Brussels, Bucharest, Budapest, Buenos Aires
10) Brasilia, Brazil, and Paris, France (5,427 miles apart) - French Guiana, which borders Brazil, is a part of France, just as Alaska or Hawaii are part of the United States.
11) Astana, Kazakhstan - 51.2 degrees north latitude
12) Argentina - Malvinas Argentinas International Airport, Ushuaia, Argentina, at 54.8 degrees south latitude
13) 32 - Australia, Bahamas, Barbados, Belize, Brunei, Canada, Dominica, East Timor, Ecuador, El Salvador, Fiji, Grenada, Guyana, Jamaica, Kiribati, Liberia, Marshall Islands, Micronesia, Namibia, Nauru, New Zealand, Palau, Saint Kitts and Nevis, Saint Lucia, Saint Vincent and the Grenadines, Singapore, Solomon Islands, Suriname, Taiwan, Tuvalu, United States, Zimbabwe
14) Cairo, Egypt
15) Guatemala
16) Great Victoria Desert - 220,000 square miles
17) Ankara, Turkey - 32.9 degrees east longitude
18) Transantarctic Mountains - 2,200 miles
19) Montreal
20) Somalia - 2,071 miles

Quiz 26

1) What is the most populous national capital city in Europe?
2) What is the second deepest lake in the world?
3) What country has the longest coastline in North America?
4) What country has the easternmost point in Africa?
5) What country has the largest number of paid newspapers?
6) Besides its canals, what river flows through Amsterdam, Netherlands?
7) What is the deepest river in the world?
8) What is the highest mountain in the United Kingdom?
9) What is the warmest ocean?
10) What was the capital of West Germany before Germany was reunited?
11) Until it gained its independence in 1825, what country was known as Upper Peru?
12) What country is the leading producer of uranium in the world?
13) What is the largest island in the Philippines?
14) What is the most densely populated Canadian province?
15) What country has the world's highest unclimbed mountain?
16) What are the three city-states in the world?
17) What is the highest coastal mountain in the world?
18) Unimak is the largest island in what chain?
19) What country is bordered by Colombia, Brazil, and Guyana?
20) What is the only carbon negative (produces less carbon dioxide than it absorbs) country in the world?

Quiz 26 Answers

1) Moscow, Russia
2) Lake Tanganyika - 4,820 feet deep in southeastern Africa
3) Canada - 125,567 miles
4) Mauritius - Rodrigues, Mauritius at 63.5 degrees east longitude
5) India
6) Amstel
7) Congo - up to 750 feet deep
8) Ben Nevis - 4,409 feet in Scotland
9) Indian Ocean
10) Bonn
11) Bolivia
12) Kazakhstan

13) Luzon - 42,458 square miles
14) Prince Edward Island
15) Bhutan - Gangkhar Puensum at 24,840 feet is the tallest unclimbed mountain in the world. It has been off-limits to climbers since 1994 when Bhutan prohibited all mountaineering above 6,000 meters due to spiritual and religious beliefs.
16) Vatican City, Monaco, Singapore
17) Mount Logan - 19,551 feet in the Saint Elias range in the Yukon province of Canada
18) Aleutian Islands – It is 1,571 square miles.
19) Venezuela
20) Bhutan – About 72% of the country is still forested.

Quiz 27

1) How many stars are on the flag of China?
2) What is the highest mountain in Russia?
3) What is the capital of the Canadian province of Alberta?
4) What is the capital of the Canadian province of Nova Scotia?
5) What is the largest island in the Atlantic Ocean?
6) How many continents are entirely in the Northern Hemisphere?
7) Based on volume, what continent has the largest man-made lake in the world?
8) What is the deepest river in Asia?
9) What is the largest island in the Indian Ocean?
10) What is the easternmost national capital city in Asia?
11) How many national anthems have no official words?
12) What are the only two countries with coastlines on the Aegean Sea?
13) What is the longest river in the European Union countries?
14) What country has the southernmost point in Europe?
15) On the Amazon River, what is the Pororoca?
16) What country has the highest percentage of its energy consumption from renewable resources?
17) What country has the northernmost point in South America?
18) By area, what is the largest Australian state or territory?
19) Canada has a strategic reserve of 2.4 million gallons of what food item?
20) What country has the northernmost point in mainland Europe?

Quiz 27 Answers

1) Five - One large gold star representing communism and four smaller stars representing the people
2) Mount Elbrus - 18,510 feet
3) Edmonton
4) Halifax
5) Greenland - 836,300 square miles
6) Two – Europe and North America
7) Africa - Lake Kariba on the Zambezi River in Zambia and Zimbabwe contains 43.3 cubic miles of water.
8) Yangtze - 656 feet maximum depth, 2nd deepest in the world
9) Madagascar - 226,658 square miles
10) Tokyo, Japan - 139.7 degrees east longitude
11) Four - Spain, Bosnia and Herzegovina, Kosovo, San Marino
12) Turkey and Greece
13) Danube - 1,771 miles
14) Greece - Gavdos Island at 34.8 degrees north latitude
15) Tidal bore wave - It is up to 13 feet high and travels up to 500 miles inland upstream on the Amazon river. The wave occurs during new and full moons when the ocean tide is the highest and water flows in from the Atlantic Ocean.
16) Iceland
17) Colombia - Santa Catalina Island at 13.4 degrees north latitude
18) Western Australia - 975,598 square miles
19) Maple syrup - It is kept to ensure the global supply in the case of emergency; Quebec province produces about 75% of the global supply of maple syrup.
20) Norway - Cape Nordkinn at 71.1 degrees north latitude

Quiz 28

1) What country is bordered by Belgium, France, and Germany?
2) What is the southernmost national capital city in South America?
3) By population, what is the second-largest city in Asia?
4) What country is bordered by Peru, Brazil, Paraguay, Argentina, and Chile?
5) What country has the southernmost point in mainland Asia?
6) What country or territory has the northernmost national park in the world?

7) What is believed to be the oldest continuously inhabited city in South America?
8) What is the oldest lake in the world?
9) English is the official language of more countries than any other language; what is the second most popular official language?
10) What is the second highest elevation national capital city in the world?
11) What country has the westernmost point in North America?
12) In what country or territory is the northernmost island in the world?
13) What is the highest active volcano in Europe?
14) What country is bordered by Brazil, French Guiana, and Guyana?
15) What is the capital of the Canadian province of Prince Edward Island?
16) What country has the northernmost point in Africa?
17) What country has the oldest operating zoo in the world?
18) By population, what is the largest city entirely in Europe?
19) What very small country generates as much as 10% of its entire national revenue from the sale of its postage stamps to foreign collectors?
20) What is the westernmost national capital city in North America?

Quiz 28 Answers

1) Luxembourg
2) Montevideo, Uruguay - 34.9 degrees south latitude
3) Delhi, India
4) Bolivia
5) Malaysia - Tanjung Piai at 1.3 degrees north latitude
6) Greenland - Northeast Greenland National Park at 76 degrees north latitude is also the largest national park in the world at 375,291 square miles, which is larger than all but 29 countries in the world.
7) Quito, Ecuador - founded in 980 AD
8) Lake Zaysan - about 65 million years old in eastern Kazakhstan
9) French - 29 countries
10) Quito, Ecuador - 9,350 feet
11) United States - Amatignak Island, Alaska at 179.2 degrees west longitude
12) Greenland - Kaffeklubben Island (Coffee Club Island) is a small island off the northern tip of Greenland at 83.7 degrees north latitude.
13) Mount Etna - 10,810 feet in Sicily, Italy
14) Suriname
15) Charlottetown

16) Tunisia - Iles des Chiens at 37.5 degrees north latitude
17) Austria - The Vienna Zoo has been open to the public since 1779.
18) Moscow, Russia
19) San Marino
20) Mexico City, Mexico - 99.1 degrees west longitude

Quiz 29

1) What is the highest mountain in Antarctica?
2) In what country can you swim between the European and North American tectonic plates?
3) What is the northernmost national capital city in Europe?
4) What country contains the geographic center of South America?
5) How many continents are entirely in the Southern Hemisphere?
6) What is the only country outside of Europe where Dutch is spoken by most of its population?
7) What country has the most cities with a population of over 1 million?
8) What two islands in the Mediterranean Sea are independent nations?
9) In what ocean is the Republic of Seychelles located?
10) What is the highest mountain in Turkey?
11) What country has the world's heaviest building?
12) What country has the largest percentage of its area devoted to national parks?
13) What is the most populous national capital city in the world?
14) What is the only African country that borders the Mediterranean Sea and the Red Sea?
15) What country is bordered by Nicaragua and Panama?
16) What is the most populous island in the Mediterranean Sea?
17) The most remote inhabited island in the world is part of what country?
18) What country has the oldest mountain range in the world?
19) What is the deepest lake in Africa?
20) What is the highest mountain in Pakistan?

Quiz 29 Answers

1) Mount Vinson - 16,050 feet
2) Iceland - The Silfra fissure in Thingvellir National Park is a crack between the two continental plates and is the only spot in the world where you can swim directly between the North American and European continents. The crack is filled with extremely clear cold water

that remains about 35-39 degrees Fahrenheit all year.
3) Reykjavik, Iceland - 64.1 degrees north latitude
4) Paraguay
5) Two – Australia and Antarctica
6) Suriname - former Dutch colony in South America
7) China - over 100 cities
8) Cyprus and Malta
9) Indian Ocean - off the east coast of Africa
10) Mount Ararat - 16,854 feet
11) Romania - The Palace of Parliament in Bucharest is 275.6 feet high and covers an area of 1.41 square miles with a volume of 2.55 million cubic meters and weighs about 9 billion pounds. It is the second-largest building in the world by surface area.
12) Zambia - National parks make up 32% of its area.
13) Beijing, China
14) Egypt
15) Costa Rica
16) Sicily
17) United Kingdom - Tristan da Cunha Island in the South Atlantic is a British overseas territory and is 1,511 miles off the coast of Cape Town, South Africa. It is 38 square miles and is only accessible via boat, a six-day trip from South Africa.
18) South Africa - The Barberton Greenstone Belt is 3.5 billion years old with a maximum elevation of 5,900 feet.
19) Lake Tanganyika - 4,820 feet deep in southeastern Africa
20) K2 - 28,251 feet

Quiz 30

1) By area, what is the second-largest freshwater lake in the world?
2) Since the 1940s, Canada has had a policy of naming thousands of its unnamed lakes after whom?
3) What is the second largest desert in Asia?
4) What country has the most United States emigrants?
5) What is the deepest canyon in the world?
6) What is the most densely populated Asian country?
7) What is the southernmost national capital city in Africa?
8) What was the first European country to create national parks?
9) How many states does Brazil have?
10) What country is bordered by Latvia, Lithuania, Poland, Ukraine, and

Russia?
11) What is the largest island in Canada?
12) What country is bordered by Ecuador, Peru, Brazil, Venezuela, and Panama?
13) What is the least densely populated African country?
14) What is the highest active volcano in Asia?
15) What desert contains the largest continuous body of sand in the world?
16) What island has the longest river?
17) What is the capital of the Canadian province of Saskatchewan?
18) What is the oldest city in Canada?
19) What is the second largest desert in Africa?
20) What is the lowest elevation national capital city in the world?

Quiz 30 Answers

1) Lake Victoria - 26,950 square miles
2) Fallen soldiers from all three branches of its armed forces
3) Gobi Desert - 500,000 square miles in China and Mongolia
4) Mexico
5) Yarlung Tsangpo Canyon (Tibet) - 19,714 feet maximum depth
6) Singapore
7) Cape Town, South Africa - 33.9 degrees south latitude
8) Sweden - 1909
9) 26 - plus the Federal District for the national capital
10) Belarus
11) Baffin - 195,928 square miles
12) Colombia
13) Namibia
14) Mount Damavand – 18,406 feet in Iran
15) Arabian Desert - The contiguous sand body within it is known as the Rub 'al-Khali or the "Empty Quarter" and is about 250,966 square miles.
16) Borneo - The Kapuas River is 710 miles long.
17) Regina
18) St. John's, Newfoundland – founded in 1497
19) Kalahari Desert - 360,000 square miles in Namibia, Botswana, and South Africa
20) Baku, Azerbaijan - 92 feet below sea level

Quiz 31

1) What is the third-longest river in the world?
2) What is the only country that borders the Black Sea and the Mediterranean Sea?
3) What is the largest volume lake in Europe?
4) By area, what is the second-largest island nation in the world?
5) What country has the largest number of rivers at least 600 miles long?
6) What country is bordered by Turkey, Iran, Syria, Jordan, Saudi Arabia, and Kuwait?
7) What is the most populous national capital city in North America?
8) How many letters are in the shortest country name in the world?
9) In what country or territory is the northernmost point of land in the world?
10) By area, what is the largest country in the world without any mountains (points greater than 2,000 feet elevation)?
11) How many countries are in Central America?
12) What country changed its name to Myanmar in 1989?
13) Where are the Thousand Islands located?
14) What country has the longest national anthem?
15) What country has the northernmost skyscraper (at least 150 meters tall) in the world?
16) What is the oldest national capital city in Europe?
17) What is the most populous national capital city in Africa?
18) The Pacific Ocean is so large that at some points it is antipodal to itself; what does antipodal mean?
19) What is the westernmost national capital city in South America?
20) What are the only three countries with coastlines on both the Atlantic and Indian Oceans?

Quiz 31 Answers

1) Yangtze - 3,915 miles
2) Turkey
3) Lake Ladoga - Russia
4) Madagascar - 226,658 square miles
5) Russia - 36
6) Iraq
7) Mexico City, Mexico
8) Four letters - Chad, Togo, Mali, Iraq, Iran, Oman, Laos, Niue, Fiji,

Cuba, Peru
9) Greenland - Kaffeklubben Island (Coffee Club Island) is a small island off the northern tip of Greenland at 83.7 degrees north latitude.
10) Belarus - 80,155 square miles with a maximum elevation of 1,130 feet
11) Seven - Belize, Costa Rica, El Salvador, Guatemala, Honduras, Nicaragua, Panama
12) Burma
13) Saint Lawrence River - They are an archipelago of 1,864 islands between the United States and Canada.
14) Greece - Its national anthem, "Hymn to Liberty," has 158 verses. The anthem is a poem written in 1823 by Dionysios Solomos and set to music by Nikolaos Mantzaros.
15) Russia - Vysotsky Business Center in Yekaterinburg, Russia at 60.0 degrees north latitude
16) Athens, Greece - founded in about 3000 BC
17) Cairo, Egypt
18) Two points are antipodal if they are on diametrically opposite sides of the earth, so in some points of the Pacific Ocean, you could go straight through the center of the earth and come out the other side and still be in the Pacific Ocean.
19) Quito, Ecuador - 78.5 degrees west longitude
20) Egypt, Israel, South Africa

Quiz 32

1) By population, what is the second-largest island nation in the world?
2) What country has the most beaches?
3) What is the southernmost city in the world with a population of over 10 million?
4) By area, what is the largest country in the European Union?
5) What is the main river that flows through Tokyo, Japan?
6) What country has the highest percentage of its population in the military (active, reserves, and paramilitary)?
7) What island is nicknamed "The Spice Isle" for its production of nutmeg and mace?
8) What is the deepest river in Europe?
9) What two countries share the island of New Guinea?
10) What is the highest mountain in Europe?
11) What country is the largest mango producer in the world?
12) Portuguese West Africa is the former name of what country?

13) What is the deepest lake in Europe?
14) What country has the highest percentage of its area that is desert?
15) By population, what is the largest city in Canada?
16) Which country has the longest official name?
17) What is the highest active volcano in North America?
18) What is the oldest national capital city in the world?
19) What is the highest mountain range in North America?
20) What is the least populous country in the world?

Quiz 32 Answers

1) Japan
2) Australia - Its coastline is over 16,000 miles long and has over 10,000 beaches.
3) Buenos Aires, Argentina - 34.6 degrees south latitude
4) France
5) Sumida River
6) North Korea - over 30%
7) Grenada
8) Danube - 584 feet maximum depth, 3rd deepest in the world
9) Indonesia and Papua New Guinea
10) Mount Elbrus - 18,510 feet in Russia
11) India
12) Angola
13) Hornindalsvatnet - 1,686 feet in Norway
14) Libya - about 99%
15) Toronto
16) United Kingdom - Its official name is the United Kingdom of Great Britain and Northern Ireland.
17) Popocatépetl - 17,802 feet in Mexico
18) Damascus, Syria - inhabited for about 11,000 years
19) Alaska Range - 20,343 feet maximum elevation
20) Vatican City - less than 1,000 people

Quiz 33

1) What country has the westernmost point in mainland South America?
2) By population, what is the second-largest city in North America?
3) What is the longest mountain range in Africa?

4) What is the longest river in the world that flows entirely within one country?
5) What country is bordered by Ecuador, Colombia, Brazil, Bolivia, and Chile?
6) Zanzibar is part of what country?
7) What province or territory has the northernmost point in Canada?
8) What is the highest mountain in Argentina?
9) What is the longest mountain range in Europe?
10) What country has the most desert area in the world?
11) What river flows through more countries than any other in the world?
12) What country has the world's widest waterfall?
13) By population, what is the largest island nation in the world?
14) What country only borders France?
15) What country is bordered by Yemen, Saudi Arabia, and the United Arab Emirates?
16) Not including the United States, how many countries use the U.S. dollar as their official currency?
17) What country consumes the most milk per capita?
18) By area, what is the largest country with no natural rivers?
19) What country is bordered by France, Italy, Austria, and Germany?
20) What is the highest mountain in India?

Quiz 33 Answers

1) Peru - Punta Pariñas at 81.3 degrees west longitude
2) New York City
3) Atlas Mountains - 1,600 miles through Morocco, Algeria, and Tunisia
4) Yangtze - 3,964 miles entirely in China
5) Peru
6) Tanzania
7) Nunavut
8) Aconcagua - 22,835 feet
9) Scandinavian Mountains (Scandes) - 1,095 miles through the Scandinavian Peninsula
10) Australia - 965,000 square miles of desert
11) Danube (10 countries) - Germany, Austria, Slovakia, Hungary, Croatia, Serbia and Montenegro, Romania, Bulgaria, Moldova, Ukraine
12) Laos - Khone Falls on the Mekong River in the Champasak Province of Laos has a width of 35,376 feet.

13) Indonesia
14) Monaco
15) Oman
16) Seven - Ecuador, El Salvador, Zimbabwe, Timor-Leste, Micronesia, Palau, Marshall Islands
17) Finland
18) Saudi Arabia - 12th largest country
19) Switzerland
20) Kangchenjunga - 28,169 feet

Quiz 34

1) What is Australia's most significant mountain range and the third-longest range in the world?
2) What is the southernmost national capital city in North America?
3) What country has the southernmost point in mainland South America?
4) What is the only country that borders the Persian Gulf and the Red Sea?
5) What is the highest mountain in Japan?
6) What country has the southernmost university in the world?
7) What is the highest mountain in Nepal?
8) What country is bordered by Angola, Zambia, Botswana, and South Africa?
9) What is the southernmost national capital city in Asia?
10) What city of 1 million or more is closest to the equator?
11) By population, what is the largest city at least partly in Europe?
12) What country has the westernmost point in Asia?
13) What are the two main tributaries of the Nile River?
14) In what city do the two main tributaries of the Nile River come together?
15) What national capital city's full official name is Krung Thep Mahanakhon Amon Rattanakosin Mahinthara Yuthaya Mahadilok Phop Noppharat Ratchathani Burirom Udomratchaniwet Mahasathan Amon Piman Awatan Sathit Sakkathattiya Witsanukam Prasit?
16) What country is bordered by India, Afghanistan, Iran, and China?
17) What is the largest peninsula in the world?
18) In what country or territory is the northernmost active volcano in the world?
19) What country only borders Saudi Arabia?
20) What is the highest mountain located on an island?

Quiz 34 Answers

1) Great Dividing Range - 2,300 miles
2) Panama City, Panama - 9 degrees north latitude
3) Chile - Cape Froward at 53.9 degrees south latitude
4) Saudi Arabia
5) Mount Fuji - 12,388 feet
6) Argentina - National University of Tierra del Fuego in Ushuaia, Argentina, at 54.8 degrees south latitude
7) Mount Everest - 29,020 feet
8) Namibia
9) Dili, East Timor - 8.6 degrees south latitude
10) Quito, Ecuador - 15.9 miles south of the equator
11) Istanbul, Turkey
12) Turkey - Cape Baba at 26.1 degrees east longitude
13) White Nile and Blue Nile
14) Khartoum, Sudan
15) Bangkok, Thailand
16) Pakistan
17) Arabian Peninsula - 1,250,006 square miles
18) Norway - Beerenberg volcano on the Norwegian island of Jan Mayen in the Arctic Ocean at 71.1 degrees north latitude
19) Qatar
20) Jaya Peak - 16,503 feet in New Guinea

Quiz 35

1) What country is Sulawesi island part of?
2) By area, what is the largest bay in the world?
3) What is the only Central American country that doesn't border the Caribbean Sea?
4) What country has the longest coastline in mainland Asia?
5) What river flows through the city center of Berlin, Germany?
6) China has the largest Buddhist population of any country; what country has the second largest?
7) What is the least populous country in South America?
8) Going west from Ecuador, what is the next country the equator passes through?
9) By population, what is the second-largest city in South America?

10) What is the most densely populated South American country?
11) What country has the world's oldest working library?
12) What is the largest volume lake in Australia?
13) What two countries are connected by the Karakoram Pass?
14) What island country has the Bahamas to the north and Jamaica to the south?
15) What is the highest active volcano in South America?
16) What country has the southernmost point in mainland Europe?
17) By area, what is the largest of the Canary Islands?
18) The island of Borneo is shared by what three countries?
19) What is the least densely populated Asian country?
20) What is the least visited country in the world?

Quiz 35 Answers

1) Indonesia - 11th largest island in the world at 69,761 square miles
2) Bay of Bengal - 839,000 square miles
3) El Salvador
4) Russia - 23,396 miles
5) Spree River
6) Thailand
7) Suriname
8) Kiribati
9) Buenos Aires, Argentina
10) Ecuador
11) Morocco - The al-Qarawiyyin library in Fez is the world's oldest working library operating since 859 AD.
12) Lake Eyre
13) China and India - The pass is a gap between two mountains in the Karakoram Range and is about 148 feet wide at an elevation of 18,176 feet.
14) Cuba
15) Ojos del Salado - 22,615 feet on the Chile and Argentina border
16) Spain - Punta de Tarifa at 36.0 degrees north latitude
17) Tenerife - 785 square miles
18) Malaysia, Indonesia, Brunei
19) Mongolia
20) Tuvalu - It is the fourth-smallest country in the world with 10 square miles across nine islands in the Pacific midway between Hawaii and

Australia. It has about 2,000 visitors annually.

Quiz 36

1) What is the northernmost city in the world with a population of over 10 million?
2) How many states does India have?
3) By area, what is the third-largest freshwater lake in the world?
4) What is the southernmost national capital city in Europe?
5) What tiny country is the world's biggest exporter of false teeth?
6) What country is bordered by Eritrea, Djibouti, Somalia, Sudan, South Sudan, and Kenya?
7) With the dissolution of the Soviet Union, how many independent republics were created?
8) What is the only South American country with English as an official language?
9) What country has the shortest national anthem?
10) By area, what is the largest lake in Central America?
11) By area, what is the largest plateau in the world?
12) How many countries lie on the prime meridian (0 degrees longitude)?
13) What is the easternmost national capital city in Africa?
14) In what ocean are the Solomon Islands located?
15) What is the highest elevation city in the world with a population of over 5 million?
16) What country has the easternmost point in Europe?
17) By population, what is the second-largest city entirely in Europe?
18) What is the easternmost national capital city in Europe?
19) The Kremlin is on the bank of what river that flows through Moscow, Russia?
20) What city has the highest number of American emigrants?

Quiz 36 Answers

1) Moscow, Russia - 55.8 degrees north latitude
2) 29
3) Huron - 23,000 square miles
4) Valletta, Malta - 35.9 degrees north latitude
5) Liechtenstein - Vivadent AG in the city of Schaan is the largest manufacturer of false teeth in the world.
6) Ethiopia

7) 15 - Russia, Ukraine, Georgia, Belarus, Uzbekistan, Armenia, Azerbaijan, Kazakhstan, Kyrgyzstan, Moldova, Turkmenistan, Tajikistan, Latvia, Lithuania, Estonia.
8) Guyana
9) Japan - "Kimigayo" is the title of Japan's four-line national anthem; it is one of the oldest anthems in the world and has a total of 32 characters and runs a length of eleven measures.
10) Lake Nicaragua - 3,191 square miles
11) Tibetan Plateau - 970,000 square miles in China and Pakistan
12) Eight - Algeria, Burkina Faso, France, Ghana, Mali, Spain, Togo, United Kingdom
13) Port Louis, Mauritius - 57.5 degrees east longitude
14) Pacific - northeast of Australia
15) Bogota, Colombia - 8,596 feet
16) Russia - Cape Flissingsky at 69 degrees east longitude
17) Paris, France
18) Moscow, Russia - 37.5 degrees east longitude
19) Moskva River
20) Mexico City

Quiz 37

1) Outside of Asia, what is the highest mountain range in the world?
2) What country is bordered by Botswana, Mozambique, South Africa, and Zambia?
3) What country has the oldest restaurant in the world?
4) How many countries don't have any natural rivers?
5) By population, what is the largest city in Australia?
6) What is the most populous island in the world?
7) What is the northernmost national capital city in South America?
8) What is believed to be the oldest continuously inhabited city in North America?
9) What is the least densely populated North American country?
10) What country has the most tornadoes per square mile?
11) What South American country has a higher percentage of its land covered in forest than any other country in the world?
12) What is the largest desert at least partially in North America?
13) Measured from base to summit, what is the tallest mountain in the world?
14) What country has the longest coastline in South America?

15) What is the deepest river in North America?
16) What country is completely surrounded by Russia and China?
17) What country has the longest coastline in Africa?
18) What is the northernmost city in the world with a population of over 5 million?
19) What country has the northernmost permanent airport with flights, but none scheduled?
20) What is the second-longest mountain range in the world?

Quiz 37 Answers

1) Andes - maximum elevation of 22,841 feet
2) Zimbabwe
3) Austria - St. Peter Stiftskulinarium restaurant in Salzburg, Austria, is the oldest restaurant in the world and has been in operation since 803 AD.
4) 18 - Bahamas, Bahrain, Comoros, Kiribati, Kuwait, Maldives, Malta, Marshall Islands, Monaco, Nauru, Oman, Qatar, Saudi Arabia, Tonga, Tuvalu, United Arab Emirates, Vatican City, Yemen
5) Sydney
6) Java - Indonesia
7) Caracas, Venezuela - 10.5 degrees north latitude
8) Cholula, Mexico - founded in 2000 BC
9) Canada
10) United Kingdom
11) Suriname
12) Arctic Desert - 5.4 million square miles in Canada, Greenland, Norway, Russia, Sweden, United States
13) Mauna Kea in Hawaii - Measured from the seafloor where it starts, Mauna Kea is about 33,500 feet tall, almost 4,500 feet taller than Mount Everest; it only reaches 13,796 feet above sea level.
14) Brazil - 4,934 miles
15) St. Lawrence River - 250 feet maximum depth, 8th deepest in the world
16) Mongolia
17) Madagascar - 3,000 miles
18) St. Petersburg, Russia - 59.9 degrees north latitude
19) Canada - Alert Airport in Alert, Nunavut, Canada, is about 520 miles south of the North Pole at 82.5 degrees north latitude.
20) Rocky Mountains - 3,000 miles through Canada and United States

Quiz 38

1) After the Himalayas, what is the second-highest mountain range in the world?
2) What is the largest island in Norway?
3) At the population density of New York City, the entire population of the world would fit in an area closest to what U.S. state?
4) Based on average depth, what is the shallowest of the Great Lakes?
5) How many African countries does the equator pass through?
6) What is the second-most populous island in the world?
7) What famous city is built on 118 small islands?
8) What is the highest mountain in Kenya?
9) Does the Northern Hemisphere or the Southern Hemisphere contain more of the world's land area?
10) What is the least densely populated South American country?
11) What country has the most visitors annually?
12) What is the largest desert in South America?
13) In what country was the first mile of concrete highway in the world built?
14) Based on the number of islands, what is the largest archipelago in the world?
15) What is the highest mountain in Ecuador?
16) What country has the westernmost point in Africa?
17) What mountain has the largest base circumference of any non-volcanic mountain in the world?
18) What country only borders Germany?
19) What country has the southernmost point in Asia?
20) What is the only African country that borders the Mediterranean Sea and the Atlantic Ocean?

Quiz 38 Answers

1) Karakoram Range - Pakistan, China, India
2) Spitsbergen - 14,546 square miles
3) Texas - about 4% larger
4) Huron - 195 feet average depth
5) Seven - Sao Tome & Principe, Gabon, Republic of the Congo, Democratic Republic of the Congo, Uganda, Kenya, Somalia
6) Honshu - Japan
7) Venice, Italy

8) Mount Kenya - 17,057
9) Northern Hemisphere - 68% of the total land
10) Falkland Islands
11) France
12) Patagonian Desert - 200,000 square miles in Argentina and Chile
13) United States - In 1909, Wayne County (Detroit, Michigan) built the first mile of concrete highway in the world.
14) Norwegian Archipelago - at least 240,000 islands, coral reefs, cays, and islets
15) Chimborazo - 20,561 feet
16) Cape Verde - Santo Antão at 25.4 degrees west longitude
17) Mount Logan – It is 19,551 feet elevation in the Saint Elias range in the Yukon province of Canada and has 11 peaks over 5,000 meters (16,400 feet).
18) Denmark
19) Indonesia - Pamana Island at 11 degrees south latitude
20) Morocco

Quiz 39

1) By area, what is Japan's second-largest island?
2) What is the least densely populated European country?
3) What is the capital of the Canadian province of British Columbia?
4) What country is bordered by Ethiopia, Somalia, South Sudan, Tanzania, and Uganda?
5) What country is Ellesmere Island part of?
6) What country has the northernmost university in the world?
7) What city of 5 million or more is closest to the equator?
8) What is the only South American country that borders the Caribbean Sea and the Pacific Ocean?
9) How many South American countries does the equator pass through?
10) Going by land, what is the minimum number of countries you would have to cross going from Norway to North Korea?
11) What country has the northernmost airport with scheduled flights?
12) What river flows through Madrid, Spain?
13) By area, what is the smallest island country?
14) What is the largest non-polar desert in the world?
15) What is the official language of Greenland?
16) Based on cargo volume, what is the busiest port in the world?

17) What is the highest mountain in Tanzania?
18) What is the only country in the world that doesn't have either a rectangular or square flag?
19) What is the deepest lake in South America?
20) What is the easternmost national capital city in North America?

Quiz 39 Answers

1) Hokkaido - 32,210 square miles
2) Iceland
3) Victoria
4) Kenya
5) Canada - 10th largest island in the world at 75,767 square miles
6) Norway - University of Tromsø in Tromsø, Norway, at 69.7 degrees north latitude
7) Singapore - 85 miles north of the equator
8) Colombia
9) Three- Ecuador, Colombia, Brazil
10) One – Russia
11) Norway - Svalbard Airport, Longyear in Svalbard, Norway, at 78.2 degrees north latitude
12) Manzanares River
13) Nauru - eight square miles in the South Pacific
14) Sahara - 3.3 million square miles
15) Greenlandic - It is an Eskimo–Aleut language closely related to the Inuit languages in Canada.
16) Shanghai, China
17) Kilimanjaro - 19,331 feet
18) Nepal - It has a combination of two triangular pennants.
19) O'Higgins/San Martin Lake - 2,743 feet deep on the Chile-Argentina border
20) Bridgetown, Barbados - 59.6 degrees west longitude

If you enjoyed this book and learned a little and would like others to enjoy it also, please put out a review or rating. If you scan the QR code below, it will take you directly to the Amazon review and rating page.

Made in the USA
Monee, IL
15 February 2023